Global Governance, Economy and Law

This book provides a critical examination of the most important institutions of global governance in the world today. Drawing on history, political science, law and economics, the authors examine institutions such as the United Nations, the World Trade Organization (WTO), the International Monetary Fund (IMF), the World Bank and also the global private sector.

In a series of comprehensive analyses, the inability of these institutions and entities to promote and protect human rights and international peace is revealed. The authors examine the failure of the United Nations to prevent the most fundamental violation of human rights, including genocide; the inability of the WTO to remedy its democratic deficit, prevent exploitation of vulnerable workers, and integrate into its framework the protection of the environment; the consequences of the increasing power of multinational enterprises without the acceptance of their global responsibilities by the global private sector; and, in the case of the international finance institutions, the inability to prevent the financial catastrophes that have occurred in Asia and elsewhere while losing the battle against poverty in many countries in the South. While examining the failures of the past, the authors enthusiastically propose far-reaching reforms, suggesting how these global institutions and their member states can reform themselves to prevent the exploitation of the most vulnerable in the global economy and bridge the gap between the high vision that saw the birth of these institutions and their present-day failures. *Global Governance, Economy and Law* calls for nothing less than a global Marshall Plan, a new global political vision and a new system of international taxation to finance the integration of justice into the world economy.

This book will interest not only advanced students and academics in international law, international relations, and trade and development studies, but also those with an interest in globalization and international governance.

Errol Mendes is a professor of law at the University of Ottawa, Canada. His work focuses on globalization, corporate integrity, international law, human rights, and constitutional law. **Ozay Mehmet** is a professor of international affairs at Carleton University, Canada, and a visiting professor of economics at the Eastern Mediterranean University in Cyprus. His work focuses on labor economics, social justice, and the impact of globalization on the most vulnerable workers in the global economy.

Routledge Studies in International Law

1 International Law in the Post-Cold War World
Essays in Memory of Li Haopei
Edited by Sienho Yee and Wang Tieya

2 The Break-Up of Yugoslavia and International Law
Peter Radan

3 International Human Rights, Decolonisation, Globalisation
Becoming Human
Shelley Wright

4 Global Governance, Economy and Law
Waiting for Justice
Errol Mendes and Ozay Mehmet

Global Governance, Economy and Law

Waiting for justice

Errol Mendes and Ozay Mehmet

LONDON AND NEW YORK

First published 2003
by Routledge
11 New Fetter Lane, London EC4P 4EE

Simultaneously published in the USA and Canada
by Routledge
29 West 35th Street, New York, NY 10001

Routledge is an imprint of the Taylor & Francis Group

© 2003 Errol Mendes and Ozay Mehmet

Typeset in Baskerville by Taylor & Francis Books Ltd
Printed and bound in Great Britain by
TJ International Ltd, Padstow, Cornwall

British Library Cataloguing in Publication Data
A catalogue record for this book is available from the British Library

Library of Congress Cataloging in Publication Data
A catalog record for this book has been requested

ISBN 0–415–28263–2

Contents

Illustrations

Tables

Figures

Preface

The idea for this book arose in the dying days of the twentieth century. Both authors felt that the implications and impact of the historic times that we have been living through will not fully be understood for many years, perhaps decades, to come. However, we felt that there was an obligation to those who have waited for justice to no avail, to describe and analyze one of the most important evolutions in the history of humanity in the twentieth century, namely the emergence of the institutions of global governance. The idea for most of these institutions emerged during one of the most destructive and cruel of human conflicts to have ever taken place: the Second World War. It is there we start our book in Chapter 1.

Organization of the book

In Chapter 1 we focus on the historical paradoxes that gave birth to the United Nations and the system of protection of international human rights. We have chosen the area of human rights, the global secular religion, to examine the moral regime of the present-day structures of international peace and security. The conclusions of our examination are both pessimistic and optimistic given what we see as the "tragic flaw" in the institutions of global governance and, indeed, in humanity. In our attempt at a multidisciplinary analysis, we have tried to show how history, philosophy, ideology, military strategy, international law, and international politics have clashed with each other to evolve a most fragile system of protection of international human rights, peace, and security. This fragility has been underscored by the events of 11 September 2001.

In Chapter 2, we focus on the main institution of global trade and commerce, formerly called the General Agreement on Tariffs and Trade, now the World Trade Organization. Again, we begin the chapter by discussing the historical origins of this institution and its present-day status. We focus on two areas in particular to examine the moral regime of this area of global governance, namely the discussions surrounding trade and labor standards and trade and the environment. We also examine the question regarding who is presently benefiting and losing from the regulation of global trade and the democratic deficit of such regulation. In our conclusions to this chapter, we are again both pessimistic and optimistic about the benefits of global trade.

In Chapter 3, we focus on the most unregulated of global activities, the operations of the global private sector. In this chapter, we discuss the challenges of the exercise of great economic, and increasingly political, power without responsibility by the multinational enterprises. In this largely unregulated area of global governance, we examine how these new global giants are learning that there are consequences to not internalizing their responsibilities as global players. We look at how such consequences can range from damage to corporate reputations to increasing legal regulation of the global private sector. Finally, we consider the emergence and effectiveness of values-based codes of ethics and corporate integrity.

In Chapter 4, the direction of the text switches to a primarily economic analysis of the functioning of the global labor market and the need for integration of social justice into the workings of this fundamental aspect of global governance. We argue for upward harmonization of wages and labor standards to prevent a "race-to-the-bottom" that can marginalize and exploit the most vulnerable on the planet. We demonstrate how the hotly contested "race-to-the-bottom" actually comes into being, and the critical reforms that must be taken by national and international institutions of governance to promote a fair global labor market.

In Chapter 5, we describe and discuss the history and evolution of the international financial institutions that were designed to promote economic and social stability in the aftermath of the Second World War but in the view of many have failed in their basic missions. We examine the shortcomings of the key institutions in this area, namely the International Monetary Fund and the World Bank. We then consider and analyze the potential for their reform, in order to effectively prevent the kind of financial crises that we saw in Asia in 1997 and Argentina in 2002. We also discuss how these institutions can most effectively promote sustainable development in the South. We conclude that present or even increased aid or other forms of charitable flows to the South will not suffice to deal with those marginalized or missed by the globalized economy. We propose, and discuss in the conclusion to the chapter, a global Marshall Plan that is funded, in part, by the main beneficiaries of globalization, the multinational enterprises.

In our concluding Chapter 6, we propose a new vision for the task of integrating justice into the institutions of global governance. "Global pluralism" is the title we give to this vision, which attempts to depart both from the insularity of national self-interest bound only by international law and also from the empty rhetoric of global universalism. We propose that this new vision will be the foundation of creating a global community of solidarity, dignity, and compassion among all members of the human family that will not only take into account national and cultural differences but will also transcend them.

Throughout our long careers in the area of law and economics we have written, taught, and advocated a return to the high visions that were first dreamed of for the institutions of global governance discussed in our text. Our book discusses how the loss of those original high visions today has abandoned and marginalized billions of our fellow human beings and made the future of so many so uncertain. It is for them that we have written this book. However, because this book would also not be possible without the support and love of our own families, we also dedicate it to them. Finally, we also wish to acknowledge and thank those who have professionally supported our efforts to complete the book.

Acknowledgements

Professor Errol Mendes dedicates this book to his family, Sharon Lefroy, Alexander Mendes, and William Mendes. They are among my chief reasons for living a good life and desiring to write. I would also like to thank some professional supports and intellectual motivators, who were key to the completion of my work on this text. First, I want to thank Alan Fleichman, one of the great information specialists in the field of human rights, and documentalist at the Human Rights Research and Education Centre at the University of Ottawa. His assistance in obtaining research materials and logistical support to the book was indispensable. Second, I want to thank Bruce Newey for his great work as a research assistant and editor who was not afraid to question or red-pencil his former professor's writing. I also want to thank Aya Bouchedid for her assistance in the research task. The intellectual motivators for this book, who are also friends, are numerous. I wish to mention, in particular, Richard Goldstone, Justice of the Constitutional Court of South Africa, the first Chief Prosecutor of the Ad Hoc War Crimes Tribunal for the Former Republic of Yugoslavia and co-chair of the Independent International Commission on Kosovo; Paul Martin Jr, a leading thinker and actor on the reform of the international financial architecture and a former Canadian finance minister, who included me in his discussions on global governance; Marcus Gee, one of Canada's most eminent journalists in the area of international peace and security; and finally, all my friends and colleagues in the Office of the Secretary General of the United Nations with whom I have worked on the Global Compact. In this text, we have critiqued the workings of the United Nations. However, to adapt Winston Churchill's quip: The UN is the worst institution of global governance, except for all the others which are much worse. It is also clear that we owe much to the inspiration of the great historian of the international human rights movement, Paul Gordon Lauren; Amartya Sen, winner of the Nobel Prize in Economics in 1998; author and philosopher Michael Ignatieff; and my Canadian law professor colleagues, Bill Schabas and Anne Bayefsky.

Finally, I want to thank the former Rector of the University of Ottawa, Marcel Hamelin, and the present Rector, Gilles Patry, who gave me the opportunity to continue my life's work in the field of globalization, justice, and law. Of

xii   *Acknowledgements*

course, it also goes without saying that my co-author Professor Ozay Mehmet has continued the intellectual jousting and companionship that I so cherish and which led to the completion of this book.

Professor Mehmet would like to acknowledge his appreciation for his long association, on and off since 1968, with the International Labor Organization. The opportunity to work with the ILO in various countries in Southeast Asia, Africa, and the Middle East sparked a lifetime dedication to the pursuit of social justice, and the insights gained in these policy assignments put a "human face" on his economics in the classroom and in his research writings. In the ILO, past and present, he wishes to record, in particular, his debt of gratitude to Don Snyder, Eddy Lee, and Frank Lisk.

Professor Mehmet would also like to express his thanks to numerous academic and professional colleagues in several countries for the fruitful discussions and exchanges over the years. Though not always ending in agreement, these discourses clarified his ideas on international development and the great themes of equity and growth, investment and technology, human and social capital, justice and exploitation in the global village. In Professor Mehmet's global village, Southeast Asia has occupied a special place. Without slighting anyone by omission, it is a pleasure to record the influence of Malaysian friends past and present, Ungku Aziz, Yip Yat Hoong, K.S. Jomo, S. Husin Ali, and James Puthucheary. Similarly, it is with gratitude that his Indonesian friends Sayuti Hasibuan and Sritua Arief are remembered. In his country of birth, North Cyprus, Professor Mehmet acknowledges the support and encouragement of President R.R. Denktas, M. Tahiroglu, Ergun Olgun, and Tareq Ismael.

In Ottawa, Professor Mehmet wishes to express his thanks to his colleagues at Carleton University, in particular Martin Rudner, John O'Manique, and Fraser Taylor. A particular word of thanks is due to his co-author, Errol Mendes. The idea of "waiting for justice" in this book is Errol's, but their collaboration goes back many years. This has been a productive as well as an enjoyable collaboration, a happy blending of law and economics tempered by their own personal experiences in the developing world, resulting in an earlier book co-authored with Robert Sinding, *Towards a Fair Global Labour: Avoiding a New Slave Trade* (Routledge, 1999), to which the present volume is a sequel. They both share an abiding commitment to justice for all in the global village, the foundation stone of global governance, based on global pluralism, dignity, and equality. Their joint work is but a small testament of this commitment.

Professor Mehmet wishes to dedicate this book to his wife, Karen Ann Mehmet, as a token for all the love and support over the years.

1 The "tragic flaw" of humanity reflected in the United Nations and the struggle for human rights

Prelude to the United Nations: the Age of Hope

The institutions of global governance and law that we know today have their roots in one of the darkest periods of human history. Their beginnings showed a mirror up to the tragic flaw within the nature of humanity.

In this work we define global governance to include not only the institutions set up to deal with issues of global scope, but also the situations that evolve in the absence of appropriate and effective institutions to deal with such global matters. Our concept of the "tragic flaw" is adapted from Shakespearean tragedy, and encapsulates the notion that there can be one or more particular characteristics of an individual, a group, a nation, or indeed institutions organized by humans that can eventually undermine their other good qualities and potentially threaten their existence. We describe human nature as including the inclination toward justice which promotes human progress as well as the inclination toward domination and exploitation that retards such progress. The history and texts of moral philosophy worldwide are filled with both the analysis of and the tension between these two fundamental characteristics of human nature. In this chapter, and to a lesser extent throughout this text, we will use this notion of the tragic flaw as an instrument to critically examine the moral regime of some of the key institutions of global governance. Finally, given our above definitions of these universal contradictions in human nature, the simple definition of justice we use in this work is one based on the notion of the universal moral Golden Rule, or is one that approximates the Kantian categorical imperative, which can be recast as a Golden Rule of Justice to "do unto others as you would have them do unto you."

In this first chapter, our thesis is that the aspirations of humankind to eradicate the conditions that led to the Second World War and the evils that occurred during the war were soon overwhelmed by the tragic flaw within the nature of humankind. This tragic flaw, as we will demonstrate in this chapter, is the urge in human nature, which is then reflected in the institutions of global governance, to seek the supremacy of territorial integrity over human integrity and dignity in the pursuit of perceived collective power and self-interest. We argue that this occurred even among those who showed the greatest enthusiasm for advancing human progress and human rights through institutions of global governance in the aftermath of the Second World War. We will demonstrate how these enthusiasts even turned the other way in the face of the most brutal genocides since the Holocaust during the Second World War.

It was August of 1941, "somewhere in the Atlantic," that President Roosevelt agreed to meet and discuss with Winston Churchill the growing threat of aggression from Hitler's Nazi Germany and the increasing desire for world dominance of the Axis Powers. The United States (US) was still not at war, but the pressure was building from within the US to assist the British in what increasingly looked like a last-ditch attempt to save Europe, and Britain itself from the shadow of Fascist totalitarianism.

The location of the naval force that brought the two world statesmen together should be of special interest to Canadians, for it was at Placentia Bay in the waters off Newfoundland. A leading historian of human rights, Paul Gordon Lauren, describes the meeting of the leaders as an almost desperate attempt to save the peoples of Europe and the rest of the world from a cataclysm of evil.[1] The primary focus of the discussion between the two leaders, according to Lauren, concerned the role of the United States in the war. While the United States was still a non-belligerent, discussions took place on how it could assist in the fight for the survival of freedom and human dignity in Europe, North Africa, and Asia. The plan needed a foundation of principles that could serve to inspire and lead their respective populations into action. Those principles, drafted in haste by Churchill and Roosevelt on the waters off the coast of Newfoundland, were announced to the world as the Atlantic Charter. The Charter would become the catalyst for the idea of the United Nations (UN). The Atlantic Charter was the first international document (conceived in the midst of the greatest carnage ever seen in human history) in which two great world leaders had the courage to declare the right of all peoples to "live out their lives in freedom from want and fear," and the need for "a wider and permanent system of general security for the world." It should also be noted that at this time, before the General Agreement on Tariffs and Trade (GATT), the World Trade Organization (WTO), the International Monetary Fund (IMF) or the World Bank had taken shape, the Atlantic Charter contained principles that linked the imperative for a new global security institution and respect for human rights with improved labor standards, economic advancement, and social security.[2]

The approval of the Atlantic Charter was swift from all the Allied powers at the first meeting of the Inter-Allied Council (which included the Soviet Union).

With the torpedoing of American isolationism at Pearl Harbor in December of 1941, the need was great for the Atlantic Charter to galvanize more nations, especially in the Asian theater of war, into the fight against the evil of the Axis Powers. Lauren describes vividly how in January of 1942, twenty-six nations at first, and later forty-six nations, endorsed the Declaration of the United Nations. In doing so, these nations vowed to unite in the struggle against the Axis Powers and to adhere to the Atlantic Charter, including its call for the human rights of all peoples to be respected and for the creation of a global institution to ensure international peace and security. There was a consensus among the nations that agreed to the Declaration of the United Nations that sovereignty and territorial integrity could not be had at the expense of the fundamental rights of all human beings. The principles contained in the Atlantic Charter would be the rallying cry for the "people's war" against the crushing of human dignity and rights perpetrated by the Axis Powers.[3]

However, history seemed determined to show the other side of human nature in operation, thereby demonstrating the tragic flaw in the character of humankind. In stark contrast to the conception of the Declaration of the United Nations, Lauren reveals that it was also in January of 1942, when the Declaration was being promulgated, that an unspeakable act of evil was also being planned. It was during this month that the Wannsee Conference was held just outside Berlin, where the genocide of entire races, and one in particular, was being planned with meticulous care and attention to detail. This plan was called the "final solution of the Jewish Question." What was planned at Wannsee translated into the deaths of over eleven million people, including six million Jews, exterminated with the utmost cruelty solely on the basis of their race, ethnicity, religion, language, disability, sexual orientation, or simply because they were too young, too old, or too sick to be of any use to the Nazi forces.[4]

What is staggering about this dark period of human history is that Germany did not enter into this program of genocide devoid of an intellectual, religious, and moral history that would have proffered a myriad of reasons for not engaging in this barbaric plan. The instinct for dominance, self-interest, and territorial grandeur seems hardwired into the nature of humankind. This instinct creates a moral blind spot that centuries of intellectual, religious, and moral learning cannot undo. The only restraint against this blind spot that afflicts those with pretensions to civilization, and all others alike, is an effective rule of law together with regional and global governance institutions that ensure the rule of law, not individuals.

January of 1942 was the point in history when the tragic flaw in human nature became truly global. As discussed above, we define the tragic flaw in the nature of humankind as the struggle between the desire for dominance, self-interest, and territorial grandeur against the universal appeal of human dignity, conscience, and compassion. In the early millennia of human history, these human instincts battled against each other in small places on the planet, between and within tribes, settlements, villages, fortified towns, and cities and ultimately nations. But the defining moment when this struggle became global and laid the foundations for the institutions of global governance that included this tragic flaw was in the month of January of 1942.

However, no sooner was the end of the Second World War in sight, than the states that promoted the instinct toward human dignity, conscience, and compassion, contained in principles of the Atlantic Charter and the Declaration of the United Nations, also seemed to succumb to the temptations of the quest for dominance, self-interest, and territorial grandeur. As Lauren has stated:

When pressed, most of those leaders who spoke so eloquently about human rights quickly noted that statements like the Atlantic Charter and the Declaration of the United Nations represented only goals rather than legal agreements that might jeopardize national interests or threaten national sovereignty. It is in this context that Churchill made his celebrated statements about not allowing stated principles such as that of the right of self-determination to precipitate the liquidation of the British Empire, and describing the Atlantic Charter as "no more than a simple, rough and ready, war-time statement of a goal" toward which the supporting governments "mean to make their way" instead of a binding treaty with firm commitments.[5]

Even in Churchill, the tragic flaw was beginning to take hold in the scramble for collective power and self-interest in the aftermath of the Second World War.

Birth of the United Nations: one step forward, two back

While many nations had joined with the Great Powers in the fight to win the war against the Axis Powers, they were excluded from the first deliberations at Dumbarton Oaks in the fall of 1944. It was at Dumbarton Oaks that the United States, Britain, the Soviet Union, and China met to sketch out the Charter of the new global security organization that would come to be known as the United Nations. All but one Great Power agreed that the Charter would not contain any substantial provisions on human rights.[6]

It is an irony of history that the only participant at Dumbarton Oaks that wanted a reference to the right of all people to equality and non-discrimination was China. China reflected the concern of many countries of the South, and Asian countries in particular, that the new institutions of global governance would allow the colonial powers to prevent decolonization and self-determination of colonized peoples.

And so at Dumbarton Oaks in 1944, the struggle swung entirely in favor of the human instinct for dominance and self-interest when the Great Powers developed a post-war global security institution which was to be dominated by them. The Great Powers were able to ensure their dominance by creating a new Security Council that gave them both permanent membership and the power of veto. Their design for the organization, which involved the formation of a weaker General Assembly where the secondary powers could "blow off steam" without endangering the interests of the Great Powers, also assisted in cementing their hegemony. The emphasis by the Great Powers at Dumbarton Oaks and in the period that followed was on national sovereignty, territorial integrity, and political independence, which meant non-interference in the domestic affairs of the Great Powers. The only reference to human rights was in the context of general economic and social cooperation.[7] According to Lauren, the then US secretary of state, Cordell Hull, poured derision on the efforts of his own undersecretary, Sumner Welles, to promote an International Bill of Rights, stating that no concept of universal human rights would undermine the national sovereignty of the United States.[8]

In the struggles of human nature that comprise the tragic flaw of humankind, the history of the Second World War and its aftermath show that enfeebled law-making that promotes dominance, self-interest, and territorial grandeur usually comes out stronger in the short term. Justice takes much longer to surface.

The catalyst for justice often begins with an outcry against law-making that does not include it. So it was with the creation of the United Nations Charter that we know today. When the Dumbarton Oaks proposals for the creation of the United Nations were made known, there was a storm of criticism that went around the world from citizens, non-governmental organizations (NGOs), and those countries left out of the Great Powers' self-interested power structures inherent in the proposed Security Council and the General Assembly. There was particular anger over the omission of any substantial global protection of human rights and the right to self-determination. In 1945, with the end of the war in sight, the Great Powers eventually accepted that another conference, this time involving states from all parts of the world, should be held to hammer out the final version of the Charter of the United Nations. This conference would take place in San Francisco in April of 1945.

While the gathering constituted the largest number of states assembled at that time to lay the foundations of the United Nations, they were also mindful of the failure of the product of the last similar gathering at the end of the First World War which led to the ineffectual and ultimately doomed League of Nations.[9]

The rhetoric for the ideals of peace, global security, human dignity, and human rights flew high at San Francisco, but the Great Powers stuck in large part to their Dumbarton Oaks proposals. Before the conference was over, the surrender of Germany also saw the first stirring of the Cold War at the birth of the United Nations. This reinforced the non-human-rights focus of the Great Powers. It was the representation from the rest of the international community, such as from India, South Africa, New Zealand, Australia, Egypt, the Philippines, and the countries of Latin America, that pushed for the democratization of the Dumbarton Oaks deliberations as described by Lauren.[10] It was from these countries that proposals to amend the Dumbarton Oaks text came. In particular, these proposals called for the insertion of the primacy and protection of human rights into the Charter. These countries were joined in their efforts by an army of individuals, groups, and NGOs from around the world. Of particular concern to many of the smaller nations that were either former colonies or were fighting for independence were the human rights of those in colonies and dependent territories.

The Great Powers eventually succumbed to the pressure from the rest of the world. They agreed to a substantial number of their demands to put in place provisions for human rights in the Charter and for specific parts of the new United Nations to take lead roles in the promotion and protection of human rights, but without substantially altering the entrenched power structures agreed to at Dumbarton Oaks. The stage was being set for the insertion of the tragic flaw in the Charter of the United Nations. In particular, the drafters of the United Nations Charter seemed determined to include the supremacy of territorial integrity and political independence, while allowing weaker language on human rights to enter the constitution of the global body.

On 26 June 1945, there was a signing ceremony for the world leaders assembled at San Francisco, two months after the work on the United Nations Charter had begun. Fresh from victory in the war and with the chill of the Cold War starting to take effect, the Great Powers had managed to insert the two dueling concepts into the United Nations Charter at the signing ceremony in the Veterans Building Auditorium in San Francisco.

One of the concepts, as noted above, was the supremacy of territorial integrity. The central purpose of the new world body as stated in Article 1 was to maintain international peace and security. The principal condition for such peace and security was territorial integrity and the concomitant principle of political independence of the nation-state. The five permanent members of the new Security Council, whose primary responsibility would be to maintain international peace and security, could guarantee their own territorial integrity and political independence (and those of their allies) by the veto powers that the Charter bestowed on them.

The foundational principle based on territorial integrity and political independence in the United Nations Charter was that, if one nation did attack the territorial integrity of another, the Security Council would have the means through the Chapter VII enforcement powers to take effective collective measures. These powers allow for the prevention and removal of threats to the peace, and for suppression of acts of aggression and other breaches of the peace. Indeed, so sacred was the principle of territorial integrity and political independence that at the San Francisco conference, most of the Great Powers were adamant that not even the United Nations itself could intervene within the domestic jurisdiction of the nation-state. While, in theory, the new powerful Security Council could conclude that serious human rights violations might constitute a threat to international peace and security and follow up with its enforcement powers, as we shall see, the Cold War and the power of veto have effectively denied this potentially powerful machinery for the enforcement of global justice.

The other dueling concept concerned the references in the United Nations Charter to human rights. The reinsertion of human rights principles in the Charter, at the strong and forceful demand of the other members of the international community and the NGOs, set the stage for later conflicts between territorial integrity and human justice. However, the provisions relating to human rights allowed into the Charter by the Great Powers were never meant to be as strong as the provisions pertaining to territorial integrity and political independence. These provisions seemed in places more rhetorical than substantial. Justice waits for rhetoric to be hammered into reality. The opening lines of the Charter confirm "faith in fundamental human rights, in the dignity and worth of the human person, in the equal rights of men and women and of nations large and small." The same Article 1 that entrenches the supremacy of territorial integrity and political independence in the United Nations Charter goes on to state that the purpose of the UN is also:

> To develop friendly relations among nations based on respect for the prin-
> ciple of equal rights and self-determination of peoples, and to take other
> appropriate measures to strengthen universal peace;
>   To achieve international cooperation in solving international problems of
> an economic, social, cultural, or humanitarian character, and in promoting
> and encouraging respect for human rights and for fundamental freedoms for
> all without distinction as to race, sex, language, or religion.

Other important provisions of the Charter that touch on human rights are Articles 55 and 56. The former tasks the United Nations to promote "universal respect for, and observance of, human rights and fundamental freedoms for all without distinction as to race, sex, language, or religion." Article 56 requires that "[a]ll members pledge themselves to take joint and separate action in cooperation with the Organization for the achievement of the purposes set forth in Article 55."[11]

These provisions seem to be the rhetorical foundation for the grudging permission given to the General Assembly to discuss, study, and make recommendations concerning matters within the scope of the Charter, including human rights (Article 13). This set the stage for the unexpected victory of justice in the evolution of the Universal Declaration of Human Rights, which, while not legally binding on member states, would establish the intangible power of moral authority in the area of universal human rights. For the General Assembly to achieve even these limited goals, again permission was granted by the Great Powers to designate the Economic and Social Council as a critical organ of the United Nations that could initiate the discussions, studies, and recommendations in the area of human rights (Article 62). In turn the Council could establish Commissions in the economic and social fields, including that of human rights, to assist the Council in the performance of its functions and duties to the General Assembly (Article 68). The Charter also made provisions for the establishment of the International Court of Justice, which could adjudicate on matters relating to the achievement and maintenance of the purposes and principles of the United Nations, including those relating to human rights. This function could be carried out in either an adjudicatory or an advisory capacity. Each member state pledged to comply with the decisions of the court in any case to which it was a party. However, the Statute of the Court annexed to the Charter made the compulsory jurisdiction of the Court voluntary to member states. A court which automatically had jurisdiction in all disputes involving member states would have been a powerful force for the global rule of law. However, this same court would also have been a powerful force against the assertion of the unimpeachable sovereignty claimed by the Great Powers and many other delegations.

Although the provisions of the Charter have been lauded by some as unprecedented in human history, it must never be forgotten that the primary goal of the Great Powers at San Francisco was, as is so vividly described by Lauren, to protect their own dominance, self-interests, and territorial grandeur. This was done despite the higher vision first shown in the Atlantic Charter and the Declaration of the United Nations in the 1941–2 period. The tragic flaw was deeply entrenched in the global constitution hammered out at San Francisco.

Indeed, the way in which the Trusteeship Council and the International Trusteeship System was set up under the United Nations Charter is a prime example of high-flying rhetoric concerning the goal of self-determination and human rights for all peoples. In reality, it became riddled with exceptions for the colonial powers of Europe and the United States.[12]

Even with these limited provisions on human rights, Lauren describes how attempts to insert language which would make the provisions more legally binding on member states was fiercely resisted by the Great Powers. Certain delegations at the San Francisco conference argued that the most popular phrases concerning human rights, such as "promoting respect for human rights," "may discuss," "initiate studies," "consider," "make recommendations," were too weak legally. These delegations argued that these phrases should be substituted with stronger legal language such as to "enforce," "guarantee," "implement," "assure," "protect" or "promote," or require the "observance" of human rights. This language was rejected by the Great Powers and some of the other delegations.[13] The imperatives of territorial integrity, self-interest, and political independence led to the weakening of the human rights legal language in the United Nations Charter. Many of the nations opposing the stronger provisions on human rights in the Charter had concerns about whether the human rights abuses within their own territories would become open to world censure. In this regard, Russia under the Stalinist dictatorship, in addition to the fears of the United States over the civil rights situation in its southern states, would prevent any further strengthening of the human rights provisions. Indeed Article 2(7) of the Charter[14] was written specifically to prevent such intrusion into human rights abuses within the domestic jurisdictions of both the Great Powers and the other nations at the San Francisco conference. The provision read: "Nothing contained in the present Charter shall authorize the United Nations to intervene in matters which are essentially within the domestic jurisdiction of any state or shall require the Members to submit such matters to settlement."

Whether the suffocating of the human rights provisions in the United Nations Charter by weak language and the primacy of territorial integrity and political non-interference was deliberate or not, the tragic flaw was set that July in 1945. The legacy of the Atlantic Charter had almost evaporated. Indeed, the power structures of the United Nations and language relating to human rights would promote the rule of clashing ideologies, not law.

Many delegations and NGOs present at the San Francisco conference felt that the provisions on human rights were so weak that the Charter would have to be followed with a stronger International Bill of Rights, a proposition that ultimately even President Truman accepted in the closing speech at the conference. His words seem to indicate that he knew that a post-war world that talked human rights in the United Nations Charter but practiced oppression would be a very troubled one:

> We have good reason to expect the framing of an international bill of rights, acceptable to all the nations involved. That bill of rights will be as much a part of international life as our own Bill of Rights is a part of our Constitution. The Charter is dedicated to the achievement and observance of human rights and fundamental freedoms. Unless we can attain those objectives for all men and women everywhere – without regard to race, language or religion – we cannot have permanent peace and security.[15]

The evolution of the International Bill of Rights: rekindling the Age of Hope

As discussed, we have opted to base our definition of justice on the Golden Rule that is widely accepted by most of the world's religions and cultures. We argue that this simple concept of justice regards the promotion and protection of human dignity as an end in itself. There can legitimately be debate concerning the meaning of human dignity. In this regard, we would argue that the minimum content of human dignity would be the universally recognized human rights that we discuss in this chapter. As we shall see in this and subsequent chapters, our concept of justice as the promotion and protection of human dignity can also encompass fundamental social, economic, and environmental rights.

Justice in the institutions of global governance often has to take second place to the quest for territorial integrity and self-interest. But justice has also learned to be adept at grabbing at whatever is rationed out to its sphere, and at creating greater opportunities for the dignity of humankind to be promoted. This is the lesson we learn from the evolution of the International Bill of Rights.

The Charter of the United Nations came into force on 24 October 1945. In the autumn of the same year, a preparatory Commission of the Economic and Social Council chaired by one of the greatest champions of justice in modern history, Eleanor Roosevelt, the former First Lady of the United States, recommended that the Council set up a Human Rights Commission. It was also recommended that such a Commission be directed to begin work immediately on an International Bill of Rights. After fighting between the member states over the composition and membership of the proposed Commission subsided, the eighteen members began, in 1947, to develop the process for the drafting of the first part of what would be a three-part International Bill of Rights. The first part of such a Bill would be a Universal Declaration of Human Rights, which was to be drafted by a nine-member team with the assistance of the Director of the Human Rights Division of the UN Secretariat, Canadian law professor John Humphrey. Many, especially Canadian experts, have credited Professor Humphrey with being the author of the first draft of the text of the Universal Declaration of Human Rights.[16] The final draft was submitted to the full Commission which, after the final revisions were made, sent the draft to the Council which eventually passed it to the Third Committee of the General Assembly, which itself made more revisions and finally passed it on to the General Assembly for a vote on 10 December 1948.[17]

It should be noted that, despite the great energy given to each and every word of the Universal Declaration of Human Rights, at least one of the Great Powers was determined that it would not take on any semblance of a legal obligation that would intrude on national sovereignty. Lauren reveals that

> Right in the midst of these deliberations, Eleanor Roosevelt received most unwelcome instructions telling her to focus her efforts on a declaration of principles on human rights, where the United States government felt "on safer ground," and that any discussion about legal commitments and enforcement "should be kept on a tentative level and should not involve any commitments by this Government."[18]

It is perhaps because most nations realized that the Great Powers did not intend major legal consequences to flow from the Universal Declaration that the Declaration was adopted with no votes against on 10 December 1948. While it has been stated that the Declaration received unanimous approval of the member states of the United Nations, there were eight abstentions, six from the Soviet bloc, as well as from both South Africa and Saudi Arabia. These abstaining votes could not be regarded as being merely neutral to the Declaration. Yet the mystique of the unanimity of the Universal Declaration took root and has contributed to its evolution as the most potent moral force for justice in the community of humankind. This evolution is testament to the ability of justice to wait, but at the same time to spring on to any platform that will allow it to flourish against the towering edifice of territorial integrity and self-interest that is built into the institutions of global governance. Justice is the greatest antidote to the tragic flaw within the nature of humankind.

The contents of the Universal Declaration were a huge advance on the tentative and vague wording of the human rights provisions of the Charter. The preamble dares to talk with vigor about the counterforce to the values of territorial integrity, dominance, and self-interest. This counterforce includes "recognition of the inherent dignity and of the equal and inalienable rights of all members of the human family is the foundation of freedom, justice and peace in the world." Referring specifically to the actualities and possibilities of evil without this counterforce, the preamble, in implicitly referring to the Holocaust that had just occurred, stated that "disregard and contempt for human rights have resulted in barbarous acts which have outraged the conscience of mankind."

The actual extent of such barbarous acts done in the name of racial dominance and superiority had been revealed with seemingly unending accounts of chilling horrors at the International Military Tribunal at Nuremberg, since the start of the Tribunal's hearing in November of 1945.[19] The first Article of the Universal Declaration, that "all human beings are born free and equal in dignity and rights," must have seemed so hollow to those who saw their loved ones perish in the concentration camps of Nazi Germany without mercy, let alone without freedom, equality, or dignity.

The rest of the content of the Universal Declaration affirmed, again with vigor and courage and without pandering to cultural relativism, that all members of the human family were entitled not only to the fundamental civil, political, and legal rights so cherished by the West, but also to the fundamental economic, social, and cultural rights. This latter set of rights was equally cherished by the developing world and the emerging powerful Communist bloc of countries on the other side of the Cold War's Iron Curtain.

What is stunning about the Universal Declaration of Human Rights is not its content of rights, which in 1948 must have seemed unattainable to all member states of the United Nations, even the richest and most democratic. Rather, the surprise in the evolution of the modern history of humanity is the fact that even though the Universal Declaration was pushed through as a non-binding statement of principles, it began to develop a moral force and authority throughout the world during the latter half of the twentieth century. The provisions of Articles 2 to 21 of the Universal Declaration, dealing with the fundamental civil, political, and legal rights, have also come, in the view of many jurists, including this author, to have legal force through the evolution of customary international law on human rights.[20] It has also been the catalyst for much stronger and legally binding international and regional Conventions on Human Rights, in particular the European Convention on Human Rights and Fundamental Freedoms. There is much to study and discuss as regards the reasons why the Universal Declaration achieved such moral force. The lofty rhetoric by the high-profile supporters of the Declaration played a part. Chief among these rhetorical champions was Eleanor Roosevelt, who proclaimed that the Declaration was "first and foremost a declaration of the basic principles to serve as a common standard for all nations. It might well become the Magna Carta of all mankind."[21] Some would argue her prediction has come true, but the reasons why are unclear. There was no blanket coverage of the Universal Declaration deliberations and proclamation around the world. Global television channels such as CNN and the BBC World Service were not ubiquitous, as they are today. Perhaps the Declaration is the ultimate example of the power of the universal conception of justice that has its foundation, the promotion and protection of human dignity, assisted by the power of words used by champions of human dignity. It should also not be forgotten that while the high ideals of the Universal Declaration were being hammered out, the War Crimes Tribunals at Nuremberg[22] and Tokyo[23] reminded the international community that there were limits to the conduct of war, which if broken would be such an affront to humanity that punishment would follow on the basis of universal jurisdiction. While such laws of war had existed in some form since the fifteenth century, the Geneva Conventions of 1949, which now have universal membership, consolidated the duty of all states to prosecute and punish individuals who had committed grave breaches of such humanitarian laws.[24] The 1977 Protocol to the Geneva Conventions extended the reach of such laws to internal conflicts.

Again we see that while justice has to wait for the opportune time to build its moral structures against the tragic flaw imbedded into the main institutions of global governance, it seems determined to create such opportunities, even when unexpected.

UN legal standard-setting in human rights: more law, but less moral force

The resolution of the General Assembly that approved the Universal Declaration of Human Rights also approved the development of two other parts of the International Bill of Rights. First was a legally binding multilateral treaty, called a Covenant, which would impose a legal obligation to promote and protect human rights. Second was a legal document that would detail the implementation measures for the human rights obligations. The Human Rights Commission had already produced a draft "International Covenant on Human Rights," so it was expected that the rest of the International Bill of Rights would evolve quickly.

This did not happen. Once again ingredients of the tragic flaw, self-interest and national sovereignty, asserted themselves. In the Commission, the Council and the General Assembly member states promoted either the sections on civil and political rights or economic, social, and cultural rights according to their perceived national self-interest. In the end, it was decided that there would be two separate Covenants on each of the two categories of rights, with the right to self-determination in both, at the insistence of the developing world. There was also considerable disagreement and tension concerning the implementation measures for the two Covenants. These differences took between 1950 and 1966 to resolve. The Covenants were finally unanimously approved by the General Assembly on 16 December 1966, with over a hundred member states voting in favor. The Optional Protocol, which permitted individual communications and petitions to the Human Rights Committee, was approved by a smaller margin of sixty-six votes in favor, two against, and thirty-eight abstentions.[25] A second Optional Protocol on the elimination of the death penalty was later added to the International Covenant on Civil and Political Rights.

However, even though the number of states approving legally binding obligations concerning human rights had risen dramatically from the number approving the Universal Declaration, there was something lacking. There was much less enthusiasm for the acceptance of legally binding obligations. The Cold War had intensified and made concerns about human dignity secondary to reinforcing hegemonic alliances on either side of the ideological Iron Curtain.

The moral authority of the Universal Declaration seemed lacking with these legal standard-setting instruments on human rights. The time frames for the drafting, approval, and ratification of the two International Covenants alone tell the story of the political vacuum. The drafting of what emerged as the two Covenants began in 1948, and it took eighteen years for the Covenants, amended and revised many times, to be finally approved on 16 December 1966. It took another ten years before the necessary thirty-five ratifications for both Covenants took place. While in February 2002, there were 148 ratifications to the Civil and Political Rights Covenant and 145 for the Economic, Social and Cultural Rights Covenant, many of them riddled with reservations, the human rights records of the majority of these states show that such ratifications are nothing more than UN "diplomatic decorations."

If hypocrisy in the observance, or lack thereof, of human rights is the main script of many of the member states of the United Nations, the same cannot be said of many individual champions within the United Nations system who are determined to make a difference. These individuals have fought and continue to fight battles for human dignity in the treaty bodies and other implementing mechanisms under the International Bill of Rights and other legal human rights standards. The wait and battle for justice is often a case of individuals struggling against all odds.

Such is the case of many of the past and present eighteen members of the Human Rights Committee serving in their individual capacities, who examine the countless reports by state parties to the International Covenants on their compliance with the obligations contained in the Covenants. The Committee also manages the inter-state complaint mechanism and receives individual communications and petitions under the Optional Protocols as regards the Civil and Political Rights Covenant.[26] These individual champions have developed jurisprudence and advisory opinions that have strengthened the edifice of human dignity against that of territorial integrity and political independence.[27]

The model of inserting individual champions, albeit elected by ratifying states, into the implementing treaty bodies and other monitoring mechanisms has spread from the International Bill of Rights to a host of other human rights legal standard-setting documents. These include the 1965 Convention on Elimination of All Forms of Racial Discrimination, the 1981 Convention on the Elimination of All Forms of Discrimination Against Women, the 1987 International Convention Against Torture and Other Cruel, Inhuman, or Degrading Treatment or Punishment, and most recently, under the most diplomatically decorated treaty ever, the 1990 International Convention on the Rights of the Child, ratified by 192 nations.[28]

However, the periodic reporting system, which is the most widely used method of implementing human rights legal standards, is increasingly coming under fire for being a way to keep the legal and political implications of ratification free of substance. One of the most well-known individual champions, Philip Alston, associated with many of the treaty bodies, in his Final Report on Enhancing the Long-Term Effectiveness of the United Nations Human Rights Treaty System, stated that "the present system is unsustainable and … significant reforms will be required if the overall regime is to achieve its objectives."[29]

At an international conference held in Canada in 1997, which examined the overall effectiveness of the implementation of the six major legally binding United Nations treaties on human rights, the organizer and rapporteur, Professor Anne Bayefsky, summing up her own views and those of the leading jurists and practitioners, many of whom were associated with the treaty bodies, described the shortfalls in the UN Human Rights Treaty System as follows:

- State reports, due to each treaty body, are overdue to an enormous extent. A large number of overdue reports are initial reports. States having the largest number of overdue reports are frequently those with extremely poor human rights records.
- If all the overdue reports were actually to be submitted, expunging the backlog would take years. Even with respect to reports which have been submitted, the meeting time now available to treaty bodies means that delays in considering those reports for some treaty bodies runs into years.
- The treaty bodies spend only a few hours considering a single report, on average every four years. The time spent in an actual dialogue or exchange with a state party when treaty bodies consider reports is often severely circumscribed.
- The proceedings of the treaty bodies in general are often poorly attended, particularly by national non-governmental organizations (NGOs) and national and international media.
- The availability to the treaty bodies of reliable, independent information on human rights conditions in state parties is a significant problem: the treaty bodies generally do not engage in fact-finding, state party reports are less than candid, NGO material can be highly selective or focused, and the UN secretariat is ill-equipped to produce in-depth country studies.
- In the case of two of the six treaties the individual complaint procedure is not available. In the case of three treaties which include a right of petition, access is limited by the rate of ratification of this optional mechanism. (The fourth petition system for the Women's Discrimination Convention is not yet in force.) Even in the case of the most widely ratified individual petition mechanism, the Optional Protocol to the Covenant on Civil and Political Rights, there have been relatively few cases over the years in comparison with the potential complainant population in ratifying states.
- The follow-up of treaty body conclusions is often minimal and reduced to promises of answers in a next state report years away.
- Access to the process is circumscribed both because actual attendance of the treaty body meetings is difficult, and because a comprehensible (in sufficient languages), timely, written account of the proceedings in the form of the questions asked, the answers provided and the record of the dialogue, is difficult, if not impossible, to obtain.
- Concluding observations, which follow the consideration of a state report by a treaty body, often lack sufficient specificity in their critique of domestic laws and practices to serve as useful domestic tools for governments and NGOs alike.

- There is a significant level of non-compliance with the Human Rights Committee's views on individual communications under the Covenant on Civil and Political Rights.
- Although the General Assembly, and other UN bodies such as the UN Commission on Human Rights and the Commission on the Status of Women, have responsibility to follow up treaty body conclusions, they generally do not do so.[30]

This is a damning description of how flaws in the institutional structures of the United Nations can render illusory the work of those individuals who champion the cause of human dignity. There is a general consensus on the part of the international human rights community that things have gone badly wrong. Some would argue that deliberate ineptitude and ineffectiveness is part of the tragic flaw that characterizes the United Nations mandate in the human rights area.

In the Vienna Declaration at the 1993 World Conference on Human Rights, the participants expressed "dismay and condemnation that gross and systematic violations and situations that constitute serious obstacles to the full enjoyment of all human rights continue to occur in different parts of the world."[31] The Vienna World Conference on Human Rights is significant in the formal history of human rights in that the Universal Declaration of Human Rights, originally adopted by only forty-eight nations in 1948, received reaffirmation, this time by 171 nations from all parts of the world representing the entire human kaleido-scope of cultures, religions, and traditions. The Vienna Declaration went further and proclaimed, "All human rights are universal, indivisible and interdependent and interrelated."[32] There was also an agreement at Vienna to create the United Nations Office of the High Commissioner for Human Rights to be the highest champion for human dignity. The second holder of the office, Mary Robinson, on the occasion of the fiftieth anniversary of the Universal Declaration in 1998, seemed frustrated at the lack of progress in the cause of human dignity:

> Just two months after taking office last year, I spoke of a worry that many in the United Nations appeared to have "lost the plot" and allowed their work to answer to imperatives other than those set out in the UN Charter. I suggested that this distraction from the core principles of the Charter could be a root cause of much of the criticism that is leveled at the Organization – couched in terms of complacency, of bureaucracy, of being out of touch, and, certainly, of being resistant to change.[33]

She stressed that she had hope that under the leadership of Secretary-General Kofi Annan, "the gap between the rhetoric and action on human rights" would narrow. She also stressed that this gap was not small:

> The record of the past fifty years does not encourage any "business as usual" approach. Twice in this decade we have witnessed genocide. Rape has become a weapon of war. Torture, arbitrary detention, and disappearance

remain commonplace. Hundreds of millions live in extreme poverty, suffering from malnutrition, disease, and a lack of hope. Many billions of dollars have been spent and much rhetoric expended for disturbingly little result. This massive failure of implementation shames us all.[34]

On 19 March 2001, Mary Robinson announced her intention to resign (which she subsequently delayed to September of 2002) stating that she could be a much more effective champion for human rights outside the constraints of the United Nations. She also cited the fact that the United Nations allocates less than 2 per cent of its US$20 million budget to cover the ever-increasing tasks confronting the Office of the High Commissioner for Human Rights. In addition, she noted the unfair pressure that had been placed on her staff as but another reason for her not to seek another term as the UN-designated global champion for human rights.[35]

As for the body that crafted the Universal Declaration of Human Rights, the UN Human Rights Commission, its evolution has taken a similar path. At its six-week annual session in April of 2001, a leading human rights activist, Reed Brody of Human Rights Watch, concluded that the foxes were guarding the chickens. Fourteen of the new members of the Commission included representatives from countries with very bad human rights records, such as the Democratic Republic of Congo, Kenya, Libya, Syria, and Vietnam. A description by *The Economist* of the workings of the Commission at its annual session in 2001 described the annual majority voting in the following manner: "Governments tend to club together to defend their mutual self-interest, especially when they have a record of brutality that is criticised by non-governmental organisations (NGOs) or by western governments."[36] Predictably, resolutions sponsored by the United States or a European country concerning human rights abuses in China are voted down. In addition, it is often alleged that the Commission gives little help or resources to the Special Rapporteurs, Special Representatives, Independent Experts, and Working Groups that it appoints to inquire into specific human rights situations, and that, moreover, when they issue their reports, there is little follow-through, often with tragic results.[37] Warnings from one of the Commission's own experts on the planning of the genocide in Rwanda were given to and ignored by the Commission before the genocide actually occurred in 1994.[38] The Commission, in the view of many, has failed to perform the critical implementation role envisaged for it by the founders of the United Nations. The present-day members of the United Nations seem determined to have the Commission slide into further ineffectiveness. On 3 May 2001, the United States, for the first time since it helped to establish the Commission in 1948, was voted off the fifty-three-member Commission in a secret ballot at the UN Economic and Social Council. China, which continued to be a member, rejoiced in this result, accusing the United States of using human rights as a political weapon.[39] However, the United States was voted back on to the Commission early in 2002 after its allies on the Commission were embarrassed by its absence.

It will take time, resources, and determination to turn the UN diplomatic decorations of ratified human rights treaties into meaningful protection for human rights and dignity for all members of the human family through such treaty bodies and monitoring mechanisms. The longer the wait, the greater the effect of the tragic flaw will be.

However, the long-term perspective must not also be lost. As the eminent human rights jurist Henry Steiner has noted,

> In a world rich in human rights norms and ideals but wanting in political will and enforcement of those ideals, the universal institutions have played a modest role ... We are much better off having our institutions, whatever their inadequacies, than resting with declarations and law-making treaties that lack permanent human rights organs. They give us a start. We can exploit the politically possible to work toward a next half-century that will give international institutions and processes greater capacity to aid peoples.[40]

While Steiner's optimism is not unrealistic, for his hopes to be accomplished, the fundamental principles behind the institutions of global governance will have to change, to stand a chance of breaking down the barriers and inertia against giving the individual champions and institutions of human rights greater capacity to ensure the human rights of the peoples of the world. The treaty bodies of the various international human rights treaties and the Human Rights Commission must start being treated as quasi-judicial bodies that are a critical part of the international rule of law and justice, rather than as instruments of those who view the body of international human rights law more as diplomatic decorations than binding obligations.

Genocide, the Cold War and complicity: the Age of Hypocrisy

In the half-century since the end of the Second World War, we have seen emerging in both greater frequency and intensity the most evil form of violation of human dignity: genocide. As discussed in the opening pages of this chapter, the horrors of the path to the genocide of over eleven million people at the hands of the Axis Powers during the war was one of the driving forces for the creation of the United Nations. As we have seen, the motivation to secure the human rights of all humanity that started with the Atlantic Charter and the Declaration of the United Nations in 1941 was not forcefully entrenched in the provisions of the United Nations Charter.

One day before the Universal Declaration of Human Rights was adopted in 1948, the General Assembly adopted a Convention which, although not as celebrated as the Universal Declaration, is deemed by the most eminent jurists to bind both signatories and non-signatories alike because of its most fundamental principles on human rights.[41] The treaty is the Convention on the Prevention and Punishment of the Crime of Genocide, adopted by the United Nations General Assembly on 9 December 1948.[42]

The Genocide Convention came into force in a shorter time frame than the International Covenants described above after the necessary twenty ratifications in 1951. By October of 2001 it had fewer ratifications than the International Covenants, with 137 states ratifying, and like the Covenants is again stricken with reservations, even by the United States.[43] The Genocide Convention was intended to go beyond the principles of the Nuremberg Charter, which required a link between what was called in the Nuremberg Charter "crimes against humanity" and the international conflict of the Second World War. The critical provisions of the Genocide Convention made it clear that genocide could be committed during a war or during peacetime:

Article I

The Contracting Parties confirm that genocide, whether committed in time of peace or war, is a crime under international law which they undertake to prevent and punish.

Article II

In the present Convention, genocide means any of the following acts committed with intent to destroy, in whole or in part, a national, ethnical, racial or religious group, as such:

(a) Killing members of the group;

(b) Causing serious bodily or mental harm to members of the group;

(c) Deliberately inflicting on the group conditions of life calculated to bring about its physical destruction in whole or in part;

(d) Imposing measures intended to prevent births within the group;

(e) Forcibly transferring children of the group to another group.

Article III

The following acts shall be punishable:

(a) Genocide;

(b) Conspiracy to commit genocide;

(c) Direct and public incitement to commit genocide;

(d) Attempts to commit genocide;

(e) Complicity in genocide.

Article IV

Persons committing genocide or any of the other acts enumerated in Article III shall be punished, whether they are constitutionally responsible rulers, public officials or private individuals.

These provisions of the Genocide Convention reach beyond the traditional ambit of international law that focuses on juridical relations between states, and imposes individual responsibility for the most atrocious of human rights abuses even where such abuse is done in the interests of the state. Thus the Convention should have been one of modern history's greatest instruments for breaking down the armor of territorial integrity and political independence and for allowing human dignity and justice to prevail. It is no surprise that once again the wait for justice will have to be agonizingly long. As one eminent jurist in this area, William Schabas, has noted:

> Almost inevitably, the criminal conduct of individuals blazes a trail leading to the highest levels of government, with the result that this aspect of human rights law has been difficult to promote. While increasingly willing to subscribe to human rights standards, States are terrified by the prospect of prosecution of their own leaders and military personnel, either by international courts or by the courts of other countries, for breaches of these very norms.[44]

As we shall see with the prosecutions of the former president of Chile, General Augusto Pinochet, and the war criminals in the Balkans who are still free, these are and always will be obstacles, albeit not insurmountable, to the implementation of the most fundamental human rights norms in global governance. In addition, Professor Schabas correctly concluded that until 1992, "the Convention definition of genocide has seemed too restrictive, too narrow. It has failed to cover, in a clear and unambiguous manner, many of the major human rights violations and mass killings perpetrated by dictators and their accomplices."[45]

This problem was hugely increased by the fact that, during the Cold War, the dictators were often the proxies of the two superpowers. The accomplices were not only individuals within these proxies, but also the two superpowers themselves. The Soviet Union, whose state ideology was opposed to the very notion of human rights, acted with immense cruelty, both within the Soviet bloc and elsewhere. The signatures of the Soviet bloc on human rights legal documents meant very little in light of the profound violations of human rights within the Gulag, the mass murders during Stalin's brutal rule, the torture chambers of the secret police, and the mass persecution of religious and other minorities.[46] These horrible affronts to human dignity were extended and multiplied in the territories of their allies around the world.

The second major external accomplice was not infrequently the other superpower, which professed to be fighting the Cold War on behalf of liberty, freedom, and human rights: the United States of America. The ultimate external accomplice was the Security Council of the United Nations.[47]

The *Oxford English Dictionary* defines hypocrisy as "the assumption or postulation of moral standards to which one's own behaviour does not conform." The Cold War initiated an age of human rights hypocrisy. It was entered into by the West for seemingly noble reasons. When the Russians tightened their grip on Eastern Europe after Churchill pronounced the fall of the Iron Curtain in March of 1946, and increased their armed forces to present a clear danger to the West, all the while stoking Communist insurrections elsewhere, President Truman declared the start of the Cold War. In March of 1947, in a speech which later came to be known as the "Truman Doctrine," President Truman stated that the world had a choice between two forms of human governance:

> One way of life is based upon the will of the majority, and is distinguished by free institutions, representative government, free elections, guarantees of individual liberty, freedom of speech and religion and freedom from political oppression. The second way of life is based upon the will of a minority forcibly imposed on the majority. It relies upon terror and oppression, a controlled press, framed elections and the suppression of personal freedom.[48]

Just as the Atlantic Charter and the Declaration of the United Nations had made a call for action against evil based on the value of human dignity, so too did the Truman Doctrine, stating that it would be the policy of the United States "to help free people to maintain their institutions and their integrity against aggressive movements that seek to impose upon them totalitarian regimes." Later, President Eisenhower would push the rhetoric even further when he stated, "Forces of good and evil are massed and armed and opposed as rarely before in history. Freedom is pitted against slavery, lightness against dark."[49] President George W. Bush, would use similar words in the days following 11 September 2001, targeted this time at a worldwide network of terrorists.

Critics from the left have argued that when the forces of the West, called to arms by the Truman Doctrine, became enmeshed in the battle strategies of the Western military complex, reinforced by powerful economic interests, the means devoured the ends. Noam Chomsky and others have asserted and detailed this slide as regards the involvement of the United States in the gross human rights violations in Indo-China, Central America, Argentina, and Chile. All were done in the name of containing the forces of evil.[50]

The destruction of human dignity as a means to the end of containing the Soviets had major implications for the main institution of global governance, which was effectively controlled by the two superpowers that manufactured the Cold War. Perhaps the greatest implication was to be found, not only for historical purposes but also for the future evolution of the United Nations, in the genocide of the people of East Timor.

On 7 December 1975, Indonesian troops invaded the former Portuguese colony of East Timor. Before the invasion of East Timor, there was a population of approximately 688,000 that was growing at a rate of around 2 per cent a year. By 1981, the population had dropped to approximately 500,000. A third of the population, more if one takes into account the normal growth rate, had been slaughtered. In terms of the percentage of population killed, the slaughter in East Timor has been one of the worst since the Holocaust of the Second World War.[51]

The president of Indonesia who had ordered the invasion of East Timor had come to power with the assistance of the United States. Indonesia was a vital ally in the fight against the Communist expansionism in Southeast Asia that had triggered the involvement of the United States in Vietnam, Cambodia, and Laos. Others have well described how the United States was involved in the overthrow of the former President Sukarno and the coup of General Suharto which led to the slaughter of approximately half a million of his own people under the banner of an anti-Communist crusade. On Suharto's coming to power, the ties between the United States and Indonesia grew closer. This included greatly increased military aid and equipment despite the gross violations of human rights. Whether accurate or not, the taint of complicity hangs in the air of history.[52]

It is also alleged that the invasion of East Timor was delayed by President Suharto for a few days to avoid embarrassing President Gerald Ford and Secretary of State Henry Kissinger, who were in Jakarta at the time.[53] Some have argued that the United States condoned – or at least did not stop – the invasion, because East Timor controlled the strategically important waters of the Ombai–Wetar straits, which linked the waters of the Indian and Pacific Oceans, vital for the naval forces of the United States.[54]

The invasion of East Timor was also a confirming sign that the main institution of global governance had failed in even its primary goal of the protection of territorial integrity and political independence under Article 2(4) of the United Nations Charter. Resolutions passed by the Security Council and the General Assembly calling for Indonesia to withdraw and respect the territorial integrity of East Timor and its people's right to self-determination failed to elicit any response from Indonesia. Over time, the number of states opposed to these unheeded resolutions grew to the point that the importance of not offending Indonesia and its Western allies was of greater significance than the genocide of the East Timorese.

The Security Council passed two resolutions. Resolution 384, which was passed unanimously in December of 1975, called on all states to respect the territorial integrity of East Timor and for Indonesia to withdraw its troops without delay. Nothing happened. In April of 1976, the Security Council essentially repeated its earlier resolution. This time the United States and Japan abstained. Again, not surprisingly, nothing happened. The Security Council then stopped discussing the unfolding genocide.[55]

Other bodies of the United Nations, such as the Human Rights Commission, proved equally ineffective, as did UN-sponsored talks.

While the West was rightly outraged over the genocide in Cambodia by the Khmer Rouge, the genocide in East Timor, which was proportionately of a larger scale, was met with silence because of the exigencies of the Cold War.[56] The genocide in Cambodia was also a result of superpower rivalries, as has been well discussed elsewhere.[57] The history of the genocide in East Timor posed one of the most significant moral, political, and legal challenges to the institutions of global governance and international law, challenges that were doomed to be repeated in the later genocides in Rwanda, the Balkans, and yet again in East Timor in the last decade of the twenty-first century.

In the tragedy of East Timor, the main institution of global governance and international law was unable to meet the two main goals of protecting territorial integrity and human rights, the same goals that brought the institution into existence. In part, this was because the Cold War had driven the United States to partner with leaders and countries whose values were far removed from the ideals of the Atlantic Charter, the Universal Declaration of Human Rights, or even the Truman Doctrine. Such corrosion of the moral authority of key players in the United Nations, and indeed the West, due to conflicts not only in East Timor but also in Indochina, Central America, Chile, and Argentina,[58] would outlast the Cold War. It would set the stage for a moral coma in the post-Cold War period until the turning point in Kosovo. History is a way of describing the unfolding nature of humanity. The cruelty, moral blindness, and hypocrisy of the history of humankind in the era of the Cold War describe, with chilling clarity, the tragic flaw within the nature of humanity and its institutions of global governance.

The regional human rights regime in Europe: is the wait for justice over for Europe and is it a model for the rest of the world?

As regards the triumph of justice, Europe offers great hope, but within that hope there is a sense of deep historical dismay. To begin with the dismay: does it have to take two world wars, genocide, and the threat of the Soviet Union on the doorstep to initiate a governance system where justice can triumph? If so, then to bring justice to the entire world means the future history of world would indeed have to be bleak.

In contrast to the short memories at Dumbarton Oaks and San Francisco a few years earlier, in May of 1948, the Congress of Europe met at The Hague and decided to match rhetoric with justice by stating at the end of their meeting:

> We desire a united Europe, throughout whose area the free movement of persons, ideas and goods is restored;

We desire a Charter of Human Rights guaranteeing liberty of thought, assembly and expression as well as the right to form a political opposition;

We desire a Court of Justice with adequate sanctions for the implementation of this Charter;

We desire a European Assembly where the live forces of all our nations shall be represented.[59]

The Statutes of the Council of Europe of 5 May 1948 further established that its purpose was to be "the defence of individual freedom, political freedom and the pre-eminence of law." Article 3 made respect for human rights a precondition for membership. We shall see how this condition seems to be ignored in regard to the continuing membership of the Russian Federation, undermining the great work of the European Council to date.

The Committee of the Ministers of the Council mandated the drafting of the treaty envisaged by the Congress of Europe, and on 4 November 1950 the Convention for the Safeguard of Human Rights and Fundamental Freedoms was signed in Rome. As the Congress of Europe had also envisaged, the Convention established an effective system for the regional protection of human rights in Europe with a Commission of Human Rights and the European Court of Human Rights (ECHR) to monitor and implement the European-wide respect for fundamental human rights and freedoms. However, even in an area which felt the devastation of the trumping of human rights by national sovereignty, the Convention made the individual right to petition the Commission and the right to bring a member state before the Court conditional on express approval by the state concerned. The Committee of Ministers was made the final oversight body for cases not brought before the Court, making it possible for justice to triumph in the court of European public opinion and through the imposition of political sanctions. The Convention came into force on 3 September 1953.[60]

The Convention is limited primarily to the area of civil and political rights and does not pretend to cover the huge area of economic, social, and cultural rights. With the great lack of progress on the implementation of the United Nations Covenant on Economic, Social and Cultural Rights and the evolving nature of the European Union, perhaps the limited coverage of the European Convention was the right choice. One of the founding architects of the European regime of human rights, Pierre-Henri Teitgen, stated,

Certainly, professional freedom and social rights, which have themselves an intrinsic value, must also, in the future, be defined and protected. Everyone will, however, understand that it is necessary to begin at the beginning and to guarantee political democracy in the European Union and then to co-ordinate our economies, before undertaking the generalization of social democracy.[61]

While most accept that the European human rights regime was influenced by the Universal Declaration of Human Rights, Europe, through the Council of Europe, was the first supranational institution of governance that set up an effective complaint and judicial system to protect human rights. The European Commission and the European Court of Human Rights have been far more effective in protecting human rights and the rule of law than the various organs of the United Nations, although even the European regime is not without its "stains."[62]

In recent years, the European Commission of Human Rights and the European Court of Human Rights have been merged into a single and powerful institution for the protection of human rights by Protocol 11 to the Convention which entered into force on 1 November 1998. There are now forty-one contracting member states to the Convention. States that wish to join the Council of Europe must not only accede to the Convention but must also sign on to the optional protocols for the right of individual petition, under Article 25, and agree to the jurisdiction of the European Court of Human Rights. The caseload of this judicial infrastructure has dramatically increased since its establishment. In 1999, before being merged into the Court, the European Commission on Human Rights received more than 3,000 cases every year. In 1999 the Court rendered 177 decisions.[63]

Compliance figures indicate that Europe has managed to establish, through the rule of law, the essentials of effective restraints against human rights abuses. In very large measure, the member states of the European Convention have complied with the large number of decisions handed down by the European Court in a wide array of human rights cases.[64] Indeed, that justice has become ascendant in Europe is affirmed by the fact that Great Britain has joined most other European nations in incorporating the European Convention into their domestic legal system.[65] Many domestic courts in Europe regularly cite the European Convention in adjudicating disputes involving human rights. The impact of a major European Court of Human Rights decision against one country can thus be felt across all the forty-one members of the Council. There are more than 600 major decisions of the forty-one-member Court on virtually every aspect of the Convention, with thousands of Commission precedents on admissibility decisions. One of the key admissibility factors taken into account is the exhaustion of domestic remedies, which requires applicants to the European judicial machinery on human rights to give their domestic legal systems a chance to provide adequate and effective remedies before resort is had to the European human rights system. It is claimed by some that this principle of human rights subsidiarity is one of the key factors in the success of the European system, as it allows for a dialogue between domestic and supranational human rights judicial institutions and contributes to preventing the overloading of the system. Another factor that has contributed to the success of the European system has been its ability to adapt to change and remedy shortcomings.[66] Finally, the factors of a common European culture and a common political heritage of freedom and the rule of law are cited as major reasons for the system's success and for compliance with the decisions of the European Court. However, there is concern that the addition to the Council of Europe of the Russian Federation and other Eastern European states (where there is less of a tradition of respect for human rights and the rule of law) may negatively impact on a common European human rights culture.[67] Nevertheless, there could be a fundamental reason why even the new members of the Council may eventually fully participate in the evolving culture of human rights on the European continent, and it has everything to do with the desire to secure membership in one of the world's most powerful economic clubs, the European Union (EU).

The main judicial body of the EU, the European Court of Justice, while deciding in 1996 that the Union cannot accede to the ECHR, also ruled that basic human rights such as those in the ECHR are general principles of Community law. This ruling was then confirmed by the EU in the 1992 Maastricht Treaty on the European Union, and codified in Article 6(2) of the Treaty on European Union (commonly known as the Amsterdam Treaty), which entered into force on 1 May 1999. The same Article also requires that the EU respect human rights in external relations, and human rights are now one of the five objectives of the Common Foreign and Security Policy of the EU.[68]

Article 6(1) of the Treaty on European Union proclaimed that, "The Union is founded on the principle of liberty, democracy, respect for human rights and fundamental freedoms and the rule of law – principles which are common to member states." With such a proclamation it was inevitable that the Treaty on European Union would also state in Article 49 that only a European state "which respects the principles set out in Article 6(1) may apply to become a member state of the Union." The European Council, in June of 1993 at Copenhagen, decided on "political criteria" that must be met by candidates for accession to the Union. These criteria include "stability of institutions guaranteeing democracy, the rule of law, human rights and respect for and protection of minorities."[69] Many of the Central and Eastern European candidates for European Union accession, such as Slovakia, will have to improve their human rights records, particularly in the area of protection of minority rights, if the Copenhagen criteria are to be respected.

Article 7 of the same treaty also establishes a procedure for suspension of certain fundamental rights of membership, such as withdrawal of financial benefits and voting in the Council, in the case of a "serious and persistent breach by a member state of principles mentioned in Article 6(1)." The decision as to whether there is a serious and persistent breach is made by the heads of state or government on a proposal by one-third of the member states, or by the Commission with the approval of a two-thirds majority of the votes cast in the European Parliament. The Council on a qualified majority decision can then decide to impose such sanctions on the member state, including withdrawal of voting rights in the Council and financial benefits from European Union membership.[70]

The final linking of the economic union with the human rights system in Europe occurred when the Charter of Fundamental Rights of the European

Union was jointly proclaimed by the presidents of the Council, the Parliament and the Commission on 7 December 2000, at the Nice meeting of the Council. The rights proclaimed in the Charter seem to bring the solidarity of economic and political power and union to the aid of human dignity. The Charter is divided into six main sections: "Dignity," "Freedom," "Equality," "Solidarity," "Citizens' Rights," and "Justice." These sections include civil and political rights, rights of citizens derived from Community treaties, and fundamental social and economic rights, including the right to collective bargaining and the right to strike.[71]

Europe, after being the main oppressor of human dignity in the twentieth century, has evolved a swifter path to justice than the other continents and hemispheres. But dangers still lurk. Since the fall of the Berlin Wall in 1989, several countries in Eastern and Central Europe have joined the Council of Europe to show their determination to improve their human rights record and to demonstrate that they are keen to establish the rule of law within their national boundaries, and perhaps ultimately become members of the EU. The most controversial of the recent memberships has been the Russian Federation. This recent addition has the potential to bring the entire system into disrepute. The actions of the Russian Federation in the rebel republic of Chechnya could be viewed as crimes against humanity. Yet faced with the need to build and keep an international coalition against terrorism in the aftermath of 11 September 2001, the actions of the Russian Federation in Chechnya will be largely ignored in the capitals of Europe and America. One of the leading international human rights non-governmental organizations, Human Rights Watch, has severely questioned how the Council of Europe can morally allow Russia to keep its membership in the Council, given the continuing atrocities in the Chechnya region committed by Russian security forces.[72] A leading European human rights jurist, Manfred Nowak, has stated that

> the recent admission practice of the Council of Europe in respect of countries such as Albania, Croatia, the Russian Federation, or the Ukraine, raises doubts about the seriousness of the Council of Europe in applying its own membership criteria. Membership of the Council of Europe, therefore, no longer necessarily means that the political admission criteria in Article 6(1) TEU [*Treaty of the European Union*] are met.[73]

This could be a warning that the European system of human rights, a model to the rest of the world, could be sowing the seeds of its own demise if the desire for expansion by the Council of Europe disregards its own human rights membership criteria. Even when the tragic flaw is contained, there is always the potential for it to re-establish itself.

Since the establishment of the European human rights regime, there have been attempts to establish other similar regional systems for the protection of human rights and the rule of law. None have been as successful as the European system, in part because of the effects of colonization and the anti-human rights environment of the Cold War.

The regional human rights system in the Americas

In Central and South America, the Organization of American States succeeded in establishing the Inter-American Convention of Human Rights in November of 1969, despite the fact that the region had been a proxy battleground for the superpowers during the Cold War. The Convention established an Inter-American Commission of Human Rights with a limited mandate that has expanded over time to include the power to receive petitions or communications concerning violations of human rights, scrutinize member state reports, and carry out on-site visits.[74] In 1978, the Convention entered into force. The Convention also established the Inter-American Court of Human Rights situated in Costa Rica, with the seven members of the Court sitting in their personal capacity, but elected by the General Assembly. As in the case of the International Court of Justice, the decisions of the Inter-American Court are binding only on the member states that have accepted the jurisdiction of the Court.

Europe completed its human rights and rule of law catharsis through two world wars and a genocide that the world will never forget. While the human rights regime in the Americas has the potential to follow the European model, there will have to be considerable political will and civil society pressure to ensure that the wait for justice will not take as long.

Essentially, while all of the states, except Cuba, have moved to become formal democracies, the legacy of the culture of totalitarianism and lack of respect for human rights lingers on the American continent. Until the Truth Commissions have effectively implemented the foundations of restorative justice, until the impunity of the security forces and corruption is effectively restrained, until the former generals and even presidents have gone through the Courts of Justice, until the huge differentials of power, wealth, and resources are diminished, until racism, gender discrimination, and oppression of minorities and aboriginal peoples are effectively combated, the wait for justice will be a long one in the Americas, even with formal democracies entrenched on the American continent.[75]

The proponents of a Free Trade Area of the Americas (FTAA) are just beginning to insist that a free trade zone for the hemisphere must also have a foundation of effective democracies, the rule of law, and respect for human rights. The most recent endorsement of these foundational principles occurred at the Summit of the Americas in Quebec City on 21 April, 2001, when the thirty-four leaders of the Americas linked the participation by the member states in summit negotiations leading to a Free Trade Agreement for the Americas to the maintenance of democratic order. Later, a Democratic Charter for the Americas was hammered out by the foreign ministers from countries in the hemisphere. It seems that another continent may be starting slowly down the European path to justice.[76] However, the potential for the tragic flaw to re-assert itself is especially high in the early stages of the path to justice.

Human rights in the Asia-Pacific

The Asia and Pacific region has not yet produced any regional human rights regime or inter-governmental system for the protection of human rights. Some argue that in addition to the lack of political will, there is the reality of the authoritarian instincts and cultures of many post-colonial leaders and governments in the area. One leading Asian jurist, Vitit Muntarbhorn, has suggested that the lack of an effective regional system on human rights as exemplified by the case of Europe is "partly due to the lack of homogeneity in the region; it is perhaps too vast and eclectic for a comprehensive regional system."[77] Given the slow but steady progress toward a regional system in the equally vast and non-homogeneous area of the Americas, this suggestion is not satisfactory. The same author goes on to point out that identifiable action is taking place within countries and at the regional level, such as regional workshops and meetings supported by the United Nations, to discuss the establishment of a regional system and the emergence of national plans on human rights and human rights education. Perhaps most encouragingly (given the Asian reality), we are witnessing the emergence of strong civil society groups focused on the promotion and protection of human rights as well as the establishment of national human rights institutions and ombudsmen with varying degrees of effectiveness and independence.[78] The Asia and Pacific region may well see the emergence of a regional system, developed not from the top down, as in Europe and the Americas, but from the bottom up, put together with fierce tenacity by civil society groups assisted by the more effective and independent national human rights institutions and ombudsman offices.

The African human rights system

In Africa, the wait for justice may be even longer. In June of 1981, the Organization of African Unity (OAU) adopted the African Charter on Human and Peoples' Rights. It took twenty years from when the idea was first conceived for it to become reality.[79] The Charter contains one of the most extensive lists of rights in any human rights document, including civil and political rights, economic, social, and cultural rights, and the rights to peace, solidarity, a healthy environment, and development. Duties to the family, society, the nation and the state are also included. However, the Charter has some severe drawbacks. One is the use of so-called clawback clauses, which allow fundamental rights such as the right to liberty and security of the person to be limited for "reasons and conditions previously laid down by law." Likewise, while there is a Commission established under the Charter to assist in the implementation of the rights, it was only in June 1998 that the OAU adopted a protocol to establish an African Court of Human Rights to try to bring the rule of law to human rights claims on the African continent. The protocol, which will come into force when fifteen ratifications have been deposited, will provide for the Court to hear complaints directly from individuals or NGOs as well as from state parties and African inter-governmental organizations.[80] One eminent African jurist, Adama Dieng, noted in 1998 that no inter-state communication had been filed with the African Commission. He concludes:

> In light of the grave human rights situation on the continent, the only reasonable explanation for this inaction is lack of public awareness of the Charter and its complaints procedures. It is, thus, difficult to see the African Charter as a fully effective weapon for the promotion and protection of human and peoples' rights. And yet did the African States not undertake to respect these rights when they signed the United Nations Charter?[81]

The answer is that regional charters, just as the United Nations Charter, can become prisoners of the imperative of non-interference in domestic affairs and political independence. Even with the lessons learned from the depravities of the "big man" who tortures his people across the African continent, the paradigm of non-interference in domestic affairs and political independence reigns. The respect for human rights and dignity must break down the supremacy of national sovereignty and territorial integrity if the peoples of Africa are to finally obtain the justice that they have desired for such a long time. On 9 July 2002, the leaders of Africa took a step in this direction when they replaced the Organization of African Unity with the African Union. One of the main goals of the new organization will be to promote democracy and human rights, and to develop regional peacekeeping forces to deal with conflicts that have killed hundreds of thousands of civilians. However, many observers have concluded that lack of resources will inhibit this new organization from achieving its ambitious democracy and human rights goals.[82]

After the Cold War: the era of television wars, genocides, and virtual guilt

It was barely two years since the Berlin Wall had come down. The United States rejoiced in the new reality of a unipolar world, virtually unknown before in human history. President George Bush Sr had proclaimed a new world order of international peace and security, which would be enforced by the military might of the remaining superpower and its allies. He proceeded to prove it to Saddam Hussein, who had invaded Kuwait in August of 1990. The vital national interests of the United States and her allies were at stake in terms of the security of oil supplies and the possible threats that Saddam Hussein posed to Saudi Arabia and Israel, also vital allies of the United States.[83]

A compliant Security Council backed the wishes of the huge coalition put together by the United States to use force to get the Iraqis out of Kuwait. When the overwhelming force was launched against Saddam Hussein at the start of the Gulf War on 16 January 1991, the world witnessed almost a video-game style war, with television screens around the world filled with Iraqi targets being destroyed by smart bombs shot from stealth bombers and other military aircraft. There was little battlefield television reporting, as the media were tightly controlled by the coalition forces. The United States had learned the lessons of Vietnam and the power of the battlefield image. As it turned out, with the battle won in a month and the Iraqi withdrawal from Kuwait, there were very few coalition casualties and heavy Iraqi losses. The first post-Cold War television war seemed almost painless for the forces of the new world order, and also seemed to set the stage for the possibility of a *Pax Americana*. The global dominance of the West secure, the emergence of real protection of human rights, sanctioned by the United Nations, seemed possible. The stage management of the televised Gulf War also helped in this regard. The approval by the Security Council in 1991 of humanitarian intervention by the United States and its allies to protect the Kurds in Iraq seemed to reinforce this conclusion.[84]

These high hopes began to dim, and almost die with the resurgence of ethnic conflict in the Achilles' heel of Europe, the Balkans. In 1993, President Bill Clinton was doomed to inherit the leadership of the democratic world, governed more by the CNN factor than by the institutions of global governance or the rule of law.

After a referendum on independence for Bosnia in March of 1992, in which the Croat and Muslim population voted for independence from the Federal Republic of Yugoslavia (FRY), the evil hard-wired into human nature re-appeared in Europe in a way not seen since the end of the Second World War. Supported by the soon-to-be-indicted war criminal President Slobodan Milosevic of the FRY and his army, the Bosnian Serbs, led by the similarly indicted war criminals Radovan Karadzic and General Ratko Mladic, laid siege to Sarajevo, the Bosnian capital. Pictures of innocent civilians being slaughtered by the relentless barrage of heavy guns firing into apartment buildings, markets, and streets shocked the conscience of the world but produced little action from the Security Council, the United States, or the assembled economic and military might of Europe. The cruelty of the Bosnian Serb forces who besieged Sarajevo and went on the rampage elsewhere seemed to know no bounds. The United Nations Commission of Experts report on the war crimes in Bosnia revealed horrific details of systemic rape and sexual assaults, the destruction of cultural property, and the precision of the ethnic cleansing. The report revealed that even the timing of massive shelling of residential sections of Sarajevo was made to coincide with political developments and events.[85] Over 200,000 people would die in Bosnia before the Dayton Peace Accord brought the fighting to an end. The Security Council imposed economic sanctions on Serbia and an arms embargo that included Bosnia, which some have argued aided the genocide in that country. A United Nations peacekeeping force made up of Canadian, French, British, and Dutch soldiers was sent to keep a non-existent peace. Unfortunately they were grossly undermanned, under-resourced, and with totally ineffective rules of engagement or backup support from NATO or the United States.[86]

In July of 1995, the supposed safe haven of Srebrenica, guarded by a small contingent of Dutch soldiers, was overrun by Bosnian Serb and FRY forces. It is estimated that over 4,000 Muslim men and boys were herded away from the town and slaughtered. Human Rights Watch described the fall of Srebrenica and its environs to the murderous Bosnian Serb forces as

> a mockery of the international community's professed commitment to safeguard regions it declared as "safe areas" and placed under United Nations protection in 1993. United Nations peacekeeping officials were unwilling to heed requests for support from their own forces stationed within the enclave, thus allowing Bosnian Serb forces to easily overrun it and – without interference from UN soldiers – to carry out systematic, mass executions of hundreds, possibly thousands, of civilian men and boys and to terrorize, rape, beat, execute, rob and otherwise abuse civilians being deported from the area.[87]

In this war, the television images of emaciated Bosnians in Nazi-style concentration camps, the pictures of the Dutch peacekeepers watching helplessly as the Bosnian Serb forces herded the doomed men and boys from Srebrenica to their deaths, along with pictures of men, women, and children being blown to pieces in the streets and marketplaces of Sarajevo, produced the paradigmatic virtual guilt that eventually drove the United States into action. Belated action is the overdue offspring of virtual guilt. In August of 1995, at the instigation of the United States, NATO, with the authorization of the Security Council, began air strikes against the Bosnian Serbs. This enabled the UN peacekeeping force to eventually break the siege of Sarajevo using the appropriate rules of engagement and military weaponry. With successes by the Croats and Bosnian Muslims in other parts of the country, President Milosevic began to withdraw his military support for the genocidal action of his Bosnian Serb allies, leading to the eventual cease-fire and terms of relative peace in the Dayton Accords of November 1995. NATO forces, initially at 60,000 military personnel including a strong United States contingent, would have to stay in Bosnia for a very long time to enforce the peace and protect human rights in the remaining part of Europe, where the dark side of human nature is never far from the surface.[88] In some parts of the human family, this characteristic of the tragic flaw of humankind, which has no respect for human rights and dignity, can only be contained by the muscle of its neighboring region, and ultimately in some cases only by the remaining superpower in the world.

The UN Commission of Experts on Bosnia lamented the failings of the international community and the United Nations in Bosnia's tragedy in language that is almost painful in its poignancy, given what was to transpire in Kosovo and in the troubled continent of Africa:

> The United Nations experience in Bosnia was one of the most difficult and painful in our history. It is with the deepest regret and remorse that we have reviewed our own actions and the decisions in the face of the assault on Srebrenica. Through error, misjudgment and an inability to recognize the scope of evil confronting us, we failed to do our part to help save the people

of Srebrenica from the Serb campaign of mass murder ... Srebrenica crys-
tallized a truth understood only too late by the United Nations and the
world at large: that Bosnia was as much a moral cause as a military conflict.
The tragedy of Srebrenica will haunt our history forever.

In the end the only meaningful and lasting amends we can make to the
citizens of Bosnia and Herzegovina who put their faith in the international
community is to do our utmost not to allow such horrors to recur. When the
international community makes a solemn promise to safeguard and protect
innocent civilians from massacre, then it must be willing to back its promise
with the necessary means.[89]

The UN secretary-general, Kofi Annan, signed the report and in November
of 1999 apologized deeply to the world for the UN's failing in Bosnia. It would
not be the last apology for the incompetence of the United Nations in the face of
genocide. Such failures would overshadow the successes of the United Nations in
restoring peace and democratic rule and establishing a major human rights presence in Cambodia, Mozambique, Namibia, Guatemala, Georgia, and El
Salvador, among other countries.[90]

Before the virtual guilt from the Balkans began to haunt the living rooms of
America and Europe, another form of virtual guilt was beginning to take shape
in another troubled continent.

In mid-1991, the first photos of starving Somali children, moments away
from death, hit the television screens and newspapers in the United States. By
1992, international relief agencies had assembled the needed food and medicine.
When such relief arrived, despite the presence of UN peacekeepers, it was
seized by armed militiamen of the various warring clans. Up to 2,000 people
were dying daily of starvation, while in Mogadishu and other major Somali
urban centers, the "technicals" of General Mohammed Farah Aidid and his
enemies were locked in battle.

The United Nations managed to secure a truce so that humanitarian aid
could be directed to the population whose death throes from starvation were
being piped into the living rooms in the United States and elsewhere. After being
defeated in the November 1992 election, President George Bush Sr. sent in
American troops to protect relief workers in an operation called "Restore
Hope." The coalition consisted of 30,000 American soldiers and 10,000 soldiers
from allied nations. When the US soldiers landed on the beach in Somalia, CNN
accompanied them and took pictures of the night landing and shot them back to
the living rooms of America and the world. The era of television wars, genocides, and virtual guilt had begun.

When President Bill Clinton took office, the coalition had succeeded in
curtailing the mass starvation of the Somali people as well as opening up the
ports of Mogadishu and Kismayu and the crucial supply roads that linked the
country together. In March of 1993 the majority of the US military personnel
left. The television pictures reported an American humanitarian triumph. Only
some 4,000 American logistical support personnel remained, supported by a US

rapid reaction force of 800 heavy infantry and helicopter gunships. Days after the pullout, when Pakistani UN forces were searching for hidden arms belonging to General Aidid, twenty-four Pakistani soldiers were killed in coordinated ambushes. The United Nations forces, led by the Americans, began a hunt for Aidid, which resulted in more deaths of UN military personnel and seventy-three of Aidid's followers. On 3 October 1993, two US military helicopters crashed during an attempt by the US Army Rangers to capture General Aidid. In the fierce fire-fight that followed, eighteen Americans, one Malaysian and about 300 Somalis were killed, with many more wounded. In addition to the capture of an American soldier, television screens in the United States and around the world were filled with scenes of rejoicing Somalis dragging the dead body of one of the American soldiers through the streets. There was an instant outcry in the US Congress and the American public for a withdrawal of US forces and an end to risking the lives of American soldiers in savage far-off countries. President Clinton ordered the withdrawal of all American forces by 31 March 1994.[91]

The television pictures of the dead American soldier being dragged through the streets of Mogadishu perhaps also partially sealed the fate of 800,000 people soon to be massacred in Rwanda, including close to 77 percent of the Tutsi population of that country.[92] The only remaining superpower had recovered from similar pictures of dead soldiers being brought back from Indochina. In the age of saturation television, there would be no more stomach on the part of either American politicians or public for American youth dying in far-off lands, where the vital national interests of the superpower were not at stake. The CNN factor now had to be added to the tragic flaw that plagues the institutions of global governance and international law.[93]

In the age of television wars, genocide, and virtual guilt, the image can trigger first virtual guilt, then action in the cause of human dignity. Sadly, it can also produce overwhelming inaction, unless American citizens, especially on American territory, are attacked and killed, as was demonstrated in the days following 11 September 2001.

The consequences of the electronic image to global governance and law can also be profound. As discussed above, Article I of the Genocide Convention commits the contracting parties to both punish and prevent genocide. Article VIII of the same Convention authorizes state parties to "call upon the competent organs of the United Nations to take such action under the Charter of the United Nations as they consider appropriate for the prevention and suppression of acts of genocide or any of the other acts enumerated in Article 3."

The key organ of the United Nations in the prevention of genocide should be the Security Council, which is charged with the ultimate responsibility to take action against threats to international peace and security under Chapters VI and VII of the United Nations Charter. If genocide does not qualify as a threat to international peace and security, then the United Nations surely loses its moral right to exist. Perhaps knowing this, the Security Council and its permanent members did almost everything they could to ignore the unfolding genocide in

Rwanda until it was too late.[94] Again we see the deliberate ineptitude and ineffectiveness as reinforcing the tragic flaw within this global institution of governance.

On 6 April 1994, the man who was stirring ethnic hatred in Rwanda to stay in power, President Habyarimana, died when his plane was shot down. Within hours, the group that had planned the genocide for months, perhaps years, began the mass murders of Tutsis and moderate Hutus across the country. Alison Des Forges of Human Rights Watch gives a chilling account of the ample warning of the pending genocide that was given to the Security Council:

> A January 11, 1994 telegram from General Romeo Dallaire, commander of the U.N. Peacekeeping Force, to his superiors was only one, if now the most famous, warning of massive slaughter being prepared in Rwanda. From November 1993 to April 1994 there were dozens of other signals … Foreign observers did not track every indicator, but representatives of Belgium, France, and the U.S. were well-informed about most of them. In January, an analyst of the U.S. Central Intelligence Agency knew enough to predict that as many as half a million persons might die in case of renewed conflict and, in February, Belgian authorities already feared a genocide. France, the power most closely linked to Habyarimana, presumably knew at least as much as the other two.[95]

Both Des Forges and General Dallaire himself have also recounted how the pleadings for more troops, resources, and material, together with a stronger mandate and rules for engagement, seemed to fall on deaf ears. Des Forges has speculated on why the staff of the UN Secretariat, including the future secretary-general, Kofi Annan (who was then in charge of peacekeeping), may have failed to pass on to the entire Security Council, including the non-permanent members, the gravity of warnings of crisis and the urgency of General Dallaire's requests. She asserts they did not pass these warnings on because they did not wish to displease the major powers in the Council such as the United States. The immensity of this omission is clear from the confirmation by US military experts that, if General Dallaire had received the 5,000 well-equipped troops that he had requested, perhaps most of the 800,000 lives lost would have been saved.[96] Could it be that the United States had no desire to see its military personnel back in Africa so soon after the Somalia debacle, with the possibility of similar images of dead soldiers being sent home from a country where it did not have a vital national interest? If the Genocide Convention had triggered a legal duty on the part of the international community to prevent the slaughter in Rwanda, the only remaining superpower would have had to get involved.

Another leading authority on genocide, William Schabas, has documented how some of the permanent members of the Security Council strenuously objected to the word "genocide" even being used to describe the unraveling horror in Rwanda. This included both the United Kingdom and the United States. Schabas and others have surmised that this refusal to use the word "genocide" was prompted by the fear that it would lead to increasing pressure for the United States and the other permanent members of the Security Council to take action to prevent the genocide under the Genocide Convention.[97] With the then concurrent genocidal situation worsening in Bosnia, there seemed to be no appetite on the part of most European nations or the United States to send their troops into what could well be another Somalia-type humanitarian intervention disaster. The electronic image has had a profound impact on the workings of the international law of genocide, human rights, and humanitarian intervention.

It was only on 8 June 1994, after much of the slaughter had taken place, that the Council passed a resolution stating its grave concern that "acts of genocide have occurred in Rwanda." Following this pitifully late acknowledgement, the Council then authorized the humanitarian intervention force UNAMIR II on 17 May 1994. Ironically, the size of the force was projected to be around 5,500 troops, the number which General Dallaire had asked for to prevent the genocide.[98] A member of the permanent five of the Security Council, France, decided to deploy its own troops to create a "safe humanitarian zone" in southwest Rwanda.[99]

Given the hopes for and the rationale behind the Security Council, and indeed the United Nations, from the time of the Atlantic Charter to the Universal Declaration of Human Rights, the Rwandan genocide may be looked upon by historians in future centuries as a turning point in global governance and law. Unable to prevent a preventable genocide, the Security Council would soon be ceding ground and allowing other institutions of global or regional governance to take the steering position to combat another emerging possible genocide in the Balkans, specifically in Kosovo. Another passage from Des Forges' account of the Security Council's role in the Rwandan genocide notes the increasing obsolescence of the Council in preventing genocide:

> Members of the Security Council gave more importance to maintaining diplomatic procedures than to condemning perpetrators of genocide. Rather than demand that the Rwandan representative resign from the Council, they continued collaborating with him, thus treating his government as an honorable member of the world community. They did not insist that he absent himself from discussions about Rwanda or even that he observe the usual custom of abstaining from such discussions. They thus afforded him the chance to know and communicate to his government all proposals for U.N. action in Rwanda.[100]

The report of the Independent Inquiry into the actions of the United Nations during the 1994 genocide in Rwanda produced similar views stating categorically that "the United Nations failed the people of Rwanda during the genocide in 1994."[101] The report also concluded that, when faced with both the earlier risk and then the systematic implementation of genocide, traditional principles of peacekeeping had to be "transcended" because there can be no neutrality in the face of genocide. Finally, the Independent Inquiry, among other things, made a clear recommendation that the United Nations had to develop an action plan to prevent genocide. The report urged that the obligation under the Genocide Convention to "prevent and punish" genocide had to be made a concrete reality in the work of the United Nations, and that each part of the UN system, including the member states, should examine what active steps they should take to counteract such horrific crimes. It would be ironic that the specific active steps that the United States and other NATO members did take in the emerging "horrific crimes" in Kosovo would be to ignore the Security Council, and the United Nations Charter itself, until after the bombing stopped.

In December of 1999, the secretary-general of the United Nations, Kofi Annan, apologized for the failure of his institution of global governance in Rwanda in light of the report of the Independent Inquiry. On 14 April 2000, the Security Council accepted responsibility for having failed to stop the genocide in Rwanda. They vowed to do more to stop other such massacres in the future. Responding to the report of the Independent Inquiry and other investigations relating to the genocide, the Security Council members acknowledged that member governments had lacked the political will to stop the genocide despite clear early warnings of the imminent massacre. They also acknowledged that the Council had deprived the UN peacekeeping mission, headed by Canadian General Romeo Dallaire, of both the mandate and resources needed to stop the killings. Presiding over the Council, Canadian foreign minister Lloyd Axworthy stated that the inaction of the United Nations "made a mockery, once again of the pledge 'never again'."[102]

It seems it is easier for the institutions of global governance to create tribunals and courts to indict and punish war criminals or those who have aided and abetted them, than to prevent them from committing the "horrific crimes" in the first place. Even then, there are problems of limited jurisdiction or lack of resources, both financial and political as well as in terms of military cooperation, for these tribunals to carry out their functions effectively. Professor Schabas makes the point that Article VI of the Genocide Convention of 1948, which mandates prosecution for genocide before "such international penal tribunal as may have jurisdiction" should have been a mandate to the international community to create a permanent international criminal court. The Cold War killed such a possibility. Schabas gives a short history lesson about how long justice had to wait even with the setting up of such tribunals:

> The first international tribunal giving effect to article VI, the International Criminal Tribunal for the Former Yugoslavia, was established in May 1993, with a mandate that was severely restricted in both time and space. Following the genocide in Rwanda in 1994, a second, similar body was created. The Ad Hoc Tribunals of the Former Yugoslavia and Rwanda proceeded to prosecute charges of genocide that were within their temporal and territorial jurisdiction. An initial conviction for genocide was recorded on 2 September 1998, just short of fifty years after the adoption of Article VI of the Convention. Meanwhile, preparations for a full-blown interna-

tional court of general jurisdiction culminated in the 1998 adoption of the Rome Statute of the International Criminal Court. The Court will come into existence after the deposit of sixty accessions or ratifications.[103]

The wait for justice became compounded by the inability to bring the prime instigators of genocide, such as Radovan Karadzic and Ratko Mladic, before the International Criminal Tribunal for the Former Yugoslavia at The Hague. The failure by NATO forces to bring the two war criminals to justice not only harmed the stature of the Tribunal, but also encouraged the then president of the FRY, Slobodan Milosevic, to embark on his most recent and final attempt at more "horrific crimes" in Kosovo. For these crimes, Milosevic would eventually be indicted for crimes against humanity and brought before the Tribunal at The Hague. Once there, the Tribunal would also lay charges of genocide against him and his leading co-conspirators for the slaughter in Bosnia. His trial on all these charges began on 12 February 2002.

The Kosovo crisis, universal jurisdiction, and the International Criminal Court: turning points in the wait for justice?

In Kosovo, as in Rwanda, there were many early warning signs, the main one being the revocation of autonomy for the Yugoslavian province in 1989.[104] The FRY government in Belgrade unleashed officially sanctioned discrimination against the majority Albanian province in the media, educational institutions, public sector employment, property ownership, and in language policies. There was also a dramatic increase in arbitrary arrests, detentions, and the use of torture by the Serbian police and security forces, all of which was well documented by Human Rights Watch, Amnesty International, and other NGOs. The international community did not provide sufficient support for the non-violent resistance led by Dr Ibrahim Rugova. This led to violent resistance in the form of the Kosovo Liberation Army (KLA), which emerged as a major force, especially after the resolution of the Kosovo conflict was left out of the Dayton Accord which ended the war in Bosnia. Because the international community did not assist the non-violent protests, the KLA began a plan to incite, through random acts of violence against Serbian targets in Kosovo, an ever-increasing spiral of violence by the Serb security forces in the hope that the international community would eventually be forced to intervene. Their plan worked.[105]

The Serbian massacre of fifty-eight people in the town of Prekazi in February of 1998 turned the conflict into a full-scale civil war. The Independent Commission on Kosovo, led by Justice Richard J. Goldstone, the first Chief Prosecutor of the International Criminal Tribunal for the FRY, and Carl Tham, estimated that by June of 1999, in the neighborhood of 11,000 Kosovar Albanians were killed by FRY forces, and that approximately 863,000 civilians sought refuge outside Kosovo, while 590,000 more were displaced internally. Rape, torture, and other forms of human rights abuses were also widespread.

The political will and diplomatic efforts of the Europeans and the United States seemed only to respond to escalations in the level of violence and horrific crimes. Even then, the strategy seemed confused and reactive. This culminated in the emergence of the so-called "threat diplomacy" encapsulated in the Rambouillet discussions late in 1998, where NATO threatened a bombing campaign against the Serbs if the discussions on a peaceful settlement failed. The United States and NATO were in charge at Rambouillet. The United Nations had become relegated to a minor player in this last-ditch attempt to prevent genocide in Europe by diplomatic means. The discussions failed when Milosevic refused to sign, primarily because he could not accept a NATO-led military force which would implement the Rambouillet peace terms on FRY territory.[106] In the end he got such a force on FRY territory whether he liked it or not.

On 15 January 1999, Serb police and military forces massacred forty-five civilians in the Kosovar village of Recak. The day after, an independent monitoring team of the Organization for Security and Cooperation in Europe (OSCE) visited the site, including the head of the mission, Ambassador William Walker. Ambassador Walker's shock at the barbarity that he was seeing was shared with millions around the world through the electronic media. The CNN factor was being triggered once again. The Recak massacre and other incidents of escalating violence, especially after the pullout of the OSCE–Kosovo Verification Mission (KVM) monitoring force, put the credibility of NATO into intense focus, given the threat of bombing behind the failed Rambouillet talks. On 24 March 1999, NATO began what Michael Ignatieff has called the "virtual war" against the FRY. There would be no ground troops sent in by NATO. The memories of Somalia still burned bright. NATO unleashed an aerial bombing campaign against Yugoslavia above 15,000 feet to avoid the air defenses. The virtual war was conducted between 24 March 1999 and 10 June 1999. Over 10,000 "strike sorties" were made against military targets, telecommunications installations, transportation links including bridges, electricity production facilities, and oil refineries. Some civilian targets were hit, including the Chinese Embassy; however, most of these were claimed by NATO forces to be mistakes. There was not a single NATO casualty during the campaign. It may have been the first time in human history that a major military conflict produced absolutely no combat casualties for the victorious side. There were no pictures of dead NATO soldiers flashed back to their home countries. Human Rights Watch asserts that approximately 500 civilians, mostly Serbs, died in the NATO bombing campaign.[107]

The United Nations, theoretically the main institution of global governance for international peace and security, was not in the picture. The NATO decision to start the bombing occurred without consultation or authorization of the Security Council or any other body of the United Nations. The aerial war seemed to be a clear violation of the United Nations Charter. The threat or use of force is strictly prohibited by Article 2(4). The right of self-defense in Article 51 is strictly limited to a response to a prior armed attack involving an international conflict, until the Security Council can take measures itself. The actions have to be reported to the Council and do not affect the right of the Council to take the final measures to maintain or restore international peace and security. We shall discuss later how the United States would use this Article in justification of its military action against the Taliban and the al-Qaeda terrorist network in Afghanistan in the aftermath of the terrorist horror on 11 September 2001.

As discussed above, the Great Powers were also insistent on the legal obligation of member states not to use human rights or humanitarian reasons for intrusion into the sovereignty of member states. Article 2(7) of the Charter specifically prohibits intervention into the domestic jurisdiction of member states. Finally, Article 53 of the United Nations Charter required any collective action taken under regional arrangements, such as NATO, to have the authorization of the Security Council, except in the case of self-defense.[108]

It is therefore clear from the Charter and the decisions of the International Court of Justice that it is only the Security Council that can authorize the use of force under its Chapter VII powers. The aerial war unleashed by NATO was clearly illegal by the norms of the United Nations Charter and international law. However, we can sense that history reaches a turning point when universal norms are held up for questioning, not by madmen and bloodthirsty villains like Adolf Hitler, Pol Pot, or Slobodan Milosevic, but by leaders of the free and democratic world. And that turning point was reached when many regarded the NATO intervention in Kosovo as illegal but legitimate.[109]

The Independent Commission on Kosovo concluded that the NATO military intervention rested not only on the growing humanitarian catastrophe in Kosovo right up to the intervention in 1999, but also on the "weaving together of past experience and future concerns:"

- the resolve not to allow a repetition of the 1998 scale of violence and displacement in Kosovo;
- the related resolve to avert "another Bosnia," giving a crucial political and symbolic influence to reports of the Recak/Racak massacre;
- a post-Bosnia, post-Rwanda desire to demonstrate that the international community under US leadership was generally sincere about its resolve to prevent and punish severe patterns of human abuse;
- NATO's need to maintain credibility by following through on its threats, and to show an altered relevance of the alliance for the security and well-being of Europe after the Cold War, especially in view of its upcoming fiftieth anniversary agenda;
- concern among European states to avert the potential mass migrations that could result from an extended civil war in the region;
- the underlying conviction, based on extensive experience throughout the 1990s, that Milosevic could not be trusted;
- the belief that only an armed presence in Kosovo that was not subject to vetoes in the UNSC [United Nations Security Council] could ensure a transition to restore substantial autonomy for Kosovo.[110]

Since 1998, the Security Council had issued resolutions that the human rights and humanitarian crisis in Kosovo was the result of the actions of the Yugoslavian government in Belgrade. It had called for an arms embargo on both the Serbs and the KLA. It had urged the War Crimes Tribunal at The Hague to investigate the violence in Kosovo for possible indictments for war crimes. It had promoted the setting up of an independent monitoring presence in Kosovo, leading to the endorsement of the OSCE–Kosovo Verification Mission. It had condemned the displacement of refugees, called for an end to Serb violence that spurred such displacement, and urged the return of such refugees. However, the Council also firmly confirmed Serbian sovereignty over Kosovo. These actions by the Security Council, while laudable for the most part, had no chance in putting a stop to the increasing cycle of violence set in motion by Milosevic. Only the use of force remained. Russia and China let it clearly be known that any authorization of the use of force by the Council would be met with their veto. International law demanded inaction on the part of NATO. International legitimacy, the ghosts of Rwanda and Bosnia, and the turning of history demanded action.[111]

Some jurists have tried to justify the legality of NATO's actions on the grounds of humanitarian intervention. The literature on humanitarian intervention is burgeoning, and enough has been written to try to squeeze the Kosovo intervention into previous patterns of humanitarian interventions without Security Council authorization. These have included military interventions by India in Bangladesh in 1971, by Tanzania in Uganda in 1979, and by Vietnam in Cambodia in 1978. A cynical response to such arguments is given by Professor Schabas, who, after stating these interventions could not be justified by the Charter, argues that the "look the other way" reaction of the international community to these interventions was "much as cinema-goers cheer when an aggressive policeman tortures a brutal criminal, despite their general abhorrence of police brutality and recognition that it is fundamentally illegal."[112]

Perhaps the best counter-response to the arguments that NATO's actions were justified on the basis of humanitarian intervention is the behavior of NATO itself. As the Independent Commission on Kosovo has indicated, NATO did not give any international law justification for its intervention, and most jurists who supported the NATO intervention, including this author, argued that, while it was prohibited under international law, it was a legitimate exception.[113] The Kosovo "exception," however, has major implications for global governance and law. Indeed, the "exception" was further detailed in the way the conflict in Kosovo ended.

After the aerial bombardment began on 24 March 1999, the Serb forces initiated a vicious attempt at "cleansing" Kosovo of its Albanian majority. While the Belgrade government claimed that NATO had provoked the mass expulsion, others claim it was an attempt by Milosevic to destabilize the neighboring countries and widen the conflict. Whatever the reason, the CNN factor again swung into action. The pictures of hundreds of thousands of refugees on foot or herded into trains, including the very elderly, the infirm, and the very young, resembled the nightmare pictures of the Second World War. NATO promised that the bombing would continue and that the refugees would be returned. The Independent Commission on Kosovo asserts that during the NATO bombing, approximately 863,000 civilians became refugees outside Kosovo, while another 590,000 were internally displaced. Together, these figures represented 90 percent of the Kosovar Albanian population. The Commission also claims that around 10,000 killings by the Serb forces occurred during this period, and around 3,000 more went missing. "Horrific crimes" of sexual violence and rape were visited upon the fleeing Kosovar Albanian women as well as widespread use of torture and wanton destruction of Kosovar property.

The European states (especially Germany), together with Russia, which strongly opposed the NATO intervention, were keen to find new methods to end the virtual war, given that Milosevic had not been bombed back to the negotiating table.

It is significant that it was not the Security Council of the United Nations but the G8, a powerful body usually focused on global economic matters, which brokered the end to the war. In its meeting in Cologne in April of 1999, Russia and the G7 agreed to a seven-point peace plan. This plan was then taken by the Russian foreign minister, Victor Chernomyrdin, to Milosevic on 19 May 2001. As NATO forces began preparations for a ground invasion before the winter of 1999, Milosevic finally began to negotiate under the threat of a military invasion of his territory. An envoy from another organization which had its roots in economic cooperation, namely the European Union, finished the task of obtaining a settlement to end the bombing. Martti Ahtisaari, the president of Finland, and Chernomyrdin negotiated an agreement on the G8 principles with Milosevic. After Milosevic and the Serb Parliament formally accepted the agreement, the virtual war came to an end on 10 June 1999.[114]

The terms of the agreement would again further the impact of the "Kosovo exception" on universally accepted norms. The G8 principles required a withdrawal of Yugoslavian military and police forces from what the Security Council of the United Nations resolutely stated was Yugoslavian territory. The Agreement also required an immediate and verifiable end to the human rights abuses and violence in Kosovo by the Serbs. It called for the deployment of an effective international civil and security presence and the return of all refugees. It also stated that Kosovo would enjoy substantial autonomy within the Federal Republic of Yugoslavia. These concessions by Yugoslavia spoke to the very heart of what is supposed to be protected by Article 2(7) of the United Nations Charter, namely non-interference in the domestic affairs of member states.[115]

As if in great haste to recoup its own legitimacy, on 10 June 1999, the same day that the bombing stopped, the United Nations Security Council passed Resolution 1244 which sanctioned the G8 agreement and established the necessary structures for the creation of the "interim" UN civil administration of the province and the international military security presence led by NATO. Time would tell that the peace would be equally hard to first win and then consolidate.[116]

If one of the chief aims of the NATO intervention was to get around the blockages in the Security Council to stop another Rwanda or Bosnia genocide, how successful were the ghosts of those pitiful reminders of the failure of the institutions of global governance? The Independent Commission on Kosovo concluded that the intervention was both a success and a failure:

> It forced the FRY government to withdraw its army and police from Kosovo and to sign an agreement closely modeled on the aborted Rambouillet accord. It stopped the systematic oppression of the Kosovar Albanians. NATO had demonstrated its military clout as well as its ability to maintain its political cohesion in the face of a challenge that could have torn the alliance apart.
>
> But, the intervention failed to achieve its avowed aim of preventing massive ethnic cleansing. More than a million Kosovar Albanians became refugees, around 10,000 lost their lives; many were wounded, raped or assaulted in other ways. The Kosovar Albanian population had to endure tremendous suffering before finally achieving their freedom. Milosevic remained in power, however, as an indicted war criminal.[117]

While this is a fair accounting of the "Kosovo exception" for an immediate post-conflict assessment, it is suggested that the intervention is far more significant and perhaps will have far more positive impacts in the long term for the following reasons.

First, we suggest it may have had an impact on the culture of inertia and denial in the Security Council of the United Nations as regards unfolding humanitarian and human rights catastrophes. Emerging proof of this is provided by the later Security Council-sanctioned interventions in East Timor by the Australian-led force, and in Sierra Leone by the multinational forces.

Second, the growing involvement in humanitarian and human rights issues of global organizations that are primarily focused on economic issues, like the G8 and the IMF in the case of Indonesia and East Timor, is of great significance. Even the most ruthless of villains like Milosevic and former President Suharto of Indonesia are aware that the destruction of their economies (with or without the help of NATO or other military forces) will probably lead to internal insurrections that could topple them and imperil their private wealth, which in most cases is ill gotten. Some would argue that this finally occurred with both Presidents Milosevic and Suharto. Other villains and dictators are thus put on notice.

Third, the Kosovo exception cannot be defended on the legal grounds of a valid humanitarian intervention. But there should not be a need to do so. The Kosovo exception should be taken as a turning point in the evolution of global governance and law. This turning point is an urgent call, whether heeded or not, that the institutions of global governance, in particular the United Nations, are in need of a major overhaul. Likewise, the rules and practice of international law, especially as espoused by states like China and Russia which regard national sovereignty as paramount, are also in need of an overhaul. Despite or because of the Kosovo exception, these and many other states will not accept the under-mining of Article 2(7) of the United Nations Charter by reference to human rights or humanitarian concerns. Adapting a quote from former US President Clinton, they are on the wrong side of history. That history began with the tragedies of Rwanda and Bosnia, and became solidified with Kosovo. This trend continues most recently with the near-universal acceptance that territorial sovereignty could not protect the terrorist networks using Afghanistan as their base for attacks against American and other interests. That history involves the growing impact on the global community, not of nations, but of individuals. The emerging reality of a global society, knit together by instant and constant elec-tronic and media communications, may actually be driving an as yet unheeded agenda that human rights are no longer the forgotten twin of national sovereignty. The global community of individuals, not nations, is now demanding equality between human rights and national sovereignty. History turns full circle to the vision of the Atlantic Charter, the Declaration of the United Nations, and the vision of the promoters of the Universal Declaration of Human Rights. The tragic flaw written into the constitution of the United Nations is starting to be addressed.

The most recent victories of this new global community lie in the evolution of universal jurisdiction for the prosecution of war criminals and the establishment of the International Criminal Court. With regard to both of these "victories," human history sometimes unfolds with perfect timing.

While the United States and NATO were threatening President Milosevic, soon to be indicted as a war criminal, a former president, while on a visit to Britain, on 17 October 1998 was arrested on the basis of Spanish warrants. The warrants, issued by a Spanish judge, alleged he was responsible for systematic acts, in Chile and other countries, of murder (including the murder of Spanish citizens), torture, "disappearance," illegal detention, and forcible transfers. The former president was General Pinochet, who also had been the subject of extra-dition requests for the kidnapping, murder, or "disappearance" of nationals from Switzerland and France. Other criminal proceedings had also begun against the former dictator in Belgium, Italy, Luxembourg, Norway, Sweden, and the United States.[118]

Overturning the lower court decision on 25 November 1998, the House of Lords, in a landmark decision (but with a narrow majority of three to two judges) which some say initiated the practicality of universal jurisdiction around the world, held that a former head of state did not have sovereign immunity as regards crimes against humanity.[119] However, on 17 December 1998, the House of Lords set aside its decision because one of the judges had links to Amnesty International, one of the interveners in the case, and scheduled a rehearing in the case. In the rehearing, which has been heavily criticized, the highest court in Britain limited the scope of its earlier decision considerably by stating that state immunity protected Pinochet for the charges related to murder and conspiracy to murder, but not for torture and conspiracy to commit torture. The court held that

Pinochet was subject to extradition to Spain if torture was a crime of universal jurisdiction under UK law at the time the alleged acts took place. The international crime of torture was clearly established under the Convention against Torture, which Great Britain had implemented on 29 September 1988. Since it was alleged that there was evidence that Pinochet was implicated in at least two torture cases alleged by Spain, which had occurred after Britain's implementation of the Convention in 1988, the concept of universal jurisdiction permitted the extradition of Pinochet to Spain for such crimes. The extradition would be subject to the discretion of the Home Secretary. In the decision, the House of Lords had stated that the *ius cogens* nature of torture as an international crime gives universal jurisdiction to all the courts of parties to the Torture Convention, regardless of where the torture occurs.[120] While the later decision of the House of Lords has been severely criticized for limiting the scope of the earlier decision by the same court, it did not suffocate the revival of universal jurisdiction in international law. Rather, the decision has led to other prosecutions around the world based on universal jurisdiction. This has included the arrest, prosecution, and conviction of a Rwandan mayor in Switzerland for war crimes, and the prosecution of a Mauritanian military officer in France on charges relating to torture in his country. More recently, on 9 June 2001, a Belgian jury convicted four Rwandans, a politician, a professor, and two Benedictine nuns, of war crimes in Rwanda. This was the first time a civilian jury in one country has convicted persons for war crimes or crimes against humanity committed in another country. The jury sentenced one nun to fifteen years and the other to twelve years for their role in the massacre of 7,000 people who were murdered after they sought refuge in their convent in southern Rwanda in 1994. The politician was sentenced to twenty years and the professor to twelve years.[121]

However, there are still many legal and political obstacles remaining in the revival of universal jurisdiction. On 14 February 2002, the International Court of Justice at The Hague dealt a setback to the development of the concept of universal jurisdiction. It ruled that Belgium had to cancel an arrest warrant for an incumbent foreign minister of the Democratic Republic of Congo, Mr Abdulaye Yerodia Ndombasi, for alleged crimes committed during his term of office. The Court ruled that such ministers enjoyed full immunity under customary international law against any act of authority of another state that would hinder them in the performance of their duties. This immunity, according to the Court, would extend even to where such officials are suspected of having committed war crimes or crimes against humanity under existing customary international law norms. However, in a confusing additional ruling, the Court emphasized that such officials could still have criminal responsibility for such crimes while they enjoyed jurisdictional immunity. Jurisdictional immunity could bar prosecution for a certain period or for certain offences, but may not exonerate the person to whom it applies from all criminal responsibility. The timing of the exercise of universal jurisdiction over such officials becomes paramount in light of this ruling by the International Court of Justice. One critical aid in the development of clear and sound principles of universal jurisdiction is the promulgation of the Princeton Principles on Universal Jurisdiction. Developed by scholars and jurists from around the world at Princeton University in 2001, the Principles are designed to avoid the improper exercise of universal jurisdiction, and to give greater coherence and legitimacy to the exercise of such jurisdiction.[122]

As it turned out, Pinochet did not face his accusers in Spain because the British home secretary, Jack Straw, deemed him too frail to stand trial, and he was returned to Chile. On his return, on 1 December 2000, Pinochet was placed under house arrest and charged with crimes related to kidnapping, disappearances, and homicide during his brutal rule from 1973 to 1990.[123] He sought to avoid these charges by the same tactics, relating to unfitness to stand trial, which allowed him to evade the Spanish extradition request. He succeeded. The Santiago Court of Appeals on 9 July 2001 declared the former dictator mentally unfit to stand trial and incapable of understanding the charges against him. On 1 July 2002, Chile's highest court confirmed the earlier ruling. The Supreme Court, in a four to one ruling, concluded that the former dictator could not ever be put on trial due to an irreversible condition of dementia. Even if Pinochet goes to his grave without conviction by any court of law, the greatest legacy of the former dictator will be to lend his name to the revival of universal jurisdiction for war crimes and crimes against humanity around the world. The deficits created by the tragic flaw in the United Nations are now being addressed within national jurisdictions around the world through the workings of universal jurisdiction.

The practical reality of universal jurisdiction is that there is now a much greater possibility that courts anywhere in the world may claim universal jurisdiction over a class of international criminals. These include individuals who commit acts amounting to crimes against humanity described by Amnesty International as including "widespread or systematic murder, torture, forced disappearance, arbitrary detention, forcible transfer, and persecution on political grounds."[124] Human rights jurists also claim that as prohibitions, crimes against humanity have become part of the most fundamental norms of international law (*ius cogens*) and impose a duty, *ergo omnes* all states have a legal interest in ensuring these prohibitions are enforced. Therefore universal jurisdiction cannot be revoked or modified by treaty or national laws. Many countries around the world, but especially in Europe and the Americas, have enacted legislation which expressly gives their courts universal jurisdiction over crimes against humanity, war crimes, and other international crimes such as torture.[125] The encirclement of the acts of evil constituting genocide, war crimes, and crimes against humanity by the rule of law and universal jurisdiction that gathered steam with the Pinochet rulings will be seen as another turning point in the global wait for justice. The designers and implementers of genocide, war crimes, and crimes against humanity will have fewer and fewer places to visit, or hide themselves or their ill-gotten gains. As regards the struggle for human rights, universal jurisdiction must be seen as one of the more hopeful developments in combating the tragic flaw in the institutions of global governance.[126]

The final and most recent turning point in the wait for justice is the establishment of the International Criminal Court (ICC). Again, its origins point to the synchronicity in human history. In 1989, while the Cold War was in its death throes, the small Caribbean nation of Trinidad and Tobago proposed to the General Assembly the setting up of an international criminal court to assist in the fight against the global drug-trafficking problem. The General Assembly sent the issue to the International Law Commission (ILC) for study. In 1990, the ILC reported back suggesting the establishment of a court dealing with international crimes in general. The General Assembly approved and asked the ILC to study the establishment of such a court. After reports by a Working Group of the ILC on a draft statute for such a court, and the creation of an Ad Hoc Committee of the General Assembly to review the draft, and finally an attempt at consolidation of a draft statute by a General Assembly Preparatory Committee, a Diplomatic Conference was called for Rome in June 1998 to hammer out a final statute.[127]

In the summer of 1998, a ferocious battle was to be fought in Rome by civil society groups from all over the world in consort with a group of "like-minded" countries led by Canada. At the Rome Conference, there were 160 nations gathered, seventeen inter-governmental organizations, fourteen specialized UN agencies and 250 accredited NGOs who all had a hand in the formation of a statute of the ICC.[128]

In contrast to what was about to unfold in Kosovo, the main opposition to the resolve of the civil society groups and the like-minded coalition of states to have an effective treaty to establish an international criminal court at the Rome Diplomatic Conference came from the United States.

Before the Rome Conference, the Clinton administration had stated they were in favor of establishing an international criminal court (ICC) if the right protections were built into its statute. The United States had taken the lead in pushing for the establishment of the Ad Hoc Tribunal for the FRY and had assisted a year later in the establishment of the Ad Hoc Tribunal for Rwanda. Leading experts from the United States, like Professor Michael Scharf, have argued that the experience of these tribunals, despite slow starts and lack of adequate resources (and, in the case of the Rwanda tribunal, lack of competent prosecutors) have shown the world that "an international indictment and arrest warrant could serve to isolate offending leaders diplomatically, strengthen the hand of domestic rivals, and fortify international political will to impose economic sanctions and take more aggressive action if necessary."[129] This perspective has been strengthened with the removal, on 28 June 2001, of the former president of the FRY, Slobodan Milosevic, to The Hague Ad Hoc War Crimes Tribunal for the former FRY, to stand trial for war crimes, crimes against humanity, and genocide. This is the first time a former head of state has been brought before a war crimes tribunal. Human rights jurists and NGOs around the world hailed the bringing of Milosevic to justice as the beginning of the end of the centuries of impunity enjoyed by heads of state and senior political figures for massive human rights violations.[130]

At the Rome Conference, the main goal of the United States was to have an ICC controlled by the Security Council of the United Nations. This was the same Council that the superpower would ignore in the Kosovo crisis. The justification given by the United States for its position was that it needed the comfort of its Security Council veto if, as the remaining superpower left in the world, the largest burden of intervening in humanitarian crises would fall on American military personnel. In this humanitarian role, it did not want such personnel to be subject to the potential investigation of an independent ICC prosecutor or the jurisdiction of the ICC itself.[131]

Most of the other nations at the Conference, led by the like-minded group and the human rights NGOs, vehemently opposed the view that any country's citizens would be exempt from the jurisdiction of the ICC. Professor Scharf has suggested that the attitude of the US government, in particular the Defense Department, reflected the residual mistrust of international courts arising from the decision of the International Court of Justice (ICJ) in *Nicaragua v. United States*[132] which led to the American withdrawal from the compulsory jurisdiction of the ICJ. Fears about possible ICC investigations and prosecutions of American military actions in Vietnam, Panama, Libya, and Grenada may also have been behind the US push for a Security Council-controlled ICC.[133] Such fears may be compounded by actions that the United States military forces have taken in special operations against the Taliban and al-Qaeda terrorist network in Afghanistan after 11 September 2001. Here again, such fears are unfounded as the ICC Treaty clearly states in Article 11 that the Court has jurisdiction only with respect to crimes committed after the entry into force of its constitutive statute.

On 16 July 2001, the Rome Diplomatic Conference voted in favor of a treaty to establish an international criminal court. After five weeks of grueling negotiations, which had seen the remaining superpower isolated and sidelined by its own allies, the treaty was approved by a vote of 120 to seven with twenty-one abstentions. The United States joined a most unusual alliance with China, Libya, Israel, Qatar, Yemen, and most ironically, Iraq, in voting against the treaty. It was a very sad historic event for the superpower that had shown the greatest leadership in the establishment of the Atlantic Charter, the Declaration of the United Nations, the Nuremberg and Tokyo War Crimes Tribunal, the United Nations Charter, and the Universal Declaration of Human Rights. It is even sadder when the details of the ICC Treaty are examined to reveal that many, some would argue most, of the American concerns had been dealt with in the detailed provisions of the Statute of the ICC established by the treaty at the Rome Diplomatic Conference.[134]

The ICC Statute established three forms of exercise of jurisdiction by the Court under Article 13.[135] First, the Security Council could refer situations to the Court. This jurisdiction legally binds all Member States to comply with orders of the ICC as regards the surrender of indicted persons or transfer of evidence concerning the alleged international crime. These orders would be enforceable under Chapter VII of the UN Charter, by the Security Council.

It was the second category of exercise of jurisdiction that the United States most opposed. Under this category, situations can be referred to the Court by the independent prosecutor of the ICC. The third exercise of jurisdiction can occur where situations in which crimes appear to have been committed are referred to the prosecutor by a state party. The exercise of jurisdiction under the second and third categories of jurisdiction is conditional on the state of nationality of the accused or the state where the crimes were committed being parties to the Statute or accepting the jurisdiction of the Court. In most cases, therefore, the second and third category of the exercise of jurisdiction would rely on the cooperation of the parties to the ICC Statute to enforce rather than the Security Council. It was therefore obvious to most at the Rome Conference that the most effective jurisdiction of the ICC was the first type, which was supported by the United States. According to Professor Scharf the Conference, however, also tried to modify the second and third type of jurisdiction to convince the United States to sign on to the Statute. First, the second type of jurisdiction would be subject to "complementarity." This meant the ICC under Article 17 of the Statute would only have jurisdiction if national authorities were unwilling or unable to prosecute. Likewise, at the suggestion of the United States, the complementarity principle was subject to the requirements in Article 18, that the independent prosecutor must give notice of the intention to investigate and must defer to a state who decides to investigate itself, unless the prosecutor can convince the Court that such state investigation is not genuine.[136]

Other Articles of the ICC Statute designed to meet US concerns included limiting the jurisdiction of the ICC to "serious" war crimes of concern to the international community as a whole and represents a "policy or a plan". In addition, Article 15 of the ICC Statute requires the approval of a pre-trial chamber of the ICC before the prosecutor can launch an investigation, and giving the Security Council the ability to postpone an investigation for up to twelve months on a renewable basis. These provisions, included for the benefit of the United States, were sufficiently persuasive to attract all the other permanent members of the Security Council, except for China of course, to sign on to the Rome Treaty.[137] The second type of jurisdiction was viewed as essential by both the civil society groups from around the world and the like-minded group of states. This second type of jurisdiction is a critical aspect of global justice given the abject loss of "moral authority" of the Security Council after the debacles of Rwanda, Bosnia, and Kosovo.

With the Pentagon carrying the day against American approval of the ICC Treaty, the United States began to campaign against the ICC's jurisdiction over nationals of non-state parties, arguing that it was against the general rules of international law. This is an astonishing position by the superpower that has led the world in the establishment of international human rights standards since the signing of the Atlantic Charter. The "serious crimes" that are covered by the Statute of the ICC – namely genocide, crimes against humanity, including rape, forced pregnancy and sterilization, and war crimes – are, as the Pinochet rulings have confirmed even as regards a former head of state, crimes of universal jurisdiction constituting the fundamental norms of international law (*ius cogens*). As such, the commission of any of these crimes gives a legal interest to the courts of any nation, let alone the ICC, to exercise jurisdiction over persons alleged to have committed such serious crimes without the consent of the indicted person's national state. The United States courts have themselves exercised such universal jurisdiction in the area of international crimes of universal jurisdiction created under anti-terrorism treaties.[138]

Perhaps mindful of these inconsistencies, just hours before the deadline for signing on to the Rome Treaty expired on 31 December 2000, President Clinton, in his last few days in office, sent his war crimes ambassador, David Scheffer, to sign the Treaty. However, the president and his war crimes ambassador signaled that he could not submit the same Treaty for Senate approval if it remained in its present form, and recommended that his successor should not do so either.[139] The chances of United States Senate approval was slim, especially as the Senate Foreign Relations Committee, formerly headed by the arch-enemy of global governance, Senator Jesse Helms, had long resisted any attempt to give any institution of global governance binding authority over the United States. The irrational fear of US soldiers and peacekeepers being hauled before the ICC on trumped-up and politically motivated charges will keep such resistance high and prevent ratification for a long time.

Ultimately, despite the recent withdrawal by the George W. Bush administration of the US signature from the Treaty establishing the International Criminal Court, we predict that a future United States administration will ratify the Rome Treaty after some face-saving amendments are made. We will discuss below the significance of the American "unsigning" in the context of the aftermath of the terrible events of 11 September 2001. It is likely that the United States in the future will not be willing to share the ignominy of membership in the "like-minded" group of human rights oppressors that opposes the ICC. Under the Clinton administration, the US participated in the work of the Preparatory Commission on the elements of crimes, rules of procedure, evidence, and other issues.[140] This is a good sign that ultimately the entire leadership of all the democratic nations of the world will be fully behind this vital institution of global governance. Israel also signed the treaty the same day as the US accession. China will then be isolated among the permanent membership of the Security Council in opposing the ICC. The implacable opposition of China to any incursion into its national sovereignty by international human rights standards will only be loosened with inevitable democratic and political reforms in that emerging superpower. There is increasing evidence for the need of a permanent international criminal court. In February of 2002, the US administration sought a time limit from the Security Council on the Ad Hoc International Criminal Tribunal for the Former Yugoslavia and its sister Tribunal for Rwanda. The administration is asking for the Courts to be wound up by 2007 or 2008. As the US is the principal financial supporter of the Ad Hoc Tribunals, this request is a serious threat to the continuation of the Courts beyond the suggested termination dates. In a similar setback to the establishment of ad hoc international criminal courts, the United Nations, in February of 2002, announced that it would abandon its five-year efforts with the government of Cambodia to establish an international tribunal to prosecute leaders of the Khmer Rouge for the genocide that took place in Cambodia. The United Nations was unable to get sufficient Cambodian cooperation to guarantee the independence and impartiality of the tribunal.

On 11 April 2002, the sixtieth ratification of the ICC Treaty was received by the United Nations, thereby allowing the ICC to come into force on 1 July 2002. Indeed, by 11 April 2002, sixty-six ratifications had been received. On this date, without the participation of the only superpower in the world, a major turning point in the wait for global justice occurred. The encirclement by the rule of law of the evil that produces genocides, crimes against humanity, and war crimes became tighter. History will note that the tragic flaw of global governance began to heal in these times.

Conclusion: The Global Information Age and economic and military power in the twenty-first century; can justice co-opt them?

The CNN factor has created a moral imperative that nations who profess a belief in the preservation and protection of human rights and dignity should act in the face of evil. When it comes to what exactly should be done, disorganization, ineffectiveness, self-interest, confusion, and not an insubstantial amount of hypocrisy, reign. The standard response from the international community and the United Nations is to organize some sort of peacekeeping initiative. The early part of the twenty-first century may come to be known as the era of the vicious internal small wars, such as those in Angola, Sierra Leone, the Democratic Republic of Congo, Chechnya, Macedonia, Sri Lanka, and other places primarily in Africa, the Balkans, Central Asia, and Southeast Asia. The number of UN peacekeeping missions in this era has skyrocketed. Since 1988, the thirty-eight peacekeeping missions that have taken place are double the number of such missions in the preceding forty years. Sierra Leone presents the paradigm example of the dilemma facing the institutions of global governance in the post-Rwanda, post-Bosnia, and post-Kosovo world of intervention to arrest the rampage of evil. The UN brokered the Lomé Peace Agreement in July of 1999 between what is called a rebel group, the Revolutionary United Front (RUF), and the democratically elected government. The rebel leader Foday Sankoh, a war criminal by any standards, was for the moment a peacemaker. The UN may have had in mind the triumphs that came from following a similar strategy in its success stories in Namibia, Mozambique, El Salvador, Nicaragua, Cambodia, and other places. However, in the case of Sierra Leone, the rebels were little more than organized criminals whose main objective was to secure control over diamond resources, diamond-smuggling, and thousands of civilians by hacking off limbs to terrorize them into submission.[141] It would only be a question of time before the Lomé Peace Agreement would collapse.

In 1999, the United Nations assembled a peacekeeping force (UNAMSIL) cobbled together from many different nationalities. With around 10,000 military personnel involved, it was one of the largest peacekeeping missions in the history of the United Nations. The purpose of UNAMSIL was to assist in the disarmament, demobilization, and return of internally displaced refugees.

By May of 2000, the rebels had humiliated the force by capturing hundreds of peacekeepers and stealing, or in one case buying, their weapons. Hostilities between the RUF and the government resumed. The large-scale killing, torture, maiming, and rape resumed. It became a textbook example of the ineffectiveness of UN peacekeeping even when sufficient numbers of military personnel were on the ground, in contrast to Rwanda, where there were virtually none. The British then hastily deployed special troops to defend Freetown, support UNAMSIL, and to train the Sierra Leone army, before they too substantially pulled out. Foday Sankoh was arrested but succeeded by another very dubious RUF leader, Issa Sesay. The secretary-general recommended increasing the UNAMSIL force numbers, but the 13,000 agreed to by the Security Council in May of 2000 could not be met due to the withdrawal of Indian and Jordanian forces and the reluctance of other countries to contribute troops.[142]

The United States offered to supply air transportation for the troops of other nations, but only for very high fees that the United Nations could not afford. Kofi Annan gave the example of a previous American offer to airlift Bangladeshi peacekeepers for approximately US$17–21 million. Eventually, the UN flew the troops in on a commercial aircraft for US$6 million. In early May of 2000, at the height of the crisis, US assistance had been limited to flying in one planeload of Jordanian ammunition. The Secretary-General clearly indicated that humanitarian crises such as the one in Sierra Leone needed the military assistance that primarily the United States could provide but was unwilling to give. There seemed little interest on the part of the United States to offer economic assistance in the form of free military airlifts, let alone sending in military personnel to the unfolding tragedy in Sierra Leone.[143] There was no national or strategic interest for the remaining superpower in this faraway land, and the ghosts of Somalia still haunted the Americans. Meanwhile the Security Council deployed an inadequately trained and led peacekeeping force as an alternative to doing nothing, with the memory of Rwanda still fresh in the minds of members of the Council.

Some would argue that the American position had an internal rationality to it. The lessons from Iraq, Bosnia, Kosovo, and most recently Afghanistan, taught the United States that, when faced with leaders like Milosevic, Sankoh, Mullah Omar, and Osama bin Laden, who, at the pinnacle of the mastery of evil, deceive, dissemble, and play outside the rules of civilized humanity, the only effective option is to meet them with well-coordinated and well-commanded overwhelming force, or what is euphemistically called in military circles "robust military presence." For example, the Serb security and paramilitary units were suppressed in Bosnia, after they had felt the overwhelming force of NATO troops but not before they had humiliated, kidnapped, and murdered UN and European soldiers. Such overwhelming force also has a direct correlation to the CNN factor. The more military muscle, especially in the form of high-flying bombers as in the case of Kosovo, the less chance there is of having pictures of dead soldiers sent into the living rooms back home, thereby undermining the political will to intervene in the cause of human rights and dignity. If the political will does not exist to send such overwhelming force into areas far from the economic and strategic interests of the United States, some leading experts in the United States argue that the best alternative is to do nothing, rather than send military personnel into a potential no-win conflict.[144]

The United Nations does not have the option of dispatching a well-coordinated and well-commanded overwhelming force to these troubled areas, unless provided by the United States or other member countries. The debt-ridden institution of global governance, with its renowned inefficient bureaucracy and geopolitical infighting, could not be more ill suited to put together such overwhelming force in this era of small and vicious internal wars. Secretary-general Kofi Annan has called for the creation of a reserve of rapid reaction contingents that would be on call from countries with well-equipped and well-trained troops, and who would prepare the way for the deployment of other peacekeeping forces. The standby contingents would have to be given better combat authority by the Security Council and better intelligence on what they are likely to encounter.[145]

The United Nations is unlikely to get its rapid reaction contingents. The Global Information Age has created instant virtual guilt in the face of evil around the world. However, even the most ardent supporters of human rights in the community of nations are unwilling to engage the mass murderers or war criminals if it means heavy burdens on their national treasuries or risking the lives of too many of their military personnel. This is especially so when such losses will be beamed into the living rooms of every voting citizen in the nation. The Global Information Age has, in part, created the paradox of conscience and inaction that will haunt humanity in the twenty-first century and reinforce the tragic flaw at the heart of the United Nations. It is unlikely that the United Nations will be the institution to break this paradox of conscience and inaction. The leaders of the international community must begin to look at other arrangements for global governance that can offer some hope of change.

In the search for other arrangements, the realities of economic and military power in the twenty-first century must be examined. Economic and military power capable of preventing or ameliorating humanitarian disasters is increasingly available in different regions of the world. In the case of military might, NATO demonstrated such power in the Balkans and may inevitably be assisted in the European sphere by the emergence of a European Union military force. In Africa, the two great regional military powers of Black Africa are undoubtedly South Africa and Nigeria, acting in concert with their regional allies. The Nigerian military assumed this role in 1998–9 when its troops, leading the regional ECOMOG intervention force, subdued the murderous rebels of the RUF in Sierra Leone and later returned as a major part of the UN peacekeeping force in that country. While the Nigerian troops themselves have been rightly accused of violations of human rights and of humanitarian laws,[146] as well as looting and diamond-smuggling, they have provided some level of protection against indiscriminate murder and maiming of the terrorized civilian population of Sierra Leone by the RUF.[147] More recently, a United Nations report has implicated neighboring Liberia and its president, Charles Taylor, in assisting the RUF through diamond-, arms-, and timber-smuggling. Liberia, which is now the target of UN sanctions itself, has also been accused of collaborating with the RUF in spreading the conflict to Guinea. In August of 2000, the Security Council authorized the creation of a Special Court to prosecute those who have committed war crimes, crimes against humanity, and other serious humanitarian law violations in the course of the conflict.[148]

Anxious not to have American forces drawn into such constant chaos in this part of Africa, the United States has adopted a strategy of focusing on Nigeria and its allies as the 'regional champions. The new administration of George W. Bush has pledged to help train Nigerian forces in peacekeeping operations. In a partnership called "Operation Focus Relief," through training and providing weapons the United States assisted Nigerian, Ghanaian, and Senegalese battalions to become more effective in the UNAMSIL force.[149] With the world's attention turned away from Sierra Leone toward Afghanistan and the Middle East, the relative calm in this troubled part of West Africa, backed by the large peacekeeping UN force of 17,000 troops, seems to indicate that this strategy may be quietly working. The ultimate success of the regional strategy of the United Nations, backed by Britain, Nigeria, and the United States, was the relatively peaceful presidential and parliamentary elections held on 20 May 2002, which saw the election of President Ahmed Tejan Kabbah, who pushed for the huge UN force to bring the atrocities of the rebels to an end. The rebels, who are accused of human rights atrocities against the people of Sierra Leone, did not win any seats.

In the case of East Timor, in the wake of the failure of the United Nations to provide adequate contingency plans for the security of civilians after the vote in favor of independence on 30 August 1999, another regional power came to the rescue. In the weeks following the vote, Indonesian soldiers and the pro-Indonesia militia had slaughtered hundreds of people and had turned over 200,000 people into refugees. After Indonesia declared its inability to handle the security of civilians in East Timor on 12 September 1999 and agreed to a UN-sanctioned intervention, an Australian-led international force (INTERFET) of 10,000 personnel was sent to East Timor as an interim measure. INTERFET managed to successfully provide security for the civilians and eventually put a stop to the violence. Australia provided approximately 6,000 military personnel. In February of 2000, a UN peacekeeping force replaced the Australian-led force and a UN transitional administration was also set up.[150] In his farewell to INTERFET commander Australian Major General Peter Cosgrove, Timorese independence fighter Xanana Gusmao stated, "When the children of our nation learn of the sacrifices made by all of our martyrs, they will learn also of the role of INTERFET."[151]

On 30 December 1999, the United Nations issued its third apology in six weeks (the prior two were for Rwanda and Bosnia) when Sergio Vieira de Mello, head of the UN Transitional Administration, asked the people of East Timor for forgiveness for the UN's failure to deal with a predictable human disaster. Long before the independence vote, the pro-Indonesian militia had threatened a civil war and the slaughter of its opponents.[152] The lack of political will in the Security Council had again failed the people of East Timor.

History will record the courage of the battered but unbeaten people of East Timor who ultimately showed the world their determination for democratic self-rule, and the promotion and protection of their human dignity would be invincible. On 20 May 2002, East Timor became the world's newest independent nation, after three years of UN administration and the election of their heroic new president, José Alexandre Gusmao (also known as Xanana) on 17 April 2002.

Military enforcement by regional powers against designers and implementers of genocide, crimes against humanity, and war crimes is expensive, as even Australia found out. One of the most challenging pieces of the global governance puzzle as regards the struggle for human rights and dignity is where the economic leverage will come from to assist in regional humanitarian intervention.

If one seeks to identify the seat of economic power in global governance institutions today, the G7/8 group readily comes to mind. As we shall see, this relatively new institution of global governance is increasingly going beyond the economic sphere to encompass the traditional territory of the United Nations in areas such as human rights and conflict prevention and resolution. In its short life, it has already been successful in bringing about the end of one major human rights disaster, namely Kosovo.

The G7/8 origins lie, again quite ironically, in a meeting in November 1975 at Chateau Rambouillet in France, the same place that gave birth to the term "threat diplomacy" in the context of the Kosovo crisis. The six most powerful economic powers of the world, namely the United States, Germany, Britain, France, Italy, and Japan, focused on the pressing economic problems of the day, such as exchange rates and the stagflation that occurred in the wake of the OPEC oil crisis. Canada was invited to join at the Puerto Rico Summit in 1976. The European Union was invited to meet with the group on specific economic subjects in 1977, as were the leaders of the Soviet Union, and after its demise Russia, in 1991. Russia became a core member in 1998, but the G7 group still meet separately on core economic matters.

A leading expert on the G7/8, Professor John Kirton, has argued that the G7/8 has moved increasingly into the areas of human rights, human security, democratization, and conflict prevention, culminating in the Cologne Summit of 1999 where a peaceful settlement to the Kosovo crisis was devised. Kirton even asserts that President Ronald Reagan attributed the end of the Cold War and the rapid spread of democratic governance throughout the world to "the concerted action of the G7 countries in 'hanging together' to ultimately find and implement the correct combination of firmness and accommodation in pursuit of the democratic cause." In support of this assertion, Kirton points to the fact that, when the G7 leaders first met President Gorbachev at their 1991 summit, they "wisely refused to respond to his desperate plea for financial assistance, thus paving the way for the accession to power of his democratically oriented successor, Boris Yeltsin."[153] Although "democratic" is a relative term in relation to Russia, the G7 did pave the way for large-scale financial assistance to Yeltsin's turbulent country.

Kirton gives other examples of the human security agenda of the G7/8, such as debt relief, democratic conditionality on development assistance, coordination of assistance to end the apartheid regime in South Africa, taking China to task for the Tiananmen Square massacre, and other human rights issues, including those related to the handover of Hong Kong to China in 1997. But it was the Cologne Summit in June of 1999 which left the impression that the G7/8 could possibly emerge as a new global force in the struggle for human security and rights. The Cologne Summit was the testing ground for Boris Yeltsin's and Russia's commitment to the democratic values of the other members of the G8, given the traditional support of Russia as an ally of the Serbs. Kirton and others have suggested that the abandonment of Milosevic by his Russian allies at the G8 Summit left him no choice but to agree to the G8 plan and withdraw his troops from Kosovo.[154]

Another positive result of the G8 meeting in Cologne was the establishment of the G20 group of nations to focus on reform of the architecture of the international financial system in the wake of the Asian financial crisis of 1997. The group was to be headed by Canadian finance minister Paul Martin.[155]

The success of the G8's peace and security agenda at the Cologne Summit led to the establishment of the G8 foreign ministers' meetings, the first of which was held in December of 1999. These meetings began to focus on conflict prevention and human security. However, when confronting one of their own members, Russia, on its brutal war in Chechnya, even the mightiest military and economic powers in the world demonstrated their impotence. At the December 1999 meetings of the G8 foreign ministers, Russia refused to budge under a barrage of criticism from the other foreign ministers. Indeed, while the meeting was taking place, the Russians intensified their shelling of the Chechen capital, Grozny, endangering the lives of the 45,000 civilians who remained there.[156] Despite the setback with their Russian colleagues, the G8 foreign ministers issued a communiqué stating that a priority for the group's political agenda would be to develop sustainable strategies in conflict prevention, regional security, and arms control. The communiqué called for "an integrated comprehensive approach encompassing political, security, economic, financial, environmental, social and development policies based on the principles of the United Nations Charter, the rule of law, democracy, social justice, respect for human rights, a free press and good governance." Unfortunately France broke the consensus, and the G8 failed to adopt an action plan on these human security strategies.[157]

Expanding the human security agenda of the G8, in the preparatory process to the 21–23 July 2000 meeting in Okinawa, there were meetings of education ministers, finance ministers, and environmental ministers, together with meetings on cyber-crime and the digital divide between the haves and the have-nots in the Global Information Age. Again, there was a reaffirmation by the G8 foreign ministers, meeting at Miyazaki in July of 2000, of their commitment "to human security through the creation of an environment where the dignity, well-being, safety and human rights of all people are ensured."

The communiqué of the G8 reflected the outcome of these meetings, but with the additional rhetoric that comes with a millennium meeting:

> During the last quarter of the twentieth century, the world economy has achieved unprecedented levels of prosperity, the Cold War has come to an end, and globalization has led to an emerging common sense of community. Driving these developments has been the global propagation of those basic principles and values consistently advocated by the Summiteer-democracy, the market economy, social progress, sustainable development and respect for human rights. Yet we are keenly aware that even now in many parts of the world poverty and injustice undermine human dignity, and conflict brings human suffering.[158]

In the same communiqué, these leaders of the most powerful nations in the world again pledged to focus on conflict prevention and resolution in accordance with the Charter of the United Nations.

At the G7/8 meeting in Kananaskis, Alberta, in June of 2002, there was a concerted attempt by the Canadian host government to implement the vision of the 2000 G7/8 communiqué, at least as far as the African continent was concerned. Having promised to do so at the previous year's summit in Genoa and urged to fulfill their promises by the Canadian government, the leaders of the leading industrialized countries conditionally pledged that they would dedicate to Africa at least half of the US$12 billion in increased aid money promised at a UN conference in Monterrey, Mexico, in March of 2002. The action plan developed at the Canadian summit, called the New Partnership for African Development (NEPAD), promised that the development assistance "could" be directed at those African nations judged by a yet-to-be-established peer review system to be governing "justly" by promoting democracy, human rights, anti-corruption, and economic freedom. Skeptics have pointed out that there were no new funds promised for Africa and that even the conditional promises could be evaded if donors felt that the peer review system was inadequate. In addition, many have pointed out that the increased trade protectionism by the industrialized countries, especially the United States in the agricultural sector, can prevent these same African nations from growing themselves out of poverty. However, the Kananaskis Summit was also successful in getting the agreement of those attending to raise US$20 billion for Russia to decommission its nuclear materials and develop better controls over biological, chemical, and other materials that could be used by terrorists for weapons of mass destruction. Finally, the summit also announced increased debt relief for the most impoverished nations, cooperation on transport security, and the full membership of Russia in the group who will also host the G8 in 2006.[159]

Paying attention to the views of the critics of the G7 and now the G8 summits, the time is overdue for powerful words at future G8 summits to be matched by commensurate powerful action that deals head-on with the tragic flaw found at the heart of many of the institutions of global governance.

Proposals to engender a new Age of Hope

The economic and military might of the democratic world is concentrated in the G8 group. Despite its failure to rein in Russian brutality in Chechnya, this emerging institution of global governance has shown promise, as indicated by its leadership on Kosovo. The goal of the G7/8 should be to use its economic and military power to force the reform of the institutions of global governance, particularly in the area of international peace and security. We will argue below that the key aspects of such reform should be the development of a Global Human Security Fund and a World Development Fund. Such reforms can and should start with the Security Council of the United Nations.

The G8 should support the enlargement of the Security Council by starting with the admission of Germany, Japan, and one major Islamic nation, such as Indonesia, to the permanent membership of the Council. Consideration should be given to developing a permanent membership of the Security Council that does not carry the veto power. This could pave the way to allowing other regional powers such as Brazil, South Africa, and India to join. Enlargement of the Security Council should come with commitments by the major economic and military powers on the Council, including Germany and Japan, to develop a Global Human Security Fund to assist the new peacekeeping burdens of the United Nations. The Human Security Fund should also be used to give additional resources to the Office of the High Commissioner for Human Rights and the treaty bodies that oversee the implementation of international human rights treaties by member nations. Those who provide such funds will have the right to demand reforms to the ineffective bodies that monitor the core human rights treaties. There needs to be much streamlining and consolidation in such bodies before they can fulfill their mandate. Until this happens, the integrity of the Atlantic Charter and the Declaration of the United Nations by the architects of the United Nations will never be restored.

In Chapter 5 we also assert that the G8 group, and other states that have major multinational corporations headquartered within their jurisdictions, can build on the US$1.3 billion Health Fund to fight AIDS and other infectious diseases that ravage poor countries, especially in Africa, established by the meeting in Genoa in July of 2001. Similarly, we argue that the G8 can go much further than the proposed New Partnership for African Development (NEPAD) announced at the meeting of the group in Kananaskis, Canada, in June of 2002. We propose the development of a much larger World Development Fund. In

Chapter 5, we argue that part of the revenues for the World Development Fund must come from an indirect form of taxation on multinational corporations.

There have been various attempts at dialogue on reform of the Security Council, none of which have met with much success or hope.[160] This is due, in part, to the slim possibility of obtaining the required support of two-thirds of member states, including the permanent five in the Council, to amend the United Nations Charter.[161] The Commission on Global Governance has suggested a staggered reform, including the abandonment of the use of the veto power by the permanent five by 2005.[162] These suggestions are well-meaning, but somewhat unrealistic.

At some stage, the international community, perhaps with the G8 group in a leadership role, will have to consider developing the practice that, in the prevention or abatement of grave human rights or humanitarian crisis, the veto power cannot be used or threatened in the Security Council. The "Kosovo exception" can be considered the start of just such a practice.

At the Berlin meeting of G8 foreign ministers, it was agreed that the G20 should include in its agenda the financial measures for conflict prevention and the coordination of the international financial institutions' work in the area of conflict prevention and human security.[163] Such an agenda should include the establishment of a Global Human Security Fund with contributions coming from members of the G8 and other developed nations. The G20 group should also focus on how the international financial institutions, especially the International Monetary Fund and the World Bank, can link economic development and financial stability to the establishment of the rule of law and the promotion and protection of human rights.[164]

One of the main purposes of a Global Security Fund would be to bolster the peacekeeping and peacemaking functions of the United Nations and, with the authorization of the Security Council, to assist regional powers such as Nigeria, South Africa, and Australia in the prevention and curbing of humanitarian disasters in their respective regions. Middle powers, such as Canada, the Scandinavian countries, members of the Council of Europe, and the other countries of the Americas that are not permanent members of the Council, could assist in the development of effective global peacekeeping and peacemaking functions. Such assistance could include the training of regional militaries in effective military leadership, peacekeeping coordination, and human rights promotion and protection, including the observance of all applicable humanitarian laws.[165] Some have argued that regional organizations, particularly in Africa, have shown a lackluster performance in providing effective peacekeeping that respects humanitarian law and human rights.[166] At the root of such criticism is the lack of sufficient resources and military training. This has been recognized by UN Secretary-General Kofi Annan, who has expressed concern for the increasing reliance of the Security Council on regional and subregional organizations and arrangements in conflict zones. Other than NATO, he has pointed out that "few others have, or claim to have, the same operational expertise." In a similar fashion he has also stated:

... in recent years the Security Council has been reluctant to authorize new United Nations peacekeeping operations, and has often left regional or subregional organizations to struggle with local conflicts on their own ... That puts an unfair burden on the organization in question.[167]

The world is becoming more dangerous due to the numerous threats to the security of individuals regardless of nationality and citizenship. Threats from environmental degradation and climate change, pandemic disease, the rapid increase in small arms and accompanying violence around the world, terrorism, organized crime, drug and human trafficking, corruption, human rights abuses, and the proliferation of nuclear and biological weapons are a non-exhaustive list of these threats to human security around the world. Ultimately these are human rights issues, as the quality and value of life of each member of the human family is deeply impacted by these threats. The origins of the human security concept can be traced back in part to the 1994 United Nations Development Program (UNDP) Human Development Report.[168] This report categorized human security as involving seven aspects of security of humans, namely economic, food, health, environmental, personal, community, and polit-ical. Since this original definition of human security, the concept has been used by many to focus on the threats to individuals in various types of violent conflict. This focus has had practical outcomes as witnessed by the ban on landmines orchestrated by determined civil society groups from around the world, again in consort with like-minded nations led by Canada. The Ottawa Landmines Convention[169] has created a worldwide movement to ban the use of these killers of innocent men, women, and children long after the conflicts are over. The former foreign minister of Canada, Lloyd Axworthy, was candid in his faint praise of the institutions of global governance as regards the Ottawa Convention:

> In the campaign to ban landmines, for example, we had to go outside the UN's Conference on Disarmament to get an effective ban convention. This was not because of any disdain for that venue – quite the contrary – but because we saw that, if we wanted a complete and effective ban in our own lifetimes, we would have to find another way. At a moment of opportunity, the UN found itself structurally and politically hindered from taking action.[170]

Axworthy and others have also claimed that civil society groups, acting in consort with again virtually the same like-minded nations, were key to securing the Rome Treaty on the International Criminal Court.

In these two areas, a focus by individuals, groups, and like-minded nations has managed to produce tangible results from the human security agenda. The proponents of human security see the concept as a way to reconcile the tragic flaw of the United Nations Charter, which pits territorial integrity and political independence against human rights and dignity. These proponents argue that national sovereignty and security are not ends in themselves. Rather, they are a means for achieving the security of the citizens. When the above-listed threats to human security exist, then neither the individual nor the sovereignty of the state is safe. Human security requires the tackling of the root causes of these threats to both human and national security and taking preventative measures to reduce vulnerability, minimizing risk, and taking adequate remedial measures when prevention fails. Therefore, such measures require the foreign, defense, intelligence, and development policies of the industrialized and developed world to be coordinated to focus on specific threats to human security.[171]

The G8 group, again with Canada in a leading role, has, in the past, proposed to focus on specific threats to human security not specifically addressed by the international community, such as the rapid proliferation of small arms, the eradication of exploitative child labor, and the protection of children in conflict zones together with the curbing of the use of child soldiers. While new international legal norms continue to be built by the United Nations and its agencies in these areas, enforcement lags and "invites disillusionment with the possibility of constraining power by the rule of law."[172]

International law must also adapt to the new realities of global governance and human security. In this regard, the international community should note the pioneering recommendations of the International Commission on Intervention and State Sovereignty sponsored by the Canadian government. In its report titled "The Responsibility to Protect," the Commission, made up of leading scholars and leaders from around the world, argued for the establishment of two basic principles. First, that state sovereignty implies responsibility and that the primary duty for the protection of its people lies with the state itself. Second, where a population is suffering serious harm, as a result of internal wars, insurgency, repression, or state failure, if the state in question is unwilling or unable to halt or avert it, then the principle of non-intervention yields to the international responsibility to protect arising out of the evolving norms of international law. This responsibility to protect includes preventive action, taking appropriate reactive measures, and finally includes the responsibility to rebuild.[173]

However, the broader human security agenda has faced opposition and skepticism from some experts and many members of the United Nations. There is still the desire on the part of many governments, governing parties, and individual leaders around the world to secure local, regional, and in some cases global self-interest, power, and control as a priority over combating the threats to human security outlined above, even if it means putting our species and the biosphere at risk. The global community of individuals and like-minded states has started the long and arduous task of developing strategies and legal norms to deal with this part of human nature. Until the task is done, the wait for justice will not be over and the eradication of the tragic flaw at the heart of the United Nations will not be a gift that we can bestow on our children and the generations of humankind that are to come.

Postscript: the effect of 11 September 2001, or has the world really changed?

This first chapter was largely written before 11 September 2001, the day that some say the world, including the world of global governance, changed for ever. We assert that the effect of the terrorist attacks on the United States on that day reinforces and strengthens many of our conclusions written before they occurred. The following is a short exposition of that assertion.

On 13 September 2001, President George W. Bush unveiled the "Bush Doctrine" to the world in response to the 11 September 2001 terrorist suicide attacks on the World Trade Center in New York and the Pentagon in Washington, DC, and the downed plane in Pennsylvania, that claimed the lives of thousands of innocent American citizens as well as the lives of those from dozens of countries around the world. He stated that under his administration, US foreign policy would demand that nations of the world join a global coalition against terrorism and deny terrorists safe haven or face the military, economic, and political might of the remaining superpower as an adversary.[174] On cue, the United Nations Security Council also passed two unanimous resolutions. The first resolution, on 12 September 2001,[175] condemned the terrorist attacks as a threat to international peace and security, and called on all states to bring to justice and hold accountable the perpetrators, organizers, and sponsors of the attacks, thereby implicitly authorizing the United States to use military force under the self-defense provisions of Article 51. On 28 September 2001,[176] the Security Council again unanimously passed another resolution reaffirming its condemnation of the 11 September attacks by adopting a wide-ranging resolution which set out a comprehensive framework and targets for combating the practitioners, sponsors, and financiers of international terrorism, including the creation of a committee to monitor implementation. American pressure on the Security Council pushed these resolutions through with great speed. This swift action was matched by the speed with which the US administration put together an astonishing global coalition of states to take on the al-Qaeda network and its leader, Osama bin Laden, hiding in Taliban-ruled Afghanistan.[177] Based on intelligence evidence-gathering, the US administration held the al-Qaeda network and their Taliban sponsors directly responsible for the terrorist attacks in the United States. Most European governments and Pakistan also agreed that these two groups were responsible for the attacks in the United States.[178] Later, a videotape showing a gleeful and gloating bin Laden expressing pleasure at the slaughter he had planned would prove these early judgements correct.[179] Within two days of the attacks, Russia had given its complete support to the United States' efforts to root out the terrorists and had even offered to assist NATO actions in this regard.[180] Russia no doubt saw the chance of persuading the United States that they shared the common cause of combating Islamic fanaticism, whether in Chechnya or from their bases in Afghanistan. NATO, on 12 September 2001, had invoked for the first time in its history the mutual defense clause in Article 5 of its Charter that pledged all members to come to the assistance of another member under attack.[181] History again showed its taste for irony. The mutual defense clause was primarily intended to allow the United States to come to the aid of the European members of NATO in the event of a Soviet attack against one or more Western European nations. Britain soon became second in command of the global coalition, sending its fighter aircraft and special operations forces immediately to the theater of operations around Afghanistan to work with the US forces. Canada and other NATO countries quickly followed suit.

There was much commentary that the United States had reversed its isolationist foreign policy after realizing how much it needed the United Nations, and a global coalition of countries around the world, to take on the terrorist networks responsible for the 11 September 2001 attacks.[182] This hope for a return to multilateralism was somewhat premature. These commentators pointed to how quickly the outstanding debt the United States owed to the UN had been paid, and the acceptance of a critical role of the United Nations in the reconstruction of Afghanistan after the United States had finished the first phase of the self-defense military action against the al-Qaeda network and their Taliban supporters.

However, the multilateral initiatives of the United States could also be looked at in a manner which reinforces the imperative of regional peace and security efforts, albeit within the framework of a global set of principles and strategies laid down by the United Nations guided by a superpower, itself wounded from the terrorist attacks. However, it is clear that one of the main reasons why the United States returned to the multilateral fold was because of the impossibility of achieving its aims against the terrorist networks and their sponsors without the active cooperation of regional powers. In this regard, the role of Pakistan, the Central Asian republics, and, to a lesser extent, the Arab allies of the United States became critical in the lead-up to the military campaign against the al-Qaeda network and its Taliban supporters in Afghanistan. These regional powers again demonstrated the necessity for globally sponsored regional initiatives against not only terrorism, but also human rights and humanitarian disasters. Pakistan, in particular, would prove to be a critical player in the American-led war against the terrorists and their sponsors in Afghanistan. It was Pakistan, with American backing, that had nurtured the Taliban into existence to fight against the Russian occupation of Afghanistan. The Taliban and al-Qaeda also used these resources covertly for terrorist attacks against India in Indian-controlled Kashmir. Ultimately, the incursions by Pakistan-backed terrorists into Indian-controlled Jammu and Kashmir, together with their deadly attacks on the Indian Parliament in New Delhi, would bring India and Pakistan to the brink of war, including the possibility of a nuclear confrontation. In the American-led war against the terrorists in Afghanistan, Pakistan was also deemed crucial in belatedly cutting off supply routes for military and financial support to the Taliban and their terrorist guests, while providing crucial intelligence for American military operations against their former allies. Finally, Pakistan was also crucial because it is a major Islamic nation, with its own minority of Islamic fanatics, which nevertheless joined in the global coalition against terrorism, thereby preventing the US-led campaign from being regarded as a clash of civilizations.[183]

Likewise, the Central Asian republics of Uzbekistan and Tajikistan also agreed to provide bases for American military operations. Additionally, Saudi Arabia and the United Arab Emirates, the remaining Islamic nations that had recognized the Taliban government, demonstrated their opposition to the "Crusade against Islam" portrayal by bin Laden by withdrawing their diplomatic recognition, even while some of their citizens still continued to funnel money to the terrorists.[184] Turkey, the only Islamic nation in NATO, agreed to send special operations forces against the terrorists. The statements and actions by other Islamic nations like Indonesia and even Iran demonstrated that the Islamic world desires the same global peace and security from senseless terror as the rest of the human family.[185]

President Bush on 7 October 2001 announced the start of the intense bombing of Taliban and al-Qaeda targets in Afghanistan. Using the proxy armies of the Northern Alliance rebels to capture enemy territory once the bombing degraded the enemy forces, as in Kosovo, the virtual war of high-tech aerial bombardment led to almost all the territory held by the Taliban and the al-Qaeda network being captured. Even though this time the American adminis-tration had prepared its citizens for large numbers of casualties in what it considered a retaliatory self-defense campaign, at the time of the writing of this postscript in the spring of 2002 there were only ten casualties caused by enemy fire.[186] One of those casualties, a CIA operative, was killed in a prison uprising by captured Taliban prisoners in the town of Mazar-el-Sharif. In contrast to the debacle in Somalia described earlier, while CNN, joined by its Arab equivalent, Al-Jazeera, showed horrific pictures of the slaughter of Taliban fighters and civilian casualties, there were no pictures of American casualties in the first phase of the war. This second major triumph of the American military machine that can win wars with few casualties began to spur talk in the United States of putting Iraq next on the target list in the war against global terrorism. A rumoured meeting, later disputed, between the lead hijacker, Mohammed Atta, and an Iraqi intelligence agent in Europe fuelled speculation that Iraq was also a sponsor of the terrorist attacks in the United States.[187] In the fall of 2002, President Bush signalled that the U.S. together with some of its allies were prepared to invade Iraq to disarm it and cause a regime change, if the UN Security Council did not act to disarm Saddam Hussein. In contrast to the "Kosovo exception" many of the U.S. coalition partners in Kosovo and the Gulf War regarded such unilateralism as neither legal nor legitimate.

Such actions and reactions demonstrate there was not really a return to multi-lateralism in the wake of 11 September 2001. In reality, what is occurring is that when the vital security interests of the major superpower are at stake, or its own citizens are killed, especially in its homeland, the United States will endeavor to form global coalitions and coordinate with the United Nations to ensure that those vital interests are protected. The United States demonstrated that it will, if it has to, reach across the globe to establish regional alliances to fight its enemies. That being said, the extent of the horror of 11 September 2001 has meant that terrorism finally joined the list of international crimes that warrant global coalitions and concerted action against their perpetrators and sponsors. While terrorism had claimed the lives of many thousands around the world before that date, when the front lines of the terrorism moved to New York, Washington, and Pennsylvania, terrorism joined the company of genocide, war crimes, and crimes against humanity as the most dangerous foes of global governance. Many Western nations, including the United States, Canada, Britain, and several European countries, passed severe anti-terrorism laws which some have argued have undermined civil liberties and human rights within their own multicultural communities.[188] The response has been that the new forms of global terrorism have created a new area of threat within many Western nations that lies between criminal activity and warfare. As such, all nations have the duty to pass such laws and to stop the financing and harboring of terrorists and their supporters.[189]

Ultimately, the sole superpower and its allies had to resort to the good offices of the United Nations to win the peace in Afghanistan and determine an exit strategy. With the rout of the Taliban government, the UN sponsored talks in Bonn, Germany, to allow the leaders of the various ethnic groups in Afghanistan to determine the nature of the post-Taliban government. On 5 December 2001, the four main ethnic groups agreed to the form and composition of an interim government which would be led by Harmid Karzai, a Pushtun tribal and military leader. They further agreed that, after six months, the former exiled King Zahir Shah would convene a *loya jirga*, or tribal council, which would rule for eighteen months until the holding of democratic elections.[190] This complicated nation-building agreement, while encouraged by the regional powers and the promise of billions of reconstruction dollars from the United States and its European allies, would have had less chance of being achieved without the mediation of the United Nations. To cement the "winning the peace" role of the UN, on 19 December 2001 the Security Council authorized a multinational force led by Britain to enforce the peace under its Chapter VII powers. The force, while dominated by European soldiers, significantly included contingents from Islamic countries such as Turkey.

To conclude our assertion that 11 September 2001 did not usher in a new era of multilateralism, at least not on the part of the United States, on 13 December 2001 the Bush administration unilaterally withdrew from one of the most important arms control treaties, the 1972 Anti-Ballistic Missile Treaty. The reason given by President Bush for terminating the results of decades of multilateral arms control was that America wanted to protect its territorial integrity and citizens from terrorist groups and nations by attempting to build an impenetrable missile defense shield.[191] Days before, the United States had also effectively stopped a multilateral initiative on strengthening biological weapons control despite the anthrax terror attacks across America.[192] At the very same time in the Middle East, both the United States and the United Nations seemed utterly powerless to stop the rising tide of human slaughter in Israel and the occupied territories of the West Bank and Gaza. Both watched as prospects for peace in the region evaporated further with every suicide killing by Palestinian terrorists in Israel, each countered by relentless military attacks and incursions by the Israeli army into the occupied territories.[193]

What was perhaps the most stunning unilateral move by the remaining super-power after 11 September 2001 was the revoking of the US signature to the Treaty establishing the International Criminal Court on 7 May 2002. In a letter to Secretary-General Kofi Annan, the US administration stated that the United States did not intend to become a party to the Treaty and that it had no legal obligation from its signature to the Treaty made on 31 December 2000. Indeed, the Bush administration went further, to assert that by revoking its signature to the Treaty it had no obligations under the 1969 Vienna Convention on the Law of Treaties.[194] Article 18 of the Vienna Convention puts an obligation on states not to undermine any treaties that they sign, even if they do not ratify them. Critics of this unilateralist action within the US Congress and elsewhere were quick to point out that the revoking of the signature would imply that "beyond the extremely problematic matter of casting doubt on the U.S. commitment to international justice and accountability, these steps actually call into question our country's credibility in all multilateral endeavors."[195] Some experts have claimed that, contrary to press reports, the United States did not renounce Article 18 of the Vienna Convention, a treaty that it has never ratified. However, US officials have often indicated that the Convention in large part does reflect binding customary international law.[196] The Bush administration defended its actions by repeating the arguments discussed above, claiming that the Treaty was flawed and dangerous. This, according to the Bush administration, was because the Treaty required the US to cede some of its sovereignty to a Court prosecutor who would not be accountable, and who could initiate political prosecutions of American officials and military officers, thus creating a powerful disincentive for American military engagement in the trouble-spots of the world.[197] While the present administration has promised it would not allow the US to become a safe haven for those fleeing prosecution by the Court, critics such as Richard Dicker of Human Rights Watch claim that the administration is "seeking to delegitimize it [the ICC] by casting doubt as to its credibility and effective-ness."[198] However, The President of the European Commission, Romano Prodi, and the UN High Commissioner for Human Rights, Mary Robinson, together with a host of American allies, have defiantly asserted that the Court will survive and will make a difference in accountability for human rights abuses and put an end to impunity, despite the absence of the world's only superpower.[199] It is ironic, given Samuel Huntington's thesis concerning the clash of civilizations, that the US now joins China, India, and Pakistan in being the only major coun-tries that have neither signed nor ratified the Treaty establishing the International Criminal Court.

Beyond the serious consequences of the American "unsigning" of the Treaty as regards the functioning of the International Criminal Court, the unilateral action is deeply troubling for the future of the rule of law in global governance. The chief of the UN Treaty Section, Palitha Kohona, is quoted as saying that, until the US "unsigning", it was "unheard of for a nation that signed a treaty to withdraw that signature."[200] David Scheffer, a former US ambassador for war crimes under the Clinton administration, has argued that the unilateral withdrawal has undermined both American interests and the cause of international justice. He argues that the literal removal of the Treaty from US international legal obligations constitutes a dramatic moment in international legal history.[201] The fears being raised by some of America's own leading international legal experts concern the terrible specter that the American "unsigning" may become a precedent for other nations to follow suit and attempt to withdraw from major multilateral treaty obligations, even those that they have ratified. In early July of 2002, the US began another assault on the International Criminal Court by threatening to veto the extension of the UN-mandated peacekeeping mission in Bosnia, and potentially other parts of the world, if the Security Council did not pass a resolution that UN peacekeeping forces are immune from the jurisdiction of the Court.[202] Ultimately, a compromise was reached on 12 July 2002, when the Security Council passed a unanimous resolution that, pursuant to the existing provisions in the ICC Statute regarding deferrals of investigation or prosecution, for a twelve-month period there would not be any proceedings against peacekeeping personnel from countries that were not parties to the ICC Statute. The Security Council would have to renew the deferral after that point. While most of the nations supporting the Court felt that the integrity of the new global justice institution had been preserved, the Canadian ambassador to the UN, Paul Heinbecker, regarded it as a "sad day for the UN" because the Security Council did not have a mandate to interpret treaties negotiated elsewhere because of unilateralist pressures from the United States.[203] 0In August of 2002, the US started putting pressure on states, with whom they have diplomatic, foreign and military assistance ties, to enter into bilateral agreements which would bar the surrender of US nationals and Government employees, including foreign contractors, to the ICC. Claiming that these agreements are based on Article 98(2) of the ICC statute, the US had obtained 13 such agreements by November 2002. We suggest that Article 98(2) authorises no such agreement and that another provision of the ICC Statute, Article 90(4) which gives priority to ICC requests for surrenders barring an existing extradition treaty, renders these bilateral agreements null and void under international law.

The future will tell whether these and other unilateral actions by the Bush administration could potentially threaten the foundational institutions of global governance, such as the United Nations itself, and the most important treaties of international peace, security, and human rights.

The almost universal reaction of horror to the 11 September 2001 attacks, and compassion for the innocent victims and their families, may have raised the cry for justice against senseless evil and inhumanity around the world, but the tragic flaw still lingers.

2 World trade

For whose benefit?

The evolution of governance in world trade: another loss of vision

The post-war evolution of the world trade regime reveals intersections with and parallels to the development of the United Nations and its agencies. In July of 2001, at the G8 summit in Genoa, Italy, amidst raging street battles with anti-globalization protesters, the most powerful trading nations in the world readily admitted that the poorest countries in the world, from Africa in particular, had yet to benefit from the world trade regime. In addition, it was conceded that more needed to be done to give exports from the developing world greater access to the markets of the developed world. These are some of the many admissions concerning the development of systems of global governance, as documented in Chapter 1, that demonstrate a bias in favor of the economically, politically and militarily more powerful nations of the Western world. This chapter develops the thesis further to highlight the tragic flaw within what is potentially the most powerful institution of global governance in the economic sphere, the World Trade Organization (WTO).

We discussed in Chapter 1 how the Atlantic Charter was the crucible within which the United Nations' tragic flaw was formed. Indeed, the Atlantic Charter can again be viewed as the starting point for the introduction of the tragic flaw into the world trade regime. Contained within this document, which was signed by both Roosevelt and Churchill, was the famous declaration which stated that while freedom of trade would be supported by the two Great Powers, they would also recognize the right of all peoples to have "improved labor standards, economic advancement, and social security" and to "live out their lives in freedom from want and fear."[1]

In the final stages of World War II, the Allies began a series of conferences to discuss how to prevent the reoccurrence of the economic conditions that led to the worldwide depression of the 1920s and the rise of the Nazis in Germany. The most significant of these conferences was held at Bretton Woods, New Hampshire, in 1944. At this stage, it was evident that trade, economic stability, peace, international security, and human rights were clearly linked. The Bretton Woods Conference was successful in developing the institutions and agreements that dealt with the financial aspects of the post-war global reconstruction. This was achieved through the establishment of the International Bank for Reconstruction and Development, later to become known as the World Bank, and the International Monetary Fund (IMF). The IMF was created to re-establish the international monetary and exchange rate system that had disintegrated and caused the economic and social upheavals in Europe and North America. The World Bank's main role in the post-war period was less concerned with development than with encouraging foreign investment in Europe, which had fallen victim to the pre-war economic collapse.[2] As we shall discuss in Chapter 5, the time has come to re-examine the mandate of both the World Bank and the IMF.

The third pillar of the Bretton Woods System was to be the world trade regime. Movement toward this goal began with a series of conferences from 1946 to 1948 that established the General Agreement on Tariffs and Trade (GATT). There was supposed to be an integrated coherence to the Bretton Woods System. The IMF, the World Bank, and the International Trade Organization (ITO) were to collaborate on monetary, investment, and trade policies to ensure that Europe, North America, and Japan would rebuild their economies to the benefit of all citizens. This, it was believed, would be achieved through full employment, greater investment, stable exchange rates, and the political stability that such conditions bring about. As many have pointed out, the ambitious program of the Bretton Woods System had many contradictions that upset the grand plan for post-war economic reconstruction.[3]

The leaders of the industrialized world had not envisaged that the GATT would be the centerpiece of the world trade regime. The original plan was to create an institutional infrastructure around the GATT to collaborate with the other Bretton Woods institutions. It is ironic that the idea for an institutional framework, labeled the International Trade Organization, for the GATT came principally from the United States, who saw the need for oversight of the international monetary and trade systems as crucial for global peace and security.[4]

In 1945, the United States introduced a resolution at the newly formed Economic and Social Council of the United Nations (ECOSOC), calling for a UN Conference on Trade *and Employment*. The objective of this Conference was to begin the task of initiating multilateral tariff negotiations as well as drafting the charter for the ITO. After meetings in London, New York, and Geneva from 1946 to 1947, in addition to the negotiations on tariffs, a draft of the ITO charter was prepared, and was set to be finalized in Havana, Cuba, in 1948. The GATT was drafted in Geneva in addition to the negotiations that took place on tariffs. The function of the GATT was intended to be limited: it was to encapsulate the negotiated tariff reductions as well as some restrictions and protective clauses to ensure that the tariff commitments were respected. The ITO was to have the power to oversee and enforce the GATT, which was to be an integral part of the ITO. The draft charter of the ITO was completed at the Havana Conference in 1948. The highest order of priority was to have the United States, as the most important economy in the post-war world, ratify the ITO Charter. This did not happen.[5]

Just as with the cooling off over the high vision of the Atlantic Charter and the human rights proclamations contained therein, it became clear that the US Senate would not ratify the ITO Charter. The United States Congress had become less internationalist and more concerned with American self-interest than during the war or the period immediately after it. In December of 1950, the US administration announced that it would not re-submit the ITO Charter to Congress for approval. The ITO was dead.[6] As with the development of the United Nations Charter, which was discussed in Chapter 1, the tragic flaw began to creep into the world trade regime at the point when self-interest won out over the original high aspirations of the Bretton Woods institutions, which were derived from the original vision of the Atlantic Charter.

In the annals of history, grand visions seem so often dashed by parochial politicians sitting in powerful places. The failure to ratify the ITO shares some historical bonds with the present-day challenge of having the US Senate ratify the Rome Treaty establishing the International Criminal Court, which was discussed in Chapter 1.

The death of the ITO was to have serious consequences for the development of one of the most important features of global governance today, the global trade regime. By default, the GATT, a minimal code for trade relations, became the main game for the organization and coordination of international trade rules. Unfortunately, what also died along with the ITO Charter was the intention to have a world trade regime that would be infused with the social dimensions of trade, as well as global values of justice and human rights. For example, the Havana Charter made explicit reference to the need to link the world trade regime with fair labor standards, both as a principle of justice and as the underlying rationale for a rules-based trading regime:

> [A]ll countries have a common interest in the achievement and maintenance of fair labor standards related to productivity, and thus in the improvement of wages and working conditions as productivity may permit. The Members recognize that unfair labor conditions, particularly in production for export, create difficulties in international trade and accordingly each Member shall take whatever action may be appropriate and feasible to eliminate such conditions within the territory.[7]

As we will discuss later in this chapter and in Chapter 4, it is a moral, legal, and indeed economic imperative that the world trade regime return to the original vision of the Havana Charter in the area of labor standards and trade.

Devoid of its institutional framework, the GATT proceeded to develop over several rounds of multilateral trade negotiations. The major values underlying these negotiations were non-discrimination and reciprocity. To date, there have been eight rounds of multilateral negotiations since the original GATT of 1947. These rounds have become progressively technical in nature, focusing on tariff reductions and rules to prevent the subverting of negotiated tariff concessions. When institutions of global governance develop from highly technical foundations, there is a tendency for such institutions to treat their technical objectives as ends in themselves. There is also the tendency for such institutional development, led by technical experts, to become isolated from other institutions of global governance. Experts tend to focus only on their area of expertise and talk only in their own language. Some have argued that this is what occurred with the successive rounds of the GATT negotiations.[8]

The first five rounds of the GATT dealt primarily with tariff reductions among the industrialized nations of the world and were of relatively short duration. The sixth round, called the Kennedy Round, which took place from 1963 to 1967, achieved greater reductions of tariffs and began discussions on some of the trade issues affecting developing countries. There were minor concessions to these countries in terms of exemptions, or lesser obligations in the emerging trade disciplines of the GATT. The seventh round, the Tokyo Round, from 1973 to 1979, continued with the goal of reducing tariffs, and began the complex and as yet unfinished task of dealing with non-tariff barriers. The inclusion of non-tariff barriers in multilateral negotiations has led to increasing intrusion into the domestic policies of GATT-contracting parties in order to protect negotiated concessions. These negotiations have led to the initiation of discussions on subsidies, technical barriers to trade, taxation that discriminates against imports, dumping practices, state trading, customs procedures, and other domestic practices that cause trade dislocations.[9]

The eighth round of the GATT negotiations, the Uruguay Round, belatedly established the institutional infrastructure for the world trade regime. This institution, the World Trade Organization (WTO), is mandated to continue the work of the GATT. In terms of global governance of the world economy, there is little doubt that this is the most significant change since the Bretton Woods Conference. The creation of this institutional structure could not have come sooner. With WTO membership now extending to well over a hundred nations, the global trade regime must now deal with areas formerly exempt from GATT rules or that were managed under separate agreements, such as agriculture, textiles, trade in services, and intellectual property.

The WTO is the institutionalized personification of all the GATT rounds from 1947 to the Uruguay Round and is termed the GATT 1994. Other agreements established in the Uruguay Round include the General Agreement on Trade in Services (GATS), the Agreement on Trade-Related Aspects of Intellectual Property Rights (TRIPs), the Agreement on Trade-Related Investment Measures (TRIMs), and agreements on trade in textiles and clothing. In addition, the Uruguay Round established an institutionalized dispute resolution system, a Trade Policy Review Mechanism (TPRM) and an annex with four "plurilateral agreements." With the establishment of the WTO, the "contracting parties" of the GATT became the "members" of the WTO.[10]

In April 1994, the Final Act incorporating all of these agreements was signed by 111 GATT member states in Marrakesh. The Final Act took effect in January of 1995, when the WTO was created. However, the WTO did not completely bury the ghost of the ITO. The technical success of the Uruguay Round and the establishment of the WTO is significant, although, as we shall discuss below, there remain serious problems originating from the failure of the ITO.

First, the GATT rules from 1947 to 1994 provide an impressive "code" of rules for the promotion of global free trade. These rules are designed to put limits on the ability of member states to undermine negotiated concessions, thereby creating restrictions or distortions of the policy goal of liberalized global trade. Fundamental "grundnorms" assist in this goal. These include the "Most Favored Nation Clause" (MFN), which prohibits contracting parties from discriminating against products from other members. It also includes the "National Treatment" (NT) principle of non-discrimination against imports from member states of the WTO. The tariff concessions must not be exceeded by the contracting parties and are reinforced by other GATT rules. However, there are stipulated limited exceptions to the above rules, such as those relating to national security, health and morals, as well as trade-related environmental measures. There are also safeguards or escape clauses for temporary import restrictions, permission for regional trade agreements, and a "waiver" power.[11]

The GATS extends the reach of the WTO deep into the economies of its member states to encapsulate more than a hundred different types of services. This includes services such as banking, insurance, transport, communications, etc. The GATT rounds of the 1980s extended the reach of the WTO to services because the world economy was generating more and more of its wealth from services. This has led to an increase in need for the protection of services against anti-competitive and protectionist measures by contracting parties of the GATT. The trade negotiators and experts developed rules in this area by making analogies to trade in goods, and eventually developed counterparts to the MFN and NT rules as well as schedules of concession in the area of services. The GATS went further and developed rules on competition, anti-trust, and government procurement together with similar exceptions to those dealing with trade in goods. Also included in the agreement were new provisions on transparency.

The TRIPs agreement deals with an even more complex area than trade in services. As the global economy drew more of its wealth from knowledge-based industries and activities, it was inevitable that trade rules would move from promoting liberalization in tangible goods to dealing with matters concerning intangible assets which are protected by national and international intellectual property rules.

The rules of the TRIPs agreement aim to provide a minimum level of protection for all kinds of intellectual property and to provide for the enforceability of these rules through the WTO dispute settlement mechanism. These rules include the requirement that member states provide the legal infrastructure, including legal remedies, for the protection of intellectual property. There are also the equivalent of the MFN and NT provisions in the TRIPs rules.[12]

The brief descriptions above concerning the evolution of the world trade regime and the WTO demonstrate how international trade negotiators and technical experts seem to have responded to evolving trends in the global economy, especially in the area of services and intellectual property. The power of the

WTO lies partly in the fact that its Charter ties together all the various agreements of the Uruguay Round, as well as in the fact that countries wishing to become members of the WTO must accept the entire package. This allows the GATT type of multilateral negotiations to extend to the new areas of services and intellectual property. The fact that the WTO has the legal status and the functional powers to meet the challenges of changing trends in the global trade regime is the most important institutional improvement over the original GATT.

The technical responsiveness to the changing picture of global trade shown in the establishment of the WTO is not matched by a sensitivity to existing and emerging trends in the social dimensions of trade, including labor, the environment, and human rights. Indeed, many have argued that the impressive responsiveness to the growing importance of services and intellectual property by the trade experts has ignored the possible conflict between the rules of these new trade areas and certain categories of human rights. In this regard, the Canadian Standing Committee on Foreign Affairs and International Trade expressed the concerns of many civil society groups in its report on the future of the WTO:

> For example, health, consumer, student and other social advocacy groups raised issues with respect to: the right of entry, establishment and "national treatment" for private health and educational services corporations; the extension of patent rights for pharmaceutical drug companies; trademark rights in relation to cigarette packaging; the patenting by large transnational enterprises of genetically modified organisms and other life forms. Whose rights need to be protected in the public interest? What is consistent with international human rights norms?[13]

In part, these new areas of trade rules developed rapidly because of national and international lobbies linked to multinational corporations from the developed world.[14] In Chapter 1, we discussed how the pursuit of power and national self-interest created the tragic flaw within the United Nations. In this chapter we suggest that the national self-interest of developed countries, together with the self-interest of multinational corporate lobbies from these same countries, has been the driving force behind the development of the world trade regime. If the interests of the poor of the planet are left out of the development of the world trade regime, the consequences of the tragic flaw within the WTO will run parallel to that of the United Nations.

In relation to the social dimensions of trade, the various rounds of the GATT negotiations have produced only a passing reference to "raising living standards" (in the preamble to the GATT), and an important exception to the MFN and NT grundnorms under Article XX(e). This exception permits WTO members to ban the import of goods made with prison labor. Likewise, Article XX permits trade restrictions on certain public purpose grounds. However, any measures taken under the Article XX exceptions are to be as "least trade restrictive" as possible. Many argue that this approach, reinforced by GATT/WTO panel decisions, has narrowed rather than preserved the public purpose exceptions contained in Article XX in the area of the environment and public health and safety.[15] (This will be discussed in greater detail below.)

The WTO was one of the last major institutions of global governance to become widely known to the clientele that it serves, namely the global human family. How this awareness occurred, however, will not be fondly remembered by the architects of the global trading regime. This is because it occurred through television screens and newspapers filled with pictures of the "Battle in Seattle." This "Battle" was a result of both inadequate and ineffective preparatory work which, when combined with the thousands of protestors rioting in the street, conspired to bring to an abysmal end the Third WTO Ministerial Conference in December of 1999 in Seattle. The demonstrators, who were protesting the lack of inclusion of any social dimensions of trade in the multilateral negotiations in Seattle, may not have had a democratic mandate to stop such critical talks. Nevertheless, they did ring global alarm bells and raised awareness that there was an unfinished agenda that remained despite the death of the ITO.[16] Subsequent protests around the world at the major international conferences of the World Bank, the IMF, the G8, and at the most recent Summit of the Americas have reinforced this conclusion.

The global trade regime: can it be recast in the cause of all humanity?

There was no mention in the WTO Charter of the relationship between fair labor standards and fair trade, as was expressed in the Havana Charter of the ITO. However, what is included in the preamble to the WTO Charter may be of interest to those concerned with many of the social justice questions that have been raised in relation to the global trading regime. In addition, this may be the first indication that the trade negotiators and experts realize that trade rules cannot be totally isolated from other critical aspects of global governance and law, such as sustainable development and the environment. The first two preambular paragraphs of the Marrakesh Agreement establishing the WTO state that the parties to the agreement recognize:

> [T]hat their relations in the field of trade and economic endeavour should be conducted with a view to raising standards of living, ensuring full employment and a large and steadily growing volume of real income and effective demand, and expanding the production and trade in goods and services, while allowing for the optimal use of the world's resources in accordance with the objective of sustainable development, seeking both to protect and preserve the environment and to enhance the means for doing so in a manner consistent with their respective needs and concerns at different levels of economic development,
>
> ... that there is a need for positive efforts designed to ensure that developing countries, and especially the least developed among them, secure a

share in the growth in international trade commensurate with the needs of their economic development.

Preambles can be regarded as setting the foundational constitutional principles of an entire legal text, be it a national constitution, an international treaty, or the charter of an international organization.[17] One could therefore argue that this first preambular paragraph is of tremendous significance. It states that the primary purposes of the WTO, namely the reduction of tariff and non-tariff barriers and fostering non-discrimination in global trade relations, are subject to three crucial qualifications.[18]

First, there must be an environmental qualification to the primary trade purposes of the GATT. Trade objectives must be pursued in a manner consistent with the optimal use of the world's resources and in accordance with the objective of the preservation and protection of the environment. Some may argue that this statement is simply a reinforcement of the principle of comparative advantage. This argument posits that, if nations produced only goods for trading in which they have a comparative advantage, the world's resources would be optimally used.[19] Such an approach ignores the fact that environmental concerns can be in conflict with the concept of comparative advantage. Brazil may have a comparative advantage in cutting down the entire Amazonian rainforest (thereby causing irreparable harm to the biosphere) and exporting the lumber products around the world. This, however, would not be the optimal use of the world's resources. Resource use must take into account the fragile nature of the biosphere and the need for the conservation and protection of the environment to ensure the survival of all species, including humans. This argument does not deny that in many circumstances the principle of comparative advantage may indeed contribute to a more efficient – and therefore more environmentally friendly – trading regime. However, the principle of comparative advantage is not always in friendly co-existence with environmental preservation and protection.

Second, under the Marrakesh preamble of the WTO, the main objective of trade liberalization must take into account the need for sustainable development. This is a significant concession to the social dimensions of international trade. As will be discussed below, the concept of sustainable development has substantive content, and has become entrenched in global governance thinking since the 1987 Report of the World Commission on Environment and Development (the Brundtland Report), and the 1992 Rio UN Conference on Environment and Development. In addition, even the World Bank, in a 1998 report entitled *Development and Human Rights*, acknowledged that sustainable development is an expansive principle that could include the protection and promotion of universally recognized human rights. Within the sphere of sustainable development could well fit the principles of fair labor standards that disappeared along with the ITO Charter, even though they did not expressly reappear in the WTO Charter. It would be remiss not to point out that the ITO was abandoned by the United States, the same country that champions human rights, including labor standards, around the world.

It could be argued that the two preambular qualifications to the core trade agenda of the WTO mentioned above are "a basket full of holes" because they are contingent on the member countries' "respective needs and concerns at different levels of economic development."[20] However, as will be discussed, there is growing acceptance in the international community concerning minimal levels of obligations in areas such as labor standards and human rights, which all countries are expected to meet regardless of their different levels of economic development. It is in these areas that the battle may be fought to reinstate the social dimensions of trade into the global trade regime.

The third qualification to the main objectives of the WTO requires that the attainment of trade goals must be done in a manner that ensures developing countries, especially the least developed, obtain a fairer share of the growth in global trade. Moreover, this should be achieved through an approach that reflects the individual needs of their economic development. It could be argued that this is equivalent to an "affirmative action" clause, which requires positive efforts on behalf of the WTO members in this regard. Out of such a requirement could arise the foundational principle that developing, and especially the least developed, nations should have access to differential and favorable treatment as of right.[21]

The preambular qualifications to the main objectives of the WTO could be used to promote strategies that demand that world trade and economic globalization are not ends in themselves, but rather are used to serve the cause of humanity. This is a prerequisite for combating the tragic flaw within the world trade regime, much the same as the human security agenda is a prerequisite for combating the tragic flaw within the United Nations as discussed in Chapter 1. Whether such strategies will actually be successful is another matter.

Many fervent supporters of the WTO and of the world trade regime would reply to the above critique concerning the development of the WTO with the following economic and strategic arguments.

First, the fact that GATT negotiations proceeded along a narrow and technical basis is one of the reasons for its success. This argument points to the wide-ranging activities of the UN in the area of human rights, and the International Labor Organization (ILO) in the area of labor standards, as illustrative of the fact that a wider focus is not always effective. That the WTO emerged in 1994, despite the unsatisfactory nature of the previous GATT rounds and without the backing of an institutional framework, is testimony to the effectiveness of the focus of the trade negotiators and their army of technical experts.[22]

Second, it is argued, especially by those who work for or support the limited mandate of the WTO, that global trade has led to economic growth in all parts of the world, and that the corollary of this growth has been improvements in social justice and the alleviation of poverty. Poverty is the root cause of many violations of the economic, social, and cultural rights of people around the world. This thesis, labeled "neo-liberal" by critics on the left, is also known as the "rising tide lifts all boats" argument. In a series of on-line conferences organized by the World Bank Development Forum on globalization and poverty and on trade and sustainable development, such views were often put forward by the "pure" trade experts. The World Bank recognized that Seattle marked a turning point; its "clients" were no longer governments, but also included national and international groups from civil society. The following are some examples:[23]

> A recent paper "Growth is good for the poor" by World Bank economists David Dollar and Aart Kray has shown with plenty of factual eloquence that openness to trade and investment, on average, contributes to increasing a country's per-capita growth rate and alleviating its poverty situation, and has no significant relationship with inequality in the country. In sum – Globalization is good for growth; growth is good for the poor; globalization has no effect on inequality; hence, globalization is good for the poor. This is a simple and yet forceful fact-based conclusion, and cannot be disproved by specific examples to the contrary; any such example could be countered by more examples where globalization works for the benefit of the poor. Passionate discourses do not tell the broader truth: factual statements do!
>
> (Sandeep Mahajan, Economist, World Bank)

The problem is that there seems to be a constant battle over these factual statements in regard to whether the rising tide does in fact lift all boats. There was fierce opposition to this thesis from other participants in the cyber-discussions:

> There is no justification for the claim that globalisation is delivering benefits for all, and secondly, there is ample evidence showing that millions of poor and vulnerable people have been adversely affected.
>
> ... UNCTAD's review of the evidence in the World Investment Report 1999 found no systematic link between liberalisation and the quantity of inward investment flows.
>
> (Barry Coates, World Development Movement, UK)

> A recent World Bank paper, by Lundberg and Squire, shows that "greater openness to trade is negatively correlated with income growth among the poorest 40 per cent of the population". As the population of the developing countries is over 5 billion people, the "poorest 40 per cent" amount to over 2 billion people.
>
> (John Madeley, journalist, UK)

The truth probably lies somewhere between these two positions. On the benefit side, although there are still unjustifiable restrictions on the main exports of developing countries, especially textiles and agricultural products, there are increasing trade opportunities under the General System of Preferences (GSP) scheme. In 1964 GATT members adopted the GSP, which put in place the ground rules for preferences for developing countries. The Uruguay Round established a WTO Committee on Trade and Development to examine how global trade rules affect developing countries. The WTO has no choice but to deal with the critical issues facing developing nations. This is because 80 percent of the nations that comprise the membership of the WTO can be classified as developing, with new candidates, including China, being regarded either as developing nations or economies in transition. Importantly, 38 percent of the Gross Domestic Product (GDP) of most developing countries is attributable to trade. Additionally, the share of manufactured imports in the developing world rose from 7.3 percent to 23 percent between 1973 and 1997.[24] These figures demonstrate that countries of the developing world will have the ability to increase their influence in the WTO as well as in the markets, and will consequently have the trading power to demand that they be heard.

The massive subsidies given to agricultural products by the United States and the European Union create considerable dislocations in the ability of developing countries to benefit from trading in agricultural exports. However, it is claimed that 70 percent of the exports from the least developed countries (LDCs) have duty-free tariff status in twenty-three of the major markets of the global trading system. While there are still unjustifiable restrictions on agricultural products from the developing world, before the advent of the WTO this sector was not included in any multilateral trade negotiations. With the inclusion of agriculture as part of the WTO's agenda, there is now at least the possibility that agriculture will eventually come fully under the discipline of global trade rules. This would mean that not only would agriculture have the protection of the MFN and NT grundnorms, but also that disputes involving agriculture could be settled by recourse to the dispute settlement mechanisms of the WTO. Those who proclaim such benefits, however, concede that the WTO rules-based system will not fully benefit developing countries until domestic economies have removed the structural impediments and supply-side constraints in order to create a regulatory and macroeconomic environment that promotes globally competitive, supply-side responses.[25] Other experts argue that the dramatic widening of income gaps between nations has probably been reduced by the globalization of the commodity and factor markets, at least for those countries integrated into the global economy. They go on to contend that within labor-abundant countries, opening up to international trade and factor movements has lowered inequality and that world incomes would be less unequal in a fully integrated world economy than in one that is fully segmented.[26]

On the detriment side, while some critics of the global trade regime concede that there may be "factual" evidence that the GDP of a number of developing countries may be increasing due to engagement in the global trade regime, with a consequent decline in poverty levels, they also point out that there is evidence of growing inequities within such countries. They argue that in many of these same countries the gap between winners and losers is widening, as is the gap between urban and rural residents in terms of overall poverty levels, while extreme poverty may remain unchanged. A 1997 UNCTAD report asserted that, in almost all developing nations that have undertaken rapid trade liberalization, wage inequality had increased, while the employment levels of unskilled workers had declined. In addition, it was observed that real wages had fallen significantly, as much as 20–30 percent in parts of Latin America.[27] Some non-governmental organizations (NGOs) argue that the rapid opening of weak economies to trade, combined with deflationary pressures on commodity prices, together with high interest rates and weak government supports, often destroys the very labor-intensive industries in the developing world that global trade was supposed to offer a comparative advantage. Likewise, the effects of the global agribusiness' orientation toward export markets on large segments of the population who rely on small-scale farming can be disastrous for both rural and indigenous populations.[28]

According to figures put forward by the former director general of the WTO, Renato Ruggiero, at a high-level WTO symposium on trade and development in 1999, more than two billion people live on less than US$2 per day, 1.5 billion lack access to fresh water, and 130 million children have never gone to school.[29]

Based on a more recent UNCTAD 2000 report on the least developed countries (LDCs) authored by Charles Gore,[30] there is growing evidence that becoming full members of the world trade regime may not be sufficient for the LDCs to improve their lot in the global village. For the 614 million people living in the forty-three LDCs, the future looks bleak. During the 1990–8 period, the growth of real GDP per capita was so low, just 0.4 percent per year (excluding Bangladesh), that only one of the LDCs will graduate out of this category by 2015, and only eight will do so in the next fifty years. This is despite the fact that most LDCs have liberalized their economies and retracted trade barriers more than other developing nations in order to integrate themselves into the global trade and financial markets. Indeed, 37 percent of LDCs have removed all tariff barriers or have only minor ones in place. The report found that the implications of commodity price changes for the terms-of-trade of different LDCs have been varied, depending on the nature of their trade specialization and the composition of their imports and exports. Since March of 1999, the rapid increase in oil prices has benefited oil-exporting LDCs; however, non-primary oil exporters have been hit not only by low primary commodity prices but also by rising fuel bills. Since the majority of LDCs are primary commodity-exporting and oil-importing countries, the decline in the terms-of-trade has been severe. This has contributed significantly to the inability of the poorest members of the human family to rise out of poverty and human misery through the global trade regime. The UNCTAD report reinforces the conclusion that the institutions of global governance and effective donor assistance, together with external debt relief, must provide these countries with the proper help they need to integrate into the global economy. Otherwise, the world trade and financial regimes will seem, to the hundreds of millions who live in abject human misery, as working only for the benefit of the affluent members of society rather than in the cause of all humanity.

The other losers in the global trade regime have been described in a previous text co-written by the authors.[31] These include informal sector workers, workers in export processing zones (EPZs), child workers, illegal economic migrants, and seafarers. One could add to this growing army of humanity: single mothers unable to upgrade their skills due to child care responsibilities and poverty, unskilled laborers, workers in import substituting or privatized industries, and those whose living standards are affected by government spending reductions and downsizing, which often means the most vulnerable of society. In addition, it has been argued that developing countries have been forced by the global trading system to specialize in a narrow range of export-focused commodities, which leaves their economies extremely vulnerable to commodity pricing swings and external shocks. Likewise, technical and financial resources, as well as expertise in developing appropriate infrastructure, commercial and industrial planning, and trade policy development to deal with the challenges posed by global trade, are in short supply in many developing countries. Finally, both the legal and regulatory frameworks in areas such as corporations, banking, investment, and anti-competition laws are lacking in many developing countries.[32]

While the Bretton Woods institutions and foreign donor agencies are assisting developing countries to improve their capacity to enter the global trading regime on more equal terms, the lack of such capacity is preventing much of the human family from enjoying the claimed benefits of the global trade regime, despite factual statements to the contrary.

While there is little doubt that, ultimately, developing countries will fare better from a rules-based global trading regime, there is still a need for considerable assistance to be given to developing countries through special and differential treatment. This includes longer time frames for implementation of rules-based disciplines, flexibility in tariff reduction arrangements, non-reciprocity, and preferential treatment. It has been argued that all that has been promised to the developing world in this regard has not been delivered. Consequently, the poorest parts of the human family have been forced into the global trading ring from a position of weakness.[33] Participation in the global governance system of the world trade regime under these conditions is a denial of the human dignity to the millions of poor who inhabit the developing world. Some would go further and say it is exploitation. As we discussed in Chapter 1, it is our contention that such a denial of human dignity is also a denial of fundamental justice. Where there is such a denial of fundamental justice, the consequences of the tragic flaw at the heart of the WTO will continue to undermine its mandate.

Justice requires consistency: drawing the *existing* moral, legal, and economic links between trade and labor standards

The Havana Charter of the ITO clearly recognized the link between fair labor standards and equity in the global trade regime as described above. Yet in the wake of the ITO's demise, none of the GATT rounds found time to incorporate these considerations into the rules-based trade regime. This opens the global governance system of trade to the charge that it will permit what is called "social dumping." Advocates against this practice argue that social dumping occurs when there are unfair cost advantages built into exported products. These cost advantages are the result of manufacturing processes that do not fully internalize the cost of labor and the environment into production. This may occur due to either non-existent labor or environmental standards, or because such standards are not enforced.[34] One American trade economist has argued that eliminating social dumping

> would raise living standards by eliminating negative externalities, i.e. prac-
> tices whose social costs are not reflected in the monetary costs borne by
> firms. Much like the elimination of tariffs and quotas, ending social
> dumping would encourage a more efficient allocation of resources and
> patterns of production.[35]

However, trade policy experts who are acutely aware of the possibility that linking the trade regime to labor standards could lead to protectionist measures under the guise of concern for humanity, offer qualifications to the definition of social dumping. Two such experts, in reference to the case of Mexico and the North American Free Trade Agreement (NAFTA), caution

> [t]hat Mexico, in this case, has much lower wage rates does not in itself
> constitute social dumping since, commensurate to its level of development,
> such lower costs can be a legitimate area of comparative advantage.
> Actionable dumping would only result if prices of goods for export were
> kept artificially low through a deliberate suppression of labour and other
> input costs, thereby causing a material injury to competing producers in the
> importing country.[36]

Ironically, even the majority of developing countries do not agree with such a qualification of social dumping, thereby rejecting any linkage of the global trade regime to labor standards. It was the industrialized Western nations who have tried to get labor issues on to the WTO agenda; however, they have been stymied from doing so by the developing world. Developing nations regard Western moti-vations in this area as profoundly protectionist and as a disguised attempt to take away the comparative advantage associated with lower labor costs in the devel-oping world. As we shall see in Chapter 4, this perspective can be effectively countered, not only from a moral and legal perspective but also from an economic perspective. At the first Ministerial Conference of the WTO in Singapore in 1996, the developing world was successful in blocking the WTO from adopting a fair labor standards agenda. Instead, they succeeded in having the final communiqué dress up the status quo in flowing rhetoric which affirmed that WTO members would

> renew their commitment to the observance of internationally recognized
> core labour standards. The International Labour Organization (ILO) is the

competent body to set and deal with these standards, and we affirm our support for its work in promoting them. We believe that economic growth and development fostered by increased trade and further trade liberalization contribute to the promotion of these standards. We reject the use of labour standards for protectionist purposes, and agree that the comparative advantage of countries, particularly low-wage countries, must in no way be put into question. In this regard, we note that the WTO and the ILO Secretariats will continue their existing collaboration.[37]

In essence, the developing world redirected the issue of fair labor standards to the international organization that was created to deal with it, namely the ILO. Some would argue that this was done because of the track record of the ILO, to which we now turn.

The ILO, the world's oldest international organization, was created in 1919 at the end of World War I. Its mandate was to ensure the "improvement of labor standards." Such improvement was thought to be a necessary condition of sustainable peace. The Declaration of Philadelphia in 1944 (passed concurrently with the establishment of the Bretton Woods institutions) updated and expanded the mandate of the ILO to cover the promotion of labor standards, economic advancement, and social security, without adopting a particular bias toward these issues, e.g. a trade union perspective. As we have argued elsewhere, this unique mandate has been both a strength and a weakness for the ILO.[38] In the post-Second World War era, the ILO has been sidelined by the tremendous growth of international trade and the financial markets and the institutions that oversee them, such as the WTO, the World Bank, and the IMF. This has occurred to the extent that even the ILO's own leadership has questioned its survival. The ILO was far more successful in the inter-war years, when it exercised global leadership in putting a stop to practices such as slave trading.

In the post-war years, the ILO seems to have embarked on a mission of "assembly line" standard-setting outside the realm of trade. It has adopted some 175 international labor standards covering health and safety in the workplace, social security, minimum wages, collective bargaining, freedom of association, employment promotion, training, migrant workers, women and child workers, as well as many sectoral standards. The enforcement of these standards has been abysmal. As we shall see, unlike the WTO or the IMF, the ILO has lacked an effective incentive system to ensure that the plethora of labor standards it has promulgated are in fact implemented. We have argued in a previous text that this external weakness is a reflection of an internal weakness of the ILO's governance structure. In particular, we have critiqued the Eurocentric and legalistic approach to the development of labor standards taken by the ILO. The Organization has continued to make the focus of its tripartite structure, described below, the churning out of labor standards, which are unrelated to the growing trade, and financial markets agenda, thus making its isolation greater and bringing its relevance increasingly into question.[39]

It is only recently that the ILO has turned its attention to other critical functions such as technical assistance in employment, labor force planning, and labor market development. Another critical function recently taken on by the ILO is the development of core labor standards that are binding on all member states,[40] which will be discussed in detail below. However, as we have argued elsewhere, the present structure of the ILO prevents it from taking its proper place in a system of global governance that promotes global trade and globalization not as ends in themselves, but rather in the cause of humanity.[41]

The three key structures of the ILO are the International Labor Conference (ILC), the International Labor Office (the Office), and the Governing Body (GB). The ILC was developed on a unique tripartite basis where government, employer, and worker representatives of the 170 members meet annually for three weeks to set the broad policy orientations of the ILO, including the adoption of resolutions and monitoring of the Conventions. The Office implements the policies and other directions of the GB, and is headed by a director general who is elected by the GB every five years. The GB itself is elected every three years by the ILC, with twenty-eight government representatives and fourteen representatives for both workers and employers. Ten seats are specifically reserved for "States of Chief Industrial Importance" as determined by the GB. The extent of the implementation machinery of the ILO is as follows:

> Reports on ratified Conventions are required at regular intervals – two years for the "core" and a few other Conventions, and less frequently for the technical Conventions. Workers' and employers' organizations also have the right to provide information. The reports are examined by the Committee of Experts on the Application Conventions and Recommendations (the Committee of Experts), an independent technical body, and then by a tripartite Conference Committee of the ILC (the Conference Committee), which is a political body.
>
> ... In the case of serious, long-standing violations of core Conventions, the Committee [of Experts] will decide to include the non-complying government in a special list in the Committee's report to the Conference Plenary, which usually adopts these reports with little discussion.[42]

As we will demonstrate, these extremely weak supervisory procedures are supplemented by complaints procedures that allow for more in-depth investigation and fact-finding which adds credibility to the work of the ILO. In regard to the most high profile of the complaints procedures, the Committee on Freedom of Association (CFA), there is conflicting evidence concerning its effectiveness, with at least one academic claiming there is a large degree of compliance with CFA findings, while labor organizations have lambasted the record of compliance with the Committee's determinations. If the track record of compliance with CFA determinations by Canada, against whom a large number of complaints have been lodged, is any example, then the labor organizations are probably correct.[43]

This weak supervisory structure of the ILO stands in contrast to the more powerful structure of the WTO.[44] The highest body of the WTO is the Ministerial Conference, which meets every two years and is comprised of representatives of all the member states, with the trade minister of each member state usually being the official representative. The Ministerial Conference is the highest authority over all WTO matters. The General Council holds its sessions between Ministerial Conference meetings and is comprised of member-state trade delegates. It is the main operational body of the WTO and has the authority of the Ministerial Conference between its meetings. The General Council is also mandated to function as the Trade Policy Review Body (TPRB) and the Dispute Settlement Body (DSB). The Council for Trade in Goods, the Council for Trade in Services, and the Council for Trade-Related Aspects of Intellectual Property are subsidiary bodies to the General Council and oversee their respective agreements established under the Uruguay Round, namely the GATT, the GATS and the TRIPs.

While all members of the WTO have an equal vote, initial voting is usually done by consensus under Article IX of the WTO Charter. However, if a decision cannot be arrived at by consensus, voting takes place and decisions are made by a majority vote. It has been alleged that the initial decision-making by consensus is a form of weighted voting because the mood of the Ministerial Conference and the General Council is often dominated by the powerful economic powers, especially the United States and the European Union. In addition, because the voting is by show of hands, there is considerable influence exerted by the United States and Europe in terms of how other nations, especially aid-dependent nations, will vote.

The DSB is responsible for the crucial dispute settlement system under the WTO Charter. This includes the critical functions of establishing dispute settlement panels (DSPs), adopting panel and Appellate Body reports, authorizing the use of sanctions by members pursuant to panel rulings, and monitoring the implementation of the panels' rulings and recommendations.

Under the WTO Charter, the adjudicatory model of hard rules and remedies as a means of enforcing the global trading regime was chosen over the softer and more diplomatic model of reducing trade tensions and resolving trade disputes through diplomatic talks and compromise.[45] The previous GATT system had imposed a consensus model for the approval of trade dispute rulings before they could be implemented. This had led to long and sometimes permanent delays in resolving such disputes. Under the WTO Charter, panel decisions are automatically adopted unless there is a consensus to reject them, which is the opposite of the old GATT system. Further hardening the world trade regime into a quasi-legal system are the strict time limits imposed in regard to the dispute settlement process, and the availability of recourse to the Appellate Body where there are disagreements on issues of trade law. The decisions of the Appellate Body are binding on all parties and are monitored by the DSB as described above. Under the WTO Charter, cross-retaliation is permitted, and an aggrieved member state can use tariffs to retaliate against trade practices that have been ruled contrary to the WTO Code.

What is evident in the structure of the WTO, compared with the structure of the previous GATT, is a move from somewhat soft law to increasingly harder law as a growing number of WTO member states accept the discipline of the WTO Charter as a prerequisite for being a member in good standing of the global economy. Optimists believe that unilateral trade distorting practices are likely to be used by fewer member states, given the possibility of recourse to the dispute settlement system by aggrieved member states.

It must be emphasized that the WTO does not in itself have the power to sanction member states that violate the WTO Charter. The legacy of the former soft law regime of global trade still lingers, in that after the WTO dispute panels have ruled, the preferred option is that the member in violation of the WTO rules cease the impugned practice. The second option is that the member state in violation pays compensation, or failing that, as a last resort the aggrieved state may take WTO-sanctioned retaliatory measures. In this sense, just as in soft law regimes, the WTO system could be said to rely on self-help. However, unlike the ILO, which has no enforcement or deterrent powers to get member states to adhere to adopted Conventions, the WTO dispute settlement system can impose economic costs on members who are in violation of the WTO rules, and this may have a deterrent effect.

While more dominant economic powers, like the US, can still present significant challenges to the rules-based WTO system, weaker member states now have increased access to more equitable remedies in trade disputes with more powerful members, through the dispute settlement panels.[46] However, whether this will actually be the case remains to be seen, given the fact that as of 1996 approximately 90 percent of trade disputes within the context of the WTO were between North American members, the EU, and Japan.

Nevertheless, the track record of the dispute settlement system of the WTO has been excellent since its establishment. One leading jurist, William J. Davey, writing in 2000, has detailed the success of the system as follows:

> The success of its dispute settlement system is critical to the success of the WTO itself. Only an effective dispute settlement system can ensure rule enforcement, which in turn provides predictability and stability in trade relations …
>
> So far, the record of WTO dispute settlement is impressive. It has been extensively used – around 180 consultation requests in less than 5 years – or roughly 40 per year. Roughly one-half of the requests appear to be settled or otherwise abandoned.
>
> In respect of 62 matters, where consultations have failed, panels have been established. Eight cases were later settled or dropped. Of the remaining 54 cases, reports have been adopted in 28 cases, while 26 others are now pending at some stage in the panel/appellate process …
>
> So far the record on implementation has been reasonably good. Of the 28 cases where reports have been adopted, no implementation was required in 4 cases and implementation appears to have occurred in 10 cases. Of the

remaining 14 cases, the time set for implementation has not expired in 9. Of the five problem cases, non-implementation was admitted in one case.[47]

Such an impressive record of implementation of the WTO Code stands in marked contrast to the lack of implementation of ILO Conventions by member states.

It is obvious, then, that the call, by the 1996 WTO Ministerial Conference in Singapore, to have the ILO as the competent body to deal with labor standards was a successful bid to maintain the unsatisfactory status quo concerning the linkage between trade and labor standards. From the Declaration of the Singapore Ministerial, one can assume that the ILO and the WTO secretariats are collaborating, perhaps with a view to changing this unsatisfactory status quo. Not much is publicly known about such collaboration, if it exists at all.

As noted above, since 1919 the ILO has promulgated some 175 Conventions covering a huge variety of labor matters, sectors, and categories. As also discussed, this productivity has also been the source of the ILO's ineffectiveness in having any impact on the world trade regime.

However, the ILO may well have surprised everybody by taking the lead in changing the status quo by developing core labor standards that are binding on all member states of the ILO. Since the membership of the ILO overlaps substantially with that of the WTO, the emergence of new possibilities for change are on the horizon.

In 1994, at the 81st Session of the ILO, its future orientation and the reform of the workings of the Organization were high on the agenda. Various parts of the ILO, including the International Labor Office, were tasked with developing strategies to increase the Organization's effectiveness. The work of various ILO working groups and committees revealed that there was a desire to draw a link between social and economic development. There was a recognition that developing countries had the right to progress at a different pace from that of the developed world. There was also an acceptance that lower labor costs in developing countries were a legitimate comparative advantage. However, there seemed to be a growing consensus in the ILO that three fundamental labor rights were required to counterbalance this legitimate comparative advantage. These included: (1) freedom of association (ILO Convention 87), (2) the right to bargain collectively (ILO Convention 98), and (3) the absence of forced or compulsory labor (ILO Conventions 29, 35 and 105). The ILO discussions on balancing social with economic development concluded that within the context of trade, these core labor standards were a minimum threshold requirement for establishing the legitimacy of lower labor costs as a comparative trade advantage. In essence, with these three fundamental labor rights as a minimum threshold requirement, there would be a symmetry between freedom of trade and the freedom of workers to trade their labor. Outside the parameters of the link between fair trade and fair labor standards, the ILO discussions in 1994 and thereafter added two more core labor standards: (1) the prohibition of exploitative child labor, and (2) freedom from discrimination in employment (particularly with respect to gender discrimination). At the 268th Session of the Governing Body of the ILO, the Organization seemed galvanized by the recognition given to its strengthened role in the protection of fundamental labor rights by the Declaration made at the 1995 Copenhagen World Summit on Social Development, and, ironically, by the 1996 WTO Ministerial Conference in Singapore, as discussed above. The urgency of finding a new focus for the ILO through such discussions and studies on the linkage between social and economic development, eventually led to action. The Governing Body decided to formulate a Declaration that would confirm the existing obligations of all member states regarding certain fundamental labor standards. Both the Governing Body and the director general were keen to emphasize that such a Declaration would not modify the Constitution of the WTO, but would clarify its meaning in relation to the fundamental principles of labor rights. The Governing Body finally authorized the director general to prepare a draft Declaration of principles concerning fundamental labor rights as well as a follow-up mechanism. The ILO distributed the draft Declaration and consulted with the tripartite constituents (government, employer, and worker representatives) on the contents in May of 1998. Such careful preparation proved successful when the ILC, at its 86th Session in June of 1998, voted to adopt the Declaration on Fundamental Principles and Rights at Work, which set down the five principles outlined above as the "core labor standards." The relevant part of the Declaration states:

> [A]ll Members, even if they have not ratified the Conventions in question, have an obligation arising from the very fact of membership in the Organization to respect, to promote and to realize, in good faith and in accordance with the Constitution, the principles concerning the fundamental rights which are the subject of those Conventions, namely:
>
> (a) freedom of association and the effective recognition of the right to collective bargaining;
>
> (b) the elimination of all forms of forced or compulsory labor;
>
> (c) the effective abolition of child labor; and
>
> (d) the elimination of discrimination in respect of employment and occupation.[48]

The Declaration specifically mentions that these fundamental rights should not be used for protectionist trade purposes, or to call into question the comparative advantage of any country. However, the follow-up provisions to the Declaration, in keeping with the generally weak supervisory mechanisms of the ILO, essentially involve little more than annual reports by member states and the review of these reports.

It is inevitable that those who oppose any linkage between trade and labor standards will claim that even these core fundamental labor rights are too vague to be effectively enforced through the WTO dispute settlement system. It could be argued, for example, that freedom of association has proven to be a very complex concept, even within the context of a domestic legal system as developed as Canada's.[49]

In our previous text, we argued that in domestic legal systems, labor markets and laws that regulate core labor standards resolve the complexities arising out of both equity and efficiency considerations, and, moreover, these laws address market failures rather than playing a zero-sum game of winners and losers.[50] In addition, as others have pointed out, the WTO Charter and affiliated agreements are replete with far more ambiguous and complex matters than the core labor standards outlined in the ILO Declaration on Fundamental Principles and Rights at Work. In particular, the relatively new WTO agenda on the GATS and the TRIPs agreements presents much greater challenges in terms of ambiguity and complexity than those raised by the core labor standards as promulgated by the ILO.[51]

However, in this work we wish to concentrate on the particular linkage between trade and labor standards. This linkage is virtually irrefutable, given that all 175 members of the ILO have accepted the legal obligation "to respect, to promote and to realize" the fundamental labor rights detailed above. The link between trade and labor standards must be acknowledged particularly as regards countries that have *existing legislation* that, in theory, obliges actors within those nations to respect such fundamental labor rights. The problem occurs when there is a lack of enforcement of such domestic laws or when the state is complicit in the lax enforcement of these laws, as is often the case in export processing zones (EPZs) around the world.

We have noted elsewhere[52] the rapid increase in numbers, size, and importance of EPZs around the world in the last fifteen years. Employment has grown by 9 percent per annum in EPZs between 1975 and 1986, and by more than 14 percent between 1986 and 1990. We have also noted how such zones are often characterized by unfair labor practices such as labor contracting in order to avoid employment contracts, suspension of social security laws, intimidation against unionization, and lax enforcement of health and safety laws. Often, existing laws on freedom of association, collective bargaining, non-discrimination, and child labor are either ignored or workers are coerced or harassed into avoiding unionization. The World Bank has confirmed that such unfair or even illegal labor practices have a particularly negative impact on women, who make up more than 70 percent of the workforce in EPZs. While there are exceptions to this general description of EPZs, the grave exploitation of workers in many EPZs may be leading to a new form of twenty-first-century slavery.[53] Increasing numbers of countries in which EPZs are located have in place, or will enact, laws and regulatory systems that protect the fundamental labor rights mandated by the ILO Declaration on the Fundamental Principles and Rights at Work, as "legal decorations" for the purpose of proclaiming compliance with their ILO obligations.

A compelling analogy to trade could be made to illuminate how the institutions of global governance in the trade and labor areas can deal with this undermining of human and labor rights as well as sustainable development. We suggest that it may be possible to argue that non-enforcement or complicity in the lax enforcement of labor standards is tantamount to an export subsidy under the existing WTO Charter.

A subsidy, broadly defined, is usually regarded as a benefit conferred by government on a company or product. Such action can be trade-distorting. The GATT addresses the issue of subsidies under Articles VI, XVI, and XXII, as well as under the Subsidies Code adopted at the Tokyo and Uruguay Rounds. Article XVI prohibits export subsidies on non-primary products. Article VI requires the existence of material injury or the threat of material injury before countervailing duties can be imposed. In 1979, more complex provisions were added to the GATT rules on export subsidies. These rules allow a GATT member to displace the exports of another member where there are export subsidies on primary products, material injury, and a causal connection between the subsidies and the material injury. The Uruguay Round further developed the rules on subsidies by establishing a definition of a subsidy under Article 1 of the Agreement on Subsidies and Countervailing Measures as "a financial contribution by a government or any public body" within the territory of a signatory state or "any form of income or price support in the sense of Article XVI of the GATT" conferring a benefit. In addition, the Uruguay Round added the specificity requirement, which requires that, for a subsidy to be actionable, it must be "targeted" and not one that is generally available. Export subsidies are those that are targeted only at products that are to be exported. Such subsidies are subject to countervailing duties under the WTO, in contrast to domestic subsidies, which are subject to countervailing duties only if certain conditions are fulfilled. These conditions include the degree to which the subsidy assists in the export of the products to other countries, and the degree to which imports into the country offering the subsidy are restrained.[54]

Based on the above, it becomes feasible to argue that, as regards products manufactured and exported from EPZs, non-enforcement or state complicity in lax enforcement of *existing* domestic core labor standards, that are also binding internationally through the ILO Declaration, could amount to a breach of the WTO subsidy rules. Such labor practices can and should be seen as trade-distorting in that they decrease the cost of manufacturing in the EPZs, thereby allowing a lower price for the exported products based on unfair competition that permits labor costs "below market level."[55]

We would counter the claims that such labor costs are in fact to the comparative advantage of WTO members, on both moral and legal grounds. In regard to the moral ground, it would be outrageous for any country to assert that they can claim rights arising out of a moral wrong, namely the non-enforcement of their laws. Not only is the concept of *ex inuria non oritur ius* a legal principle in many legal systems around the world, but we suggest that it is also a universal moral principle.

In terms of legal grounds, just as the WTO rules on subsidies set a bare minimum on what is or is not a permissible subsidy, the enforcement of existing laws on core labor standards in EPZs must surely be a minimum standard which must be met if labor inputs into exported products are not to be regarded as illegal subsidies. While non-enforcement or complicity in the lax enforcement of core labor standards is more difficult to identify than a specific governmental subsidy program, it is not impossible. Indeed, the expertise of the ILO, together with the growing expertise of civil society groups that focus on labor practices in EPZs, make such evidence-gathering very feasible.

The WTO agreement on subsidies and countervailing measures allows domestic industries to impose countervailing duties to offset subsidies on imported "like products." The key determination made in relation to such subsidies under the WTO agreement is whether the subsidized imports cause or threaten to cause material injury to the domestic industry producing the domestic "like product." However, proving material injury is difficult even in standard subsidy cases, and is likely to be more so in the context of below market-level labor inputs. Consequently, as we have previously argued, a rebuttable presumption of material injury could be institutionalized by the WTO, and brought into play whenever an exporting state has violated its own core labor standards in an EPZ. This is where the preamble to the WTO Charter and its reference to raising living standards and achieving sustainable development, as the context of the WTO Code, should mandate the evolution of trade principles that address material injury out of impermissible labor practices. We suggest that this context of "raising standards of living" and "sustainable development," within which the WTO Code is situated by its preambular provisions, calls for the creation of special rules to combat violations of the fundamental human rights of workers. Exploitative and abusive labor practices cannot be said to be a means to an end of higher living standards and sustainable development.[56]

We discuss below how any sanction-related actions taken by WTO members could focus on individual multinational corporations that are engaged in abusive labor practices to gain an unfair competitive advantage in the global marketplace.

As regards the question of how best to determine which firms may be receiving unfair labor subsidies, the most compelling position would be to target those firms in EPZs that are actually making use of the non-enforcement or state complicity in the lax enforcement of such fundamental labor rights. In this respect, one could make an analogy with the US ban on forced labor, which applies only to offending products and not to overall trade with the country from which the product originated.[57] Such an approach would provide an incentive to multinational firms to carry over their higher labor standards to the EPZs, and not to engage in a race-to-the-bottom in EPZs as regards fundamental labor rights.

Significant and growing amounts of foreign direct investment (FDI) are already in or going to EPZs in the developing world. As the nineteenth-century industrialized world had its slave labor, its sweat-shops and child laborers, so the twenty-first-century globalized world has its EPZs. There is growing evidence that many of these EPZs attract FDI not only because of the tax holidays, free rent, and other governmental incentives, but also because existing labor laws on unions, freedom of association, non-discrimination, child labor, and health and safety are deliberately not applied.[58]

There is a moral and legal inconsistency of the highest order in the system of global governance, if a WTO member, whose laws on fundamental labor rights are deliberately not applied in an EPZ (intended to attract foreign investment and manufacturing of products for export), does not attract the same scrutiny as it does when it develops a specific export subsidy program for products manufactured in other parts of the country. To state otherwise would be to condemn the millions of workers around the world who are, or will be, working in the EPZs to mere factors of production devoid of human dignity, with no stake in sustainable development upon which the WTO Charter is built. To state otherwise would be to regard the foundation of goods, services, intellectual property, and investment markets on which the GATT, and subsequently the WTO, were built, as ends in themselves, rather than as a means to serve the cause of humanity. Again, this would reinforce the tragic flaw within the world trade regime to much the same extent as the ineptitude and inefficiency in the face of gross human rights abuses reinforced the tragic flaw within the United Nations, as discussed in Chapter 1.

In such circumstances, it cannot be argued that the above amounts to an attack on the comparative advantage of lower labor costs. What are being attacked, however, are impermissible trade-distorting practices according to both domestic and international standards. In addition, there is compelling evidence from the Organization for Economic Co-operation and Development (OECD) that the abuse of core labor standards does not result in any long-term competitive advantage.[59] Such abuse is essentially of short-term advantage only to the firms that benefit from it, and the domestic elites who profit from such firms. Chapter 4 will further elucidate these arguments.

The above linkage between trade, core labor standards, and the use of subsidies has the unique characteristic of being *intrinsic* to the WTO trade provisions. The more traditional argument for the inclusion of a social clause in the WTO Charter is *extrinsic* to the WTO trade provisions and thus requires a political consensus.

Trade unions around the world including the International Confederation of Independent Trade Unions (ICFTU), as well as many human rights experts, advocate inserting a social clause in the WTO Charter that would make trade privileges conditional on compliance with fundamental worker rights such as those set out in the ILO Declaration. These groups envisage this social clause as imposing a loss of trade benefits, or as a trade sanction of last resort for the consistent breach of fundamental worker rights. To avoid the use of a social clause for protectionist purposes, some, like the ICFTU, advocate that the ILO and the WTO jointly administer any such clause. The ILO would use its expertise, and its somewhat ineffective supervisory mechanisms and committees, to gather evidence of non-compliance with core labor standards and to monitor abuses of core labor rights. The WTO would provide enforcement mechanisms through its dispute settlement system. Such an approach might also utilize a phased method of enforcement. Initially, there could be a censure of the offending member leading eventually to the withdrawal of the member's right of access to WTO bodies and negotiations. Recourse to sanctions could be a last resort and implemented only after an agreed period for compliance has passed, and only after technical and financial assistance has been offered.[60]

However, it is not only the governments of developing countries that are strongly opposed to such suggestions concerning the introduction of a social clause. There are some developing country NGOs, and even international human rights and development organizations, that are also fierce critics of any such clause. They fear that the introduction of a social clause into the WTO Charter would lead to protectionism, loss of comparative advantage, and an imposition of a Northern perspective of fundamental rights.[61]

In our previous text, we discussed other possible challenges to a social clause which may prevent its establishment.[62] First, as will be more fully explained in the discussion below on the link between trade and the environment, the current WTO rules and the jurisprudence from the WTO panels seem to indicate that there is a central principle of trade law that prohibits member states from imposing their domestic process and production standards on foreign suppliers. An importing country can only treat "like products" differently if the physical properties of the products differ, and not if the products differ only by method of processing or production. (There is the one exception, mentioned above, of forced labor.) Thus, carpets imported from factories using child labor cannot be treated differently from carpets made in factories without the use of such labor. The structural development of the WTO makes it very difficult to have any part of the Organization, including the dispute settlement panels, enforce policies that are outside the scope of the contractual regime underlying the agreed-upon rules of multilateral trade. Trade sanctions are extremely ill suited to changing production or process methods abroad.[63] Child labor activists as well as the United Nations Children's Emergency Fund (UNICEF) have warned against the imposition of tariffs or other sanctions against the importation of products made with child labor. The manufacturers of these products may react to the imposition of such sanctions by lowering even further the working conditions in their factories to compensate for the sanctions, or may switch to other more welcoming markets. There may also be worse fates awaiting children who lose their jobs due to the imposition of sanctions; some children may be forced into prostitution. Good intentions can bring disastrous and unintended consequences if not backed by sound strategies. We have previously argued that effective sanctions against exploitative child labor lie in gradually moving children into formal and non-formal education systems. Moreover, parents must be given the financial incentive to send their children to school, and there must be a specific tailoring of human resource development strategies for marginalized communities with the assistance of foreign and international donors.[64]

Essentially, the sanctions system of the WTO is still based on the contractual rights and duties of each member. Members cannot collectively act to impose multilateral trade sanctions against persistent violators of fundamental worker rights. If it were left to individual members to do so, it would raise the specter of protectionist or politically motivated actions in the name of worker rights.

The above discussion should not stop debate on the linkage between trade and fundamental worker rights. Indeed, the counter-arguments to the introduction of a social clause contain the possible foundations for a proper linkage between trade and fundamental worker rights. We have demonstrated that there is as much, if not more, of a solid moral, legal, and economic basis to show that abusive labor practices in EPZs are equally as trade-distorting as intellectual property piracy, which is protected under the TRIPs Agreement of the Uruguay Round.

For the moral, legal, and economic considerations outlined above, we suggest that there be a future round of multilateral talks on the social dimensions of trade, beyond those agreed to at Doha, Qatar, which involve not only the WTO but also the ILO, the World Bank, the IMF, and regional trade blocs. The aim of such talks should be to develop a new General Agreement on Development and Equitable Competition (GADEC), bringing the discussion back to the original intention of the Bretton Woods institutions, which was to collaborate in the rebuilding of the world economy for the benefit of all people of the world. Under such multilateral talks, the members of the WTO, the ILO, the World Bank, and the IMF can negotiate binding agreements on economic and social development, adherence to fundamental labor and human rights, environmental standards, competition policy, and other issues related to the contestability and sustainability of global markets. Contestability, according to economics and trade experts,[65] aims to reduce anti-competitive practices that prevent economically and socially efficient outcomes for global markets. Contestability refers to both government and private sector practices, and can include the targeting of abusive labor practices in EPZs, as discussed above. Likewise, given the context of sustainable development within which the WTO Charter is situated by its preambular paragraphs, there would be sound moral, legal, and economic grounds for linking multilateral environmental agreements (discussed more fully below) containing global environmental standards to a GADEC.

The carrot to enter into the GADEC agreement would be to have preferential access to expertise and resources supplied by a new World Development Fund (WDF) that could be developed by the United Nations and the Bretton Woods institutions to implement the agreements on economic and social development. (We will explore the nature and implementation of the WDF further in Chapter 5.) Such agreements could address the systemic problems that developing countries face in fully integrating into global trade and financial capital markets. The stick behind the GADEC would be that persistent and flagrant violation of such agreements would result in the loss of access to the benefits of the World Development Fund. While any member of GADEC could ask for an investigation into violations of the GADEC agreement, an independent, impartial, and expert dispute settlement system similar to that of the WTO could make determinations on the nature and extent of the violations.

We readily admit that such a suggestion, if agreed upon by the community of nations, would take a long time to develop. In fact, the development and implementation of such a plan would take well beyond the conclusion of the Doha Round, which was initiated in November of 2001. In the interim, the immediate debate on the linkage between trade and labor (and, indeed, the environment, as we shall discuss below) should take place in the Trade Policy Review Mechanism (TPRM) established within the WTO institutional structure. The TPRM institutionalizes periodic reviews of trade policies and practices of member countries. We have previously suggested that there is absolutely no impediment to member states that wish to show leadership working with the WTO Secretariat with the assistance of the ILO, to integrate their labor law and market policies and practices into the review of their trade policies and practices.[66] This could be done on a continual basis, thereby beginning the global debate on how labor law and policy implementation can either assist liberalized trade or distort it. If such leadership in the context of the TPRM proves successful, then the WTO can be encouraged to include, as a guideline for TPRM reports, the analysis of labor law and policy implementation and how it impacts on a member's trade policy. The assistance of the ILO can be offered to developing countries that wish to become involved in such leadership efforts to link trade and labor standards. The involvement of the ILO would also serve to allay fears that the drawing of any such link between trade and labor standards would simply be a front for protectionist measures. The WTO Secretariat could monitor the development of such trade and labor linkage reports within the TPRM and encourage other member countries to follow suit through the Trade Policy Review Body (TPRB), which reports to the WTO General Council on the implementation of the TPRM. For countries who recognize that their labor systems and markets may fall short of the standards set by the ILO Declaration, incentives could be offered by the World Bank working in concert with the ILO and the TPRB to upgrade such labor systems and enforcement regimes, in addition to giving assistance in implementing complementary human resource development strategies.

We suggest this approach to the linkage of trade and labor standards because it does not need another WTO multilateral round of negotiations in order to be achieved, and it seems to present a viable interim solution. Such an approach needs, above all else, leadership from member countries, especially those in the developed world who profess to be champions of human rights. Some may ask, what will this accomplish? Keeping in mind the transitional nature of this approach, the history of the GATT, and later the WTO, shows that much can emerge from forums that focus on the conceptual and empirical foundations of free and fair trade while avoiding the possibility of unilateralism that could be a cover for protectionism. Many developing nations would perhaps find such an approach to the linkage of trade and labor standards more palatable than the incentives-based system offered through the generalized system of preferences (GSP) of the European Union and the United States. These GSP regimes offer increased market access and extra trade preferences to those countries that meet certain labor standards. In order to be eligible for these benefits, countries must prove that they are indeed enforcing and monitoring such standards. Concerns about this generalized system of preferences include such things as the potential for protectionism; that incentives may be too low to effect meaningful change; and that there is a lack of effective technical assistance to the countries in the GSP regime. It is not surprising that many developing countries view GSP regimes with deep distrust and as a "one-sided" neo-colonial approach. Moreover, as tariff levels drop, the GSP regimes will become less and less relevant for enforcing linkages between trade and labor standards.[67]

The TPRM cannot be a vehicle for protectionism, since paragraph A.i. of Annex 3 of the WTO Charter, which establishes the TPRM, clearly states that the TPRM is not intended to serve as a basis for the enforcement of specific obligations, or for dispute settlement procedures, nor to impose new policy commitments on members.[68]

Such a soft law approach to a critical aspect of the social dimension of global trade will not satisfy those who advocate the incorporation of a social clause into the WTO Charter. However, the above approach is not meant to be the exclusive means by which the labor dimensions of trade are addressed; rather, it should be viewed as but the first step. Those who advocate the incorporation of a social clause into the WTO Charter on behalf of global social justice should consider whether it may be better to start with something small in the hope that it will develop into something more significant over time. Justice, carefully planned and nurtured, can sprout and grow with unexpected vigor. We have discussed in Chapter 1 how this happened with the Universal Declaration of Human Rights. There is no reason why it cannot happen in this vital area of global trade and fundamental labor rights.

Even if the very small step of integrating fundamental labor rights into the TPRM is not undertaken, the above analysis concerning the analogy of prohibited subsidies as regards abusive labor practices in EPZs, may entice a dispute settlement panel one day, with the right expert panelists, to rule that such practices are a violation of the *existing* WTO Charter.

In our previous text, we suggested[69] that the North American Agreement on Labor Cooperation (NAALC), adopted in 1993 in the context of the North American Free Trade Agreement (NAFTA), was a useful model to explore international trading relationships. This is because it represents a pioneering example of linking regional free trade agreements with labor cooperation in industrial relations and worker rights. The ILO has recognized the NAALC as the most noteworthy current example of a social clause in the context trade because it is a multiparty agreement involving a North–South dimension. Even some of its critics have admitted that the NAALC has broken new ground in the area of trade and labor. The NAALC parties have pledged to ensure "high labor standards" and "fair, equitable and transparent" avenues for enforcing their respective domestic labor laws. The NAALC also creates an obligation for the parties to enforce their own labor laws in eleven areas. It goes on to provide that a "pattern of practice" of violations of these obligations would in certain defined circumstances lead to an expert panel, the Evaluation Committee of Experts, being appointed to recommend compliance measures. Any persistent pattern of non-enforcement could also lead to the appointment of an arbitral panel and eventual sanctions.

However, some feel that the NAALC's focus on ensuring enforcement of national labor standards is insufficient. There is also criticism that the complaints process militates against transparency and natural justice, as complainants are unable to bring their concerns directly to the Labor Secretariat of the NAALC. Instead, they must work through a complex and lengthy review process, conducted by the appropriate National Administrative Office (NAO) in each country and by other relevant bodies. The NAOs file public reports on labor issues and can recommend ministerial consultations. In addition, there are concerns that the trade sanctions trigger is difficult to activate. This stands in contrast to the direct access to the dispute settlement panels provided for under NAFTA, and even the direct access to arbitration panels given to environmental groups under the North American Agreement on Environmental Cooperation (NAAEC). Under the NAALC, trade measures can only be resorted to in the various stages of the review process after satisfying a considerable evidence burden proving a persistent violation of domestic laws, which both countries recognize. Moreover, these violations can only have occurred in the areas of health and safety, child labor, and in setting minimum wage levels. Freedom of association complaints can only go as far as consultations and an obligation to report.[70]

Since writing our previous text, we have come to the conclusion that the NAALC model is a failure. The ministerial consultations do not seem to have any effect on persistent violations of domestic labor laws. While the consultation process seems effective in documenting abuses, the same cannot be said for its ability to take the necessary steps to end them. For example, some have claimed that workers in the industrial zones in northern Mexico, called maquiladoras (where over a million Mexicans work, many for less than the minimum Mexican wage), have found the NAALC to be totally ineffective. There are claims that workers in these maquiladoras who have brought complaints through the NAALC mechanisms have not received any redress. Instead, they have faced reprisals, intimidation, and violence in response to their claims.[71] Human Rights Watch has issued a severe critique of the NAALC in a report issued in April of 2001.[72] Among the findings of the report is the assertion that, after seven years, the three NAFTA countries have failed to live up to the commitment to work together toward broad improvement in labor rights in their respective countries, as is mandated by the NAALC. This is a result, in part, of the lack of an independent oversight body to administer the NAALC, instead of the weak bilateral and trilateral bodies that currently perform this oversight function.[73] The weakness of these bodies means that inevitably labor issues get bargained off against other pressing bilateral and trilateral issues, such as immigration, narcotics control, and the promotion of trade, according to the Human Rights Watch report. The NAALC parties had dealt with twenty-three cases by April of 2001, in which NGOs and business groups have alleged that there have been breaches of NAALC obligations. The three NAOs have issued twelve case reports, recommending ministerial consultations in all but one instance. Mexico and the United States have adopted six ministerial agreements covering nine separate cases, and Canada is currently negotiating an agreement with Mexico. However, Human Rights Watch claims that long delays, combined with a cumbersome process, create a disincentive to bring cases before the NAALC, as it could take years for a case to work its way through the system.[74] Likewise, the track record of the NAOs reveals inconsistencies in their handling of some of the most serious cases. For example, ministerial consultations have failed to resolve the problem of forced pregnancy-testing in Mexican maquiladoras, an issue raised in 1997. Mexican authorities admit that the practice violates their domestic labor laws, yet it continues.[75] This discrimination is a serious violation of both the NAALC and the fundamental labor right of non-discrimination contained in the ILO Declaration. Yet the 58 percent of the maquiladoras' workforce who are women continue to face this as well as other forms of severe discrimination in the workplace. Overall, the Human Rights Watch report condemns the timid use of the existing NAALC provisions by the NAOs and the labor ministries that take up consultations based on the NAO reports.[76] Timidity is no friend or ally of justice.

One can compare the weak enforcement structure of the NAALC with another more robust agreement that the US has recently established with Jordan in the US–Jordan Free Trade Agreement (USJFTA).[77] Under the USJFTA, the labor and environment agreements are part of the main text, rather than weak side agreements. This affirms both countries' commitments to core labor standards. The Agreement states that each party will "strive to ensure" that its domestic labor laws will reflect the ILO's Declaration of Fundamental Principles and Rights at Work, and will endeavor to improve their domestic standards. In contrast to the NAFTA side agreement on labor, the USJFTA allows the parties to skip "the non-binding remedial activities altogether by moving directly to the case reviews that could lead to sanctions for non-enforcement of the full range of labor principles that it covers."[78] The domestic labor laws of each party will be reviewed for compliance with the Agreement and "sustained or recurring" non-enforcement of those laws could lead to sanctions. While the Agreement is vague about the nature of the permissible sanctions, it states that if a dispute cannot be settled amicably, the affected party shall be entitled to take any "appropriate and commensurate measure."[79]

A former US trade representative, Charlene Barshefsky, is quoted as saying that:

> [T]he agreement is also the first to ever have, in the body of a U.S. trade agreement itself, key provisions that reconfirm that free trade and the protection of the environment and of the rights of workers go hand-in-hand. It will not require either country to adopt new laws, but rather

requires each to enforce the laws it currently has, which will join free trade and open markets with other public responsibilities.[80]

The USJFTA has the same dispute settlement mechanism for labor disputes as for disputes over free trade. However, it does not allow private parties to challenge a breach of the labor provisions, leaving it up to the two state parties to the agreement to do so. Finally, as noted above, the nature of the sanctions for the breach of the labor provisions is vague and uncertain. Despite these weaknesses, the USJFTA seems an improvement over the NAALC and, furthermore, indicates that a more robust framework is possible in a North–South free trade agreement. Given that the United States itself has moved to improve the NAALC model with the USJFTA, we can no longer endorse the NAALC as a model to be adopted in other regional free trade agreements. In addition, we would suggest that the USJFTA model is only appropriate for adoption in bilateral, multilateral, and global free trade agreements if its weaknesses outlined above are rectified.

In Chapter 1 we suggested that the regional powers of the world would be increasingly relied upon to promote international peace, security, and human rights. In this chapter, we suggest that regional trade blocs have a crucial role to play in promoting the social dimensions of trade, in particular the upward harmonization of labor standards. The NAALC model has failed to live up to its potential and there is a need for an ongoing search for a better model, which will be further discussed in Chapter 5.

In the long term do we survive? Trading off the environment

As a species, *homo sapiens* has lived for a relatively short time, barely a couple of hundred thousand years since the evolution of the first hominids. If we vanish within a short space of time, thereby extinguishing ourselves within the relative blink of an eye in terms of the history of the earth's biosphere, will the universe record an epitaph that we did so through our short-term memories and short-term interests?

The concerns over globalization, including trade, and its impact on the environment and human health, easily lead one to be pessimistic concerning the fate of the planet. The last three decades of the twentieth century saw the bell tolled so often: Chernobyl, *Exxon Valdez*, *Amoco Cadiz*, Bophal. To these one could add rapid desertification and drought in Africa, the thinning and consequent piercing of the ozone layer, global warming and climate change, the loss of large tracts of rainforest (which act as the lungs of the earth) in Asia, Africa, and especially in Latin America, the contamination of the food chain through pesticides, pollution, and toxic waste, and the emergence of "globalized diseases" such as HIV/AIDS.[81]

We tend to deal with these warnings by establishing grand commissions staffed by eminent persons, or by holding global conferences to stimulate our short-term memories and interests. However, in the long term we do not fully internalize the seriousness of these warnings. In 1987 we saw the warnings contained in the Brundtland Report produced by the World Commission on Environment and Development,[82] and in 1992 the world community came together at the Rio UN Conference on Environment and Development (UNCED).[83] Both these events emphasized that for the planet to remain habitable and for humans to survive, there could not be a win–lose game played between economic development and the environment. The concept of sustainable development was championed at both events as a means to achieve a balance between growth and the preservation of the environment. Both economic growth and environmental sustainability were regarded as mutually supportive if the right approach and technologies were utilized.[84]

There are those who question whether these two paradigms are in fact compatible, and whether an international legal approach to curbing environmental degradation as proposed by UNCED is too "neo-liberal" and "state-centric."[85] While there are many who would disagree with the critique contained in both the Brundtland and UNCED reports, and would dismiss them as disguised "neo-liberal" attempts to prioritize liberalized trade over the environment, there is at least one thing that all could agree upon. By 1992, the overwhelming majority of the world had agreed that there was indeed a link between trade, economic development, and the environment. Even the most ardent champion of liberalized trade would have accepted that, by 1992, there was no question that externalizing the environmental costs of production and trade would eventually mean more costs incurred by society, both nationally and globally in terms of remediation and impact on the lives of citizens. Also by this time, most environmentalists had modified their stance somewhat and moved away from the more radical environmentalist perspectives, such as the claim that any form of global trade would inevitably damage the environment. Moderate environmental perspectives began to accept trade as long as it was compatible with sustainable development. This debate may seem abstract, but as one author has vividly demonstrated, it can affect the everyday life of the human family:

> Barriers to markets created by environmental regulations include pesticide residues in foods, BST in milk, Chernobyl-originating radiation in agricultural products, recyclable boxes for the sale of cut flowers, regulations aimed at the way fish are caught, animals trapped or simply trade in endangered species, trade in ozone-depleting substances or hazardous waste, the labeling of products to give consumers information on environmental performance, the energy content of goods, trade in intellectual property rights based on genetic materials; all this in addition to the environmental effects of the increased volume of international trade which could be measured and internalized to account for transportation costs. This is a live, "food in the shops" debate that also brings in some fundamental concerns about international governance.[86]

Likewise, there was also a realization that environmental regulation could have a major positive impact on global trade, which has the potential to increase the standard of living of the millions of people around the world. Champions of global free trade have often argued that poverty in the developing world is one of the major causes of environmental degradation in the South.[87] By 1992, the stage seemed to have been set for some form of integration of trade and environmental issues in the lead-up to the establishment of the WTO.

However, the integration of these issues did not happen, at least not in any substantial form. Again, as with the linkage between trade and labor standards, the opposition to the linking of trade with the environment came from the developing nations during the GATT rounds and in the lead-up to the establishment of the WTO. Once again, the South's main fear was that environmental issues would be used for protectionist purposes against exports from the developing world.[88] Before the establishment of the WTO, fears of protectionism from the developed world disguised as environmental concerns resonated with the pure "free traders" from the North, who strongly argued that the GATT had neither the competence nor the mandate to deal with environmental issues. These fears led to the exclusion of any provisions dealing expressly with the environment during the Uruguay Round.[89] Those who saw the vital need for a link between trade and the environment had to place their hopes on Article XX of the GATT, which allows for exceptions to the GATT treaty, instead.[90] As we have briefly discussed above and shall explore further below, the GATT's core principles are those of non-discrimination and national treatment. This means that a country cannot prohibit or discriminate against imported products based on where they came from or the process and production methods (PPMs) used in producing those products. This also means that imported "like products" must receive the same "national treatment" in the importing country as domestically produced goods. However, these core principles are subject to the general exceptions set out in Article XX:

Article XX: General Exceptions

Subject to the requirement that such measures are not applied in a manner which would constitute a means of arbitrary or unjustifiable discrimination between countries where the same conditions prevail, or a disguised restriction on international trade, nothing in this Agreement shall be construed to prevent the adoption or enforcement by any contracting party of measures:

...

(b) necessary to protect human, animal or plant life or health; [or]

...

(g) relating to the conservation of exhaustible resources if such measures are made effective in conjunction with restrictions on domestic production or consumption.

Article XX has become the focal point of the attempt to link environmental and trade issues in the absence of any express provisions. However, as we shall see, the panel decisions under the GATT involving Article XX and environmental issues have initially proved extremely disappointing to supporters of sustainable development who expected so much from the Brundtland Report and the UNCED. The Uruguay Round, which led to the establishment of the WTO, although overlapping in its seven-year history with both the Brundtland Commission and the UNCED, had no multilateral negotiations on trade and the environment.

It could be argued that the WTO Charter contains so little on the environment that it has done the equivalent of "killing the area with faint praise." Nevertheless, there is the reference to sustainable development and the protection and preservation of the environment consistent with the needs of economic development, contained in the preamble to the WTO. While some may dismiss this as merely hortatory language, as we have seen in the context of fundamental labor rights there may be much life to breathe into such language. In addition, some experts have pointed to progress in the identification of non-actionable subsidies related to environmental retrofitting, the recognition of the Environmental Services Sector, and the creation of the WTO Committee on Trade and the Environment (CTE), as positive indications of the responsiveness of the WTO to the link between trade and the environment.[91] The CTE has been given a wide mandate to study many of the environmental issues related to the global trading regime and has also been given the task of establishing relationships with NGOs. At the 1999 High Level Symposium on Trade and the Environment and thereafter, the WTO Secretariat has given detailed accounts concerning the activities of the CTE, but to date there has been no substantial impact on the workings of the global trading regime resulting from the work of CTE.[92] The CTE is no substitute for multilateral negotiations on the environmental issues relating to global trade that should have taken place in the Uruguay Round.

Many critics would argue that these paltry concessions and weak institutional structures of the WTO concerning the environment are again an example of the fact that humans are a species with short-term memories and short-term interests. The consequences of these characteristics of the tragic flaw within the WTO parallel those within the United Nations discussed in Chapter 1.

The lifeline for the linkage between the environment and global trade remains Article XX of the GATT, which was subsequently incorporated into the WTO. However, as we shall see, the initial interpretation given to this article by the dispute settlement panels in the context of environmental concerns had been condemned by many as cutting this fragile lifeline.

The first case to engender such a critique was the *United States – Restrictions on the Importation of Tuna*[93] (the *Tuna/Dolphin I*) dispute between Mexico and the United States in 1994. This dispute arose out of a ban by the United States on the importation of yellowfin tuna caught with "purse seine" nets. These nets had been discovered to cause the death or injury of dolphins in numbers that were in violation of the standards established by the US Marine Mammal Protection Act. The GATT panel ruled that the US ban was a violation of the GATT, which could not be saved by the Article XX exceptions for three main reasons. The first reason was that the ban constituted a trade measure whose objective was to preserve resources outside the jurisdiction of the US. Second, the United States had failed to prove that the ban was aimed primarily at conservation. Third, the ban was discriminatory because it related to the manner in which the imported goods were produced, rather than to any characteristics inherent to the goods themselves. For these reasons the ban was determined to be a quantitative restriction, which is prohibited by Article XI of the GATT. One leading authority, James Cameron, gives a harsh critique of the panel ruling:

> First, how does a state deal with preserving resources, perhaps migratory, outside of its jurisdiction short of a multilateral agreement? How does the reality of somebody else's methods, perhaps even enterprises taking advantage of lower standards, get addressed in a way that survives tests of national treatment? ...
>
> Second, how did the "primarily aimed at" test get to (a) exist and (b) be so restrictively applied? ... Despite the reality of industry capture and unholy alliances (such is ordinary political life) the idea that the Marine Mammal Protection Act was really a front for protecting the US tuna industry came as a surprise to the conservationists who fought for it for many years.
>
> Third ... the issue of production and process methods (PPMs) and Article XI (the "like product" debate) remains unresolved. Of course, environmentalists don't have a thing against tuna itself, they are concerned with method. They are, more than that, concerned about fishing method and fisheries collapse, at least as much as whales, dolphins, turtles and sea birds. Frankly these are vital economic arguments, missing from the very formulaic reasoning of the panel.[94]

Contained within such a critique is the echo of the frustration of those who wished to see the GATT and the WTO deal effectively with labor standards. However, the WTO claims that its rules do not necessarily mandate conflicts with domestic attempts to protect the environment, biodiversity, or the implementation of Multilateral Environmental Agreements (MEAs), and point to a more recent Appellate Body ruling to reinforce their position.[95] The ruling in question is the *United States – Import Prohibition of Certain Shrimp and Shrimp Products* decision in 1998. The following is an edited account of the ruling given by the WTO itself on its website.[96]

In early 1997, India, Malaysia, Pakistan, and Thailand brought a joint complaint against the United States to the WTO Dispute Settlement Body, requesting that a panel be formed. Their complaint involved an import ban imposed by the US against certain shrimp and shrimp products. At the heart of the US ban was the goal of protecting sea turtles. The US Endangered Species

Act of 1973 listed as endangered or threatened the five species of sea turtles that inhabit US waters and therefore prohibited their "take" within US jurisdictional waters or on the high seas. "Take" included harassment, hunting, capture, killing, or attempting to do any of the foregoing. The US law required American shrimp trawlers to use "turtle excluder devices" (TEDs) in their nets when fishing in areas where sea turtles were likely to be located. Another provision of US law, section 609 of the Endangered Species Act, provided that shrimp harvested with technology that had an adverse impact on sea turtles could not be imported into the United States. An exception to this rule would be made only when the harvesting nation was certified as having a regulatory program and an incidental take-rate comparable to that of the United States, or when the particular fishing environment of the harvesting nation did not pose a threat to sea turtles.

The combined effect of the two laws was that any shrimp-harvesting nation where any of the five endangered sea turtle species were found had to have in place a similar sea turtle protection regime for shrimp fishing as that of the United States, if they wanted to have their shrimp and shrimp products imported into the US. This meant, in particular, that shrimp from the exporting country was required to be caught with the use of TEDs.

The WTO claims that many have missed the importance of the Appellate Body's ruling in this case, especially as regards the following:

First, the Appellate Body clearly ruled that, under the WTO rules, members can take trade action to protect the environment (in particular, human, animal, or plant life and health), or endangered species and exhaustible resources.

Second, measures to protect sea turtles could be legitimate under GATT Article XX, provided certain criteria such as non-discrimination were met.

Third, the US lost the case, *not* because it sought to protect the environment but because it discriminated *between* WTO members. The Appellate Body found that the US had provided countries in the Western hemisphere, mainly in the Caribbean, with technical and financial assistance and longer transition periods for their fishermen to start using TEDs. It had not given these same advantages to the four complainants. Therefore, the Appellate Body found that, while the US measures that instituted the ban in order to protect sea turtles did qualify for provisional justification under Article XX (g) of the GATT, they failed to meet the requirements of the "chapeau" or introductory paragraph of Article XX, which prohibits such measures from being applied in an arbitrary or unjustified discriminatory fashion.

Finally, the WTO seems keen to point out that the Appellate Body ruling stated that dispute settlement panels may receive "amicus briefs" from environmental or other NGOs as well as other interested parties.[97] It could be argued that such a ruling was largely symbolic, and was designed to counter criticism that the WTO dispute panels were non-transparent and closed to input from those with environmental expertise. As we shall see, the WTO seems to have back-pedaled on this new openness in a later decision.

It should also be noted that this and other panel rulings also seem to recognize the WTO Charter as coming within the interpretative framework of international law as mandated by Article 3 of the Dispute Settlement Understanding. Referring to international environmental law and its development since the beginning of the GATT, the Appellate Body in *Shrimp–Turtle* ruled that such international norms could be used as an appropriate benchmark for the interpretation of "conservation of exhaustible resources" as found in Article XX(g).[98]

The aftermath to the Appellate Body's ruling sheds some light on whether the decision constitutes any real improvement in the WTO's sensitivity to environmental issues. Following the ruling, the US government first tried to water down its import ban by changing the shrimp importation certification system to a shipment-by-shipment rather than a country-by-country basis. This was struck down by a US court on the basis that the changes would not give the required incentive for non-certified countries to institute or maintain national programs to protect sea turtles.[99]

In response, the United States changed the law again, this time in a manner that does not seem to have involved substantial changes to the existing law, which was the subject of the initial challenge. A list of forty countries eligible to export shrimp to the United States was published in April of 2000. Sixteen of these countries use TEDs; twenty-five are countries that do not put sea turtles at risk. Some other countries, like Brazil, have reached an agreement on a shipment-by-shipment certification basis with the United States. Some would argue that the WTO ruling seems to have had very little impact either on the trade in shrimp and shrimp products or on the environment. It has also been argued that the ruling still tends to favor trade liberalization over any unilateral measure imposed for environmental purposes that may have a discriminatory impact.[100]

There are also some ironies in certain aspects of the ruling. The decision could be used by some to argue that what the US import ban amounted to was a form of eco-imperialism: a rich developed country forcing other countries to accept its own sea turtle protection regime, placing the burden of compliance on developing countries like India. Interestingly, India, Malaysia, and Pakistan have all signed the Biodiversity Convention, but the US has not. Likewise, the impact of the Appellate Body's ruling would seem to be the opposite of the "polluter pays" principle. Here, the fact that the United States had not given resources and technical assistance to India and the other complaining countries in contrast to the Caribbean nations made the crucial difference, according to the WTO's own rendition of the facts and according to the ruling. This amounts to turning the environmental protection principle of "polluter pays" on its head, by suggesting that to fit within the Article XX exception, the United States had to pay the polluters.[101]

Even those who disagree with the Appellate Body's ruling in the *Shrimp–Turtle* case would agree that the best way to deal with problems raised by migratory species like sea turtles is to protect them through an MEA, whose signatories roughly correspond to the membership of the WTO. Leading experts like James Cameron suggest that comprehensive MEAs encourage global commitment through "a carrot and stick approach, by restricting trade in a relevant area and extending those restrictions to non-parties, and by providing financing to meet the objectives of the MEA."[102]

Examples of MEAs include the Montreal Protocol on Substances that Deplete the Ozone Layer, the Basel Convention on the Control of Transboundary Movements of Hazardous Wastes and their Disposal, and the Convention on International Trade in Endangered Species of Wild Fauna and Flora.[103] There are about 200 MEAs dealing with various environmental issues that are of sufficient concern to the entire human family that they can rightly be regarded as giving rise to fundamental environmental legal norms. Approximately twenty of these MEAs have provisions that impact on trade, by banning trade in certain products or allowing restrictions on trade in certain circumstances. The MEAs outlined above are the most well-known MEAs that contain trade-restricting provisions.

The most effective MEAs come with both the stick of trade restrictions, to deal with the problem of free riders, and the carrot of financial assistance, in addition to monitoring of compliance by the conference of the member states.

The WTO claims that the basic principles of non-discrimination and transparency under the WTO Charter do not necessarily conflict with these MEAs. Indeed, what is not known well enough is that the CTE has accepted that the most effective way to deal with the trade and environment linkage may well be through the use of MEAs. The WTO argues that the MEAs complement its work by seeking internationally agreed-upon solutions, rather than sanctioning the use of unilateral measures, to solve transboundary environmental problems.[104]

The WTO goes on to state that, so far, no action taken under an MEA that has affected trade has been challenged in the GATT–WTO system. The WTO also notes on its website that there is "a widely held view that actions taken under an environmental agreement are unlikely to become a problem in the WTO if the countries concerned have signed the agreement, although the issue is not settled completely." The WTO accepts that the real controversy will occur when one country takes a trade-related action pursuant to an MEA that it considers permissible under Article XX against another country that has not signed the MEA.[105] This is a dispute waiting to happen. Some MEAs stipulate that signatory countries must apply the agreement (including any trade-related measures contained therein) to goods and services from countries that have not signed the MEA. We follow Cameron's lead in suggesting that the WTO should make it extremely difficult for any non-signatory of an MEA to challenge actions taken pursuant to the MEA within the WTO.[106] We also strongly agree that WTO member states should have the right to implement policies mandated by MEAs that may affect trade with non-parties. In opposition to this stance, it could be argued that MEAs that allow the use of Trade Related Environmental Measures (TREMs) could result in the use of unilateral measures that are really a disguised form of protectionism. This, however, can be countered with the realization that if measures taken to deal with common global environmental problems can be disguised forms of protectionism, then there are some forms of protectionism that should be regarded as tolerable in both a moral and a legal sense! The incorporation of MEAs into the WTO regime can also be an effective counter-balance to the increasing desire on the part of the developed world to take unilateral measures to protect the environment, through mechanisms such as ecolabeling.[107]

Indeed, there is something to be said for Cameron's suggestion that the main MEAs be incorporated by multilateral agreement into the WTO, and that MEA and WTO concerns be placed on an equal footing within the dispute settlement panels.[108] There are parallels here to the discussion in Chapter 1 regarding the struggle to have human rights on an equal footing with territorial integrity and political independence.

In this area, as with labor standards, we are suggesting that the *existing* WTO Charter may provide not only a moral but also a legal basis for placing MEAs on to an equal footing within the WTO. In the preamble to the Marrakesh Agreement establishing the WTO, as we have discussed above, reference to the objective of sustainable development and the preservation and promotion of the environment provides both the moral and the legal basis for the possible resolution of this issue. Moreover, the preamble to the WTO agreement could persuade a dispute panel to dispense with the narrow focus of the *Tuna–Dolphin* decision, build upon the *Shrimp–Turtle* decision, and regard any TREMs related to MEAs as coming within the scope of Article XX, even as regards actions against non-parties to the MEA in question.

Just as we have argued that when WTO member countries permit abusive labor practices in violation of their own laws in EPZs they could be found to be in violation of the *existing* WTO Charter, the same arguments could be applied in the area of the environment. Where WTO members deliberately allow domestic environmental laws to be flouted in these same EPZs, similar arguments to the ones concerning prohibited export subsidies could be developed.

These suggestions may seem unrealistic to some but, as Cameron points out, the European Union has already shown the way by demonstrating how to balance trade, social, and environmental interests in an effective regional trade liberalization regime.[109]

A more recent Appellate Body ruling may also indicate that the *existing* WTO Charter could be applied in a way that balances trade, social, and environmental concerns. On 12 March 2001, the Appellate Body handed down an important decision in *European Communities v. Canada*, the *Asbestos* case.[110] The ruling dismissed Canada's complaint against France's ban on asbestos. Canada had claimed that the French ban was inconsistent with a number of provisions in the Agreement on Sanitary and Phytosanitary Measures (SPS) and the Agreement on Technical Barriers to Trade (TBT) as well as Article III of the GATT (dealing with the "national treatment" principle). Brazil, the United States, and Zimbabwe joined as interested third parties to the dispute. The lower dispute settlement panel had ruled that the import ban instituted by France was justified under Article XX, even though France had violated Article III by discriminating against the importation of Canadian asbestos. This finding of discrimination was a result of the panel's conclusion that asbestos, which was banned, and asbestos substitutes, which were permitted, were in fact "like products" for the purpose of Article III of the GATT. This aspect of the lower panel's ruling was heavily criticized by environmental groups for coming to the right decision for the wrong reasons. They argued that such reasoning set a dangerous precedent because it failed to distinguish between toxic (asbestos) and non-toxic (asbestos substitute) products in determining what were "like products."

The Appellate Body reversed this and other controversial aspects of the dispute settlement panel's decision. The Appellate Body held that carcinogenic asbestos is not a "like product" to safer substitute products, and that the French ban on imports of asbestos-containing products was not in violation of Article III of the GATT.

Some of the human rights advocacy groups may see in the Appellate Body ruling an opening through which human rights could be inserted into the trade regime. They argue that products which are "toxic" in the sense that they have been produced through gross human rights abuses should, in the same vein as asbestos, not be treated as "like products." Given that Article XX of the GATT already allows exceptions for "human rights toxic" products made with prison labor, the Appellate Body ruling may have reinforced the linkage between human rights and trade. Two authors, Robert Howse and Makau Mutua, have also suggested that Article XX(a), which creates a general exception to the GATT rules for the protection of "public morals," could be used to justify GATT-inconsistent measures in dealing with goods or services that involve human rights abuses.[111] For reasons discussed above, in regard to products produced by exploitative child labor, we are not in favor of using the Article XX exceptions to link human rights to the world trade regime. Indeed, Howse and Mutua accept that concerns would persist that such restrictions could be open to protectionist purposes.[112]

Leading environmental and anti-asbestos NGOs praised the Appellate Body's decision in the *Asbestos* ruling for going even further than was necessary: because the Appellate Body had found that there was no violation of Article III, any consideration of the exceptions to the GATT rules contained in Article XX was strictly unwarranted. Nevertheless, the Appellate Body did go on to consider these exceptions. In doing so, the Appellate Body upheld the lower panel's application of the health exception (under Article XX(g)), stating that it was up to each member government to decide the level of protection that it desires for its citizens. When France decided that it wanted absolute protection from cancer-causing asbestos, it was entitled to decide that there was no reasonable alternative than to implement the import ban. In setting such health policy, the Appellate Body ruled that member governments did not have to follow the majority scientific opinion as to what may constitute the appropriate level of health protection for its citizens. Some environmentalists have praised this ruling as an endorsement of the integration of the precautionary principle, as promoted by the Brundtland Report and UNCED, into trade-related disputes.[113]

The Appellate Body in the Asbestos case also overturned the panel's decision regarding the permissibility of governments to make distinctions, for the purpose of importation, between toxic and non-toxic materials. However, some have suggested that the Appellate Body's ruling leaves a serious threat hanging by accepting Canada's argument that the TBT agreement applies to health and safety measures like the French ban on carcinogenic asbestos. The ruling seems to indicate that the TBT Agreement imposes obligations on member states that may be different, but additional to the obligations under the WTO Charter. While the Appellate Body did not consider whether the French ban was compatible with the TBT Agreement, in effect this part of the ruling suggests that the WTO does have jurisdiction over public health measures that may affect trade liberalization.[114]

While the Appellate Body's substantive ruling was, in general, praised by those who do not see trade or globalization as an end in themselves, there was nonetheless harsh criticism in relation to the failure of the Appellate Body to become more open and transparent in its deliberations. After the Appellate Body had issued a notice, in November of 2000, allowing any concerned organization to file written briefs concerning the case at hand, there was intense pressure by member governments for the WTO to keep the doors closed to NGOs and the other interested parties. This was reflected in the decision by the Appellate Body to reject both the briefs of environmental NGOs and the requests to file non-party submissions under the "Additional procedure." In Kafkaesque language, the Appellate Body stated that the rejections stemmed from a failure to comply with all of the requirements of the "Additional procedure." Some applications were rejected because they missed the filing deadline, while others were rejected without any details given for the refusal.[115]

It is clear that the Appellate Body realized that it had an extremely controversial dispute on its hands, a dispute that could potentially increase the strident opposition to the WTO and other institutions of global governance seen at the Ministerial Conference in Seattle and elsewhere. The decision would have been even more contentious if it had struck down a ban on carcinogenic asbestos, which kills thousands due to the diseases it causes. In coming to a decision that seems to have attempted to achieve a balance between trade, health, and the environment, it is evident that there was clearly a fear on behalf of the Appellate Body that if it appeared too open to the advocacy of environmental and labor groups, there would be a backlash from many of the WTO members. Justice is often a very delicate balancing act, attempting to do what is practical while waiting for the possible.

Another recent advance in the social dimensions of trade has occurred in the matter of access to existing essential drugs at affordable prices for the sick in poor countries. At the Global Health Council held in Norway in April of 2001 (organized by the WTO and the World Health Organization (WHO)), there seemed to have been agreement that the differential pricing of essential drugs is fully compatible with the TRIPs Agreement and does not require countries to forego any flexibility that they may have under TRIPs. This flexibility includes issues relating to compulsory licensing and parallel imports to respond to health concerns. Such flexibility is critical to alleviate the suffering of the millions of people in developing countries who are stricken with diseases like HIV/AIDS, which can only be treated with expensive drugs. The Council noted that the TRIPs Agreement did not prohibit countries from aiding market segmentation through the prohibition of parallel imports, for example, from poor countries to high-income countries. As will be discussed, the successful multilateral trade talks at Doha reinforced the conclusions of the Global Health Council. Finally, the Council also recognized that the patent system, now protected under the WTO, while a necessary condition for critical research and development (R&D), was not sufficient to secure adequate R&D for the neglected health concerns of the poor.[116]

There is a need for "principled negotiations" on the question of how to balance trade against the environment, including the need for bringing the long-term interests of the human species and the planet into the shorter-term objectives of trade liberalization and economic growth. Such an approach is key to combating the tragic flaw within the world trade regime.

Fortunately, the Canadian-based International Institute for Sustainable Development (IISD) has made progress in this area readily possible by providing the framework for such negotiations through the widely respected Winnipeg Principles on Trade and Sustainable Development. These principles are comprised of the following:

1   *Efficiency and cost internationalization*
Efficiency is a common interest for environment, development and trade policies.

2   *Equity*
Equity relates to the distribution both within and between generations of physical and natural capital, as well as knowledge and technology.

3   *Environmental integrity*
This requires respect for limits to the regenerative capacity of ecosystems, actions to avoid irreversible harm to plant and animal populations and species, and protection for valued areas.

4   *Subsidiarity*
Subsidiarity recognizes that action will occur at different political levels, depending on the nature of issues. It assigns priority to the lowest jurisdictional level consistent with effectiveness.

5   *International cooperation*
Sustainable development requires strengthening international systems of cooperation at all levels, encompassing environment, development and trade policies.

6 *Science and precaution*
The interrelated nature of trade, environment, and development can give rise to conflicts in short-run objectives, and policies designed to address these should be shaped by objective criteria.

7 *Openness*
Greater openness will significantly improve environmental, trade and development policies.[117]

It is clear from the articulation of a common ground in the Winnipeg Principles that there should be room to have "principled negotiations" on the link between trade and the environment, without engaging in adversarial battles where one side hurls accusations of "green protectionism" and the other side responds with accusations of "uncaring profiteers." The IISD, in an assessment of the WTO made in 1996, expressed disappointment in the lack of such principled negotiations in the global trade regime. Instead, it found conservative tendencies in the entire organization and continued weakness in the CTE, which was tasked with continuing the dialogue on trade and the environment.[118] The IISD, the Canadian government, and leading experts have all urged that trade and environment concerns be "mainstreamed" across all WTO negotiations. Other recommendations by the IISD (and others) have included giving incentives to developing countries to overcome their fears of protectionism that emanate from Northern environmental concerns. Strategies to achieve this could include improvements in market access of key exports; reductions in trade-distorting subsidies in the developed world, especially in agriculture; public scrutiny of TREMs taken by developed countries that goes beyond the current transparency and notification requirements; and financially assisting in the introduction of eco-efficient technologies and environmental services.[119]

Ultimately, we can only ensure that we are not trading off the environment if we break down the isolation of trade and environmental experts. We must also break down the suspicions of the developing world concerning the green ambitions of the developed world. Green is not only the color of money. It is also the color of life.

Conclusion

Much of global civil society that rages against the institutions of global governance like the WTO, and is seeking greater protection of human rights, labor rights, and the environment across the planet, may be driven by good intentions (their critics would argue they are driven by misinformation and misguidance). Yet such rage may be also driven by a feeling that institutions like the WTO are handing over human governance to remote technocrats who usurp the democratic institutions of nations. Experts counter that the reality of the WTO is that it is seriously understaffed, underbudgeted, and that it has a much leaner bureaucratic structure than other institutions of global governance.[120] Indeed, a serious threat to the universality of the WTO regime is likely to be, according to many experts, the lack of resources, both financial and human, to assist capacity development in the developing world enabling these nations to participate meaningfully in WTO negotiations, especially in the critical areas of agriculture and services.[121] Given that the WTO is a "member-driven" organization, it has been pointed out that it is a very serious concern that two-thirds of the least developed countries do not have representation in Geneva at the WTO.[122] This is a recipe for the continued marginalization of the most vulnerable nations in the human family in both the operation and development of the global trade regime.

In addition, the structure of the WTO has been criticized for creating and exacerbating the democratic deficits within and between member nations, and between civil society groups and the global trade regime. It has been alleged that the undemocratic structure of the WTO is creating an informal and undemocratic "security council" within the global trade regime. The plenary Ministerial Conference meets only every two years, and there is no effective representative executive body that is accountable for implementation actions and overall management in between these meetings. This vacuum has been filled by the "Quad" countries, namely the United States, the European Union, Japan, and Canada. This virtual executive committee of the WTO seems to make critical decisions, such as the agreement for quick Chinese accession to the WTO, without much consultation with the other members of the WTO, who number well over a hundred.[123]

This inter-member democratic deficit is compounded by the asserted lack of effective access to WTO decision-making processes by NGOs and other civil society actors. The WTO strongly denies this and points to the recent initiatives in expanding dialogue with civil society groups. It points out that the Marrakesh Agreement includes a specific reference to NGOs in Article V(ii), which permits appropriate arrangements for consultations and cooperation with NGOs. It also refers to guidelines, adopted by the WTO General Council, which recognize the role NGOs can play to increase the awareness of the public in respect of the WTO's activities. Since 1996, these forms of consultation and cooperation have essentially entailed attendance at Ministerial Conferences, participation in WTO symposia and on-line discussions, and day-to-day contact between the WTO Secretariat and NGOs. Additionally, there have been a number of new initiatives designed to improve dialogue with civil society, such as regular briefings for NGOs, a special NGO section on the WTO website, and publication and circulation of NGO position papers received by the Secretariat.[124]

Some have suggested that such NGO inputs into the work of the WTO are more accurately described as the harvesting of diverse civil society opinions without allowing effective high-level input together with the necessary public transparency, accessibility, and accountability measures.[125] With the exclusion of the environmental and health groups' briefs from the Asbestos Appellate Body's decision-making process, the perception outlined above concerning the mere harvesting of civil society opinions will be heightened. If the WTO is to go beyond such mere harvesting, it must consider opening up the dispute settlement and Appellate Body processes to the public, and allowing NGOs with the relevant expertise to present briefs and have them considered. Likewise, if civil society input is to be meaningful, access to information and working documents must be provided before meetings are held and decisions made.

However, civil society groups will also have to deal with one major challenge themselves. There are increasing concerns about how democratic and representative civil society groups are themselves. Do they speak only for their members or special interests, or can they legitimately claim to speak on behalf of civil society, domestically or internationally? In addition, some developing countries argue that the labor and environmental lobbying by NGOs and trade unions from the developed nations can be forms of moral, legal, and cultural imperialism, or a form of disguised protectionism. We have attempted to refute some of the latter concerns in regard to the application of global standards in labor rights and the environment to the global trade regime. As regards the challenge to the democratic nature of NGOs and whom they represent, the answer is that, over time, the credibility of NGOs is tested by their own constituents and by their own actions and activities. To take just one example, the Canadian-based IISD has proven its credibility, not only to its own constituents but also to international organizations, including the WTO, which has publicized IISD reports on its own website.

Another answer to this democratic deficit challenge, both on the part of the WTO and the NGOs interested in its work, is to reinforce the role of democratically elected institutions in the work of the WTO. National legislatures around the world have very little role to play in the global trading regime. This must be rectified, as the work of the WTO and the operation of the global trade regime impacts so heavily on the mandate, mission, and functioning of members of legislatures around the world. Adverse rulings on government subsidies from WTO dispute settlement panels can throw thousands out of work in local constituencies. Decisions on sanitary and phytosanitary measures can devastate local farming and agricultural practices. The impact of the global trade regime on the mandate of members of national legislatures is becoming increasingly serious. There is a need to strengthen the role of national legislatures in the development of the global trade regime, both at the national and the international level.

At the national level, there is a need for legislatures to permit truly democratic consultations with citizens through standing committees before national positions in multilateral trade negotiations are formed. Such consultations must not again be the mere harvesting of opinions. One study of the democratic deficit in the WTO and at the national level on global trade issues revealed that "Parliament is often informed only at the end of negotiations, and is not seriously involved throughout the process."[126] This deficit is compounded by the fact that, when called to ratify the results of multilateral trade negotiations, legislatures (including the US Congress under the fast-track authority regime) can only accept or reject the whole agreement. There is thus a danger that the implementation of global trade commitments at the domestic level becomes a rubber stamp, with the real power being transferred to the executive of national governments and trade ministries in particular. This may be especially true where national legislatures are not elected, or in a parliamentary system of government where the executive effectively controls the legislative body through party discipline. Thus, the gap between the technical experts, together with the trade negotiators and the citizen, grows even wider. The wider this gap grows, the more likely it will be that the frustration of the activist component of the citizenry will spill over into protests against the remote workings of the WTO at Ministerial Conferences.

Like others,[127] we would suggest that to deal with this serious and growing problem, multilateral discussions should take place at the WTO on the need to develop a "Standing Parliamentary Assembly" to fill in the growing democratic deficit at the WTO *and within member states*. The European Parliament, the Parliamentary Assembly of the Organization for Security and Co-operation in Europe, and the Parliamentary Assembly of the Council of Europe are not perfect but are acceptable role models for such a body.[128] The fundamental purpose of such a WTO Standing Parliamentary Assembly would be to act as a highly credible advisory body to the WTO, to bring the concerns of the citizens of the member countries to the WTO. Moreover, such a body could ensure that trade negotiators pay heed to such concerns and could promote the democratization of the work of WTO internationally and within the member states. Finally, a WTO Standing Parliamentary Assembly could also assist in the crucial task of "principled negotiations" between the developed and developing world. Such negotiations are vital in areas involving linkages to fundamental labor rights, environmental protection, access to pharmaceutical products by the sick and impoverished of the human family, as well as in other critical areas that need discussing in relation to the fundamental values behind the global trade regime and its social dimensions. The WTO Standing Parliamentary Assembly could also be a catalyst for ensuring that the WTO works closely with the ILO and the international financial institutions to deal with the problems arising out of the social dimensions of trade. This could be accomplished by the Parliamentary Assembly being given the power to conduct hearings on the social dimensions of trade. It could also order key decision-makers from all the relevant organizations to reveal how problems relating to the social dimensions of trade are being dealt with.

Some may argue that the reasons why the social dimensions of trade have been largely left out of first the GATT and subsequently the WTO are because there is a clash of fundamental misconceptions about the human values behind trade and its social dimensions. On one hand, some social activists and those on the left of the political spectrum denounce the fundamental values behind the "neo-liberal" trade liberalization agenda as maximization of profit at the expense of the poor, workers, and other vulnerable groups, as well as the environment. These sectors of global civil society also claim that the global trade system is profoundly anti-democratic, unaccountable, and non-transparent. It thrives on secrecy and private hegemony with the multinational corporations who are the main beneficiaries of the whole regime.

The ardent supporters of global trade liberalization regard such perspectives as ill informed, ideologically driven, and just plain wrong. They argue that global trade liberalization is particularly good for the poor and the environment. Global trade, they argue, is a rising tide that will lift all boats and, rather, it is poverty that causes poor farming methods and other environmentally degrading practices, and gives governments little incentive to put resources into the protection of the environment. In this chapter we have attempted to show that there are misconceptions on both ends of this spectrum of opinion regarding the global trade regime. As with most areas, the reality, if there is one to be found, is somewhere in the middle of the spectrum. In that middle zone must be found the common human values that the vast majority of members of the human family can identify with and promote. We suggest that this will only happen if we can accept that globalization and global trade are not ends in themselves but are there to serve the cause of all humanity. As such, global trade must support human dignity as a fundamental requirement of justice. Human dignity is not supported by trade liberalization that involves the massive exploitation of workers in EPZs, nor is it supported by liberalized trade in goods that are toxic or harmful to sustainable life on earth. There is also little to support blindness to the reality that the poorest nations of the human family may not be able to reap the benefits of global trade without massive assistance from the developed world.

On the other hand, human progress and flourishing is also not supported by anarchists throwing deadly projectiles at police lines at WTO Ministerial Conferences. Human progress and flourishing is also not promoted by well-intentioned but misguided desires to impose sanctions on the importation of products made with child labor, without finding the resources to send those children to school rather than on to the streets as child prostitutes. The environment, fundamental labor, and human rights must be integrated into the general framework of a global trade regime which has the goal of promoting and protecting human dignity. The WTO cannot be overburdened with environmental, labor, and human rights mandates when it is barely able to find the resources to fulfill its present narrower mandate. This is also a critical reason why other institutions of global governance such as the ILO and the World Bank need to become more integrated into the work of the WTO. However, as we have discussed, there must be considerable reform of the ILO before it can begin to act as an effective partner in dealing with the social dimensions of trade. To start eradicating the tragic flaw at the heart of the world trade regime, the cause of human progress and flourishing must become the foundation of the global trade regime, as much as human security must become the foundation of any reform of the United Nations, as discussed in Chapter 1.

Some would assert that the World Trade Organization is finally returning to the idea that trade is not an end in itself, but should be for the good of all humanity. On 14 November 2001 in Doha, Qatar, at the first world trade talks since the debacle at Seattle, after going more than eighteen hours beyond the deadline for the end of the talks, the 142 members of the WTO agreed to a new round of global trade talks which they called the "trade and development" round. The meeting was also momentous in that it formally admitted China and Taiwan into the WTO. With the admission of China, the WTO can truly call itself a global institution of trade law and policy.[129]

Included among the list of items agreed to at Doha, the following moved the WTO a little further toward the unfinished agenda of the ITO:

1   There was an agreement that the intellectual property rules of the WTO should not prevent the poorer members from gaining access to cheap drugs for public health emergencies. Even this limited concession to countries that lobbied hard for it, such as Brazil and South Africa, was deemed a political agreement as opposed to a legal agreement.

2   The poorer countries would be granted a longer period to implement certain of the WTO agreements and would get assistance from the richer members to build appropriate trade infrastructure capacity.

3   In what some considered a major concession by the European Union and the United States, the Doha Agreement included a vague commitment to achieve substantial improvements in market access for farm products and the phasing out of export subsidies. Together with textiles, farm products accounted for 70 percent of the exports of the poorest members of the WTO at the time of the Doha trade talks.

4   There was a commitment to reduce peak tariffs on industrial goods that would increase the access to the developed world's markets for textiles from the poorer members when the quota-based system of textile imports is phased out in 2005.

5   There was a commitment to clarify and strengthen rules on anti-dumping used by the US and other industrialized states to keep out goods from the poorer members of the WTO.[130]

What is also significant is that there was no mention of any commitments in the area of trade and labor standards. Some have argued that this was a victory for the developing country members of the WTO, where fears about the use of this area for protectionist purposes by the richer members in part led to the debacle at Seattle.[131] As we have discussed in this chapter and will do again in Chapter 5, the perspective that linking trade and core labor standards is inimical to the interests of the developing world is long overdue for debunking and consignment to the discarded theories of global governance.

Another area viewed by the developing world as harboring the potential for protectionism fared better at Doha. There was an agreement to negotiate on the relationship between the obligations in the WTO and those found in the MEAs discussed in this chapter. Even in this area, where there should be concordance between different sets of multilateral obligations, some are warning that the developing world will be able to stop progress because of the WTO's requirement for consensus. Indeed, it has been argued that even the partial success of the poorer members of the WTO at Doha was due to their realization that there is strength in numbers, which can force concessions in a consensus-based governance system.[132] Ultimately this could prove the undoing of the WTO, because the stronger the unity of the developing world becomes in this and other institutions of global governance, the more resistance may be encountered from those with the entrenched economic and political power. This resistance became a reality in the spring of 2002 when the Bush administration passed a new Farm Bill which would provide a huge increase in subsidies to American farmers to match and ultimately even exceed those given to European farmers by the European Union. Added to the other recent protectionist measures from the United States in the area of steel and in its implementation of US anti-dumping and countervail laws, it is almost certain that the "trade and development" round initiated at Doha is now seriously imperiled.[133]

World trade must be for the benefit of all humanity. The cause of human progress and flourishing must show that entrenched economic and political power is never sustainable through exploitation and disregard of the poverty of others.

3 Power and responsibility

The ethical and international legal
duties of the global private sector

The transformation of global economic power: in search of vision

In Chapters 1 and 2 we examined the development of institutions of global governance that deal with international peace and security and global trade. The international community learned from the lessons of history that there was a need for carefully planned and developed institutions in these areas. We have discussed how, in the case of both the United Nations and the World Trade Organization, the original high visions of both institutions were superseded by the pursuit of economic, political, or military power and territorial and national self-interests that created a tragic flaw within both regimes. As we begin the third millennium, there is emerging another area of vital concern to the global community. That area involves the role played by potentially one of the most powerful players in the global arena, the global private sector.

Research done by a United States organization, the Institute for Policy Studies (IPS), has revealed that in 1996 the top 200 of the approximately 40,000 global firms have a huge share of the global economic activity. Most of these 200 firms are economically more significant than many developing countries, and control over a quarter of the world's economic activity.[1] IPS claims that of the largest one hundred economies in the world in 1995, fifty-one were corporations, while only forty-nine were national economies. Wal-Mart, as the twelfth largest corporation in 1995, could be regarded as having a larger "economy" than 161 national economies, including Israel, Poland, and Greece. Mitsubishi's "economy" was larger than that of Indonesia, the fourth most populous country in the world. Likewise, the IPS study claimed that General Motors' "economy" was bigger than Denmark's, Ford's was bigger than South Africa's, and Toyota's was bigger than Norway's.[2]

In the study, such conclusions were drawn by comparing the GDP of national economies to the annual sales figures of the top 200 corporations. With the rapid decline in both the US and global economies during the 2000–2 period, the figures may be quite different today. Many economists would argue that comparing GDP figures to sales revenues of corporations is like comparing apples to oranges, especially as GDP figures take into account the value of imports.

However, while the yardsticks may not be perfect, the figures, at minimum, present an incontrovertible picture of the growing power of the global private sector. This is also illustrated by another facet of the IPS study, which found that the combined sales of the world's top 200 corporations may exceed 25 percent of the world's economic activity and could amount to close to 30 percent of the world's GDP. The combined sales of the top 200 corporations in 1995 were bigger than the combined economies of 182 countries, which is nine fewer than all the national economies in the world in 1995. The combined sales of the top 200 corporations in 1995 was US$7.1 trillion. According to the conclusions drawn in the IPS study, *inter alia*, this meant that the top 200 corporations had almost twice as much economic power as the poorest four-fifths of humanity (some 4.5 billion people), which accounted for only 15 percent of the world's GDP in 1995.[3]

Other interesting conclusions of the IPS study include the fact that Japanese corporations in 1995 were surpassing American corporations in the top 200 rankings, with fifty-eight Japanese corporations accounting for almost 39 percent of the top 200 corporations in terms of sales in 1995.[4]

The study also noted that there was an increasing concentration in the top five industrial and commercial sectors, which accounted for over half the sales of the top 200 corporations. Borrowing from statistics published by the Morgan Stanley Capital International and Data Corporation in 1993, the IPS study, like many others, paints a picture of a growing global monopoly of giant corporations whose power seems unassailable, even taking into account the recent economic and stock market downturn. In the automobile sector, in 1993 the top five firms accounted for approximately 60 percent of the global sales of automobiles. In electronics, the top five corporations generated over half the global sales; while the top five companies in air transportation, aerospace, steel, oil and gas, computers, chemicals, and the media also had more than 30 percent of the global sales in their respective sectors.[5]

Finally, the IPS study pointed out that, increasingly, global trade is comprised of intra-corporate transactions, which also garner tax advantages from transfer pricing arrangements. A United Nations agency asserted that of the US$3.3 trillion in exports of goods and services in 1990, approximately US$1.1 trillion was intra-firm trade.[6]

These IPS analysis figures are often used by critics from the left to condemn "corporate globalization." However, the magnitude of the power of the global private sector has also been confirmed by leading academics from around the world. For example, Alan Rugman, a leading business professor at the University of Indiana and a Fellow at Oxford University, confirms the global power of the private sector, but from a different angle. He argues that globalization is a myth because of the power of multinational enterprises (MNEs) and how they are organized. He claims that the vast majority of manufacturing and service activity is organized regionally, not globally. Thus, MNEs are the engines of global business, but they think regionally and act locally. Rugman claims that a small number of MNEs operating from "triad" home bases of the United States, the European Union (EU), and Japan are at the hub of global business networks in which clusters of value-added activities are organized. He then gives his own figures to show the extent of the global power base of these triad corporations. In 2000, the world's largest 500 MNEs based in the United States, the European Union, and Japan account for 90 percent of the world's foreign direct investment and over half of world trade. These corporations control global business and trade, but operate regionally in the triad markets of North America, Japan, and the EU.[7]

Rugman goes on to state that most global trade and investment by MNEs is now intra-firm and is conducted within triad-based business networks or clusters. He concludes that regional trade and investment blocs are being reinforced by the discriminatory protectionist application of trade remedy law, bilateral invest-ment treaties with many exempted sectors, and the biased administration of health, safety, and environmental laws to benefit insiders at the expense of outsiders. Additionally, related bloc-specific institutional measures such as internal subsidies for export promotion programs and conditional national treat-ment are consolidating this trend.[8]

The 1998 World Investment Report of the United Nations also pointed to the growing power of the largest 100 multinationals, (excluding the financial sector). The report asserted that they held US$1.8 trillion in assets and generated US$2.5 trillion in sales,[9] which exceeded the 1996 combined GDPs of China, India, South Korea, Malaysia, Singapore, and the Philippines.

There is an undeniable congruence between the findings of the IPS study and those of the United Nations and Professor Rugman. The concentration of economic power in the hands of a few hundred corporations, whether on a global or a regional level, is being noted by research institutions and experts from across the ideological spectrum. Power – at least, economic power – and all that comes with such power has been shifting from nations to the giant MNEs that now dominate the global economy.

With such enormous power, there must come responsibility, not only in reality but also in perception. When power is exercised with responsibility by the institu-tions of global governance, it lays the foundation for their legitimacy. The legitimacy of institutions of global governance is of crucial importance to their continued effectiveness and indeed existence. We have seen in Chapters 1 and 2 that, when institutions of global governance like the United Nations and the WTO lose the perception of responsibility for carrying out the high visions origi-nally cast for them, there is an inevitable backlash from many quarters, and in particular from civil society.

From our discussion above, whether the global private sector corporations, with their concentration of economic power, wish it or not, they are institutions of global governance. It thus becomes crucial that they exercise such power with responsibility, unless they have grown so powerful that they cease to care about issues of legitimacy. The left-leaning critics of globalization claim that this has already happened, and that the sentiment that these corporations care little about responsibility has motivated the massive street protests that we have seen on the streets of Seattle, Washington, Prague, Quebec City, and Genoa. These critics, however, use controversial evidence to support their position. The IPS study asserts that in 1995, the top 200 corporations were net job destroyers. While they account for about a quarter of the world's economic output, they employ only 18.8 million people, less than three-fourths of 1 percent of the world's workforce. The IPS study goes on to assert that in 1995, while these corporations were cutting their workforces, their CEOs were benefiting from these job cuts and making millions in the increased value of stock options after announcing layoffs.[10] The economic downturn in the 2000–2 period, which wiped trillions of dollars off share values, may have undermined the utility of such stock options, but some would argue they have been replaced with golden parachutes and even higher CEO salaries than in 1995. The IPS study also asserts that the top 200 corporations are creating a global economic apartheid. The study gives as an example the global telecommunications sector, which was expanding its sales rapidly around the world, "while nine-tenths of humanity remained without phones." The IPS study also cites a 1996 World Bank report. The report found that, while close to 4.8 billion people lived in countries where the average per capita GNP was less than US$1,000 per year, only a handful of these people had access to credit from transnational banks, despite the fact that the thirty-one banks among the top 200 corporations had combined assets of US$10.4 trillion and sales of more than US$800 billion.[11]

We shall discuss in Chapter 5 that, whether or not the situation of what the IPS study calls "global economic apartheid" is accurate, it presents both a morally and an economically compelling case for the global private sector to tear down the system of global economic apartheid, if for no other reason than for its own survival.

The analysis of the anti-globalization theorists, such as that contained in the IPS study, is hotly contested by the supporters of the global private sector. Many of these supporters claim that the extent of the power of MNEs is vastly over-stated and that most MNEs can be, and still are, highly regulated by the countries in which they operate, especially in the developed world. Rugman argues that it is a common mistake to associate the large economic size of MNEs with political power. While accepting that the largest MNEs have total revenues greater than the gross national products of many medium and small countries, he asserts that MNEs have been observed to be bound by the param-eters of regulations and rules set by governments and international organizations. Further, Rugman contends that the political power of MNEs is overstated because their main preoccupation is with survival, profitability, and growth.[12] Supporters of the global private sector could also point to how vulnerable even the giants of the corporate world are to vagaries of the capital markets, which can wipe trillions of dollars off their share values and sales revenues, as occurred in the sudden economic slump in the 2000–2 period. Even some of the global MNEs have been teetering on the edge of potential bankruptcy in this period, with high technology companies like Lucent providing the best examples.

What cannot be contested, however, is the reality that the global private sector does have the power to profoundly corrupt the global political, social, economic, and ecological environments if it chooses to do so, or is negligent or reckless as to whether it does so. We will focus briefly on four areas to illustrate the link between the power of the global private sector and the attendant issues of responsibility.

Corruption

One writer, Sue Hawley, citing Organization for Economic Cooperation and Development (OECD) sources, claims that in 2000, bribes by Western businesses were conservatively estimated to be around US$80 billion, which she asserts is twice the amount that the United Nations believes is needed to alleviate global poverty. She also cites a 1999 US Commerce Department report which found that, in the preceding five years, bribery was believed to be a factor in 294 commercial contracts worth a total of US$145 billion.[13]

The effect of corrupt activities by MNEs in the developing world is particularly devastating. Hawley succinctly puts it in the following words:

> They undermine development and exacerbate inequality and poverty. They disadvantage smaller domestic firms. They transfer money that could be put toward poverty eradication into the hands of the rich. They distort decision-making in favour of projects that benefit the few rather than the many. They also increase debt; benefit the company, not the country; bypass local democratic processes; damage the environment; circumvent legislation; and promote weapons sales.[14]

Hawley then proceeds to give compelling evidence of corporate complicity in each of these categories of devastation in the developing world wrought by such corruption. She gives, as a paradigmatic example of MNE corrupt activities which undermine the economies and societies of developing countries, the conduct of Westinghouse Electric Corporation in the Philippines in the early 1970s. The company won a contract to build a nuclear power plant in the Philippines after allegedly giving the then dictator, President Ferdinand Marcos, US$80 million in corrupt payments. The plant cost three times as much to build as a comparable plant by the same company in Korea, around US$2.3 billion. The plant never went into operation because of poor construction and the fact that it was built near potential earthquake fault lines. Hawley asserts that even in 2000, the Philippine government is still paying US$170,000 a day in interest on the loans taken to finance the construction of the plant and will continue to do so until 2018, drawing desperately needed money away from basic services like schools and hospitals.[15]

A leading research organization in South Africa has concluded that such corrupt activities by the global private sector can involve financial and human costs which are truly staggering. The Institute for Security Studies, using World

Bank data, has suggested that if only 5 percent of the value of all direct foreign investment and imports went into countries with extensive corruption, the yearly figure involved in corrupt business practices would be around US$80 billion. This is the same figure reached by Hawley. The same organization also asserts that the Philippines lost some 20 percent of its internal revenues through corruption in the 1970s, while Nigeria and Zaire (now the Democratic Republic of Congo) lost 10 percent and 20 percent respectively in the same period.[16]

There can be no doubt, given the above, that the potential for immense damage to millions, perhaps billions, of people around the world from corporate complicity in corruption should be a serious matter of concern for global governance. We will see below how the failure to live up to ethical parameters in this area eventually triggered the evolution of international and domestic legal rules for the global private sector.

The health and safety of local communities: Bhopal almost twenty years later as a case study

The responsibility of the global private sector for the health and safety of local communities in which they operate was seared into the collective memory of humankind on 3 December 1984. On that day, an accident at the Union Carbide pesticide plant in Bhopal, India, released a deadly cloud of poison gas made up of methyl isocyanante, hydrogen cyanide, monomethyl amine, carbon monoxide, and about twenty other toxic gases. This deadly concoction killed more than 8,000 people within forty-eight hours. This figure does not take into account the many spontaneous abortions and stillbirths that took place immediately after the accident. Even today, according to news reports, more than 120,000 residents are still suffering from various illnesses related to the gas exposure, although the number could be far greater as more than 500,000 persons were exposed to the poison cloud. Local organizations claim that as late as 1999, ten to fifteen people were dying every month from the injuries and diseases stemming from exposure to the gases. One organization, the National Campaign for Justice in Bhopal, has asserted that in February of 2001, the death toll from the disaster was over 20,000. They also claim that Union Carbide, recently taken over by Dow Chemicals, continues to withhold information on the exact composition of the gases that escaped from the plant and their effects on humans, information which is vital for proper diagnosis and care. There is also continuing contamination of drinking water sources by the Union Carbide chemicals from the abandoned factory in Bhopal.[17]

Local clinics have alleged that diseases of the immune system and almost all major organs of the body continue to ravage the lives of local residents. However, a company official for Union Carbide pointed to "studies by the World Health Organization and other institutions" that show "permanent damage is limited to a very small percentage of the exposed population and that the lungs, and to a lesser extent the eyes, are the only organs that sustained permanent damage."[18]

While the company tried to lessen its responsibility by claiming that the disaster was a result of sabotage by a disgruntled employee, local organizations and residents held the company responsible and pursued redress in the courts and elsewhere. The residents did not get very much in the way of redress. In 1989, under the terms of a US$470 million settlement worked out between the company and the Indian government, each victim was to receive about US$600 for injuries and less than US$3,000 in the case of death. Local organizations assert that this amount would not be enough to cover years of medical expenses already incurred and that the sum was not even paid to all those who had suffered. Moreover, when the accident robbed the local residents of their physical strength, it also robbed them of their only source of income, physical labor. At the time of the settlement, its provisions granted company officials immunity from prosecution, but the Supreme Court of India later struck down the immunity clause but let the settlement stand. On 31 October 1991, the Supreme Court of India reinstated the criminal charges of homicide and other offences against Union Carbide and its officials, including its former chairman at the time of the accident, William Anderson. Anderson went into hiding early in 2000 to avoid a summons to appear in a US Federal Court as part of a civil compensation suit against himself and the company. The Indian government has also issued an arrest warrant for Anderson, to bring him and the company to face the criminal courts in India on charges of "culpable homicide." He and the company have also refused to accept the jurisdiction of the Indian courts on these charges, although there is a written decision by a United States District Court judge ruling that Union Carbide shall consent to submit to the jurisdiction of the courts of India. Nine senior Indian officials from the Bhopal subsidiary of Union Carbide were, however, held in custody for trial on the same charges in the Bhopal District Court.[19]

On 31 August 2000, a suit brought in the Federal Court in New York by activist organizations on behalf of seven of the victims of the Bhopal disaster, as well as five survivors seeking further compensation from Union Carbide, was dismissed. The Federal Court accepted the pleadings of Union Carbide that these additional claims for compensations should be tried in the Indian courts.

On 6 February 2001, Union Carbide merged with the Dow Chemical Company. Indian organizations urged Dow to accept the potential criminal and civil liabilities of Union Carbide and make adequate payments for medical care, research, and monitoring of the victims. They also called for release of information on the leaked poison gas, compensation for the economic rehabilitation of those affected by the disaster, and a clean-up of the contaminated soil and groundwater around the abandoned Bhopal Union Carbide factory. These local organizations claim that the early response from Dow Chemicals is to deny their responsibilities for Union Carbide's activities in India, claiming that it was "a different company." An India-wide and international network of trade unions, student organizations, women's groups, and human rights groups has formed a network in an effort to make Dow Chemicals assume responsibility for Union

Carbide's liabilities in Bhopal. The anti-globalization movement in India and around the world is also using the situation as evidence for their claims concerning the lack of corporate accountability.[20]

The Bhopal tragedy is one of several twentieth-century disasters that have shown the power of the global private sector to wreak havoc on the health and safety of neighboring communities, triggering an outcry for the imposition of corporate responsibilities. One of the earliest global incidences of a similar nature was the poisoning of the village of Minamata, Japan, by the Chisso Corporation's manufacture of acetaldehyde, used in the production of plastics, which introduced mercury into the villagers' food chain. The manufacture of acetaldehyde by Chisso in 1932 began the process of poisoning the local population. The poisoning resulted from the spillage of mercury, used in the manufacturing process, into the bay where most of the villagers' seafood diet came from. In the 1950s, dead fish could be seen floating in Minamata Bay, and animals as well as local residents began showing widespread physiological signs of mercury poisoning. In 1959, although there was direct evidence that mercury from the Chisso plant's acetaldehyde waste water caused the poisoning, this was not made public. Instead, the company installed emissions controls and made consolation payments to the victims. However, the number of victims began to widen when children began to be born with birth defects related to the mercury poisoning. It was not until 1970 that compensation was given to the majority of victims, and only in 1977 did the clean-up of the contamination begin.[21]

The pattern of immediate denials and downplaying or withholding of vital information seems a constant theme in these corporate activities which have devastating impacts on local communities. Such exercise of power without responsibility is a serious flaw in the workings of global governance.

The environmental impact of corporate activities: the Exxon Valdez *disaster, more than a decade later, as a case study*

On 24 March 1989 at a few minutes after midnight, an oil tanker, the *Exxon Valdez*, owned by one of the largest and most powerful MNEs in the world, Exxon, ran into Bligh Reef in Alaska's Prince William Sound while steering a course to avoid iceberg offshoots called "growlers." In the litigation that followed, it was alleged that the master of the tanker, Captain Joseph Hazelwood, who had a history of alcoholism and a poor record as a ship's master, had been drinking throughout the day on which the disaster occurred. Hazelwood had given directions to go outside the normal tanker lanes to an inexperienced third mate, Gregory Cousins, who was on duty despite being beyond the time limits specified by federal fatigue laws. Within minutes of Captain Hazelwood leaving the bridge, the tanker had hit the reef and 11 million gallons of oil began destroying one of the most fragile and beautiful ecosystems in the world. The spill spread across 10,000 square miles. Then, within a week, the oil slick was pushed by winds and currents out of Prince William Sound into the Gulf of Alaska.

Eventually the oil spill's effect was felt nearly 600 miles away from the stricken tanker, contaminating 1,500 miles of shoreline. The catastrophe caused more damage to birds, fish, and mammals than any other in American history. It is estimated that half a million birds died. Harbor seal and sea otter populations were decimated. The spawning and rearing habitats of fish species were critically contaminated.[22]

After a decade, while the ecosystem of Prince William Sound seems on the surface to have recovered, many assert that under the surface, the "corporate activity" of the *Exxon Valdez* still lingers with the ongoing contamination of the ecosystem. Studies by US governmental agencies estimate that only 14 percent of the oil was removed during clean-up operations.[23] Many of the species affected, from mammals to fish and birds, continue to show the effects of hydrocarbon exposure. The entire food chain of both birds and mammals is still affected, starting with the decreased numbers of Pacific herring, which is the food source for many of the mammals and birds of the area. This eventually translates into lower numbers of other species. While scientists backed by Exxon have denied the long-lasting effects of the 1989 disaster and praised the US$1.9 billion clean-up by Exxon, other scientists are discovering that weathered oil is even more toxic than previously believed. Scientists from the National Fisheries Service have found that very low levels of weathered oil from the 1989 spill (0.5 to 1 part per billion polynuclear aromatic hydrocarbons) are toxic to the early life-stages of salmon and herring. Therefore, the spill continues to have a profound effect on the reproductive and physiological health of mammals, fish, birds, and other wildlife more than ten years later. As regards the impact of the spill on the approximately twenty communities with the misfortune of being in the path of the disaster, the subsistence-hunting and -fishing by the Alaskan native communities were and are drastically affected by the spill. Many have been forced to stop their traditional way of life based on subsistence-hunting and -fishing, meaning the loss of human diversity and culture developed over many millennia. Commercial salmon and herring fisheries, initially closed immediately after the spill, have never fully recovered to their condition before the spill, spelling financial hardship and ruin for both native and non-native fishermen.[24]

More than ten years after the spill, and after a jury ordered Exxon to pay US$5.3 billion in punitive damages in 1994, Exxon has not delivered on the judgement to natives and non-natives injured by the spill. The jury had found that Exxon and Hazelwood had been reckless, and further had decided that the conduct of both required an assessment of punitive damages as a punishment and deterrent. In late September of 2000, the Supreme Court of the United States dismissed an appeal from Exxon to overrule the US$5 billion punitive damage award. Exxon had asserted that one of the jurors at the original trial had been intimidated by a court bailiff. On 16 November 2001, the United States 9th Circuit Court of Appeal in San Francisco overturned the US$5.3 billion punitive damages award and sent the issue back to the trial court in

Alaska. The Court of Appeal ruled that the 1994 punitive award was excessive under legal precedents that had been handed down since the case was first decided, and ordered the award to be reduced even if it remained punitive. With ongoing litigation related to the judgement, it will be a long time before any of the victims of the disaster get to see any of the punitive damages awarded against Exxon.[25]

What is the relationship between the power of oil giants such as Exxon (now ExxonMobil) to pollute the most fragile ecosystems in the world, and the responsibility to prevent such disasters? At minimum, one would expect the answer would be to learn from previous disasters and take the necessary precautionary steps. Yet the possibility still exists of another oil tanker or oil pipeline disaster *in the same area.*

Ten years after the *Exxon Valdez* disaster, the majority of tankers shipping oil from Valdez are aging, over twenty years old, and few are double-hulled. Some NGOs assert that there are no more double-hulled tankers today than there were in 1989. It is claimed that Exxon and other oil companies could have immediately replaced single-hull tankers with double-hull tankers, but instead lobbied for and received a phase-in period. In 1999, only three of the twenty-six tankers of the Valdez fleet had double hulls.[26]

There is yet another potential environmental tragedy in the making, which demonstrates the interconnectedness of all human activity impacting on the environment. Global warming, in part a result of the burning of fossil fuels such as oil, is causing glaciers in the Arctic to melt at an alarmingly fast rate. The Columbia Glacier is an example of this, with more iceberg calvings from the glacier threatening oil tankers in Prince William Sound. The *Exxon Valdez* had hit Bligh Reef after it had changed course to avoid the iceberg growlers in the normal tanker lanes. The impact of climate change could make a repeat of the 1989 disaster more likely. Yet there has not been an adequate response by the corporations with the power and the responsibility. As recently as February 1999, a tanker from the Valdez fleet, the *Cheasapeake Trader*, had its hull cracked by ice with a consequent oil spill in Alaska's Cook Inlet.[27]

In a similar fashion, environmentalists are warning that the Trans-Alaska Pipeline that carries oil from Alaska's North Slope to Valdez is aging, mismanaged, and in critical need of repairs. There have been many leaks from the pipeline, and allegations that employees attempting to whistle-blow have been mistreated and intimidated.[28]

The present George W. Bush administration in the United States is attempting to open up the Arctic National Wildlife Refuge to oil and gas exploration, which many assert could threaten the fragile ecosystem of "America's Serengeti." Perhaps even bigger risks lie in the fact that the lessons of the *Exxon Valdez* disaster have not been internalized by the giant corporations, which have power but need to show far more responsibility, for the sake of some of the most fragile ecosystems on the planet.

The human rights impact of global private sector activities: a case study of Shell in Nigeria

The year 1995 was a nightmare for another giant oil company, the Royal Dutch/Shell group. In addition to being accused of damaging the marine ecosystem by the sinking of the *Brent Spar* in the North Sea, it also faced accusations of complicity in the executions of nine environmental activists led by Ken Saro-Wiwa in Nigeria. Their trials – judged as gross violations of the rights of the activists by Amnesty International, the British Commonwealth, and most of the international community – and subsequently their executions, brought human rights to the forefront of discussions on the global social responsibilities of MNEs. Saro-Wiwa, a well-known writer and opponent of the military dictatorship in Nigeria, was accused by the government of conspiring to murder four pro-government Ogoni chiefs who were killed in political violence a year earlier. The fighting between the government and the Ogoni, the Ogoni and other tribal groups, as well as intra-Ogoni conflicts, had been fueled by allegations concerning environmental degradation of the Ogoni lands in the River State resulting from the oil production and distribution systems. Another factor contributing to the violence was the concerns the Ogoni had over the distribution of revenues from the oil production. Saro-Wiwa had become a leader of the Movement for the Survival of the Ogoni People (MOSOP), which campaigned vigorously against the environmental damage. Shell was the largest oil producer in the region, and indeed in the whole country, and the activists blamed the company for much of the environmental degradation affecting the food and water supplies of the Ogoni people. In addition, Saro-Wiwa and other activists felt that more of the revenues earned by Shell and the other oil companies should have been returned to the Ogoni people, who were impoverished and suffering from the oil production without reaping any benefits from what they considered were their resources.[29]

Amnesty International and other groups asserted that, in an attempt to crush MOSOP's campaign and remove the threat to the military dictatorship posed by Saro-Wiwa's growing popularity, General Sani Abacha ordered the executions to go ahead after a grossly unfair trial.[30]

Saro-Wiwa and the other eight activists were executed in November of 1995 despite appeals from world leaders such as Nelson Mandela and other heads of state of the British Commonwealth. Protests erupted around the world against Shell for its complicity in the human rights violations perpetrated by Nigerian security forces, and for failing to use its power and influence to stop the executions of the MOSOP activists. Some of these protests against the company included attacks on Shell stations in a few places, and condemnation from the press and civil society for Shell's lack of social responsibility. In addition, employees and their families felt the sting of the criticism leveled against the firm. At the time, Shell officials responded by claiming that they had done everything they could do to stop the executions through quiet diplomacy. Indeed, even after the executions, Shell continued to assert that it was using quiet diplomacy to make its concerns known about the prospective trials of a further nineteen Ogoni prisoners. Eventually Shell retracted its position in this regard and, on 15 May 1996, issued a public statement calling for a fair trial and humane treatment of the nineteen Ogoni prisoners.[31]

Amnesty International revealed that Shell had also been at the forefront of other confrontations between local communities and security forces. In November of 1990, a massacre of around eighty Etche tribespeople occurred at Umwechem after Shell had called in the Mobile Police Force, a paramilitary force, in order to protect its oil facilities and employees. In October 1993, an Ogoni youth was also allegedly killed by soldiers in the presence of a Shell employee at a flowstation. Even before the MOSOP activists' executions, Shell had expressed shock at these killings, and in 1994 developed a policy of refusing all offers of police or military protection in the Niger delta, according to Amnesty International. However, in 1996, Shell also admitted that it had, in the past, paid for imported firearms for the Nigerian police so that they could better protect Shell property and the homes of its executives. This was also the practice of many other oil companies in Nigeria at the time.[32]

The case studies described above are clear signposts for the need to attach greater responsibility to the power that corporations have to affect the world around them. Given the lessons learned from each of the cases, one could be legitimately pessimistic about the ability of some of the most powerful MNEs on the planet to fulfill any such responsibilities. Just as we have seen with nations and multilateral institutions in Chapters 1 and 2, the memories of many corporations seem to be short, and the long-term interests of both the corporation and its stakeholders are often ignored. However, this tragic flaw of the global private sector could also be on the verge of a major transformation. The desire of one of the world's major MNEs, the Royal Dutch/Shell group, to rehabilitate itself in light of its human rights disasters in Nigeria is one indicator of this potential transformation which will be discussed below.

Ethics and social responsibility in the corporate integrity risk environment

Global economic power is now being shared between the nation-state and the MNEs described above. When power is shared, the sharing of responsibility must eventually follow. Some of the most powerful MNEs will refuse to accept this. Eventually, they will either be pulled along by other MNEs who do accept this responsibility, or they will face the fate of empires, corporations, and individuals who have failed to meet the challenges of history's transformations.

Writers whose views are influential among the business community, such as Charles Handy, are beginning to state that the role of business in global governance should amount to more than that of a profit-seeking enterprise, in order to ensure that the profits sought after will be sustainable:

> The principal purpose of a company is not to make a profit, full stop. It is to make a profit in order to continue to do things or make things, and to do so

even better and more abundantly. To say that profit is a means to an end and not an end in itself is not a semantic quibble, it is a serious moral point.[33]

The evolving nature of the business environment and societal expectations of the corporate world has created a corporate integrity risk environment that MNEs ignore at their peril. This risk environment demands that the global private sector fulfill fundamental duties to the five generations of stakeholders (described below), from shareholders to the local communities and the environment. Such duties are not only ethical or social, but become a critical part of the integrity of the corporation. If neglected or undermined, as the above case studies demonstrate, the very survival or brand equity of the relevant corporation is threatened.

There are now compelling public opinion surveys that show that an overwhelming majority of citizens in Europe and North America want corporations to take into account corporate integrity, rather than the pursuit of profits as an end in itself.[34] Some writers, such as Michael J. Mazaar of the US-based Center for Strategic and International Studies, in advocating for the ethical and social responsibility duties of corporations, give the following reasons why corporations should be vitally concerned about the health of societies in which they operate:

- The need for a well-trained workforce to compete with foreign companies.
- The importance of relationships in a tribal world ... [where] a firm's network of social and business relationships can provide it with a competitive advantage over other companies.
- Competition to attract mobile, talented knowledge workers [which means firms must] pay rigorous attention to employees' family issues.
- Retention and productivity [which] rise when workers are better treated, better educated, and more in control of their own workplace.
- Public image and trust. Increasingly, companies will compete for customer loyalty.... As the knowledge era places more emphasis on values, businesses will increasingly be judged by their reliability as a civic partner.[35]

The realization of the importance of the corporate integrity risk environment has led to the global private sector responding to their ethical and social responsibility duties by developing codes of ethics, conduct, or sustainable development and, in some cases, the necessary implementation and verification systems. These codes can be divided into four categories:

1   corporate codes and compliance systems;
2   sectoral initiatives (involving coalitions from civil society and the private sector);
3   country-focused initiatives and national/regional initiatives;
4   global codes, benchmarks and verification systems.

What all these codes have in common is a search for a shared set of ethical principles which could fill the vacuum where power is exercised without responsibility. We will proceed to explore the content of such ethical principles by briefly examining each category of codes outlined above.

Corporate codes

In research based on extensive confidential interviews of dozens of officials of MNEs in Canada and around the world, Errol Mendes and Jeffrey Clark[36] have suggested that there have been five generations of issues addressed by individual corporate codes of conduct related to five generations of stakeholder expectations of MNEs. In keeping with the notion of a corporate integrity risk environment of MNEs, the five generations, as adapted to subsequent developments, are also reflective of a move from essentially the worldview of corporations being one of a player in a domestic shareholder economy to being a player in a global multi-stakeholder economy (or in Alan Rugman's thesis, to a regional triad economy). The five generations of stakeholder expectations are as follows.

The first generation is focused on protecting the assets, business opportunities, legal compliance, and intellectual property or confidential information of the corporation. This generation of issues, found in most codes, will refer to rules dealing with conflict of interest, insider trading, intellectual property, confidential information, use of corporate property, appropriate use of computers, the Internet, etc.

The major part of this group of issues found in most corporate codes of MNEs preceded the surge in interest in corporate ethics or social responsibility. It reflected the view that all corporate activity should be primarily for the benefit of the shareholders of the corporation. There was obviously special interest in these issues from shareholders, to senior officials as well as the board of corporations, but relatively little from the general public, because the public interest was limited to ensuring the survival of companies for employment and other macroeconomic reasons. With the special interests linked to the corporate structure being so strong, strict compliance with these groups of issues is a key goal for most MNEs.

The second generation of issues that began to expand the corporate integrity risk environment thinking of MNEs was the area of corruption and the role that MNEs played in subverting the rule of law and integrity of public institutions around the world. The drive to insert rules in corporate codes on bribery and corruption surged in the late 1970s. This drive was precipitated by the Lockheed Aircraft scandal that swept through the consciousness of MNEs in Japan and the United States, and the Northrop bribery scandal that led to the passing of the extraterritorial reach of the Foreign Corrupt Practices Act (FCPA) by the US Congress in 1977.[37] The United States federal sentencing guidelines (FSG) also spurred corporate action in this area.[38] Eager not to be investigated by the US Justice Department for violation of the FCPA or, if they were implicated, to obtain a lighter punishment under the FSG, many MNEs started inserting anti-bribery and corruption rules as well as strict compliance systems in their corporate structures.[39] Whether competitive pressures and the lack of a level playing field actually made such strict compliance a reality is still open to much doubt.[40]

The third category of issues found in codes of most MNEs is that relating to what some have called the voluntary stakeholders of the company, namely its employees, its customers, and its suppliers. As regards employees, the highly regulated jurisdictions of most of the MNEs in industrialized countries meant that, to act as preventive measures against regulatory risk, most MNEs have inserted employee-related provisions into their corporate codes. These provisions concern such things as the health and safety of employees, non-discrimination and harassment, as well as provisions that relate to other employment and personnel issues and provisions that promote teamwork, trust, and the retention of valuable employees. Similarly, many MNEs have provisions relating to trust, loyalty, and service or product quality guarantees (and, more recently, privacy guarantees) to customers. Again, similar commitments of trust and straight dealing are extended to suppliers.[41] While this group of issues was of special interest to the voluntary stakeholders concerned, public interest in this area surged when the debate was launched over the ethical responsibilities of MNEs to extend internationally recognized labor standards to their employees or those employed by their sub-contractors in the developing world. Such interest reached its zenith in 1996, when Nike was stung with criticisms that its Asian factories and sub-contractors were brutal sweat-shops where workers were underpaid and mistreated. Similar allegations swept across the apparel and retail sectors in the industrialized world.[42] The corporate integrity risk environment of many of these MNEs began asserting itself when consumers began to boycott goods alleged to be made with sweat-shop labor, and when labeling schemes began to appear and attract the attention of the so-called ethical consumer. Consumer boycotts have also proved effective in the context of unsafe products as witnessed by the boycotts of Nestlé over its promotion of breast milk substitutes.[43] While the regulatory and legal compliance factors made strict compliance with domestic voluntary stakeholder mandatory for MNEs, there has not been effective compliance, except in the case of a few leadership corporations, as regards the interests of voluntary stakeholders in the operations of MNEs outside their domestic jurisdictions.[44] This is particularly true of Asian MNEs. The fundamental ethical and social responsibility of the global private sector in regard to voluntary stakeholders is not to utilize bargaining or market power to exploit the range of voluntary stakeholders, from employees around the world to customers and suppliers, who are the generators of business sustainability.

The fourth group of issues that began to find its way into the codes of MNEs concerned the impact of corporations on two major sets of involuntary stakeholders: local communities and the environment. This group of issues surged to the forefront of stakeholder expectations of MNEs after the horrific tragedy in Bhopal and in the wake of the *Exxon Valdez* disaster. In part due to the potential for great damage to brand equity and huge damage awards, MNEs in Europe and North America are increasingly beginning to give greater importance to these issues in their corporate codes. Issues relating to environmental protection and conservation, sustainable development, and meaningful consultation with local communities as well as the fair sharing of benefits with such communities are beginning to appear in these codes. This is one area where special interests within the narrower range of corporate stakeholders and the wider public interest may coincide to make the corporate integrity risk environment relevant to the formerly neglected two major sets of involuntary stakeholders. One group of corporate ethics practitioners claims that the fundamental duty of the global private sector as regards the involuntary stakeholder group is to

> not ignore nor externalize stakeholder impacts for which it has a primary responsibility ...
>
> An involuntary stake is created whenever a decision-making process exposes people to direct and significant risks which they would not willingly assume or about which they have no knowledge. When significant risks or impacts are treated as externalities and ignored unless otherwise required by law, the result with a few exceptions is the creation of involuntary stakeholders. Externalizing risks and costs transfers them to involuntary stakeholders who may have little to gain by way of benefits in return.[45]

Again, as with voluntary stakeholders, externalizing risks to the ecosystem or local communities can be termed exploitation and in many cases a violation of fundamental human rights.

Finally, the fifth generation of stakeholder expectations emerged with the worldwide public debate over the role of corporations in countries with oppressive regimes and in countries where there are gross abuses of human rights by the governments and those acting in complicity with such governments. Such concerns have become issues of global debate as regards the role of MNEs during the apartheid regime in South Africa (which will be discussed further below), the role of Shell and other MNEs during the military dictatorships in Nigeria as described above, and in other parts of Africa. To this one could add the role of corporations in totalitarian regimes such as China and Burma as well as in Indonesia during the dictatorship of President Suharto. The focus of this most recent and most challenging area of stakeholder expectations of MNEs concerns their role in the promotion and protection of human rights. The private interest of the corporation is starting to approximate that discussed in relation to the fourth generation. This involves, namely, risks to brand equity, loss of property, security threats to employees due to violence and sabotage, threats of lawsuits, and ultimately, the loss of the investment if the corporation is perceived to be complicit in the human rights abuses and the government is overthrown. The public interest in this area is intense and growing more so, especially on the part of the activist civil society and human rights groups around the world. There are increasing demands that MNEs live up to minimum internationally recognized standards of human rights wherever they operate.[46] While most MNEs are afraid to address this generation of stakeholder expectations in corporate codes, leadership companies are showing the way, as we shall discuss below.

The five generations of corporate ethical and social responsibilities could be regarded as the framework for the corporate integrity risk environment of the global private sector. Most of the major MNEs around the world have developed codes, policies, and practices in the areas of the first, second, and third generation rights. Leadership corporations have also tackled the fourth generation.[47] Studies have shown that implementing these five generations of corporate integrity as reflected in corporate codes has been disappointing.[48] Other research has indicated that compliance seems strongest when the self-interest of the corporation, in both the short term and the long term, is paramount.[49] For this reason, it is primarily in the first generation corporate integrity issues, namely conflict of interest and protection of corporate assets, where words in the corporate codes match actions. Even where it is in the vital long-term interests of MNEs to match words with actions in other areas of the first three generations, such as in the area of bribery and corruption, in too many instances the words in the codes are empty rhetoric, as the above discussion on corporate corruption reveals. The short-term incentive to win the contracts but help destroy the business environment through corruption is succumbed to by too many MNE officials too many times. The destruction in early 2002 of the Enron Corporation, formerly the seventh largest company in the United States, is also testament to the failure to walk the talk on conflict of interest issues. Here, there seems a direct correlation to the tragic flaw that we discussed in the other institutions of global governance like the United Nations and the WTO in Chapters 1 and 2.

Too few MNEs have developed adequate corporate values and compliance integrity systems based on all five generations of ethical and social responsibilities in the corporate integrity risk environment. Some of the leadership corporations that have attempted to develop comprehensive provisions in these areas have done so in reaction to environmental, social, or human rights disasters that they have found themselves in. Paradoxically, this may not be a bad thing. The paradigm shift toward the notion of a business corporate integrity risk environments may only occur when the largest and most powerful of MNEs realize that there is a discipline of ethical behavior and social responsibility that must govern *even* their actions. The paradigmatic example of such an eventual paradigm shift is the reaction of the Royal Dutch/Shell group after its human rights disaster in Nigeria.

When the 1995 crises in Nigeria and the North Sea hit Shell, together with the attendant protests and consumer boycotts, a senior Shell official was quoted as saying that the company suddenly realized "how out of tune we were with the world around us."[50] Two authors, Peter Schwartz and Blair Gibb (the former was a senior Shell insider), give an account of how the company resisted the instinct to become completely defensive on the environmental and human rights disasters in which it was implicated. Instead, it embarked on worldwide consultations and dialogue with stakeholders interested in all five generations of the corporate integrity risk environment, but with a special emphasis on the environmental and human rights experts and groups.[51] In the spring of 1997, out of such consultations came a revised worldwide corporate code of conduct binding on all Shell companies. The revised code, titled the Statement of General Business Principles (SGBP), is one of the few corporate codes that contain all five generations of ethical and social responsibilities, including specific references to a commitment to "express support for fundamental human rights in line with the legitimate role of business." Many NGOs have expressed dissatisfaction with the vagueness and limited extent of this wording, claiming that it does not amount to any more than a public relations exercise. Schwartz and Gibb disagree. They argue that Shell's code represents a critical change in the core identity of this giant MNE, and by long-standing practice the code becomes part of major contractual undertakings by Shell:

> A commitment to supporting human rights, in whatever form the company may define them, that becomes an equal or higher part of Shell's identity than its present values are could mean great changes indeed in the way the company operates. Shell's contracts with indigenous NGOs to provide independent monitoring of its operation in Camisea, Peru, and its newly promulgated Rules of Engagement for security forces may be early indicators of such changes.[52]

Another indicator that the Royal Dutch/Shell group is keen to show proof of such changes is an annual public report on its performance under the SGBP presently titled "People, Planet and Profits." Controversy remains, however, with questions over the nature of the independent verification of such performance carried out by two accounting firms. To the credit of Shell, it publicizes such criticism in its annual report. One Spanish critic was published as stating, "The 'report from the verifiers' makes clear that these accountants verify little beyond financial and operational figures and the existence of certain reports."[53] While Shell has taken very credible steps to redeem itself and trumpets the paradigm shift of its full acceptance of the full range of corporate integrity issues in major world publications, the ghosts of the executed Ogoni activists still haunt Shell. This happens through the continuing condemnation from many anti-globalization activists and relatives of the executed Ken Saro-Wiwa. The future is easier to shape than is the erasing of the past.

Other companies who have found a similar painful path to developing more comprehensive and effective codes and compliance systems after environmental, human rights, or labor standards controversies, include Unocal, Rio Tinto, Nike, Freeport-McMoran, the Gap, and British Petroleum. The Enron Corporation would also have been in this list before it self-destructed.[54]

Perhaps the real champions of the evolving paradigm shift to the corporate integrity risk environment are the corporations who incorporated all five generations of the ethical and social responsibility categories without being implicated in an ethical or social responsibility disaster. These champions, who seemed ahead of their time, include Reebok, Levi Strauss, The Body Shop, and Nexen Inc. Many of these companies were at the forefront of corporate integrity in the 1990s, beyond the five generations discussed above, and became catalysts in this area.

In 1991, Levi Strauss adopted the "Global Sourcing and Operating Guidelines" which extended its ethical standards to its business partners. It also pulled out of Burma (Myanmar) in 1992 when it felt it could no longer do business there without complicity in the abuse of human rights by the military dictatorship.[55]

Likewise, Reebok, through its "Human Rights Production Standards," adopted in 1992, as well as through other activities, has made the fifth generation of human rights compliance and promotion the hallmark of its corporate culture within its own operations and within those of its business partners.[56] In a similar fashion, The Body Shop, through its 1994 "Trading Charter" and other activities, made the environment, protection of indigenous and minority cultures, and human rights part of its own trademark.[57]

Finally, Nexen Inc, a major independent Canadian oil and gas company, took a leadership role in drafting (together with fourteen other corporations and the assistance of Professor Mendes) an International Code of Ethics for Canadian Business, which was the first national code that incorporated all five generations discussed above. Adopting the code within its own corporate structures, Nexen has also promoted the code as a template for adoption by other corporations across Canada and internationally within the global oil and gas sector.[58] The human rights principles in the code were also incorporated into the Global Compact by the Office of the secretary-general of the United Nations, as will be discussed below.

Most of these leadership companies have also developed the most effective independent monitoring and verification systems, which include public reporting to ensure that the words in their codes match reality. They have, for the most part, not relied on accounting firms for such functions, given the perceived lack of independence of such firms. Indeed, some of these companies, like The Body Shop, Reebok, and Levi Strauss, have taken criticism from activist groups when the results of such independent monitoring have been made public. However, these companies have also been praised for having the courage and integrity to subject themselves to effective independent monitoring, verification, and reporting.[59] The other MNEs, like Nike and Shell, are also developing independent monitoring and verification systems, but tend to rely excessively on accounting firms to perform this task. These firms, as noted, often have not gained the perceived credibility and independence necessary to do such verification work.[60]

In contrast to these examples of positive reinforcement of corporate integrity, most of the research done in this area indicates that the majority of corporations with codes, which often do not match the comprehensiveness of the codes of the leadership MNEs, have very ineffective compliance mechanisms and virtually non-existent monitoring and verification systems.[61] The antithesis of justice in the realm of business is making ethical corporate behavior into purely a public relations exercise.

The combination of the private sector proactive champions of corporate integrity, together with the giant MNEs who came to espouse the full range of corporate integrity issues after painful episodes, has led to a dramatic burgeoning of activity within the field of corporate ethics and social responsibility.[62] This has also spurred the increasing interest in sectoral codes of conduct.

Sectoral initiatives (involving coalitions from civil society and the private sector)

In part because of the lack of effective monitoring and verification systems, there has evolved an increasing number of sectoral codes with their own monitoring and verification systems. Two examples will suffice to illustrate.

In 1996, at the instigation and urging of former President Clinton, the Apparel Industry Partnership (AIP) – a coalition of apparel and footwear MNEs such as Nike, Reebok, and Liz Claiborne, together with labor and human rights NGOs – developed a Workplace Code of Conduct and Principles of Monitoring. After the initial coalition splintered into two over disagreements about how far to go, the AIP transformed into the Fair Labor Association (FLA) which was tasked with certifying the independent monitors, and, if necessary, expelling any MNE that failed to live up to the standards of the Workplace Code of Conduct. The splinter group, led by the Union of Needletrades, Industrial, and Textile Employees (UNITE), the largest apparel union in the United States, opposed the FLA in critical areas such as the failure of the FLA members to guarantee a living wage, to incorporate local NGOs as independent monitors, and to avoid those countries that violate core labor standards. This opposition, together with various university student groups, has developed what it considers its own more rigorous standards and independent monitoring systems. Several universities have agreed to abide by the more rigorous systems for apparel bearing the universities' trademark.[63]

While some have bemoaned the splintering of the AIP into several camps, it should be regarded as part of the evolution of the corporate integrity risk environment of the apparel industry. There is a dialectic in the evolution of appropriate ethical and social responsibility standards that requires thesis and antithesis, which will eventually produce the synthesis of justice in the realm of corporate integrity. While the emerging sectoral code and compliance initiatives in the apparel and footwear sector are having their teething problems, there is a general consensus among both the MNEs and the civil society groups involved that the corporate integrity risk environment of the sector, in particular the labor standards of those who work in the sector worldwide, constitute an imperative that cannot be overlooked.

Another sectoral initiative, the Responsible Care (RC) initiative of the members of the Canadian Chemical Producers Association, focuses on health and safety and the environment, and is generally regarded as one of the most successful sectoral initiatives. The initiative has become global and has spread to the chemicals sector in forty countries. Reinforcing the inevitability that most sectors will come to accept the reality of the corporate integrity risk environment, the Responsible Care initiative was developed in the wake of the Bhopal disaster. The program was developed by industry associations in the chemical sector and their individual member corporations. The focus of the RC program is a complex series of principles and codes of practice aimed at the safe handling and transportation and environmental management and protection of chemicals throughout their lifecycle. The corporate integrity risk environment of the sector takes on a collective character under the RC program.

For example, in Canada the RC program is managed by the Canadian Chemical Producers Association (CCPA), one of the pioneers of the global RC initiative. Both the carrots and the sticks behind the RC program in Canada are that membership in the CCPA is contingent on member corporations complying with the RC principles and six codes of practice within a time limit of three years of joining the sector association. In addition, there is a requirement to file an annual report on compliance with the CCPA, which then makes available to the public the aggregate compliance data. An additional beneficial feature of the CCPA program is that in one of the most decentralized federations in the world, with Canadian provinces and the federal government having different regulatory standards for the chemical industry, the RC program has in effect created a single national program and standards for the sector. Moreover, the program provides a more effective single governance system than the various regulatory systems of the different levels of government in Canada.

Compliance verification is mandatory under the RC program in Canada, which includes on-site visits by four external verifiers. These verifiers must consist of two industry representatives who are not affiliated with the corporation being audited, and two other representatives, one of whom must be a community representative. Environmental NGO representatives have been part of many verifying teams. The corporation being inspected shoulders the cost of the verification and compliance investigation.

In Canada, the RC program is overseen by a National Advisory Panel, whose membership consists of twelve to sixteen external and independent experts or members of civil society groups. There are academics, independent consultants, and members of environmental NGOs on the panel at present.

The RC program in Canada is receiving widespread acclaim both in Canada and internationally. It is also extremely effective, if the figures produced by the CCPA are to be believed. From 1992 to 1994, the CCPA has reported that its member corporations achieved a 50 percent reduction in the total emissions of substances, compared to 1992 figures, even while the industry output had grown significantly.[64]

Finally, a third example of another sectoral attempt to regulate the business ecosystem of a particular industry is the Forest Stewardship Council (FSC). The

FSC has evolved into a global sectoral coalition that includes some of the leading environmental groups, like Greenpeace International, and major retailers of forest products, such as Home Depot, based in the United States. The focus of this sectoral initiative is to ensure and monitor effective and sustainable forest management practices globally through voluntary third-party certification and auditing. The certification process provides both carrots and sticks, as those who meet the FSC standards are entitled to market their forest products with the FSC logo. Those who do not or are not involved in the FSC sectoral initiative may face the consequences of boycotts or other measures by the relevant consumer markets. The FSC Assembly, whose approximately 130 members from twenty-five countries combine environmental groups, aboriginal representatives, and industry representatives, managed to develop a set of ten principles and standards which must be adhered to by the participating corporations if certification is to be granted. The ten principles and standards are further elaborated at the regional and national level by local FSC working groups. The FSC determines who will be the independent organizations that will carry out the certification and auditing process. This sectoral initiative has also been successful, and in 1996 over five million hectares of forest had been certified by the third-party organizations.[65]

As in the apparel industry, rival coalition and industry initiatives have also sprung up in the forestry sector to give healthy competition in the creation of a collective corporate integrity risk environment in this sector also.[66]

These sectoral initiatives demonstrate that the rhetoric of corporate ethics, integrity, and social responsibility can be turned into reality by collective action. However, as the next section will reveal, one can never forget the power of determined individuals within corporations, and indeed countries, to effect change in the global private sector.

Country-focused codes and national/regional initiatives

Country-focused codes

The late Rev. Leon H. Sullivan championed the development of six principles to promote racial equality in the employment practices of US corporations operating in the apartheid-era South Africa.[67] Sullivan was a shareholder and a member of the board of directors of General Motors (GM) and lobbied hard for GM to show leadership in South Africa. His ideas were based on a firm conviction that "within the fence" of their corporate operations in South Africa, GM and other companies could make a difference. After failing to persuade GM to withdraw from South Africa, and upon being advised by anti-apartheid activists that MNEs in South Africa could be agents of change, Rev. Sullivan proposed the adoption of his principles by US companies as a country-focused code.

The Sullivan Principles asked signatories to take specific actions in six areas. These areas encompassed the elimination of segregation, equal and fair employment practices, equal pay for equal or comparative work, affirmative action for non-white workers in management and supervisory positions, and improving the living conditions of workers. These improvements entailed advocating social, economic, and political justice for black workers in areas such as housing, transportation, schooling, recreation, and health facilities.

By 1986 about 200 of the approximately 275 US corporations investing in South Africa had signed on to the code. Several other countries followed Rev. Sullivan's lead and drafted their own South Africa-focused codes, including the British Code, which was eventually adopted by the European Economic Community. Canada also adopted a monitoring mechanism for Canadian companies operating in South Africa. The Sullivan Principles also contained auditing and monitoring provisions for ensuring compliance with the six principles. Voluntary application of the Sullivan Principles was initially monitored by an independent organization, Arthur D. Little Inc., for the industry support unit, an organization of companies subscribing to the country-focused codes. Eventually the muscle of US legislation was put behind the Principles, which denied any US support for corporations that did not subscribe to and implement the code.

Some critics argued that the Sullivan Principles were ineffective because the reporting provisions were inadequate, or because apartheid continued to exist long after the Principles were established, or because the US companies employed only a small percentage of the black workforce.[68] These criticisms ignore the fact that the Sullivan Principles impacted on the ethical environment of MNE activity in South Africa. The impacts according to one expert, J. Perez Lopez, included the elimination of discrimination in the workplace in approximately 130 companies, comprising 95 percent of all signatories. Thousands of black workers and students received scholarships, better-resourced schools, advanced training, and educational opportunities they would not otherwise have had. The Principles resulted in non-whites attaining 30 percent of management and supervisory positions in signatory corporations. The chief impact, according to Rev. Sullivan himself, was the fact that US corporations had shown they could create a moral conduit using their own resources to work toward the elimination of apartheid and improve the lives of the victims of the system at the same time.[69]

Perhaps the most powerful impact of the Sullivan Principles was expressed to the authors by a former South African ambassador to Canada and a close confidant of Nelson Mandela, the father of the modern multiracial South Africa. The ambassador stated that the main benefit of the Sullivan Principles (and other similar initiatives around the world) was to give comfort to the front-line soldiers in the struggle for equality and democracy in South Africa. This comfort lay in the belief that the world had not forgotten them; that the lure of making profits in the apartheid regime was tempered by a desire to be morally and socially responsible. Ultimately, the ambassador asserted that this intangible support was indispensable to the triumph of justice and democracy in South Africa.

The history of the Sullivan Principles demonstrates that there is a strong moral foundation to the establishment of a corporate integrity risk environment. It serves as a model to remind those MNEs who assert today that they have no role to play in promoting justice and democracy in countries and jurisdictions which afford them profits in the short term but, due to oppressive regimes that violate the rule of law, offer an unsustainable business environment in the long term. It has gone virtually unnoticed by the world that, in May of 1999, the Global Exchange and the International Labor Rights Fund established a code titled "US Business Principles for Human Rights of Workers in China" which focuses on internationally recognized human and labor rights. Three major US companies, Levi Strauss, Reebok, and Mattel, are reported to have announced that they will sign up to the ten principles in the code.[70]

National/regional initiatives

A variation of the sectoral codes and the inverse of the country-focused codes are corporate ethics and social responsibilities originating from specific countries or regions. These are important initiatives because they can demonstrate that there is a growing consensus among certain parts of the human family that societal values must include the ethical and social responsibility duties of their own private sector corporations.

In this regard the most well-known examples include the following:

• The Ethical Trading Initiative (ETI), based in the United Kingdom, which was in part driven by a growing number of consumers in the retail sector who want assurances that the goods they buy "should be produced in conditions that are safe and decent and which enable working people to maintain their dignity and a reasonable standard of living."[71] The ETI, established by a coalition of major retailers in the United Kingdom along with NGOs and with the assistance of the British government, combines standard-setting with monitoring, verification, and auditing systems to improve labor standards around the world.[72]
• The 1998 European Union Code of Conduct on Arms Exports, which sets out the criteria, including human rights criteria, that should be taken into account when licensing the export of arms, together with "operative provisions" for exchanging information and annually reviewing the implementation of the Code.[73]

More recently, two of the countries that have the largest MNEs in the extractive and energy industries, the United States and Great Britain, have spearheaded the development of a coalition of NGOs and leading MNEs in the extractive industries and have developed a set of Voluntary Principles on Security and Human Rights. The aim of the principles is to guide companies in maintaining the safety and security of their operations within an operating framework that ensures respect for human rights and fundamental freedoms. The principles focus on risk assessment, interactions between corporations and public security, and interactions between corporations and private security.[74] It can be deduced from the content and support given to the Voluntary Principles that there is a growing consensus between corporations in this sector, their home governments, and NGOs, that human rights disasters involving security forces, such as those experienced by the Royal Dutch/Shell in Nigeria, are extremely damaging to the corporate integrity of the entire sector.

Danish[75] and Norwegian national business associations have developed guidelines and checklists in collaboration with local NGOs, academics, and governments to assist their corporations to deal effectively with human rights issues.

In conclusion, national or regional initiatives will only be successful if the political will of the society is there to promote the ethical and social responsibility duties of MNEs. This includes the political will of both governmental and corporate leaders. An example of a failed initiative due to lack of political will is furnished by the so-called Clinton Code. This code, which was established in May of 1995 with the title of "Model Business Principles," was a one-page document with fewer than 200 words that attempted to create minimum human rights and labor standards for US companies operating abroad. It was roundly criticized by NGOs for being vague and incomplete in terms of standard-setting and for having no implementation or enforcement systems. At the same time, US MNEs also attacked the code, claiming that they would become uncompetitive if they had to adhere even to these minimal standards. Two years after it was rolled out, it was reported that the Clinton administration had done little to promote the Model Business Principles, which subsequently seem to have vanished quietly, perhaps overtaken by the joint initiative with the United Kingdom on security and human rights in the extractive and energy sectors.[76] Hopefully, this initiative will not face the same fate.

Global codes, benchmarks, and verification systems

NGO and business initiatives on global codes, benchmarks, and verification systems

The first major attempt by the United Nations to develop a code of practice for what were termed transnational corporations (TNCs) began in 1977, and a draft code was completed in 1990. Within two years, it was dead. The TNCs and Western governments who fiercely opposed the code had killed it.[77] In the vacuum left by the inability of the institutions of global governance to act, a plethora of attempts by NGOs and business groups has endeavored to develop codes of conduct, benchmarks, and verification systems applicable to the global private sector. These codes are said by their critics to share a common weakness. They have been formulated by a limited number of participants, whether business or NGOs. They are also critiqued for being either too vague, too detailed, or too rigorous for the global private sector to adopt and implement. Such codes include:

- The Council on Economic Priorities, a New York-based NGO which has developed a set of global standards on labor and human rights, including the call for a living wage. The standards called SA 8000 include an accreditation system to certify external monitors who will audit and verify compliance with the SA 8000 standards.[78]
- The Interfaith Center on Corporate Responsibility based in the United States, the Ecumenical Council for Corporate Responsibility based in Britain and Ireland, and the Taskforce on Churches and Corporate Responsibility based in Canada developed in 1995 and revised in 1998 the "Principles for Global Corporate Responsibility." The 1995 document contained fifty-five detailed principles, seventy-six criteria for assessing corporate policies, and sixty-six benchmarks to assess corporate compliance with the principles.[79]
- The Caux Round Table Principles for Business are primarily an attempt by a coalition of US, European, and Japanese business leaders, with assistance from academics in Minnesota, to develop general principles of ethical behavior and corporate social responsibility. Developed in 1995, the Caux Round Table Principles are significant in that they demonstrate that there can be consensus on fundamental principles of corporate integrity across widely differing cultural traditions.[80] Given the growing importance of Japanese MNEs as described above, the Caux Round Table Principles are and will be a key instrument to demonstrate that the global corporate integrity risk environment is not cultural imperialism imposed by Western societies.
- Before his recent passing away, the late Rev. Sullivan on 2 November 1999 launched the Global Sullivan Principles (GSP), which promote a worldwide set of corporate ethics and social responsibility standards.[81] The Global Sullivan Principles were endorsed by both the Clinton administration and Kofi Annan, the secretary-general of the United Nations.

While some critics have argued that the growing list of codes, benchmarks, and verification systems by NGOs and business groups could create a system overload, one could also present a more positive result of all this activity. The growing global consensus on corporate integrity has been furthered by those who have developed and consulted on this plethora of codes, and by those who have agreed to comply with these codes. One can see these codes as ripples coalescing in the pond of ethical consciousness of the global human family.[82]

Initiatives by multilateral organizations

In the wake of the failure of the United Nations to promote a universal code, other multilateral organizations have attempted to develop their own. We have already discussed, in Chapter 2, the positive development at the ILO in terms of the focus on core labor standards, which has led to the tripartite consensus on the 1998 Declaration on Fundamental Principles and Rights at Work. This

Declaration was preceded by the 1977 ILO Tripartite Declaration of Principles Concerning Multinational Enterprises and Social Policy, aimed at encouraging the positive contribution of MNEs to economic and social progress and at minimizing and resolving the difficulties to which their various operations may give rise.[83]

The OECD Guidelines for Multinational Enterprises, first adopted in 1976, also attempt to set ethical, social, economic, and most recently human rights standards for MNEs. The twenty-nine members of the OECD, together with Argentina, Brazil, Chile, and Slovakia, adopted a revised version of the Guidelines in June of 2000. The standards include those related to worker rights and industrial relations, environmental protection, bribery, consumer protection, competition, taxation, disclosure of information, and, for the first time, a provision relating to respect for the human rights of those affected by corporate activities. The Guidelines are accompanied by detailed but rather weak implementation procedures that are binding on OECD member states.[84]

Finally, UN Secretary-General Kofi Annan, in a dramatic address to the global private sector at the World Economic Forum in Davos in January of 1999, proposed that the world's most powerful MNEs enter into a Global Compact with the United Nations. The goal of this Global Compact is to promote universal values in the area of human rights, labor standards, and the environment. Its acceptance by these MNEs is crucial if they wish to see the benefits of globalization sustained. The secretary-general chose these areas for reasons that are fundamental to the evolving nature of global governance. First, because he and others believe that, in these three areas, the global private sector can make a real difference. Second, these are three areas in which universal values, according to the secretary-general, have already been defined by international agreements, including the Universal Declaration of Human Rights, the ILO's Declaration on Fundamental Principles and Rights at Work, and the Rio Declaration of the United Nations on the Environment and Development in 1992.[85]

These critical foundational documents of global governance have been discussed in Chapters 1 and 2 and, through the initiative of the secretary-general as regards the Global Compact, bind the discussions in those areas to the analysis in this chapter. The final reason given by Kofi Annan also binds the discussion and analysis in these first three chapters. He stated that the three areas of the Global Compact were also chosen because they are the ones which, in the absence of positive action, could pose a threat to the open global market, and especially to the multilateral trade regime.[86] These words seemed prophetic in light of what was to come at Seattle, Prague, Quebec City, and Genoa. The secretary-general pointed out that there is a need to "humanize" the global market though effective promotion of human rights, labor standards, and the environment.

In light of these fundamental reasons for humanizing the emerging features of global economic governance, the secretary-general outlined nine principles that the global private sector should embrace, through advocating a stronger

United Nations charged with principal responsibility for these three areas. Additionally, the secretary-general urged the global private sector to implement the principles within their corporate management practices and within their sphere of influence, and to work with UN agencies to aid in their implementation. The nine principles are as follows:[87]

1 Human rights
Business should

- support and respect the protection of international human rights within their sphere of influence; and
- make sure their own corporations are not complicit in human rights abuses.

2 Labor
Business should uphold

- the freedom of association and the effective recognition of the right to collective bargaining;
- the elimination of all forms of forced and compulsory labor;
- the effective abolition of child labor;
- the elimination of discrimination in respect of employment and occupation.

3 Environment
Business should

- support a precautionary approach to environmental challenges;
- undertake initiatives to promote greater environmental responsibility;
- encourage the development and diffusion of environmentally friendly technologies.

The Global Compact partnership was launched at a high-level meeting at the United Nations on 26 July 2000, and was attended by leaders and senior executives from over fifty corporations and representatives of labor, human rights, environmental, and development organizations.[88]

The message in the preamble to the Global Compact may be of great surprise to many. It states clearly that the Compact is not intended to be a code of conduct or to provide an independent monitoring or verification system for those MNEs who have signed on to it. Rather, it professes to be, above all, a "values based platform" to promote institutional learning and implementation of best practices based on the nine universal principles outlined in the Compact.[89] By the end of 2002, the Global Compact hopes to have 100 major multinationals and 1,000 other corporations committed to internalizing the nine principles into their corporate management practices. The Global Compact has also assisted in initiating dialogues between the global private sector, multilateral organizations, and civil society groups on areas critical to the nine principles.

The first of these dialogues focuses on the role of the global private sector in zones of conflict.[90] In addition, the Global Compact is establishing a learning bank of best practices in the nine areas, as well as promoting partnership projects between the global private sector and other partners that reflect and advance the nine principles.[91] The human rights principles of the Global Compact could appear to present the greatest challenges to the global private sector. These principles were based on the International Code of Ethics for Canadian Business established by a group of private sector companies in Canada led by Nexen Inc. Professor Mendes was also one of the principal drafters of the Code, and assisted the Office of the Secretary-General in the formulation of the human rights principles in the Global Compact. The intellectual foundations of the human rights principles in the Global Compact are based on the following premises.

First, there are few who would expect MNEs to duplicate the role of Amnesty International or Human Rights Watch. What is expected of MNEs, however, is that they appreciate the role they can play in promoting universally recognized human rights norms, and that they lead by example within their respective spheres of influence. The secretary-general gave some sound examples at the Davos Forum in 1999:

> Don't wait for every country to introduce laws protecting freedom of association and the right to collective bargaining. You can at least make sure your own employees, and those of your subcontractors, enjoy those rights. You can at least make sure that you yourselves are not employing under-age children or forced labour, either directly or indirectly. And you can make sure that, in your own hiring and firing policies, you do not discriminate on grounds of race, creed, gender or ethnic origin.[92]

However, more difficult is the notion of non-complicity in human rights abuses. Here, there is a need for the global private sector to begin a dialogue on what constitutes both the worst and best case practices. The international legal dimensions of complicity must also be taken into account, as will be further discussed below.

The clear message that the Global Compact is not intended to be a regulatory instrument, a code of conduct, or any verification or compliance system promoted by the main institution of global governance, reveals a significant turning point in the evolution of the role of the global private sector in global governance. The major interest of the global private sector in participating in the Global Compact should be their concern for making the global free market system sustainable. The Global Compact has also developed links with the Global Reporting Initiative (GRI), the framework developed by multi-stakeholders for corporate reporting on economic, social, and environmental performance. These links will help corporations meet some of the participation requirements of the Global Compact through meeting GRI reporting standards and having such reports examined by those in the Global Compact network. In addition, Secretary-General Annan has set up an Advisory Council to the Global Compact made up of internationally respected business representatives and labor and global civil society groups, together with observers from five member states from both developed and developing nations. One of the main functions of the Advisory Council will be to make recommendations on the standards of participation that will protect the integrity of the Global Compact.

We now have an endorsement of the corporate integrity risk environment from the highest ranks of the institutions of global governance. The fundamental monitoring and verification systems of the Global Compact, and indeed of all the other variations of codes described above, should come from the realization that with power comes responsibility. If this does not happen, ultimately the backlash against this denial of responsibility, even among the MNEs who have endorsed the Global Compact, will undermine the very sources of corporate power.[93] Before that happens, we will also see increasing attempts to impose greater legal duties on the global private sector by domestic and international law, an area to which we will now turn in the final part of this chapter.

The international legal duties of the global private sector

The classical notion of international law is that it governs relations between sovereign states, with some exceptions, such as the rules governing international institutions. At the time these rules were developed, states were virtually the exclusive subjects of international law with rights, duties, privileges, and immunities given primarily to states and their representatives.[94]

However, as we have seen in Chapter 1, this classical notion of international law is retreating, especially under the onslaught of developments in international human rights law and in particular with developments in international criminal law. As we have discussed in Chapter 1, the evolution of the concepts of universal jurisdiction and humanitarian intervention, together with the establishment of the Ad Hoc International War Crimes Tribunals and the establishment of the International Criminal Court, has made major incursions into territorial integrity and national sovereignty as being the supreme principle of international law. Why has this happened? Some would argue that, ultimately, legal regulation follows what society regards as unethical, socially irresponsible, or beyond the norms of acceptable behavior. The relevant society for international law is no longer the community of nations, as we have discussed in Chapter 1, but the community of individuals in the human family brought together to share common reactions to the unethical and the unacceptable by the information revolution.

It is clear under the evolving rules of international criminal law and responsibility that if employees or officers of a corporation are directly linked to war crimes, crimes against humanity, genocide, torture, or other international crimes under customary international law, they could be prosecuted in their home country or any country under the principles of universal jurisdiction. They could also be prosecuted under the Statute of the International Criminal Court when it comes into operation.[95]

Under article 25 of the Rome Statute of the International Criminal Court, corporations as an entity cannot be prosecuted for a crime under the statute. However, when an employee or officer of a corporation knowingly "aids, abets or otherwise assists in its commission or its attempted commission, including providing the means for its commission" or "in any other way, contributes to the commission or attempted commission of such a crime," those individuals can be subject to prosecution. For example, there have been allegations that some coffee companies in Rwanda aided in the genocide by storing arms and equipment used in the massacre, and that a local radio station, Radio-Télévision Libre des Milles Collines, helped create the environment that precipitated the genocide by broadcasting hate propaganda.[96]

These provisions should be taken very seriously by MNEs in their decisions on where and how to invest in conflict zones around the world. For example: an oil and gas MNE invests in a conflict zone. As part of their operations they build an air-strip, which is then used, with the knowledge and consent of the corporation, as a military staging post for aircraft to bomb civilians as part of the genocidal strategy of those in power. There could be international criminal liability attaching to the officers of such a company, which could destroy the reputation of the corporation in its worldwide activities. This highlights the need of a corporation to engage in an appropriate risk assessment before investing in conflict zones, as it is often too late for such a corporation to do anything about such a situation after it has invested in the operations and built the air-strip.[97] The possibility of such complicity in international crimes should be a key factor in the decision of MNEs to invest in conflict zones around the world.

Other forms of complicity that could engage the international criminal liability of corporations include the following:

- Exerting pressure on governments to crack down on certain parts of society that may be opposed to some of the corporation's activities, which leads to executions, torture, and other forms of human rights abuses. There have been many allegations of such corporate complicity in developing countries with authoritarian governments.[98]
- Contracting or agreeing with governments and local officials to authorize army or police personnel to use deadly force against civilians for site and personnel security, or to encourage forced labor on corporate projects. Again, there have been allegations of corporate complicity in such situations in developing countries with authoritarian governments.[99]
- Encouraging rebel groups to use child soldiers and to inflict heavy civilian casualties to gain access to mineral wealth. Tragically, allegations of such corporate complicity are frequent in the many conflict zones in the African continent where there also happens to be abundant mineral wealth. The human rights disaster in Sierra Leone, described in Chapter 1, is just one sad example.[100]

The next tier of international legal duties of the global private sector comes from what some may term the commercial or white-collar crimes of MNEs, such as bribery and corruption, money laundering, and complicity in organized crime activities. As discussed above, such crimes should not only be viewed as commercial or white-collar crimes, but should be regarded as a cancer of the International Bill of Rights, profoundly affecting both the civil and political rights and the economic, social, and cultural rights of billions around the world.[101]

The emergence of major corporate complicity in bribery and corruption, as described above, led to the United States striking back in the form of the 1977 Foreign Corrupt Practices Act with its extraterritorial reach to most of the major MNEs in the world through its linkage with the US capital markets. Since then, the United States has led a ferocious campaign[102] to get most of the major industrialized countries in the world to first develop anti-bribery and corruption treaties, and then agree to implement in their respective private sectors the provisions of such treaties. The focus of attention in this regard was not the United Nations, where treaty obligations have become diplomatic decorations, as discussed in Chapter 1. Instead, the industrialized world gave the mandate to the OECD, the club of rich industrialized nations of the world together with some aspiring developing nations. The United States and others leading the anti-corruption fight knew that multilateral norms stood a greater chance of being implemented domestically, at least in the industrialized world, in the home jurisdictions of the vast majority of MNEs, through the OECD rather than through the United Nations.

Based on initial recommendations of the OECD and on discussions with its members since 1995, OECD members and several non-members have successfully concluded negotiations on the creation of a Convention on Combating Bribery of Foreign Public Officials in International Business Transactions (the Bribery Convention) in 1997, which came into force on 15 February 1999. All twenty-nine members of the OECD, comprising the vast majority of the most industrialized nations, have signed the Convention, together with five non-members, Argentina, Brazil, Bulgaria, Chile, and the Slovak Republic. More importantly, as of 25 June 2001, twenty-nine of these countries have passed implementing legislation which is now in force. The OECD describes the Bribery Convention as targeting the offering side of the bribery transaction, to eliminate the "supply" of bribes to foreign officials. Each signatory commits to take responsibility for the actions of its own MNEs for their corrupt activities anywhere in the world. This is done by legislating a clear definition of bribery of foreign public officials, imposing deterrent sentences on officials and employees of corporations (and the corporations themselves) who violate such provisions. The Convention also provides for mutual legal assistance to make compliance with the Bribery Convention more effective. In addition, the Convention creates regular co-ordination through a Working Group on Bribery and requires signatories to initiate programs to follow up and to monitor effective compliance with the provisions of the Bribery Convention.[103]

The Convention is, we suggest, a prototype of how international legal duties on MNEs will increasingly be created in areas where the global private sector has either failed or not shown sufficient progress in self-regulation through the development of ethical and social responsibility regimes described above. There may not be a direct imposition of international legal duties on MNEs, as in the case of direct involvement or complicity in serious international crimes by MNEs. However, the indirect imposition of international legal duties on MNEs through effective multilateral treaties promoted by multilateral organizations with political clout such as the OECD is potentially the most effective form of legislated corporate integrity.

Indeed, the OECD itself has followed up its success with the Bribery Convention by other Recommendations that place an expectation on member countries to take steps to ensure that corporations have adequate accounting and other internal controls and audit systems to dissuade corrupt activities. There are also OECD Recommendations for combating corruption in the area of public procurement, including aid-funded procurement, the disallowance of tax deductibility of bribes, and money laundering.[104]

The United Nations has followed suit with Declarations in 1996 and 1998 against bribery and corruption of public office holders. UN-affiliated agencies have also developed anti-corruption programs that would directly or indirectly penalize MNEs that are involved in the programs for corrupt activities. These agencies include the World Bank and the UNDP. There have also been several regional initiatives along the same lines. Noteworthy in this regard are the increasing efforts in the Americas to combat this evil, which has afflicted too many of the nations in the Americas. In 1996, the Organization of American States (OAS) established the Inter-American Convention Against Corruption, which came into force in March of 1997. Subsequently the OAS General Assembly adopted a comprehensive Plan against Corruption in Peru in June of 1997. The Plan takes a multi-stakeholder approach that includes local populations and multilateral organizations, including the OECD, to combat the corrupt activities of MNEs and others. The Inter-American Development Bank also provides direct support and financing for anti-corruption, transparency, and accountability strategies to Latin and Central American Countries.[105]

A similar imposition of indirect international legal obligations is being imposed on MNEs in an ever-increasing number of areas from the environment, through the implementation of the Multilateral Environmental Agreements discussed in Chapter 2, to more recently in the area of money laundering. In response to the growing influence and power of global organized crime and its critical need to launder money derived from illegal activities, the G7 finally developed a framework to ensure that the MNEs in the financial sector and their home jurisdictions joined the battle against this growing global criminal activity. The Financial Action Task Force (FATF) was established at the G7 Summit in Paris in 1989. In April of 1990, the FATF produced a set of forty Recommendations to establish a comprehensive framework to combat money laundering. The membership of FATF has expanded to twenty-eight countries. The focus of FATF is to develop a complete set of counter-measures against money laundering covering the criminal justice system, law enforcement, the financial system, and its legal regulation and multilateral monitoring, as well as mechanisms for self-assessment and peer review. The enforcement regime developed by FATF provides another evolving paradigm for the indirect enforcement of legal obligations of MNEs. Where member countries have systems and practices by financial institutions which are not in compliance with the forty Recommendations, a graduated approach aimed at enhancing peer pressure on member governments is taken in order to tighten anti-money-laundering systems in the member country in question. As a final sanction, membership in the FATF is suspended if there is ongoing violation of the forty Recommendations. Suspension then becomes a signal to the international community that the country in question and the financial institutions in that country should be avoided in terms of legitimate financial relationships. Therefore, there are then substantial legal and economic incentives on the part of both the government and the financial institutions to comply with the FATF recommendations.[106]

In contrast to these emerging forms of indirect international legal obligations of MNEs, there is a growing advocacy and jurisprudence that argues for direct international legal obligations on MNEs. The International Council on Human Rights Policy has argued that the Universal Declaration of Human Rights (UDHR), discussed in Chapter 1, imposes direct obligations on MNEs as an "organ of society" expressly mentioned in the UDHR's preamble, to promote and protect the rights contained in the Declaration. As discussed in Chapter 2, preambles to international treaties and declarations can provide foundational principles by which to interpret the substantive provisions of the document.[107]

As discussed in Chapter 1, there is a strong argument that the UDHR has become binding on all member states as a matter of customary international law. As was also discussed in Chapter 1, the rights in the UDHR were translated into binding treaty obligations for signatories to the Covenant on Civil and Political Rights and the Covenant on Economic, Social and Cultural Rights. In addition, the preambles to both these Covenants state that the individual is under a responsibility to strive for the promotion and observance of the rights recognized in both documents.[108]

As further discussed in Chapter 1, in legal terms regional human rights treaties have further entrenched these rights. The African Charter on Human and Peoples' Rights imposes duties on individuals to respect fundamental rights. Likewise, the American Declaration of the Rights and Duties of Man includes an entire chapter on individual duties. Provisions in the Convention on the Elimination of All Forms of Discrimination against Women (CEDAW), and the Convention on the Elimination on All Forms of Racial Discrimination also direct states to prevent violations by a range of entities and individuals, including corporations.[109] Where there are references to the duties or responsibilities of individuals in human rights documents, one could make a strong argument that they encompass legal persons such as corporations, and certainly encompass individual employees and officers of such artificial persons.

While many, if not most, of the signatories to these binding treaty obligations treat their ratifications as diplomatic decorations (as discussed in Chapter 2), there is mounting jurisprudence that these international legal obligations may extend to MNEs directly. These international legal obligations may also be indirectly enforced against corporations under domestic legal rules.

Treaty bodies discussed in Chapter 2, such as the Committee on Economic, Social and Cultural Rights, have included the private sector as having responsibilities in regard to the right to adequate food and the right to health.[110] The Human Rights Committee has issued a General Comment that the right to privacy encompasses state protection from "natural or legal persons," which encompasses corporations.[111] The European Court of Human Rights has also ruled that under the European Convention on Human Rights, more general human rights protections, such as the right to privacy, may entail positive obligations on states to take the necessary measures, even against private entities, to ensure respect for the right.[112] A broad right such as respect for privacy could encompass many areas of activity of corporations from treatment of employees to the performance of public functions by the private sector.

These last categories of direct and indirect legal obligations of MNEs may be less subject to stringent enforcement and compliance systems[113] than those put in place by an international criminal law regime presided over by a future permanent International Criminal Court described in Chapter 1. They are also less subject to the powerful regimes that have been created by the OECD in the area of bribery and corruption, or by the G7 in the area of money laundering. However, the direct and indirect forms of international legal obligations on MNEs are rapidly growing, as evidence mounts that a global free market without ethical and legal parameters can lead to profound abuse of power by those who can deploy more influence and resources than many sovereign nations. MNEs that are in a position to wield such power, and that fail to understand the corporate integrity risk environment, become free riders on those who do. For these reasons, the international legal duties, both direct and indirect, will be backed by increasingly effective enforcement and compliance systems. As an example of this tendency, there is a growing effort, by those who see themselves as victimized by MNEs that have major assets in the United States, to initiate civil actions under the Alien Tort Claims Act. This Act permits, under certain conditions, foreign claimants to sue in the United States for damages for corporate complicity in the violation of fundamental customary international laws in the area of human rights. While some of these claims have proved unsuccessful, this avenue of legal redress may eventually prove to be a deterrent to MNEs from engaging in complicity in human rights abuses, if not legally, at least in terms of the reputational damage caused by such suits.[114]

Conclusion

The global governance system cannot be complete without an effective and constructive part played by the global private sector. With the fall of the Berlin Wall in 1989, the environment in which the global private sector thrives has, essentially, come to dominate the planet. That environment is one of free markets backed and secured by two other global governance regimes. First is the international peace and security regime constructed in the aftermath of the Second World War as described in Chapter 1. Second, and perhaps more importantly in a unipolar world dominated by the United States, is the global business environment which is also backed and secured by the institutions and laws of international trade as described in Chapter 2.

As the success of the free markets of the world has led to the increasing power of MNEs, we have seen how there are increasing pressures for ethical and legal parameters that set out the responsibilities of these major players in the realm of global governance. In this chapter we have described how there is a plethora of activities to implement ethical and social responsibility regimes. In part, these activities have been undertaken by the leadership MNEs because they understand that there is a corporate integrity risk environment that is ignored at the peril of even the largest of the MNEs. In part, these activities have also been undertaken because there is a general consensus among the MNE community that self-regulation is immensely preferable to legal regulation. However, as we have discussed above, self-regulation can often take on a public relations format when actions do not match the rhetoric of corporate ethics and social responsibility. There is also the problem of the free rider, which can be even the largest MNE in a sector, as witnessed in at least one of the case studies described above.

The exercise of power without responsibility will eventually attract the imposition of both direct and indirect legal duties on MNEs. The direct imposition is most evident as regards international criminal law rules as described above. It will not stop there, however. While classical conceptions of international law are concerned primarily with relations between states, it must not be forgotten that the goal of international law is to meet the needs of the global family. In the past, that last concept would be stated as the global family of nations. With the exponential increase in contacts between individuals, groups, and private entities across borders, the global family is as much a family of individuals as of nations. The development of international law has responded to this evolution of the human family, as discussed in Chapters 1 and 2, through the development of international human rights law that challenge traditional notions of territorial integrity and national sovereignty. We conclude that there is mounting evidence that international law is also responding by imposing directly, or indirectly, international legal duties on MNEs.

We have also argued, in Chapter 2, that the rules of international trade and the institutions of global governance that oversee them, established by sovereign nations, must also take into account the fundamental rights of workers and the protection of the biosphere on which all life depends. In this chapter we conclude with the observation that the unifying principle of the discussion in the first three chapters is that where power is exercised without responsibility, the legitimacy of both the players and the institutions that govern them can become fractured, perhaps beyond repair. Recent accounting and corporate ethics scandals in the United States, Europe, and Canada, as exemplified by the Enron, Arthur Andersen, Adelphia, Tyco Industries, and WorldCom debacles, have demonstrated this imperative of justice most dramatically.[115] It therefore becomes imperative to act before it is too late.

4 From a "race-to-the-bottom" to social justice in the global labor market

This chapter carries further the discussion in Chapter 2. We will argue, primarily from a labor economics perspective, that a lack of rules and standards in the world market may tend to create exploitation of weak and vulnerable labor groups, such as women and children, along the global assembly line. However, such a tendency is neither inevitable nor permanent. It can be arrested and reversed by means of upward harmonization, which is a necessary step "towards a fair global labour market," the title of our previous book. Upward harmonization is contingent on the adoption of universal core labor standards. We suggest that core labor standards such as those laid out in the ILO Declaration on the Fundamental Principles and Rights at Work, discussed in Chapter 2, be implemented in the labor markets of all trading countries so that workers everywhere can enjoy the same basic rights and working conditions. Upward harmonization does not mandate the immediate raising of wages that would undermine comparative advantage or reduce profitability. It requires institutional reform and, in particular, investment in higher worker productivity through human capital formation. Such reforms take time, active policy formulation and implementation. In particular, upward harmonization depends on cooperative management by the international community to adopt universally valid core labor standards. Given such cooperation, we believe upward harmonization is the path to social justice in the global labor market. Demonstrating this prospect is the overall aim of this chapter.

The chapter is organized in four sections. The first examines empirical evidence on working conditions in the global market that suggest current trends toward a "race-to-the-bottom" (RTB) effect or a downward harmonization. From this evidence, a theoretical RTB model is constructed to highlight the main dynamics and relationships in what amounts to exploitation of global workers, a problem that awaits rectification.

Arresting and reversing the RTB trend is a necessary condition for the pursuit of social justice in the global labor market. Accordingly, the second section is devoted to highlighting measures and action for upward harmonization. This section examines in some detail the economic arguments for and against such upward harmonization. The third section of this chapter argues for social justice reforms in aid of vulnerable groups such as women, children, and migrants through the application of core labor standards. However, this task is bedeviled by a knowledge barrier that exists in the North, even amongst trade specialists, regarding the realities of labor market conditions in the South. This knowledge barrier in the North is a major stumbling block on the path of upward harmonization. There is also a second impediment, which is inter-agency cooperation in the international arena. Therefore, in the final section, the topic of inter-agency cooperation is addressed in the context of social justice in the institutions of global governance.

A race-to-the-bottom world?

The globalization of production is creating a global assembly line with standardized technologies, but with widely differing wages and working conditions for workers often producing the same brand products for the same markets for the same global employers. A good example is garment industry workers in different countries and political regimes. Table 4.1 summarizes the hourly base wage-rates of workers in *maquiladoras* and similar industrial zones in the apparel industry in two high-income countries (USA and Canada) with nine developing countries in different parts of the world.

What emerges from the table is a picture of glaring disparities in the global labor market for the same category of workers. Apparel workers in the United States earn almost fifty times, while Canadian workers earn almost forty times, more than their counterparts in Bangladesh. The wages of apparel workers in other developing countries are not much better. Yet all these workers work in the same industry, producing similar products, using similar technologies. These workers are often working in labor-intensive industries for the same companies, such as Nike or their suppliers.

Similar patterns exist in other major labor-intensive industries such as the textiles, clothing, and footwear (TCF) industries. Table 4.2 summarizes recent data from a comprehensive study conducted by the International Labor Office (ILO) covering all major regions of the world.

Table 4.1   Hourly base wage in the apparel industry (1998, US$)

Country	Hourly base wage	Ratio (Bangladesh = 1)
United States	8.42	49.53
Canada	6.70	39.41
Philippines	0.62	3.65
El Salvador	0.60	3.53
Mexico	0.54	3.18
Honduras	0.43	2.53
China	0.30	1.76
Nicaragua	0.25	1.47
Indonesia	0.22	1.29
India	0.20	1.18
Bangladesh	0.17	1.00

Source: http:/www.maquilasolidarity.org/resources/garment/labour-label3.htm

Table 4.2 refers to average wages (not just base rates as in Table 4.1) and covers all major regions of the world. The overall picture that emerges is one of significant disparities between worker compensation in the same industries between low- and high-income countries and regions. In the TCF industries, European workers earn about seven to eight times more than their African counterparts. Furthermore, during the period between 1985 and 1995, the disparities between European and African workers worsened. Asian TCF workers managed to catch up, benefiting from the rapid growth of the "Asian Miracle,"[1] although these wages started from relatively low rates. However, it is almost certain that the gains of the Asian workers, shown in Table 4.2, suffered a significant setback as a result of the Asian financial crisis of 1997.[2]

The wage disparities are paralleled when we examine hours of work in TCF industries in different parts of the world economy. Table 4.3 utilizes the same ILO source to indicate average weekly hours in these industries during the decade 1985–95.

The evidence in Table 4.3 demonstrates that workers in the same industries in different regions of the global economy work different hours. African and Asian workers in the TCF industries work substantially longer hours compared to their counterparts in Europe and the Americas. The difference in working hours cannot be explained simply on the basis of higher productivity of Northern workers. These longer hours are exacerbated by results-based compensation schemes such as piece-rates and home-based production systems that result in workdays in excess of 10 hours per day. The presumption here must be that European and American workers in these industries enjoy better protection under labor laws. This, we believe, violates common norms of social justice. Workers with unequal fundamental rights are waiting for justice.

What emerges from the above wage and hours of work data is a picture of growing disparity in working conditions between workers in the same industries who are located in different regions and countries. Clearly, location makes a

Table 4.2 Average hourly wages in the textile, clothing, and footwear (TCF) industries (1995, US$)

	Textiles		Clothing		Footwear	
			Africa = 1			
(a)	*$*	*Ratio*	*$*	*Ratio*	*$*	*Ratio*
Africa	1.05	1	1.01	1	1.25	1
Americas	5.88	5.6	5.2	5.1	3.18	2.5
Asia	3.66	3.5	3.66	3.6	3.81	3.0
Europe	9.25	8.8	6.5	6.4	8.29	6.6
(b)			*Percentage change over 1985/95*			
Africa	47.6		39.1		26	
Americas	76.5		94.2		21.6	
Asia	227.8		161.6		202.6	

Source: ILO *Labour Practices in the Footwear, Leather Textiles and Clothing Industries* (Geneva: ILO, 2000) located at www.ilo.org/public/english/dialogue/sector/techmeet/tmlfi00/tmlfir.htm (Fig 1.12)

Table 4.3   Average weekly hours of work in the TCF industries (1985–95)

	Textiles	Clothing	Footwear
Africa	50	48.5	48.5
Americas	39.7	40.4	39.8
Asia	44.4	42.1	46.2
Europe	38	36.4	37.1
Oceania	40.4	38	39.2

Source: ILO *Labour Practices in the Footwear, Leather Textiles and Clothing Industries* (Geneva: ILO, 2000), at www.ilo.org/public/english/dialogue/sector/techmeet/tmlfi00/tmlfir.htm (Fig 1.13)

significant difference to wages and quality of working conditions in given industries. We shall now construct a simple economic model to explain the dynamics
of these disparities and explain why cooperative international action for upward
harmonization is essential to avoid globalized exploitation of workers.

In Figure 4.1, Panel (a) refers to labor market conditions in a high-income
country (HIC), whereas Panel (b) similarly refers to a low-income country
(LIC). What is uniquely important in Figure 4.1 is the infinite supply of labor
in LIC, reflecting overcrowding and surplus in the labor market. Hence the
labor supply is shown by the LRS line, parallel to the horizontal axis
measuring quantities of labor. LRS corresponds to subsistence wages, SW
measured on the vertical axis.

In HIC, on the other hand, there is an upward-sloping labor supply, LS,
reflecting the relative scarcity of labor. The wage rate in HIC settles at MW,
well above SW in LIC. In fact, in HIC labor is protected thanks to a variety of
progressive labor market policies which not only guarantee worker rights (such
as freedom of association and collective bargaining) but also provide "safety
net" benefits. One such benefit of particular relevance to the analysis in Figure
4.1 is the existence of minimum wage legislation in HIC which fixes a floor at
MW in Panel (a). The impact of this legislation is first to create a disparity in

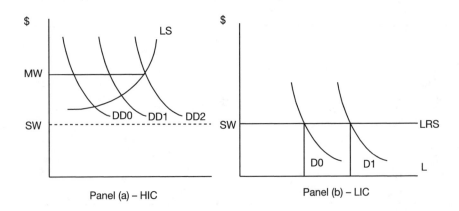

Figure 4.1   Race-to-the-bottom (RTB) in the global labor market

wages in the global labor market equal to (MW−SW). At the same time, the minimum wage legislation may also generate involuntary unemployment in HIC if labor demand is, for example, DD1. However, as a result of private investment or government macroeconomic policy (e.g. expansionary fiscalism), if labor demand increases from DD1 to DD2, then this involuntary unemployment in Panel (a) would be eliminated. By contrast, the same increase in labor demand in LIC would still keep wages at SW due to infinite supply elasticity, which would merely expand the volume of employment at this subsistence level.

Figure 4.1 can be helpful in explaining the race-to-the-bottom (RTB) trends observed to date. The RTB involves a downward slide of wages in the LIC labor market due to the absence of social protection. In particular, the RTB exists due to a lack of labor institutions to protect worker rights comparable to what exists in HICs. It should be noted that the RTB does not mean pushing wages down to zero. That, of course, would be a practical impossibility. What it realistically means is pushing the wages of global workers all the way down to subsistence level, represented by SW in Panel (b).

The logical foundation of an RTB is persuasive and supported by evidence. Suppose an international company wishes to expand its operations in the global economy from its United States, Canadian or European base. It has several options in terms of location of its expansion plans. It can remain at home, increasing its labor demand from DD1 to DD2 in Panel (a) of Figure 4.1. The company would then pay home-country workers higher wages, raising W to MW, the wage established under minimum wage legislation protecting workers. Saving these additional labor costs at home would naturally mean higher profits. So the company may opt to seek lower-cost locations in the South without sacrificing labor productivity, an objective that encourages reliance of even greater capital-intensive technology in labor abundant regimes. Moving into LIC, Panel (b) of Figure 4.1, would satisfy these corporate objectives. The company can expand employment in LIC from D0 to D1 at the prevailing subsistence wage, SW. It is important to observe that in LIC there is an infinite supply of labor at SW, implying that inflow of investment simply creates additional jobs at this subsistence wage. Labor demand at the home country would then decline to DD0 and may decline further toward SW, depending on the rate of investment relocation from HIC to LIC. The end result would be reducing wages in HIC toward the sweat-shop rate, which is the bottom. At this level, corporate profits would be at their highest. Additionally, there would be rent-seeking and transfer-pricing opportunities for corporate investors in LICs (a topic we discuss later).

Table 4.4 shows actual data in support of the analytical model illustrated in Figure 4.1. The data, tabulated from ILO sources, demonstrates that over 1980–93 employment in the TCF industries relocated from several HICs to manufacturing sites in LICs where cheap labor is plentiful.

Figure 4.2 illustrates the RTB in the global market within an integrated model. As explained above, the existence of abundant labor supply in LIC at SW acts as a magnet for foreign investment by a profit-seeking international

Table 4.4   Global relocation of employment in TCF industries (1980–93)

Country	Percentage change	Country	Percentage change
Finland	-71.7	Mauritius	344.6
Sweden	-65.4	Indonesia	177.4
Norway	-64.9	Morocco	166.8
Austria	-51.5	Jordan	160.8
Poland	-51.0	Jamaica	101.7
Syria	-50	Malaysia	101.2
France	-45.4	Mexico	85.5
Hungary	-43.1	China	57.3
Netherlands	-41.7	Islamic Republic of	
		Iran	34.0
United Kingdom	-41.5	Turkey	33.7
New Zealand	-40.9	Philippines	31.8
Germany	-40.2	Honduras	30.5
Spain	-35.3	Chile	27.2
Australia	-34.7	Kenya	16.1
Argentina	-32.9	Israel	13.4
United States	-30.1	Venezuela	7.9

Source: ILO, *Globalization Changes the Face of Textile, Clothing and Footwear Industries*. See ILO, *Globalization of the Footwear, Textiles and Clothing Industries. Report for Discussion at the Tripartite Meeting on the Globalization of the Footwear, Textiles and Clothing Industries: Effects on Employment and Working Conditions* (Geneva: ILO, 1996).

company which relocates its operations into LIC from HIC where workers are protected, among other things, under a minimum wage, MW. As a consequence, labor demand becomes more elastic, shifting from D0 to D1 as shown in the left-hand side of the figure. In LIC profits rise from ABC to ABD due to lower average cost AC^1 relative to AC^2, illustrated in the right hand side of the figure, where AR, average revenue, refers to decimal conditions.

Employment falls in HIC and expands in LIC, but while wages decline in the former, SW remains in force. In other words, foreign investment fails to generate an upward convergence of wages or, put another way, a wage trap exists in the global labor market.

The way out of this RTB trap at the subsistence wages in LIC is through upward harmonization based on two specific conditions. In the first place, there must be investment in human capital (via education and skill training) in order to raise worker productivity and wages. Second, there must be legal reform of worker rights as well as social protection of groups that are vulnerable to exploitation and unfair treatment. The result of upward harmonization is a trend of convergence of wages and working conditions in the global labor market. The dynamics of this convergence is illustrated in Figure 4.3.

In Figure 4.3, the vertical line WSL refers to the fixed quantity of world labor supply, determined by demographic forces. It is the aggregation of labor force in all countries of the globe at a given point in time. On the demand side, WDL is

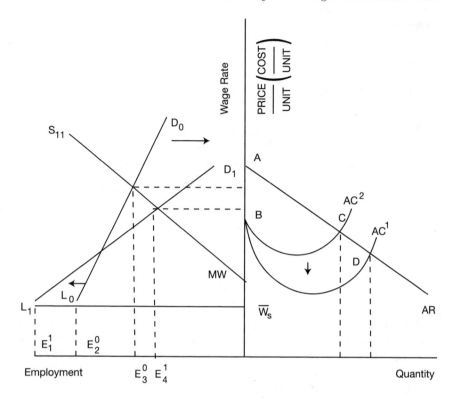

Figure 4.2   RTB model of wage exploitation with rent-seeking investment

the world demand for labor at the same point in time. MW, the policy-fixed minimum wage, coincides with the wage rate in HIC. On the other hand, in LIC the prevailing wage is at subsistence level of wages SW, all marked on the vertical axis. Under these conditions, there is involuntary unemployment, CD, in HIC and open unemployment in LIC denoted by AB. Upward harmonization could shift WDL upward along CE creating an equilibrium in the global labor market at E with GEW as the global equilibrium wage rate. There will be no out-migration from LIC to HIC, yet the wage disparity between MW and SW would be reduced to MW−GEW. In other words, investing in upward harmonization in LIC is an alternative to out-migration from LIC to HIC.

Of course, Figure 4.3 is an ideal, competitive labor market designed to illustrate upward harmonization. It is far removed from existing realities which entail all sorts of immigration and refugee barriers, work visa requirements, occupational licensing regulations, trade and non-trade barriers in developed countries, which all work to restrict the mobility of job-seekers in the global labor market. Yet the model has the merit of capturing the essence of the benefits of freedom of movement for global workers.

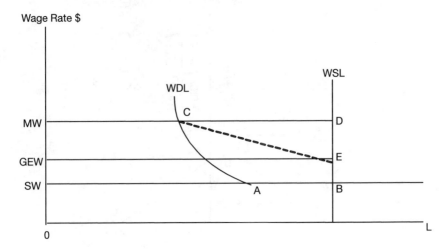

Figure 4.3   Upward harmonization model

A freely functioning global labor market is a good thing and is deemed essential for the efficient allocation of labor. However, labor market efficiency must be balanced with equity to ensure a social safety net. In HICs, freedom requires that labor market institutions, such as trade unions, and core labor rights, such as the right to strike and form free unions, exist to achieve better wages and working conditions. Economic justice in HICs is unthinkable without unions and basic labor rights. Moreover, wages are not entirely set by free labor markets; they are also set by such social policies as minimum wages. There is no compelling evidence that suggests these labor market institutions and policy interventions that balance equity and efficiency are any more responsible for cost-push inflation than macroeconomic policy. The Asian Tigers paid dearly for ignoring social protection in the labor market, and "one of the clearest lessons to emerge from the [Asian] crisis is that existing systems of social protection were unable to cope with the social consequences. Thus, strengthening of social protection is an important priority for future action."[3]

Social protection in the labor market promotes long-term stability and efficiency as is demonstrated by the experience of HICs. Therefore, trade unions and worker rights in LICs can be justified on the same efficiency and equity arguments. Thus, upward harmonization can be expected to reduce over-crowding and raise wages above subsistence wages in proportion to rising worker productivity following investment in higher labor standards. In addition, world welfare will be enhanced. These are the global benefits of upward harmonization of working conditions and greater social justice in the world economy. We now apply this conclusion to the pursuit of social justice.

Social justice in the global marketplace

Social justice is a vital element of human dignity that permeates the thesis of the different chapters in this text. As such, social justice in the global economy rests on economic justice. It is a normative objective which aims at paying labor of a given quality equitable wages, and ultimately the same wages regardless of location, race, or gender. Given enabling institutional reform and adequate resources, social justice in the global marketplace would ensure that work of equal value in the production of traded goods and services is rewarded equitably and ultimately equally in different national jurisdictions. In short, social justice in the workplace is dignifying the worker by paying labor's due in production.

Labor's due in the paragraph above consists of two components: the first is payment of equitable and ultimately equal wages to workers of the same productivity. Worker productivity is governed by technical conditions of production, principally technology, and by worker attributes such as education and training. One of the most significant manifestations of an integrating world economy is the globalization of technology that promotes equalization of worker productivity. Thanks to global sourcing and technology transfer and global assembly lines, workers around the world are increasingly producing standardized products, utilizing increasingly uniform technologies. There is evidence that in labor-abundant countries in the South, which have attracted imported capital intensive technologies, the productivity of workers producing brand products is becoming comparable despite social and cultural differences. For example, Javanese, Chinese or Mexican workers may work in different subsidiaries of a given parent firm, or they may produce similar products under a product-licensing agreement in a joint venture between a local firm and an international corporation. These workers generally produce the same, physically undifferentiated products, such as Nike shoes or electronic parts and components used in computer or telecommunication industries. To the extent that technology tends to equalize worker productivity along the global assembly line, social justice would demand that workers everywhere ultimately receive equitable and ultimately equal monetary benefits for work of equal value.

The second component of labor's due refers to institutional and personal differences of global workers in terms of education, training, and legal rights pertaining, for example, to their rights of association and collective bargaining. Institutional reform is thus an essential component of social justice in the global labor market. Technology may tend to equalize labor productivity across national boundaries, but that is not enough. Of equal significance is domestic institutional reform, which is required for the uniform protection under labor law for workers everywhere in the world. Along the global assembly line, working conditions are increasingly being standardized, but institutional harmonization is essential as well. Thus, production and assembly workers in electronics or garment industries, producing similar products in different regimes but for the same markets and often for the same companies, should enjoy equitable and ultimately equal wages and benefits. Similarly, with regard to working conditions, to the extent that hours of work and schedules are homogenized in workplaces through flexibilization[4] or by feminization[5] and other standardardized management techniques, so too should worker rights and working conditions be equalized under labor codes in the global workplace. If the treatment of capital and technology in export processing zones (EPZs) (see Chapters 2 and 5 for extended discussion of this topic) is being harmonized globally, so too should labor's treatment be harmonized under labor laws. This is the way to bring justice to global workers based on "core" labor standards as articulated, for example, in the 1998 ILO Declaration of Fundamental Principles and Rights of Work discussed in Chapter 2.

The realities of the global labor market: a synopsis

A national labor market is real: it allocates labor amongst industries, occupations, and regions while determining wages and working conditions. In elementary labor economics textbooks, the labor market is ideally presented and analyzed as a perfectly competitive market. Whenever shortages exist, labor market dynamics generate corrective labor mobility from labor-surplus regions into labor-shortage regions. Wages and working conditions should ultimately adjust toward a national equilibrium level in the labor market. In actual reality, any deviation from such an ideal is explained, as with other types of economic markets, in terms of "market failure." This failure is attributable to the lack of labor market information, occupational licensing, as well as other entry barriers into professions and skilled occupations. Equally, such market failure may be attributable to residence or visa restrictions limiting inter-regional labor mobility.

In the global labor market no such equilibrium adjustment is possible because shortage in one country and surplus in another do not automatically lead to labor mobility across national boundaries. What is worse is that there is a growing asymmetry between the treatment of capital and labor in the global economy, as described at length in our previous book.[6] Unlike free capital mobility, there is no freedom of movement for migrants who, however rational their motives, cannot simply move from one country to another in expectation of maximizing wages or net advantages.

Shortage (destination) countries

High-income countries, typically shortage destinations acting as a magnet for labor-exporting countries, have restrictive immigration policies. These policies tend to be pro-cyclical, meaning that immigration flows tend to rise and fall with the business cycle: whenever there is a boom and critical labor market shortages emerge in destination economies of the North, expansionary immigration policies are followed, but when these economies experience a slowdown and rising unemployment, immigration policies become restrictive. Over the business cycle, labor markets in labor surplus countries are obliged to function in subordination to conditions prevailing in rich Northern countries.

The destination countries are also "welfare" countries[7] because they have social safety nets and welfare programs to protect workers. To a large extent, such protection does not exist in labor surplus countries. As a result, the social costs of shifting unemployment over the business cycle fall inordinately on the low-income, labor surplus countries of the South. In times of rising unemployment, the rich countries mitigate social costs of unemployment with "welfare programs" and social safety nets. No such programs exist in most developing countries. Labor markets are always overcrowded in labor surplus countries, as evidenced by long hours and low wages in informal sectors.[8] When demand for labor declines in rich Northern countries due to a downturn in the business cycle, these labor market conditions in sending countries of the South become even more precarious.

The brain drain problem

The pro-cyclical immigration policies in rich Northern countries generate for these countries significant "free-rider" benefits. These benefits take the form of "brain drain,"[9] whereby highly educated and skilled workers, whose education and training costs were incurred by sending countries of the South, migrate and join the labor force in rich Northern countries, contributing value to the GNP in those countries. The sending countries lose twice from brain drain: first because they bear the cost burden of educating and training workers who migrate out once they graduate; and second because the GNP in these sending countries is reduced in proportion to lost productivity due to departing workers.

However, there may be compensating gains from such a brain drain. Workers from labor surplus countries who successfully integrate into labor markets in Northern countries may send remittances back home to parents, relatives or friends. These remittances, typically in the form of valuable foreign exchange, help sending countries at the macroeconomic as well as at the micro-levels. In the former case, remittances in foreign exchange may reduce balance of payment deficits; in the latter case, they clearly provide valuable income to families and households who would otherwise be in dire poverty.

However, these remittances, as in the case of the volume of labor exports, fluctuate with the business cycle. Periods of economic boom generate rising demand for labor exports. Then there are gains in the form of a steady flow of remittances from the rich countries of the North to the poor households of the South. This, however, is temporary. In times of economic slowdown and recession, declining demand for labor in rich Northern economies automatically reduces remittances back to sending countries, while labor exports also dry out.

Labor exporting countries

What then happens in labor exporting economies in times of economic slowdown? Typically, labor market overcrowding worsens. Even in the best of times these countries are overcrowded and jobs are at a premium, especially higher-quality, secure, "white-collar" jobs in the government or foreign companies. Rising unemployment, due to declining foreign demand for labor, then spills over first into the informal sector that operates as a "reserve army of job-seekers,"[10] and then increasingly into the underground economy. Human trafficking, prostitution and the sex trade, drug dealing, and other criminal activities expand in proportion to the lack of employment and income opportunities in the formal regular economy.

Snakeheads and networks in the underground global economy

In the globalizing world economy, there are two markets: the formal and the underground. Regulation, through the World Trade Organization (WTO) and international trade agreements, is focused on the first one, while the second is entirely unregulated, and therefore statistics and information on how it works, how much it is growing, and how it impacts on the vulnerable in the global village is lacking. The underground world economy is controlled by criminal networks and syndicates involved in a wide range of illegal activities including money laundering, drug dealing, arms dealing, prostitution rings, and networks involved in human trafficking.[11]

In terms of the illegal migration, the biggest destinations are high-income countries such as North America and Europe. Such migration is a profitable business, controlled by smugglers and led by snakeheads that operate global networks to move desperate people without papers and official identity across borders. In exchange for a small fortune, sometimes running to tens of thousands of dollars, snakeheads and their networks of smugglers provide the services of both a visa office and a travel agency to potential migrants and asylum seekers desperately trying to escape war-torn countries to the safety and security of stable destinations such as North America, Europe, or Australia.

How these networks operate can be illustrated with reference to Australia, a particularly attractive destination for asylum seekers escaping such war-torn Muslim countries as Iraq and Afghanistan. First, asylum seekers from these countries enter Malaysia, which does not require an entry visa from visitors arriving from other Muslim countries. Then they cross by boat into neighboring Indonesia. For an average price of US$4,000 they then obtain the services of smugglers who typically use unseaworthy vessels to take them to Australia. "About 1,600 have been caught in Indonesia this year, while another 3,000 are estimated to be in the country looking for boats to take them south, government officials say."[12]

Trafficking of women

Young women are the most vulnerable group in the global underground economy. The traffic in female sex slaves occurs worldwide and involves big money. It is estimated that the global trade in women for the purpose of prostitution and other illicit sexual activity is currently worth US$7–12 billion annually.[13] This most likely is an underestimate, given the lack of information about this odious trade in human beings. Other estimates put the figure of women in trade at four million, a quarter of whom are used for the global sex market, comprising sex tourism, mail-order brides, prostitution in brothels, pornography, militarized sexual services, factory work, and even forced domestic labor.[14] Although women are trafficked for money within their own countries, the global sex trade is expanding most rapidly across international borders, primarily from low-income sources in the developing countries to high-income markets in the North, largely due to the inadequate regulation of existing international conventions and inadequate surveillance by under-funded agencies such as the International Organization for Migration.[15]

Exploitation of girls and women in the sex industry is a global problem and it is a gross infringement of human dignity and human rights. In particular, it is a flagrant violation of the 1949 United Nations Convention for the Suppression of the Traffic in Persons and of the Exploitation of the Prostitution of Others,[16] as well as the ILO Conventions, specifically Convention 105 which bans forced and compulsory labor. The definition of "forced and compulsory labor" indicates the difficulties inherent in the application of this Convention. The term refers to "all work or service which is exacted from any person under the menace of any penalty and for which the said person has not offered himself [sic] voluntarily."[17] Strictly speaking, at least some females seeming to consent to work in prostitution rings may be driven by fear or poverty in the sending countries. Given an opportunity to reveal preference, they may well claim to be working "voluntarily," even if in reality this is not the case. This might appear to invalidate applicability of Convention 105. In fact, it merely illustrates the difficulties in applying Conventions on human trafficking in the service of social justice in the global village.

This problem can be further elaborated with reference to foreign workers working as maids, servants, and service workers in the Persian Gulf countries, one of the major labor-importing regions of the world.[18] Systematic exploitation and substandard working conditions for female workers imported from labor-surplus South and South-Asian countries regularly make headlines in the world news media. What gets reported, however, is no more than the mere tip of the iceberg. Typically, these female workers are afraid to report abuse and exploitation, which their employers heap on them, simply because they need the money and they are aware of the bonding obligations under which they are obliged to work. Once they complain, the bond is broken and they are almost certainly kicked out of employment, and may have to sink further into the hands of syndicates and snakeheads in charge of the global sex and prostitution industries.

In the short term, publicity and exposure of exploitative and unfair labor practices in the world media is probably the most effective remedy. But the root cause of the problem of female slavery and exploitation requires a long-term solution. Long-term investment in human resource development is the surest way of protecting generations of women from such exploitation and injustice. This is social preventive action. It requires investment in the education of young girls, and productive employment generation for poor households. The funds necessary for these purposes must come from sources such as the World Development Fund, discussed in the next chapter.

Women along the global economy

Feminization of the labor force is now a global phenomenon. Indeed, according to the ILO,

> women have provided the bulk of new labor supply in both the developed and developing countries over the past two decades. Women's labor force growth since 1980 has been substantially higher than labor force growth for men in every region of the world except Africa.[19]

Unfortunately, feminization of the labor force has not provided women with economic liberation. Rather, this transformation has generally created a "new global underclass [of] women in poverty,"[20] because the vast majority of working women are concentrated in secondary labor markets, either in substandard jobs in "informal sectors"[21] or in low-wage, labor-intensive sectors such as electronics, garments, and textiles.[22] As discussed in Chapter 2, many of the workers in *maquiladoras*, export processing zones (EPZs), or other industrial estates are women. As also discussed in Chapter 2, these women may be subject to exploitation because they do not enjoy core labor rights protection under social security or labor codes. Even if such protection does exist, it is often not enforced. Even in comparison to gender disparity in wages in the North, women in EPZs often receive much lower wages compared to men, although they are performing similar tasks. Additionally, they may be dismissed for marriage, absenteeism, or even pregnancy, and sometimes they even have to submit to virginity tests.[23] In Chapter 2, we discussed how such unfair working conditions in these EPZs and maquiladoras constitute a flagrant violation of worker norms under international conventions such as the ILO Declaration on the Fundamental Principles and Rights at Work. They also constitute violations of ILO Conventions 100 and 105, which mandate equality and non-discrimination in pay and working conditions. As also discussed in Chapter 2, where the exporting country is complicit in not enforcing the non-discrimination standards under their own laws, then a case can be made that illegal subsidies under the WTO rules may exist.

Women are not only over-represented along the global assembly line in low-paying jobs, they are also overcrowded in the informal sector dominated by low-income trading on the street. The combination of these trends implies that women are increasingly impoverished because, typically, they are obliged to "double shift," looking after household chores and engaging in income-generating trading in the informal sector. The condition of African women in the informal sector is especially precarious as women's share of informal sector employment in the non-agricultural African labor force often exceeds 80 percent, whereas it is somewhat less in East Asia and Latin America.[24]

A new trend in the global economy is the growth of home-based work. This practice, reminiscent of the putting-out system in pre-Industrial Revolution days, entails the production of consumer goods at home, typically by women workers who are supplied parts for final assembly by contractors in a global chain. A typical example of home-based work is the garment industry, whereby women, in addition to domestic chores such as cooking, child care, etc., are provided by suppliers and contractors with pre-cut parts of garments for sewing at home.[25] Home-based work is not only cost-saving for suppliers and contractors because of the low wages paid to home-workers, it is a labor practice that is entirely outside the purview of labor codes. Women involved in this process receive no protection against accidents and sickness, and beyond minimal wages, get no fringe benefits such as vacation or over-time pay.

Child workers

Women are not the only vulnerable group in the global economy. Under-age child workers are also victims, increasingly overcrowding sweat-shops and informal sectors as well. These young persons should be at school, not working long hours for a pittance in sweat-shops producing goods for export.

The latest estimates on economically active children aged 5–14, worldwide, summarized in Table 4.5, put their number at 250 million. The countries with the highest incidence of child workers include African countries such as Kenya and Senegal, whereas the country with the largest absolute number is India, with some 111 million. Child slavery is also widespread in India.[26] The worst forms of child work include the trafficking of children, child prostitution, children as soldiers, and domestic and hazardous work.

As we discussed in our previous book,[27] the root cause of child labor in poor countries is "cultural entrapment" which includes the following:

1   a culture of poverty whereby poor parents expect children to contribute to household income to ensure socio-economic survival;
2   unrelenting poverty that validates larger families for short-term economic survival and security for parents in old age;
3   environmental degradation and deforestation in the countryside, causing mass exodus to the cities to escape the slow death of the rural economy;
4   emergence of export-oriented, labor-intensive industries that pay low wages, especially attractive for unskilled women and under-age workers; and
5   lack of labor and social policies and enforcement procedures to safeguard minimum standards of safety and protection of workers at work.

The common factor behind all of these causal factors is the lack of resources in poor countries to invest in anti-poverty programs in order to create productive jobs and provide income generation for the benefit of vulnerable groups. To the extent that upward harmonization in the global labor market is a global chal-lenge, it must be recognized that bringing justice to global workers can only become a realistic target if and when global resources to this end are committed and delivered.

Table 4.5   Child labor data

Worldwide number of economically active children, aged 5–14[a]			250 million

Countries with the highest percentage of working children aged 10–14[b]

Kenya	41.3	India	14.4
Senegal	31.4	China	11.6
Bangladesh	30.1	Egypt	11.2
Nigeria	25.8	Mexico	6.7
Turkey	24	Argentina	4.5
Côte d'Ivoire	17.7	Portugal	1.8
Brazil	16.1	Italy	0.4

Worst forms of child labor[b]

Child trafficking	Estimated 0.7 to 2 million
Child prostitution	"Each year some one million children enter the sex trade … between the ages of 13 and 18, although there is evidence that very young, even babies, are also caught in this horrific trade."
Child soldiers	Approximately 300,000 under the age of 18
Domestic child servants	ILO estimates that domestic work is the largest employment category for girls under the age of 16, some as young as 5 or 6
Other hazardous child labor	ILO estimates that over 50 million children under 12 work in hazardous circumstances

Note
[a] = UNICEF, *The Progress of Nations 2000* (New York: UNICEF, 2000); ILO, *Child Labor, Targeting the Intolerable* (Geneva: ILO, 1996)
[b] = www.globalmarch.org global data (accessed: July 2001)

Bringing justice to global workers: the knowledge barrier

Knowledge is not the same as information. The latter is technical or statistical data, usually compiled in financial and economic reports, analysis, policies, manuals, and texts relating to market transactions. Knowledge, on the other hand, refers to a deeper understanding of the human condition that requires more than statistical information to understand and appreciate. In order to increase understanding and appreciation of the human condition, knowledge requires social, cultural, and often qualitative facts and observation of a more profound nature than mere statistical or technical analysis and reporting.

The boundary between knowledge and information has been blurred as a result of the new information technology, which has greatly facilitated statistical and technical data transmission, storage, and dissemination. No less a body than the World Bank has jumped on this bandwagon to establish a direct equality between knowledge and information. Thus, the Bank's World Development Report 1998/9 is titled *Knowledge for Development* whereas, in fact, the Bank seems to focus on information in the report, more specifically on information technology, rather than knowledge as defined above.

Although there are extensive normative rules contained in the various Declarations and Conventions of the ILO as discussed in Chapter 2, the global governance of labor in the global marketplace is virtually non-existent. This is especially so in contrast to rules and regulations relating to the treatment of capital and technology movements in the global market. A good part of this asymmetrical treatment of labor stems from a knowledge barrier, or more specifically from the failure of economists to go beyond statistical and technical information and drill down further to seek knowledge.

The debate on upward harmonization has been dominated by trade economists who are victims of this knowledge barrier. Conventional trade specialists are dedicated to the abstract theory of free trade, as any standard textbook on international trade will testify. Yet, in practice, the world of international business is far removed from the textbook models of perfect competition. As such, the debate on upward harmonization gets distorted by professional bias and a systemic knowledge barrier on labor issues and actual working conditions in developing countries. In particular, Western trade specialists' knowledge of labor markets in the developing world is limited. In fact, abstract theorizing based on perfectly competitive markets takes the place of actual realities.[28] Trade theory homogenizes the developing world to derive some abstract conclusions and policy recommendations. Far from being homogeneous, there is a bewildering diversity and complexity in developing world labor markets and working conditions. Much detailed research is required in order to develop a comparative understanding of how different labor markets function and the impacts of their legal and institutional contexts. Knowledge is also required as to how institutional efficiency of the labor market process can be enhanced in specific developing countries.

The latest trend among these economists is a call for open markets and "deep integration," a concept that is defined as "integration not only in the production of goods and services but also in standards and other domestic policies."[29] In other words, there is a strong implication that domestic policies, from the banking and financial sectors to labor market policies, education, and even cultures, should be reformed in line with trade agreements.

In principle, we favor the reformist thrust of "deep integration"; after all, that is what the upward harmonization advocated in this book is all about. However, there is a significant difference between our position and that of the traditional Western trade specialists. We believe reform is required globally, both in the South and in the North, for better global governance based on partnership. The New Partnership for African Development spearheaded by key African countries, pushed by Canada, and endorsed at the G8 Summit in June of 2002 in Kananaskis, Canada, may be the start of such partnerships.

However, it is appropriate that there is suspicion of the advocacy of openness in trade only as a prescription in the South, and as an immediate goal without prior institutional development within developing countries and without reciprocal openness in trade in developed countries, especially as regards trade in agricultural goods and textiles.

As argued by Professor Rodrik[30] of MIT, we believe that, without investment in workers and labor markets as a first step, openness and "deep integration" would undermine national autonomy, as happened in the case of excessive capital mobility, for example, in the Asian financial crisis. Hasty and premature "deep integration" would be dangerous. It would let the business cycle and market conditions in Europe and North America determine domestic policies in the developing world. The welfare of the inhabitants of these countries would therefore depend on external priorities and ignore critical and much-needed internal reforms. Prior to the 1997 financial crisis, Asian economies, while based on the inevitably ruinous crony capitalism networks, were also strongly committed to "open regionalism."[31] The welfare losses which they suffered after the crisis clearly demonstrate the risks involved in such strategy. The North must provide better trade access for the exports from developing countries, phase out agricultural subsidies in the European Union (EU) and North America, and facilitate more resource transfers from the North to the South for greater global equity and upward harmonization.

In this book, we propose the establishment of a World Development Fund (see Chapter 5) to help pay for upward harmonization, because we agree that "distributive justice [is] an international public good."[32] We endorse the argument of Rodrik that there is a risk that globalization may tend to go too far, running the risk of spilling over into social conflict if and when there are insufficient social safety nets and other domestic policy safeguards.

Most conventional trade specialists take a skeptical position on linking labor standards to trade, in effect rejecting the case of upward harmonization advanced in this book.[33] We shall now critically deal with some of these counter-arguments.

Jagdish Bhagwati,[34] one of the most influential trade economists, argues that labor standards are private goods reflecting consumer choice revealed in the marketplace. Those consumers who believe repugnant working conditions in low-income countries exist may simply refuse to buy the goods and services produced under such objectionable conditions. Ultimately, firms producing or selling such goods and services in world markets will either lose their market share or get the message and opt for higher labor standards. Bhagwati's thesis depends on the fact that the consumer is well informed. The real problem here is lack of adequate information about production or working conditions. Accordingly, "social labeling" of products in consuming countries may be the only basis for ensuring the market power of ethical consumerism. Such labeling schemes are rife with problems of authenticity, monitoring, and verification. Moreover, there is no guarantee that such schemes lead to improved working conditions in developing countries. For these reasons we disagree with the technical fix to the market as suggested by Bhagwati in regard to the problem of exploited labor.

The view that higher labor standards represent private goods is also questionable on a principle of human dignity. It puts consumers' ethics in the North in the driver's seat, making welfare of workers in the developing world subject to consumers' choices in the rich markets of the North. Even under conditions of full information and perfect foresight, these workers would only enjoy remedies against unfair working conditions if and when Northern consumers reveal with their spending power that they disagree with these unfair conditions. In other words, the workers themselves are passive, or do not have the capacity to judge the quality of their own working conditions.

Another group of economists, those who believe in the doctrine of laissez-faire economics and idealize the free market,[35] argue against higher labor standards in the South on the grounds that labor standards interfere with the free operation of the market. Deepak Lal[36] is one of the most vocal proponents of this school. In a recent article, Lal has condemned higher labor and environmental standards "as a conspiracy against the Third World" that has the effect of robbing "the world's poorest of their comparative economic advantage and doom[ing] them to continued poverty by pricing them out of the world's markets."[37] This is similar to the arguments that bad jobs are better than no jobs. This view ignores the dynamic benefits of productivity-enhancing investment in labor (as happened in the Asian Tigers) to speed up escape from the unlimited supply trap. We have discussed this human resource development strategy extensively in our previous text and continue to do so in this work.

Yet another group of economists object to higher labor standards on institutional grounds, arguing that building unions or worker organizations may create inequality. For example, some experts have argued that higher labor standards, in particular unionization in line with ILO Conventions 87 and 98, may lead to pockets of labor aristocracy, since typically a small minority of Southern workers are union members. The fact, however, that unions in developing countries are small and weak is no argument to reject worker rights, as these deficiencies are often due to the effects of authoritarian or repressive regimes.[38] In view of these political and institutional obstacles, workers' rights may take root and grow gradually, but they cannot grow automatically simply due to market forces under laissez-faire conditions. These institutions in the South need to progressively reform themselves with financial support from the North. Indeed, the speed of upward harmonization depends primarily on available resources to pay for it, a topic to be discussed in the next chapter. Without adequate financial resources, arguments for higher labor standards in the South will reinforce the position of protectionist interests in the North, or those favoring trade sanctions against exporters from the South on ethical grounds. In our judgement, a more effective alternative to these positions would be the "incentive" system relying on the human resource development (HRD) -productivity -investment approach, a topic to be taken up in Chapter 5.

Why countries avoid higher labor standards

Unfortunately it is not only conventional trade economists that oppose higher labor standards. They are also often opposed by repressive politicians, anti-globalists, and cultural nationalists in the South. The quality of debate on the asserted beneficial effects of the avoidance of higher labor standards in developing countries is also suspect and inconclusive. It can be summarized on the basis of four arguments:

1   the public good argument;
2   the blocking minority argument;
3   the endogeneity argument; and
4   the economic development argument.

The public good argument views labor standards as public goods, representing "social moral consciousness."[39] As such, regimes or countries that avoid higher standards expect to realize some kind of free-rider benefit relative to those countries willing to adopt higher standards. These international differences, in turn, give rise to charges of "social dumping."

The second unjust incentive for elites in the South (the blocking minority) to advocate, as they do, against higher labor standards, is in effect similar to the free-rider problem discussed above. This unjust incentive focuses attention on social groups within a given country, and helps to explain the absence of labor standards on the basis of the political clout of a minority which stands to benefit from the avoidance of such standards.[40] Thus, politically powerful elites, representing what Mancur Olson has called "distributional coalitions,"[41] resist higher labor standards for personal gain. Thanks to poor labor standards, they extract rents from exploitation or discrimination of their own workers in the labor market. This kind of political power enables members of these privileged coalitions to shift income distribution in their favor and at the expense of workers.[42]

The third argument[43] explains inter-country differences in labor standards on the basis of country-specific values and institutions. For example, for historical and cultural reasons Asian countries tend to prefer enterprise unions, placing restrictions on Western-type collective bargaining rights. Despite these differences, these Asian economies have achieved growth with equity, implying that Western-style unionization may not be a necessary condition for higher labor standards.

The fourth argument on the avoidance of higher labor standards is the oldest and relates specifically to the EPZs. It explains non-observance of core standards in EPZs as an explicit low-wage policy to attract foreign investment or promote exports. Lack of labor standards, especially suppression of unions, may be a deliberate EPZ strategy. This policy tends to attract footloose investment that may be transitory, and contributes to the race-to-the-bottom argument which we have discussed above.

Some economists have argued that low-paying jobs are better than no jobs at all. While this is a valid argument so far as it goes, it is no excuse to keep creating low-paying jobs or to deny workers in the developing world basic rights that are available in the North. By the same token, the arguments of authoritarian ruling elites in the South defending worker exploitation on grounds of comparative advantage in the global marketplace must be opposed.

These four arguments concerning why developing countries tend to avoid higher labor standards are inconclusive because they do not lead to any clear path. In particular, they do not promote international cooperation for global governance of the labor market. In an age of globalization, a meaningful North–South partnership is essential to manage the global labor market. Global social justice through upward harmonization is at the core of this partnership for global governance. The challenge at the start of the new millennium is how to design and manage a new system of adequate incentives in order to bring poor countries of the developing world to the international table to support a program of upward harmonization. We believe upward harmonization constitutes a global public good and deserves to be pursued for the collective good of humanity. Instead of an "Us–Them" mindset, there must be joint action against exploitation and inequality in the global marketplace to deal with the ugly realities of exploitation in the labor markets.

Exploitation of workers in the global marketplace

Millions of participants in the global economy are waiting for justice because they are being systematically subjected to institutional and economic forces that lead to exploitation. We shall briefly review below three principal catalysts for market-based exploitation in the global marketplace:

1   indefensible forms of transfer pricing and tax avoidance by multinational enterprises (MNEs);
2   rent-seeking by domestic elites;
3   social dumping by exporting countries.

Transfer pricing by MNEs

Much of international trade is currently conducted not by countries, as envisaged under the old Ricardian free trade model, but by MNEs. These MNEs include many who are world-class monopolies or oligopolies. They may seek to maximize global profits by a variety of strategies, sometimes seeking cheap resources, sometimes seeking new markets, and often utilizing monopoly–monopsony powers to manipulate prices and corner markets.[44]

What is even more controversial for theory as a guide to trade policy is that there is now the problem of intra-firm trade. According to a recent study at the Institute of International Economics, no less than 86 percent of total exports in the world in 1995, valued at US$170 billion, were between affiliates and subsidiaries of MNEs, with only 14 percent representing inter-company trade.[45] The same ratio applied for imports.

What is the explanation for the dominance of intra-firm trade in the global economy? The chief reason is transfer pricing, the ability of MNEs to fix prices for arm's-length trade by means of manipulating invoicing. Transfer pricing is one of the most powerful means at the disposal of MNEs to maximize global profits and shift tax liability across boundaries. These are artificial or accounting prices used in intra-firm sales and purchases, such as sales at inflated prices from a parent company to a subsidiary, or sales in the reverse direction at understated prices. As a result of these manipulations, revenues are shifted across national jurisdictions from the country hosting a subsidiary of the MNE to the home country. Consequently, while corporate tax liability in the host country is minimized, or sometimes reduced to virtually nothing, profitability of the parent company in the home country is overstated to artificially drive up share values.

Not all forms of transfer pricing are unjust and undermine social justice concerns, but clearly some are and do. Some of the more dubious forms of transfer pricing are ethically questionable trade practices, as they distort pricing in markets and rob national treasuries of critically needed revenues in both Northern and Southern countries. Even in the richest countries of the North, lack of tax revenues combined with deficit and debt reduction has imperiled much-cherished education and health systems in countries such as Canada and the United Kingdom. As domestic business in these countries becomes more global in scope and takes advantage of such transfer pricing, the tax base may shrink even further. If even the most developed countries are feeling the effect of a diminishing tax base due to transfer pricing, the countries of the South will be even more drastically affected in their attempt to provide basic social services or promote higher labor standards from a tax base which is often without an effective tax enforcement and collection infrastructure.

Compounding this situation is the fact that national regulations governing accountability and transparency in corporate accounting and governance vary enormously in effectiveness. The United States, for example, has extensive internal audit regulations under the Foreign Corrupt Practices Act of 1977, discussed in Chapter 3, in part to ensure that the US multinationals keep their books, records, and accounts "in conformity with generally accepted accounting principles."[46] In the South, however, in many instances no such auditing regulations exist. As a result, corruption, illegal forms of transfer pricing, and other unfair trade practices are widespread. Some of these practices involve the complicity of MNEs from the developed world, as discussed in Chapter 3. Indeed, thanks to legal loopholes, poor administrative capacity, but above all collusion between domestic elites and foreign corporate interests, there is systemic rent-seeking and gate-keeping behavior. One of the most crucial impacts of such unjust corporate practices by many MNEs is to rob the ability of national treasuries individually, and the international community collectively, to finance the development of a fair global labor market.

Rent-seeking by domestic elites

Rent-seeking generates personal monetary gain for ruling elites in charge of developmental policies in host countries. In Suharto's Indonesia, foreign investment was controlled by gate-keepers in the public service who sold investment and manufacturing licenses to willing foreign investors.[47] These investors bribed Indonesian officials in order to get fiscal concessions, such as tax exemptions and duty-free imports of machinery, free land, and above all cheap labor without any safeguards under labor laws and social security legislation. Theoretically, these payments were financed from the profits and rents illustrated as ABC in Fig 4.2 on p.159.

In this type of institutionalized corruption, the ruling elites and foreign investors win, while workers lose. Clearly these ruling elites have a personal stake in the cheap labor policies that exploit and subordinate workers. Over and above these corrupt practices, there are serious infractions of human dignity flowing from such unfair labor policies. These implications give rise to arguments such as "social dumping" in international trade. When host countries deliberately practice social dumping, they may not only be violating WTO rules as discussed in Chapter 2, they also short-change their own citizens. For both reasons, they must be held accountable under rules of global governance.

Inferior labor standards as social dumping

From the point of view of the exporting developing countries, avoidance of higher labor standards may appear to create short-term cost advantages. The basis of this cost advantage is labor abundance in the labor market. The theory behind this competitive edge is illustrated in Figure 4.1 earlier in this chapter. Lower wages and inferior working conditions in the South may act as a magnet for some foreign investors who simply do not care for the welfare or justice of workers who have been abandoned by self-seeking domestic elites.

To this extent, some interest groups in Northern (rich) countries may be prompted to promote upward harmonization in the global labor market for domestic protectionism against import-competing sectors, such as the labor-intensive garment and textile industries. When such motives are hidden behind Northern agendas for upward harmonization, clearly it would add weight to Southern fears of Northern protectionism, or new forms of cultural neo-colonialism.

Upward harmonization is good economics for humankind; paying workers their due enhances economic welfare. Higher labor standards should not impoverish, but generate demonstrable gains and benefits for rich and poor countries, for workers everywhere, not just workers or consumers in the North. Accordingly, those sincere groups in Northern countries without any protectionist agendas must remove skepticism in the South that upward harmonization is simply an extension of protectionist trade policy in the North to exploit Southern resources and workers. MNEs in particular, as argued in Chapter 6, must behave as good global corporate citizens and assume responsibility for promoting social justice in the marketplace.

At the same time, we support the argument that in certain situations the absence of higher labor standards can amount to social dumping. It is unacceptable for emerging countries to seek comparative advantage or international competitiveness by exploiting their workers. As we have discussed in Chapter 2, in many cases such exploitation is in violation of their own laws which could amount to an illegal subsidy under world trade rules.

Managing the global labor market

This topic opens the delicate question of inter-agency cooperation in the international arena where institutional turf battles and jealousies abound. The challenge of inter-agency cooperation at this point in time is further complicated by the fact that the trade–labor standards debate has been articulated and conducted within the WTO more as a North–South confrontation.[48] However, a significant potential opening exists for inter-agency cooperation because the G77 members of the South have expressed solidarity with the ILO while opposing the WTO. A good part of the underlying reason for this is that the G77 countries view the WTO as a Western club, even though their numbers in the WTO are increasingly becoming a way to bargain for their interests, as the Doha trade talks illustrated, as discussed in Chapter 2.

At the present time, the WTO, the ILO, and the international financial institutions (IFIs) function quite independently of each other, and all suffer from a fundamental democratic deficit as discussed in Chapter 2. Yet the policies, programs, rules and regulations they develop affect the economic and social lives of workers everywhere. There are two specific problems of global governance here. First, the democratic deficit implies lack of accountability of the international bureaucracies in the WTO, the ILO, and the IFIs, whose actions may often supersede or restrict the authority of elected governments. Second, so long as these international agencies are themselves undemocratic, they lack legitimacy in the eyes of the global family of workers and citizens. In Chapter 2 we have discussed how the democratic deficit could be narrowed in the WTO through the establishment of a Standing Parliamentary Assembly. Meanwhile, in the absence of such reforms, an important manifestation of these structural deficiencies in the existing international agencies is the lack of inter-agency cooperation.

Upward harmonization through higher labor standards in the global labor market is an important component of global governance. The challenge of global governance is more than strictly economic; it requires major reform of several international agencies and regional bodies currently involved in the field. After fifty years, the World Bank and the International Monetary Fund (IMF) need to be reinvented,[49] while the missions and mandates of the WTO and the ILO must be updated and coordinated, as argued in Chapter 2. We have discussed the vital subject of inter-agency cooperation elsewhere (in particular Chapter 2), and we shall further examine the failure of the World Bank and the International Monetary Fund in Chapter 5.

We believe a first step toward implementation of upward harmonization in the global labor market would be an adequate "incentive" package (like a World Development Fund discussed in the next chapter) to bring developing countries to the table and reach a global agreement on trade-standards linkage. Making such an agreement work, in turn, requires cooperation among such international agencies as the WTO, the ILO, and the IFIs to implement and manage the agreed "core" labor standards as "best practice," or ideal models, for domestic or regional labor laws. These models can be adopted regionally or as domestic laws by individual countries. An integral step in this direction would be minimum labor standards typically as part of HRD investments in the South, financed from a World Development Fund. Evolution of this prospect, however, will critically depend on how far powerful countries in the North might be willing to rise above national interest and endorse such a reform proposal. Of equal significance in this regard is the position of the private sector, especially the MNEs who must inevitably be called upon to pay a small part of their global profits to make a World Development Fund a reality. We examine this subject in Chapter 5.

5 The failure of the international financial system and financing global justice

The World Development Fund: a global Marshall Plan

This chapter builds on the arguments presented in Chapters 2 and 4 for both the international community and institutions of global governance to develop a global equivalent of the Marshall Plan. The realization and implementation of such a plan is necessary if the benefits of globalization are to be sustainable. For many, globalization creates an insecure world due to a variety of risks. These risks are embedded in the global public bads (such as international terrorism, poverty, injustice, and exploitation), as well as global public goods (such as international development, global justice, and human rights), all of which require global governance.[1] We have argued in Chapter 1 that the global good of human rights comes with a preventative cost for the institutions of global governance that is immensely less than the reactive costs involved in dealing with humanitarian disasters once they materialize. We have also argued in Chapter 1 that the development of a Global Security Fund by the international community would lessen reactive costs and, moreover, is sound global risk management. Risks in the globalized world can be classified to include such things as natural disasters, disease pandemics, humanitarian catastrophes, economic and financial crises, terrorism, and environmental disasters.[2]

We have discussed in Chapters 2 and 4 how workers in the poorest parts of the world, whose livelihoods depend increasingly on trade and foreign markets, face an uncertain future as business cycles fluctuate and currency and commodity markets rise and fall. The marginalized poor live daily a life of lost dignity and identity. The young, too, often feel alienated as new technology fails to provide adequate career opportunities. The worst form of economic insecurity in the integrating world today is the joblessness, under-employment, and poverty faced by 1.2 billion persons who live on less than one US dollar a day, according to the latest World Bank estimates.[3] The great majority of these people are working poor without any social protection, struggling to make a living either in agricultural endeavors that produce less than subsistence incomes or in the industrial sector sweat-shops or in informal sector activity. Job insecurity is greatest for female-headed households and working children, two of the most vulnerable groups in the world today, as we shall document in the pages below.

Employment creation with living wage compensation is the efficient and equitable path to overcome global insecurity and poverty, as we have discussed in Chapter 4. A productive job with a living wage is more than rewarding; it gives self-dignity while also affording an individual the opportunity to become more integrated into society. This chapter proposes the creation of a World Development Fund (WDF). Such a fund could be created by exacting a small levy on international business, to raise funds for a long-range war on world poverty and injustice. The aim of this long-range international development war is the pursuit of social justice in the global labor market to provide productive and decent jobs and to secure living wage employment income for all workers everywhere. This is our concept of upward harmonization, which can be achieved through international investment in human resource development and higher labor standards. It will take nothing less than a global Marshall Plan to accomplish this next challenge for human progress.

This chapter is organized in five sections. The first section provides a brief historical account of the failure of the international financial institutions, principally the World Bank (WB) and the International Monetary Fund (IMF), to provide the financial leadership for building an efficient and equitable development in the Third World. The WB and the IMF are now in crisis. While they could be reformed, as discussed in this chapter, it is unlikely that these agencies will become principal sources of development finance. New sources must be found and tapped.

The second section examines the changing responsibilities of multinational corporations in the international financial system. With the WB–IMF system in crisis, it is now essential to launch a fresh approach at promoting a global economic order based on social justice. The private sector must assume a leading role in generating revenues to finance upward harmonization in the global marketplace.

The third section extends the argument of Chapter 2 concerning the growth of multinational enterprises (MNEs). In the post-war period, despite unprecedented expansion, many parts of the international business community have ignored labor standards in developing countries. This private sector failure, unfortunately, must now give way to new – and bold – ways of corporate social and fiscal responsibility to shape a better global order. The foundation of this order must be human resource development (HRD), a process of investing in people. Accordingly, the fourth section puts forward an HRD investment model, centered on human capital formation, which demonstrates the dynamic efficiency gains of upward harmonization. These efficiency implications are analyzed in the context of an integrating world economy to highlight the linkage between the global labor market and international trade. Finally, in the fifth section, the key elements of a WDF are elaborated for financing upward harmonization in the global labor market.

The record of the World Bank and the IMF in global development and avoiding financial crises: justice demands reforms

The WB and the IMF are in serious crisis. After fifty years of struggling to fulfill the hopes and vision of their architects to contribute financial resources toward building a world free of hunger and poverty, these institutions of global governance have failed to live up to their promise. These Bretton Woods institutions, initially designed to be integrated into other multilateral agencies as discussed in Chapter 1, are bogged down in inefficiency and face irrelevance. The Bank cannot provide the quality and quantity of development finance required to defeat poverty and underdevelopment in the Third World. The Fund is unable to prevent successive rounds of financial crises and instability in currency markets. Both suffer from moral hazard problems deep-rooted in their structure and management style. The Argentinian crises of 2001–2 show yet again that the IMF is unable to prevent such financial crises, which destroy the living standards and the social and economic rights of millions of people in the developing world.

What went wrong? Why and how did the high hopes of fifty years ago at Bretton Woods vanish? A brief historical overview may be in order.

For the first twenty years, the Fund operated reasonably well, providing global financial stability on the basis of a gold exchange standard and a fixed rate of exchange, known as the par system. The Vietnam War provided the first shock to the system: the United States flooded the world economy with US dollars, but when Europe, particularly the French, objected to the "dollar glut," President Richard Nixon in 1970 suddenly ended the gold convertibility, causing a global inflation. Then the OPEC embargo hit the world economy and resulted in the quadrupling of oil prices. In turn, this created an excess supply of petro-dollars and reckless lending in the world financial markets.[4]

The IMF system never recovered from these shocks. This was in large measure because its original mandate and its heavily US-dominated quota and voting system were never updated or adjusted to keep pace with fundamental structural changes in the global economic landscape. Instead, it plodded along, muddling its way through successive policy shifts imposed on helpless and corrupt Third World regimes. Gradually, the IMF and WB appeared to converge, becoming partners in the goal of development, but subject to a worsening moral hazard problem. The moral hazard problem was imbedded in the nature of WB–IMF lending, and it resulted in several biases and market distortions. Indeed, the moral hazard problem was a two-headed cancer, with an internal and external dimension. Internally, WB–IMF lending created economic mismanagement, sheltering political corruption at home, such as "crony capitalism,"[5] and worsening income distribution between privileged rent-seekers at the top and vulnerable groups. Externally, this lending distorted the global banking system, as bailouts merely seemed to benefit Western banks and speculators involved in bank runs.[6] The Fund stopped acting as the lender of last resort to manage short-term balance of payment deficits; it became a crisis lender with increasing frequency, an alternative to private finance. Yet this lending function seemed to be done in a discriminatory manner, favoring US allies and, some would argue, punishing its enemies.

After 1980, the IMF shifted to a highly deflationary stabilization program, complementing the Bank's structural adjustment lending that had now replaced its conventional project lending. In return for WB–IMF bailouts, Third World governments, though often corrupt and barely accountable to their population, were obliged to accept strict conditionalities and submit to close supervision from a Washington that did not shoulder any political accountability. In the end, stabilization programs failed to promote domestic stability, fiscal responsibility, and external equilibrium because there was little or no effort to design and supervise efficient monetary policy. In other words, the WB–IMF bailouts failed on just about all grounds: they did not succeed in overcoming poverty and underdevelopment in the developing countries where they were implemented, and, more than likely, they ended up further distorting markets already reeling under severe problems of corruption and domestic mismanagement. In the end, the programs imposed by the WB–IMF failed to stem, and indeed in some cases exacerbated, the currency crises in Mexico (1994–5), Asia (1997–8), Russia (1998), Brazil (1999), Turkey and Argentina (2001–2), often spilling into social conflict. There is no suggestion that these financial crises were always and entirely due to faulty advice or intervention by the WB–IMF. Moral hazard, corruption, and inefficiency had both domestic and external determinants, with a large element of what George Soros, the speculator par excellence, has called "reflexivity."[7]

Leading experts such as Steven Radelet and Jeffrey Sachs[8] have suggested the following main suspects, especially in the context of the 1997 Asian financial crisis, as the source of financial crises that can sweep countries, regions, and potentially the entire global financial system:

1   weakness within economies, especially poor financial, industrial, and exchange rate policies;
2   over-investment in dubious activities resulting from the moral hazard of implicit guarantees, corruption, and anticipated bailouts;
3   financial panic; more precisely, what began as moderate capital withdrawals gathered momentum with great speed and evolved into a full-fledged panic, because of weakness in the structure of capital markets and early mismanagement of the crisis;
4   exchange rate devaluations (e.g. Thailand in mid-1997 and, later in the same year, Korea) that plunged the economy into crisis;
5   the ineptitude of the IMF response, especially in Indonesia, which may have actually exacerbated the financial crisis in that country.

Other experts, such as Joseph Daniels, give the following additional factors:[9]

6   transmission of shocks and contagion due to integrated financial markets as shown by both the US stock market crash of the 1980s and, perhaps, the

one we are now in. Currency crises can easily give rise to regional contagion as the Asian financial crisis has shown;

7   increased risk from complex financial instruments, as illustrated by the 1995 Barings Bank derivatives fiasco and the Long-Term Capital hedge fund bail-out;

8   regulatory arbitrage, where financial institutions set up foreign offices to avoid domestic regulation and where the mega-banks increasingly are able to avoid or even undermine the attempts of sovereign governments to regu-late and skirt around the supervision of national banking regulators.

Radelet and Sachs[10] argue that, while most of these factors contribute to finan-cial crises, the main culprits behind the Asian financial crises were creditor panic and pegged exchange rates *preceding* devaluations. There is a link between the two: when pegged rates become overvalued, countries are forced to deplete foreign exchange reserves to defend the peg. Ultimately such defense proves useless and a forced devaluation occurs. The same experts claim that the combi-nation of depleted reserves plus the broken peg then makes the economy vulnerable to creditor panic. However the greatest culprit, in the view of Radelet and Sachs,[11] seems to be creditor panic in situations where there is a high level of short-term foreign liabilities relative to short-term foreign assets, the so-called impact of "hot money." The short-term creditor knows that it must flee the country before other similar creditors do, in the event of a sudden and massive withdrawal of foreign capital, since there will not be enough liquid assets to pay off all creditors on short notice.

Radelet and Sachs give some hard evidence that this was the primary cause of the Asian financial crisis. They recommend the following key reform to the inter-national financial architecture to deal with this main culprit of the Asian financial crisis, for economies that are increasingly relying more on private funds than on IMF bailouts:[12]

First, they recommend processes drawn from domestic bankruptcy proceed-ings in industrialized countries and international workout mechanisms for developing country sovereign debt. These could include:

1   Like the Chapter 11 Bankruptcy process in the US and sovereign debt workout mechanisms under the Paris and London Club committees, a new international mechanism should be evolved to impose a generalized stand-still on the failing economies' debt-servicing obligations, while bringing debtors and creditors, both private and public, for collective rollovers and debt renegotiation, with public sector funds also stabilizing the banking system and preventing bank failures that could threaten the entire payments system. Radelet and Sachs point to the successful use of this process by Korea. Of necessity, such a generalized system of debt standstill has to be coordinated at the international level.[13]

2   If the debtors are a large number of private firms, as was the case in Indonesia, the paucity of accurate information on the firms, especially if

they are private and plagued with corruption and cronyism, will work with the weakness of the regulatory and judicial system to complicate any such generalized standstill. Reforms of corporate governance, accounting regulatory, and judicial systems have to be dealt with on a national level, before international cooperation can become effective.[14]

3   Effective mechanisms must be put in place to stop international financial panics in emerging markets. Industrialized countries have developed domestic mechanisms to prevent such panics in domestic economies, such as lender of last resort, effective banking supervision and regulation, deposit insurance, and bankruptcy laws. There is, according to Radelet and Sachs, a need for such institutions at the international level to provide a more solid foundation for the vulnerable capital markets. They claim that the IMF is not suited to be this lender of last resort in its present structure. They and others suggest that the IMF open a new facility that would be available only to countries that fulfill strict requirements, just as central banks allow banks to operate only if they meet certain standards, such as an effective regulatory and supervisory system for the banking sector. Outside of crisis times, eligibility for such a facility could lower a country's risk premium in international capital markets, creating incentives for vulnerable economies to set up effective national regulatory and supervisory institutions, especially in the banking sector. If a crisis were to occur, interim financing could be obtained from the IMF without the controversial conditionalities, as these would probably already be met. Such a facility should not be used to prop up an overvalued currency, and private lenders should be bailed in rather than bailed out in such a process. Radelet and Sachs argue that such a facility would act proactively to prevent financial crises, rather than react to them ineffectually.[15]

4   National governments should consider restrictions of short-term capital inflows without reducing the total capital inflows. Radelet and Sachs seem to approve of Chile's taxation of short-term capital inflows (by requiring a partial deposit of the foreign investment in a non-interest-earning account for one year). They suggest that Chile's ability to avoid financial crisis in the wake of the panics in Mexico, Argentina, and Asia can be attributed to these restrictions as well as to Chile's overall small stock of foreign short-term debt.[16]

The political/institutional challenges to reform of the international financial architecture

While the analysis and suggestions by Radelet and Sachs are without doubt in the right direction, they may underestimate the following important political and institutional challenges posed to their suggested reforms:

1   Yilmaz Akyuz, an expert with the United Nations Conference on Trade and Development (UNCTAD) offering a Southern perspective, has suggested

that "political constraints and conflict of interest, rather than conceptual and technical problems appear to be the main reason why"[17] there are real difficulties in reforming the international financial architecture along the lines suggested by Radelet, Sachs, and others. These reforms have to be reconciled with national sovereignty, the diversity of needs of different economies, and conflicts of interest. Akyuz suggests these are the main barriers to the establishment of international financial safety systems involving global regulation and supervision.

2   The political challenges are not only between developing and industrialized countries, but also within the G8, in large part because of the position of the United States on many of the suggested reforms. According to experts like Akyuz, such opposition to a rules-based global financial system is due to the fact that the present case-by-case approach gives considerable discretionary power to the IMF and the World Bank. In large part this discretionary power is controlled by the United States.[18]

3   Even in a rules-based system analogous to the WTO, developing countries would still feel that there is an imbalance of power between international debtor and creditor nations. This is one reason why Akyuz and others tend to place national sovereignty and policy autonomy concerns over the critical need to reform the international financial system. Likewise, they have often resisted attempts to reduce capital inflows, even of hot money, or raising their costs during the up side of the financial cycle in order to reduce the potential for financial instability and crises.[19]

4   Emerging markets have been reluctant to accept collective action clauses until creditor nations also follow suit.[20] Again, this reluctance stems from a desire to be seen as equals in the community of nations.

5   Likewise, Akyuz argues that there is resistance to differentiation among sovereign risks by international banks under the Basel capital requirements. As regards the role of the IMF in this area, developing countries are loath to have the confidential information provided to the IMF used to turn it into a credit-rating agency.[21]

Given the above realities, it is not surprising that, by the end of the twentieth century, the WB's leadership was also being severely attacked for its recent friendly response to environmentalism and the NGO movement by developing nations. Initially the Bank resisted these new challenges, but after 1995, under the presidency of James Wolfensohn, the Bank has changed course, and in the process gained the enmity of American neo-Conservative circles. These circles describe the Bank under Wolfensohn as "rudderless and lacking strategic direction," and consequently what was once the "world's premier development institution" has now become "softheaded, less analytical and therefore less relevant."[22] The charge of irrelevance is reflected in the high volume of private sector capital flowing to some parts of the Third World, excluding Africa. These private sector flows dwarf the total amount of aid monies going to the South.

Where is progress possible?

Now, at the start of the new millennium, fundamental reform of the WB–IMF is on the agenda. It may be a good sign that some observers[23] are going to the extreme of advocating the abolition of the Bretton system because the Fund is blamed for the global financial instability as well as for market distortion. Extreme positions do not usually get implemented, but they can force change from the status quo. Typical of the abolitionist position is the view of Osterfeld:

> The World Bank has, on balance, probably retarded rather than promoted development and has supplemented private capital rather than facilitated its flow to the LDCs ... The IMF has not only failed in its efforts to maintain monetary stability, but has pursued a policy that has inflicted needless suffering on some of the poorest peoples of the world ... Neither the Bank nor the Fund were necessary in 1944; neither is needed now. Both have caused more harm than good. They should be abolished.[24]

More moderate reformers include the Meltzer Commission (2000), named after its chairman, the Carnegie Mellon economics professor Allan Meltzer. The Commission, created by the US Congress in 1999 to examine the consequences of the systemic currency fluctuations on the efficacy of the Fund, produced a comprehensive report. In brief, the Meltzer Commission recommended a rather dramatic scaling back of the IMF operations by establishing a clear boundary between the Fund and the Bank. Under the Meltzer reform, the Fund would cease to be a development organization, abolish its poverty facility, and concentrate strictly on banking and early warning by means of the following three main tasks:[25]

- to act as a quasi-lender of last resort to solvent emerging economies by providing them with short-term liquidity;
- to collect and publish financial and economic data from members and disseminate those data in a timely and uniform manner; and
- to provide advice (but not to impose conditions) relating to economic policy as part of Article IV consultations with member countries.

There are several other voices calling for the reform of the Fund. Thus, a group of British NGOs have sponsored a Bretton Woods Project that focuses attention, among other things, on "the lack of democratic governance at the IMF" and recommends a fixed quota or population-weighted system of decision-making in place of the present system, which effectively turns the Executive Board and the International Monetary and Finance Committee into instruments of the United States.[26] To counter some US legislators critical of the Fund for domestic reasons, the US Treasury has made calls for an increased US quota, and has also supported a more efficiency-focused system, including some kind of equity-based expansion that would involve a greater role for private capital. This is a scheme that is also endorsed by the G7 countries.[27]

Other moderate proposals that could be implemented to quicken the pace of global social justice include the following:

Transparency and disclosure

There is general consensus that greater transparency and disclosure of information regarding the activities of domestic and international banking and other financial sector institutions, together with public sector reform and anti-corruption strategies, are critical for emerging markets. Some would argue that the same is needed for the international financial institutions, particularly the IMF. Akyuz suggests that there is some indication that greater transparency and disclosure are already taking place, as is evidenced by the increasing timeliness and quality of information being supplied on vulnerable economies on critical macroeconomic variables and fiscal, monetary, and financial policies.[28] The critical financial and banking sectors, including offshore markets as well as highly leveraged institutions, have a long way to go to meet transparency and disclosure standards able to assist in the establishment of an international financial structure that can deal with financial crises in a more effective fashion.[29] With these laggards, the G8 and the G20 must find both the carrots and the sticks to bring them up to minimal transparency and disclosure standards.

As regards the transparency and disclosure of information at the IMF, there need to be more independent reviews of its operations along the lines of the Inspection Panel of the World Bank.[30]

National implementation of global standards

Experts such as Akyuz argue that there should be much more room to have global standards to combat financial crises implemented by national authorities rather than new global regulatory agencies. A multilateral round of negotiations, such as those under the GATT and subsequently the WTO, should establish such global standards. A reformed IMF could then have the task of developing the appropriate surveillance processes to make sure that such standards are adopted and implemented.[31]

The G7/G8, the G20 and the Financial Stability Forum

These institutions must urgently deal with the need for tightened regulation of highly leveraged institutions such as hedge funds that can trigger financial crises. There is potential for indirect control of such funds through imposing greater transparency requirements on their creditors.[32] Akyuz argues that there needs to be coordinated action both at the national and the international levels in this regard. The bailout of the Long-Term Capital hedge fund has also produced a moral hazard in this area that has to be dealt with at both the national and the international levels.

National governments' actions to impose controls on short-term private capital
inflows must be endorsed by the IMF and the G20 and not opposed

There is little doubt that Radelet and Sachs are right when they pinpoint the
rapid outflow of such hot money as a key factor in the Asian financial crisis.
Controlling such capital inflows through market-based measures such as taxes
or reserve requirements should not be opposed by industrialized countries.
Indeed, commentators such as Akyuz suggest that there is a need for the IMF
to recommend such capital controls, especially for countries where a rapid
build-up of such short-term capital inflows could lead to excessive currency
risk. Such an endorsement would encourage vulnerable economies to impose
the controls without risking market confidence and overall access to capital
markets.[33]

Improving coordination of exchange and interest rates worldwide

Akyuz also argues that the spotlight on improvements in exchange and interest
rate regimes in developing countries should be extended to improvements in
exchange and interest rates between the industrialized countries, in particular
the G3. Financial crises can also be the result of large shifts in exchange and
interest rates in industrialized countries, particularly the G3, as witnessed by
the debt crises of the 1980s and the volatile capital inflows and outflows to
Latin America in more recent years.[34] To give the IMF any role in the surveillance of industrialized countries' macroeconomic policies, particularly those of
the United States, its voting and governance structure would have to be
dramatically changed to give a greater voice to the developing countries. As
discussed, this is highly unlikely at the moment, given the influence of the US
Treasury Department on any changes at the IMF. Perhaps the issue could
better be tackled at the G20 first, to build the momentum for future change at
the IMF.

Redesigning the IMF bailouts

Much has been said and written about the moral hazard for international
lenders that results from traditional IMF bailouts for countries experiencing
payment difficulties linked to their capital accounts. Similarly, much has been
said and written about the policy conditionality accompanying such bailouts,
which can have severe impacts on the citizens of the country, without any form
of participation and consent on their part. It has been suggested by Akyuz,
following the same path as Radelet and Sachs, that pre-qualification could be
one way of avoiding such problems. Countries would have to pre-qualify for
lender of last resort financing, with final eligibility resting on Article IV consultations. There will always be major hurdles in the monitoring and responding
to changing conditions if the pre-qualification approach is adopted.[35]

Getting the Canadian Emergency Standstill Clause over the political hurdles

This Standstill Clause proposed by Canada would be mandated by the IMF members, together with a rules-based system for crisis management directed at both the public and private sectors. The private financial sector (especially in the US) has been opposed to the idea of an involuntary standstill mechanism and collective action clauses that allow debtors to suspend payments. Not surprisingly, the US has also been opposed, preferring the case-by-case approach that gives them discretionary power at the IMF.[36] Again, there is a need for the G20 to take up this challenge and to create the momentum that could precipitate an eventual change of policy by the United States. There may be a need for a global network of civil society groups to lobby for such a change by opposing governments, on the model of the landmines ban and the establishment of the International Criminal Court discussed in Chapter 1.

On 22 April 2002, finance ministers from the G7 countries went some distance toward accepting the proposals for international financial architecture reform pushed by Canada and its then finance minister, Paul Martin. At the semi-annual meeting of the G7 finance ministers, the IMF and the WB, there was an agreement to develop a system to limit the amount of IMF bailouts and develop collective action clauses in emerging market debt that would promote private sector involvement in any bailout negotiations. However, the meeting did not endorse the plan proposed by the IMF to develop the equivalent of an international bankruptcy court under its auspices. The group intended the plan to be ready to be implemented sometime in 2003, after endorsement by the G8 leaders.

Conclusion

While there is clearly room for optimism for slow but steady change in the reform of the international financial architecture, the challenges are quite daunting. Canada and a group of like-minded nations at the G20 must persist in pushing the envelope as far as possible, as suggested above. Such leadership through the G20 could also push for regional action by like-minded governments to prevent financial crises in one country that can spread by contagion to others in the region. Europe, through its Exchange Rate Mechanism (ERM), provides the model. Akyuz, among others, has suggested that regional exchange rate agreements, coordination of macroeconomic policy, regional surveillance and regional cooperation on capital flows, as well as provision of international liquidity, could be an interim step to greater stability, while the larger challenges to establishing a global system are being dealt with by the G20 under Canada's leadership.

Clearly, the Bretton Woods institutions are in crisis and fundamental change is on the way. What is uncertain at this stage is the timing or the exact nature of these changes. One thing can be safely predicted: it is virtually certain that neither the World Bank nor the International Monetary Fund will, or should, stay the course and carry on with business as usual. We believe that in future the private sector, in particular the multinational corporations, should assume a greater burden in Third World development. Indeed, MNEs, not armies, must be in the forefront in this global war on poverty, exploitation, and injustice, factors that are also the root causes of global terrorism. The private sector must take the lead in this fight because MNEs are the leading actors of the private sector in international business.

Multinational enterprises in the global economy

As discussed in Chapter 3, the global private sector witnessed an unprecedented expansion in the post-war period, not just in the industrialized economies but also in the developing world. The multinational enterprise (MNEs), or transnational corporation (TNC), reflecting multiple national identities, has led this private sector expansion. In addition to the think tanks and academics mentioned in Chapter 3, the United Nations Conference on Trade and Development (UNCTAD) is one international organization that has been monitoring this growth, publishing valuable statistical and economic information in its annual *World Investment Report*. According to UNCTAD,[37] in 2000–1 there was a total of 63,312 parent corporations and some 821,818 affiliates. The details are tabulated in Table 5.1. Although, as can be expected, the great majority of parent corporations are in the developed countries (indeed, in what UNCTAD calls the "triad," consisting of the EU, North America, and Japan), it is noteworthy that there are 12,588 parent corporations in the developing countries where most of the affiliates are located.

Direct foreign investment (DFI) has been a principal vehicle of the growth and expansion of MNEs in the post-war period. DFI has transferred new technologies while joint ventures, subsidiaries, and affiliates of MNEs have opened new markets bringing new products and brands to customers. According to the latest information from UNCTAD, summarized in Table 5.2, the volume of DFI worldwide has grown from just US$57 billion in 1982 to about US$1271 billion in 2000 – a twenty-fold increase.

Table 5.1 Number of parent corporations and foreign affiliates by area and economy

Area/economy	Parent corporation based in economy	Foreign affiliates located in economy
Developed economies	49,944	95,485
Developing countries	12,588	489,504
Total	63,312	821,818

Source: UNCTAD, *World Investment Report 2001* (New York and Geneva: UNCTAD, 2001), Annex A, Table AI.2, pp. 239–42

Table 5.2   Direct foreign investment flows and related indicators (1982–2000)

Item	Value at current prices (billions of US$)			Annual growth rate (percent)		
	1982	1990	2000	1991–5	1996–9	2000
DFI inflows	57	202	1,271	40.8	44.9	18.2
Cross-border mergers and acquisitions	–	151	1,144	23.3	50.0	49.3
Employment of foreign affiliates (thousands)	17,454	23,721	45,587	5.3	7.8	12.7
Sales of foreign affiliates	2,465	5,467	15,680	10.5	10.4	18.0

Source: UNCTAD *World Investment Report 2001* (New York and Geneva: UNCTAD, 2001) Table 1.1, p. 10

Significantly, almost all of this inflow was in the form of mergers and acquisitions, reflecting the fact that the favored strategy of direct foreign investment was control of affiliates and subsidiaries. The sales of these foreign affiliates has been considerably higher than the value of DFI inflows, no doubt indicating the large volume of intra-corporate transactions.

Moreover, developed countries were the prime destination of DFI, accounting for more than 75 percent of global inflows. Inflows of DFI to developing countries accounted for 19 percent, down from the peak in 1994 of 41 percent. China was the leading destination, as well as East Asia, reflecting a rebound from the Asian currency crisis of 1997. At the other end, Africa and the forty-nine least developed countries remained "marginal in terms of attracting FDI, with 0.3 per cent of world inflows in 2000."[38]

When we explore the employment creation effects of DFI inflows, Table 5.2 indicates that this contribution has been rather limited, no doubt reflecting the relatively high capital intensity of DFI inflows. As discussed in Chapter 3, high levels of DFI do not always translate into high employment by the MNEs worldwide. Thus, in 2000 total employment of foreign affiliates was only 45,587,000, a little over 1 percent of the global labor force of 2.9 billion.[39] Moreover, this employment began to register significant growth only after 1995. As discussed in Chapter 2, this job creation pales in comparison with the value of sales generated.

In Chapter 2 the main ethical expectations and legal duties of MNEs were discussed with one exception, transfer pricing. We began our discussion of the controversial topic of transfer pricing in Chapter 4. We will further expand on the impact of the ethical and legal challenges in this area in this chapter. Minimizing job creation, which we discussed in Chapter 3, and the more dubious forms of transfer pricing do not make MNEs good corporate citizens in the eyes of host country populations and authorities. Many MNEs have minimized job creation as a result of inappropriate technology transfer to the host countries. Often they paid little or no tax, as a result of transfer pricing that allowed these firms to maximize global profits. These actions are perceived by many to add up to exploitation of the host countries and their citizens. In home countries, many of the actions of MNEs are subject to close surveillance and audit to ensure that they do not constitute illegal, unfair, or anti-competitive behavior that violates or undermines competition and anti-corruption laws, regulations, and policies. But, as we have discussed in Chapter 3, in many parts of the developing world, legal and administrative institutions are inadequate, and MNEs are often not closely monitored.

All in all, it can be stated that, in the post-war period, the activities of large parts of the global private sector in the international economy did not constitute an engine of equitable global development, especially in so far as the developing world is concerned. In the new global marketplace, however, as we have discussed in Chapter 3, a new, more ethical and socially responsible corporate culture is required as a fundamental aspect of the corporate integrity risk environment. We have also seen in Chapter 3 that flagrant unethical or corrupt conduct will inevitably lead to the imposition of domestic and international legal duties. If MNEs wish to avoid a progressively heavier legal and regulatory burden, they must do more to contribute toward global equity and social justice, in particular, by investing in social capital formation in host countries. After all, they are the principal stakeholders *and beneficiaries* of a healthy and sustainable global economy.

The next round of value creation in the knowledge-based global economy (KBE)

As the world moves toward a KBE, we believe the next round of value added for MNEs will be in the densely populated, but under-serviced, developing countries of the world. These countries, especially India and China, have witnessed rising literacy levels as well as growth of income per capita. However, they are extremely deficient in terms of access to new information. Thus, as of 1999, over 60 percent (or 64 million) of all Internet users worldwide resided in North America, which accounts for a mere 5 percent of the world population.

In the twenty-first century, the digital divide between the rich and poor countries will diminish in proportion to income growth and literacy achievements in the latter. The rate at which these positive trends can be accomplished can be significantly influenced by responsible action on the part of MNEs. Table 5.3 summarizes some interesting statistics from the United Nations. What can be observed from the data presented in Table 5.3 is that three of the world's most populated countries, China, India, and Indonesia, located in or near the dynamic Asia-Pacific region, are severely deficient in terms of access to new information which limits their capacity to participate in the KBE. To take one

Table 5.3   Access to global information

Per 1,000 people 1996–8	Main telephone lines	Cellular phone subscribers	TV sets	Personal computers
China	70	19	272	9
India	0.4	2	115	3
Indonesia	27	5	136	6
High-income countries	142	54	253	315

Source: UNDP, *Human Development Report 2000* (New York: United Nations, 2000), Table 121, pp. 198–200

extreme example, the disparity in main telephone lines (per 1,000 people) between India (which in several respects is a leader in information technology in the developing world) and high-income countries is over 1,000 in 1996–8. The ratio is much better in terms of TV sets and in the case of cellular phone subscriptions, while personal computers fall somewhere in between.

Clearly, improvements in access to new information technology, as with other market goods and services, are a function of purchasing power, which in turn depends on employment income. Accordingly, to the extent that international business can work as an instrument of job and income creation in countries like China, India, and Indonesia (as well as elsewhere), there will be value creation, and a rising share of increasing purchasing power will be returned to the investing companies themselves.

The evidence presented in Table 5.3 relates to only one sector, the new information technology. Similarly, in the twenty-first century investment opportunities in other sectors will shift globally from North America and Europe to regions in the South. There is huge untapped potential for value creation in India, for example, where, unlike China, highway and expressway development is lagging. Likewise, in Indonesia it can be expected that the center of economic development will shift away from over-populated Java to outer islands, resulting in huge investment opportunities for infra-structural projects in such sectors as communications, transport, construction, and human services.

Global corporations can cash in on these investment and value-creation opportunities in proportion to the extent to which they become better global citizens than they have been in the past. Of course, international business is a risky business, subject to political and conflict impact risks (due to sudden regime changes caused by civil war, social unrest, etc.), as well as economic risks (due to unexpected market conditions). To some extent, these risks can be measured and insured against, and, in extreme cases of loss, potential compensation may be available against confiscation or expropriation. There is a large literature on risk assessment that deals with mitigating these particular business risks.[40] However, we do not believe the traditional political risk assessment methods are the most adequate approaches for international business in the current integrating world economy. Rather, in keeping with our discussion and conclusion in Chapter 3, we believe future corporate social responsibility in the new marketplace will be based increasingly on *social capital formation* to minimize business risks. *Social capital*[41] develops relationships and trust with stakeholders in a mutually enriching, bottom-up approach. In financial terms, social capital requires replacing traditional cash-flow analysis with social cost–benefit analysis[42] in a manner that produces win–win outcomes while optimizing political and risk management.

This new corporate responsibility based on social capital would imply forging strategic relationships in host countries based on trust and social networking with stakeholders, not just close business partners as in joint ventures. Foreign investors must become active partners in civil society in host countries. In more practical terms, this means that DFI should not be judged narrowly on a strict cash-flow, bottom-line basis. Thus, to give one example, technologies transferred to developing and emerging countries should not be "old" and obsolete, but modern, top-of-the-line technologies that are also employment and environmentally friendly. DFI should contribute to sustainable development by promoting local employment and income creation while also protecting the environment.

The new corporate social responsibility: paying for upward harmonization

In the integrating world economy, MNEs must assume a new broader social responsibility in the global war on poverty. Indeed, in keeping with our conclusion in Chapter 3, as the greatest beneficiaries of international business and "knowledge-based economy,"[43] international corporations that opt for doing business according to "best practices" will be the biggest winners from upward harmonization. One has merely to recall Henry Ford's experiments around a hundred years ago at the outset of the new technology of the automobile age. Likewise, upward harmonization in the global labor market is efficient because it is capable of generating productivity gains as predicted by the classical as well as the new growth theories. These productivity gains accrue partly to the workers (as higher wages) and partly to employers or companies (as higher profit), in particular to international corporations doing business in the world economy.

We believe a new age of global corporate social responsibility is beginning. We shall now explore the key dimensions of this new responsibility in the following order. First, we shall argue in favor of a "development levy" on MNE sales to promote global justice through upward harmonization in the workplace. Second, we shall construct a human capital model in order to illustrate the "win–win" dynamic benefits of the new global corporate responsibility, for MNEs as well as workers of the world. Third, to allay any skepticism that these dynamic benefits are illusionary, we demonstrate them from the actual experience of the Asian Tigers.

A development levy for global workers

What is the best way MNEs can contribute toward upward harmonization in the global labor market? By contributing funds for the educational upgrading and skill training of global workers. This can be either voluntarily, in the form of pledges and contributions, or as international taxation. The latter is clearly more ambitious and we shall argue for a particular method of international taxation in the last section of this chapter, where a World Development Fund is proposed.

The idea of voluntary contributions from the MNEs for the benefit of global workers is the least ambitious proposal. It can be illustrated with the aid of a General Training Facility (GTF), modeled on the Global Environmental Facility (GEF) created under the Montreal Protocol[44] for financing environmental projects in developing countries. Funds for the GEF are raised from voluntary contributions from rich countries to encourage compliance of developing countries with emission standards under the Montreal Protocol.[45] Likewise, a General Training Facility may be set up on a purely voluntary basis by willing MNEs, to raise funds to upgrade and train workers in developing countries. Contributions would be designated as a levy because they are viewed as regular, say annual, pledges and contributions. As the levy would be voluntary, there would be no need to specify any conditions or terms relating to its payment; but clearly companies making these pledges will have an important say in the manner in which these funds will be utilized and managed. Perhaps the UNDP itself can take the initiative to launch this GTF idea, given the leadership of the United Nations secretary-general, Kofi Annan, in the establishment of the Global Compact which focuses on human rights, labor standards, and the environment, as discussed in Chapter 3.

There is, however, a major problem with the voluntary levy for the GTF: the free-rider problem. Because of its voluntary nature, some MNEs may decline to pledge any contributions. Yet these same companies will be able to recruit workers upgraded and trained under the GTF. If this free-rider problem is allowed to prevail, it is possible that, in the long run, free-rider MNEs will realize higher profits relative to the paying MNEs. Accordingly, the voluntary levy system cannot be sustainable in the long run; it must be replaced by a universal taxation on all MNEs so that all carry their fair share of the burden.

Some may claim that the idea of an international taxation on MNEs may be too premature. The idea of international taxation is not new, having been discussed by historians and economists for quite some time.[46] Vito Tanzi of the IMF has recommended the creation of a "world tax organization,"[47] a sort of tax coordination body, as a first step in this direction. He argues that such an organization could collect cross-country tax statistics and provide technical assistance in tax policy and administration, survey tax policy developments and arbitrate tax disputes amongst countries.

The strong implication is, however, that the world may simply be too far removed from an international tax system, no matter how desirable it may be from the perspective of global governance. In particular, rich countries may resist any attempt to undermine or weaken their own sovereignty. Therefore, a levy on MNEs may be more acceptable in the meantime, especially if its collection is done in cooperation with home countries (i.e. where MNE headquarters are located). Thus, once it is agreed multilaterally to set up a GTF, home countries may simply collect the funds from the MNE levy, on terms and rates previously agreed, and then transfer these funds to a central agency administering the Facility, similar to the GEF.

However, the GTF idea is subject to a further significant weakness, already apparent in the GEF. It would have a narrow focus, dealing only with one component (i.e. worker upgrading and training) of upward harmonization. Creating other agencies to handle issues such as protection of women or under-age workers would fragment management of the global labor market. Clearly, there are economies of scale in having an integrated, unified management of the global labor market. That is why we tend to favor a WDF, a more comprehensive system of funding upward harmonization than a GTF. But it is readily conceded that progress comes usually in small steps; accordingly, for practical reasons, a GTF may be viewed as a first experiment, similar to the GEF.

Modeling the productivity–HRD relationship: the case of under-age child workers

In economic modeling of labor standards–trade linkage, labor productivity is the key variable on which to focus. Higher worker productivity enables a win–win outcome: the worker can earn a higher wage, while the firm can realize a higher profit. In the illustration below we focus on raising the productivity of child workers through schooling and training to provide them with literacy and skills for higher-paying employment following graduation. Child workers fall into several categories, such as "street children" or under-age workers obliged to help a poor family. In all cases, these children can be helped, with financial support from the WDF, to escape poverty through schooling and training. Attending school to gain productive skills enables these children to earn higher-paying employment following graduation.

A human capital model of child workers

We now utilize the productivity relationship to construct a formal model based on the human capital theory, originally formulated by Schultz.[48] Subsequently, evidence from numerous countries around the world has confirmed the validity of the human capital theory.[49] The model is illustrated in Figure 5.1, where the horizontal axis measures time (t) measured by age, and the vertical axis measures earnings (e) or income (y).

We begin by assuming that there is a cohort of under-age children workers who start work at $t = 1$ and through their lifetime realize earnings (either in cash or kind or a combination) as denoted by the lifetime earnings profile $y0$. These under-age child workers may work in sweat-shops or in bondage or some other exploitative situation. What is analytically significant is that they receive little or

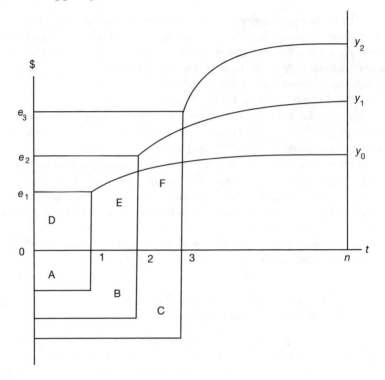

Figure 5.1   Upgrading under-age child workers

no schooling, and therefore any wage gains they realize are strictly a return on job experience, denoted by rectangle A.

Now, suppose that this cohort of under-age child workers is induced (most appropriately under a compensation scheme similar to the Bangladesh model, see below) to be released from work and placed in a school or training center; they will acquire human capital in proportion to skill acquisition. Figure 5.1 exhibits two options: a shorter and a longer release time. Under the first one, a child worker receives schooling from $t1$ to $t2$ and then starts employment, with initial earnings of $e1$ progressing over time along $y1$. The second option allows the child worker to remain at school longer, i.e. until $t3$, in which case higher initial earnings, $e3$, are realized progressing along $y2$.

Schooling is an investment activity, and the costs of the two options are denoted as direct tuition costs by rectangles B and C, along with foregone earnings D, E, and F. These investment costs generate the well-known returns to education in the form of additional lifetime earnings. These earnings are captured, and discounted to present value, as the sum of the difference of alternative life-earning profiles, $y1$ and $y2$, relative to $y0$, the control group. In the normal set of circumstances these returns to investment in schooling for under-age workers will be positive – indeed, significantly so, because the productivity of the children should rise matching their skill acquisition, allowing these child workers to escape poverty. For every child thus enabled to escape poverty, there will be a new family placed on the path of sustainable development.

Similarly, labor market efficiency can be enhanced through policies that provide timely labor market information to job-seekers about job vacancies and employment opportunities, wages and working conditions. As well, government policies can remove institutional and legal impediments such as birth registration and other similar entry barriers into certain occupations, which result in discrimination in the labor market rather than promoting market efficiency. Of critical importance is the right of workers to organize themselves in free unions and be granted legal rights for collective bargaining. These worker rights are enshrined under the ILO Declaration on the Fundamental Principles and Rights at Work discussed in Chapter 2. Such rights are absolutely fundamental in defense of all other worker rights in the job market.

The workers' right to freedom of association would also improve labor market efficiency, empowering workers through direct participation in wage determination by giving them a say in collective bargaining with management. This participation, however, needs to be accompanied with greater workers' education about the nature of their participation in wage determination and productivity sharing. The actual experience of Singapore with wage councils during the transition from labor market slack to full employment provides a useful case study to explore the mechanics of this experience.[50]

Additionally, women workers may be subject to various forms of legal discrimination, and child workers may be coerced into under-age employment. These are forms of labor market discrimination that undermine its efficiency. They represent "labor market failures" and can be corrected by progressive policy reforms – such as legal, institutional, and capacity development. However, these reforms for upward harmonization require funding, because no matter how willing a developing country may be to implement them, typically the required resources will not be adequately available. The WDF, therefore, can be the essential incentive.

To the extent that investments in upward harmonization are successful, higher productivity would be realized in line with the standard human resource development–human capacity (HRD–HC) strategies. Specifically, investment in HRD–HC can generate dynamic benefits of increased productivity, potentially offsetting any negative effects of labor standards on production costs.

How these dynamic HRD–HC benefits can result from higher labor standards can be demonstrated in Fig 5.1, most clearly illustrated with reference to under-age child employment (although similar analysis would apply in the case of all core international labor standards). Adoption of ILO Convention 138 (now updated in Convention 178) would require transferring child workers from sweat-shops to school, thereby raising their productivity and lifetime earnings. Gender equality as provided under ILO Conventions 100 and 111 would create higher lifetime productivity and earnings for women, assuming that these women were provided with greater access to education and training, and subsequently with equal employment opportunity.

Perhaps the clearest case of the potential gains of human capital formation, but at the same time undoubtedly the most stubborn form of abuse, is the case of slavery and forced labor practices. These are prohibited under ILO Conventions 29 and 105 as well as under the ILO Declaration on the Fundamental Principles and Rights at Work. But these prohibitions are considerably violated in several countries, with most extensive violations occurring in Myanmar, India, and China.[51] We believe these inhuman practices could be attacked, if the developing countries involved are both diplomatically and economically pressured and are also provided with financial incentives to phase out the offending practices, replacing them with the more humane type of human resource development programs.

The experience of East Asian NICs with HRD

That labor productivity can be significantly raised and income equality can be enhanced, through substantial investments in human resource development (HRD) as well as through schooling and training, has been demonstrated in the case of the Tigers in the "Asian Miracle."[52] These countries, following the lead of Japan,[53] harmonized education with the labor market through curriculum design and other made-at-home reforms to fit national manpower requirements for rapid economic development. They invested heavily in middle-level, practical, skill-oriented, technical/vocational education, achieving in a relatively short time frame equity-with-growth[54] (GwE), although systemic rent-seeking and gate-keeping have undermined this success, ultimately contributing to the currency collapse of 1997–8.

The GwE model was state-led economic development based on shared growth. It rejected the Western classical growth theory popularized by such noted economists as Kaldor and Kuznets, who argued that inequality in income distribution was good for higher growth rates in the early stages of development. The Asian Tigers, instead, chose a development strategy that deliberately combined wealth sharing with early growth. This wealth sharing was not only good economics: it was good politics, as it created political legitimacy in such fragile states as South Korea, Taiwan, and Singapore. The point has been well put by Campos and Root:

> Wealth sharing insured broad social support, thereby reducing the threat that the regime would fall to destructive rent seeking or insurgency. It encouraged the belief that the government was acting on behalf of citizen interests, so that unpopular decisions could be made more easily acceptable.[55]

The key in the GwE model was HRD, which matched perfectly the Asian idea of education as the virtuous circle: higher educational attainment and skill formation contributes to growth as well as personal upward mobility. Thus, public investment in education and skill development occupied the central place in the GwE model that generated the Asian Miracle. The results in terms of equality were as impressive as the growth rate in terms of GNP per capita. Thus, the Gini coefficients[56] in each one of the four Tiger economies declined sharply during 1965–90, dropping on the average by 5–10 percentage points in a period when incomes rose in excess of 7 percent annually.[57]

The Asian GwE model based on HRD is significant, and remains a valuable model for development elsewhere. It confirms the high value-added impacts of social investments in HRD through education and training. But it also demonstrates that HRD means more than education and training. It is the basis of social capital and it is also the foundation for institutional development, capacity building, and civil society/good governance reforms.[58]

Of course, the importance of HRD as an engine of development is not new. The intellectual roots of the modern theory of HRD lie in the Residual Growth debate of the 1960s, which stressed the lifetime (or dynamic) benefits of schooling, leading to the Total Factor Productivity (TFP) theory. The TFP stresses productivity gains due to innovations and entrepreneurship in determining the rate of growth of an economy, whereas neo-classical growth models stress the more fixed productivity levels of capital, labor, and land. In recent years, the TFP has been reformulated in terms of a "New Growth theory" emphasizing the endogeneity of knowledge-based skills.[59] All these contributions reconfirm the human capital theory as originally advanced in the early 1960s by T.W. Schultz, Dennison, *et al.*[60]

HRD investments and labor market policies provide a crucial link to efficiency-enhancing higher labor standards. There are multiple advantages of upward harmonization in the labor market because HRD and higher standards work in a positive, reinforcing relationship to promote growth and development: HRD is the policy path for higher labor standards in development. Higher human capital investments raise productivity, making possible higher profits and earnings. Similarly, better labor standards promote healthier and safer working conditions and have beneficial effects on the economy in terms of reduced absenteeism and reduced turnover. Additionally, there are external benefits resulting from higher standards at the workplace. For example, higher levels of education lead to greater social cohesion, and social capital formation. When workers are better educated and enjoy greater income, they will increasingly demand greater democratic rights at work and better protection for weaker and vulnerable fellow workers.

An international development levy

The HRD investments and interventions outlined above require resources. We have argued that these resources should be raised through an international development levy as part of global governance. International compensation, as argued above, can most efficiently be viewed as a levy on international business. This is the way to pay for higher core labor standards in developing countries.

What are the arguments justifying such international compensation? One line of argument in favor of the international development levy is that these higher standards are largely a reflection of tastes and preferences of Northern parties. In other words, they are extensions of Northern ethics. Therefore, to facilitate their implementation, there must be adequate financing in the form of international compensation, for neither the children nor their families or governments in the Third World can afford the direct and indirect costs of upward harmonization themselves.

The argument for our WDF proposal does not derive exclusively from an ethical perspective, but is also based on a fundamental economic premise. We argue that international business paying into the WDF will, in the long run, realize higher returns as profits and dividends from the higher worker productivity. This is what our human capital model for child workers above has demonstrated. Initially, however, the model may be introduced experimentally as a pilot project funded through voluntary corporate development financing.

A recent example from Bangladesh demonstrates how such corporate development financing and international resource transfer in aid of higher labor standards may work. The relevant case is the Memorandum of Understanding (MOU) reached between the Bangladesh Garment Manufacturers and Exporters Association and the ILO and UNICEF.[61] Under this MOU, Bangladesh garment exporters, facing an international boycott of their products on grounds that they were exploiting child workers, agreed to terminate this practice and facilitate transition of children from the workplace to school for education and skill development to enable higher productivity and earnings potential. To minimize income loss for both the children and their families, an income support program was arranged based on the compensation principle. UNICEF and the ILO agreed not only to fund the schooling of the children, but also to provide income support for the affected families for the duration of school attendance. As well, the manufacturers agreed to hire relatives of the children so as to minimize hardships for these families. The MOU was only to be valid for an experimental three-year period; however, it clearly demonstrates how the international compensation principle can work in practice to support upward harmonization.

A global HRD action plan under the ILO

The ILO, through its technical assistance and research programs, has done extensive work linking HRD with labor market analysis, monitoring employment trends and working conditions.[62] The World Bank emphasizes human capital theory in its educational sector lending, most recently linked to the new concept of "social capital."[63] Sirageldin defines social capital as the "fourth form of capital ... as the essential premise of a functioning society ... grounded in a sense of belonging by members of that society."[64]

The HRD approach suggested here could become the central thrust of efficiency-enhancing multilateral responses to promoting international labor standards and working conditions in labor markets in developing countries. In addition, such HRD investments in higher labor standards can raise the efficiency of labor markets because HRD builds and expands on the experience of such important actors as the ILO, the WB, and bilateral aid agencies in this field. In the first instance, a Global Skill Development Fund can be set up under the ILO to be financed from revenues accruing into the WDF (see below). Young workers in particular can become the beneficiaries of such a skill development program. Examples of how these cooperative solutions can be put into action are now beginning to accumulate, as is demonstrated by the Bangladesh garment exporters case mentioned above.

A World Development Fund (WDF)

The global HRD action plan needs adequate funding to be realized. These funds cannot be raised in poor countries; they must be contributed by rich, industrialized countries. Nor can this contribution be viewed as aid or charity, justified on ethical criteria alone. Official Development Assistance (ODA), as measured by the Organization for Economic Cooperation and Development (OECD), has been declining for several years, as a result of "aid fatigue" in donor countries and disappointment with aid effectiveness in recipient countries.[65] It is unlikely ODA flows will increase sufficiently to meet the needs of a global HRD action plan in future years, despite the best efforts by some G8 countries like Britain. In this financial environment, what can be done for increased funding and resource flows for Third World development, a necessary precondition for global governance?

We have argued that a World Development Fund (WDF) must be created as a central component in the architecture of global governance. This requires collective consent and inter-cultural approval (see our concluding chapter). The WDF should be financed from a levy on MNEs, as has been argued by others as well as one of the present authors.[66] Without global fiscal resources, it is futile to talk of global governance. We have also suggested that a development levy on international business is fully justified on the economic arguments of upward harmonization, specifically as HRD investments in long-term productivity of workers.

We now explore the fiscal aspects of the levy on international business, enabling global corporations to be good global citizens. As discussed in Chapter 3, many of these corporations have annual sales well in excess of the national income of most developing countries.[67]

In the practical example used below, we shall illustrate the implementation of a development levy on the world's top 500 international corporations. These top 500 companies are derived from the annual list compiled by *Fortune*, a leading US magazine on international business. The *Fortune* top 500 list is a detailed source of corporate information. As a data source, it is also larger and more up to date than UNCTAD's list of top 100 corporations,[68] and hence preferred in the illustration here. It includes the home country of these corporations, their annual sales revenue, profits, and the number of employees.

Table 5.4 illustrates all of this data for the world's top twenty-five corporations, while Table 5.5 illustrates the impact of a small (0.005 percent) annual development levy on revenues and profits of these corporations.

Table 5.4   Revenues and profits of the world's top twenty-five corporations in 2000

Rank	Corporation	Home country	Revenue in US$ million	Profits in US$ million	Employee number	Per employee: Revenue in US$ million	Profit
1	ExxonMobil	US	210,392	17,720	99,600	2.11	0.178
2	Wal-Mart Stores	US	193,295	6,295	1,244,00	0 0.16	0.005
3	General Motors	US	184,632	4,452	366,000	0.50	0.012
4	Ford Motor	US	180,598	3,467	345,991	0.52	0.010
5	Daimler Chrysler	Germany	150,070	7,295	416,501	0.36	0.018
6	Royal Dutch/Shell	Britain/ Netherlands	149,146	12,719	90,000	1.66	0.141
7	BP	Britain	148,062	11,870	107,200	1.38	0.111
8	General Electric	US	129,853	12,735	341,000	0.38	0.037
9	Mitsubishi	Japan	126,579	833	42,000	3.01	0.020
10	Toyota Motor	Japan	121,416	4,262	215,648	0.56	0.020
11	Mitsui	Japan	118,013	467	33,712	3.50	0.014
12	Citigroup	US	111,826	13,519	237,500	0.47	0.057

Table 5.4 continued

13	Itochu	Japan	109,795	638	36,651	3.00	0.017
14	Total Fina Elf	France	105,870	6,380	123,303	0.86	0.052
15	Nippon T&T	Japan	103,235	4,197	215,200	0.48	0.020
16	Enron	US	100,789	979	20,000	5.04	0.049
17	AXA	France	92,782	3,608	95,422	0.97	0.038
18	Sumitomo	Japan	91,168	365	30,715	2.97	0.012
19	IBM	US	88,396	8,093	316,303	0.28	0.026
20	Marubeni	Japan	85,351	136	31,342	2.72	0.004
21	Volkwagen	Germany	78,851	1,896	342,402	0.23	0.006
22	Hitachi	Japan	76,126	944	340,939	0.22	0.003
23	Siemens	Germany	74,858	8,560	447,000	0.17	0.019
24	ING Group	Netherlands	71,195	11,075	92,650	0.77	0.120
25	Allianz	Germany	71,022	3,197	119,683	0.59	0.027
	Total		2,973,320	145,702	5,750,762	0.52	0.025

Source: *Fortune*, 23 July 2001, p. 154

Table 5.5   Impact of 0.005 percent development levy on the revenues and profits of the world's top twenty-five corporations in 2000

Rank	Corporation	Home country	0.005 percent levy in US$ million	After-levy-per-employee profits in US$ million
1	ExxonMobil	US	1,051.96	0.167
2	Wal-Mart Stores	US	966.475	0.004
3	General Motors	US	923.16	0.010
4	Ford Motor	US	902.99	0.007
5	Daimler Chrysler	Germany	750.35	0.016
6	Royal Dutch/Shell	Britain/ Netherlands	745.73	0.133
7	BP	Britain	740.31	0.104
8	General Electric	US	649.265	0.035
9	Mitsubishi	Japan	632.895	0.005
10	Toyota Motor	Japan	607.08	0.017
11	Mitsui	Japan	590.065	0.004
12	Citigroup	US	559.13	0.055
13	Itochu	Japan	548.975	0.002
14	Total Fina Elf	France	529.35	0.047
15	Nippon T&T	Japan	516.175	0.017
16	Enron	US	503.945	0.024
17	AXA	France	463.91	0.033
18	Sumitomo	Japan	455.84	0.003
19	IBM	US	441.98	0.024
20	Marubeni	Japan	426.755	0.009
21	Volkswagen	Germany	394.255	0.004
22	Hitachi	Japan	380.63	0.002
23	Siemens	Germany	374.29	0.018
24	ING Group	Netherlands	355.975	0.116
25	Allianz	Germany	355.11	0.024
Total			14,866.6	0.023

Source: data from Table 5.4

While the overall impact on corporate profitability would be small (reducing profit per employee for the top twenty-five corporations by about US$2,000 in 2000), there may nevertheless be some significant impact on individual corporations, for example, by prolonged recession and slumping sales. This is illustrated in the case of some Japanese corporations in the list of the top twenty-five corporations in Table 5.5, whose after-development-levy-per-employee profits turn negative. In such cases, the levy collection would require further investigation and discussions with the corporations concerned. One plausible compromise solution might be to devise a moving average for the development levy so that its imposition does not become unduly burdensome.

Another problem area with the levy is the potential of an MNE suddenly going bankrupt. This is exactly what happened to the number sixteen company in the *Fortune* 500, Enron, in early 2002. The Enron debacle clearly demonstrates the risk and fragility of even the largest corporations in today's global market-place. No doubt, in future, other cases will occur because the world of international business is not fail-safe. The important implication for our develop-ment levy proposal is that the list of eligible corporations for collection will have to be revised and updated annually.

Turning to the benefit side of the levy, such a small development levy on world trade would generate a huge amount of resources for world develop-ment. Thus, a 0.005 percent levy on global revenues of the top 500 *Fortune* corporations, estimated to approach US$15 trillion in 2000, would generate US$70.3 billion for the WDF, an amount that exceeds the total official devel-opment aid from OECD Development Aid Committee (DAC) countries during 2000 by 32.4 percent (see Table 5.6). Alternatively, however, if the Levy were to be based on profits[69] of MNEs, the yield would be small, unless the rate of the levy would be correspondingly adjusted upwards. In this latter event, the net effect would be the same as using revenues as the basis of the Levy.

How could the levy on MNEs be collected? There are alternatives, but the preferred method would be for home country treasuries to collect the levy and then transfer it to the WDF. A practical application of this method is illustrated in Table 5.7 in the case of the top twenty-five *Fortune* corporations. Collection of the levy by home country treasuries would not diminish existing national sovereignty of these countries. The funds thus collected would simply be trans-ferred to the account of the WDF.

If, however, at some point in time it were possible for countries to surrender some part of national sovereignty for the sake of global governance, then a direct levy could be imposed by the WDF itself to generate autonomous revenue. The WDF would then be directly responsible for updating the list of MNEs for purposes of the levy and all its administrative aspects.

Table 5.6 Total development levy payable by the world's top 500 corporations in 2000

	US$ billon	*Percent*
Revenue in 2000	14,065	
0.005 percent levy	70.325	132.44
Total ODA from DAC countries in 2000	53.1	100.0

Source: *Fortune*, 23 July 2001, and OECD

Table 5.7   Collection of development levy in the case of the top twenty-five corporations

Home country treasury	US$ million
US	5,998.9
Japan	4,158.4
Germany	1,874.0
France	993.3
Britain	740.3
Britain/Netherlands	745.7
Netherlands	356.0
Total	14,866.6

No doubt the levy would imply a tax burden, ultimately to be shifted to consumers of products and services supplied by the MNEs. Most of these consumers would reside in rich countries of the North, and it is assumed that most would recognize the benefits of this tax burden as being a catalyst of greater global stability and justice. Some, however, might object to higher prices and shift to cheaper substitutes in the market. In this case, market competition would eventually level the field, as international companies could advertise the levy as a visible benefit of better corporate citizenship and even increase market share accordingly. In the long term, as discussed in Chapter 3, global ethics and social responsibility could play a major role in consumer choice. As consumers in the high-income countries show an increasing appreciation of global security and justice, they can be expected to regard the WDF levy as investment in good global governance, yielding global public goods, in much the same way that national taxation has been seen as indispensable in the provision of public goods within national boundaries. Of course, countries cooperating in the collection of the development levy would be entitled to sit on the managing board of the WDF, and thus have a say in its management. Indirectly, the same would apply for the MNEs that would, in the first instance, pay the development levy. Ultimately, of course, the levy would be paid by the consumers of goods and services in the global markets.

We believe our suggestion for a development levy on international companies is superior to a number of alternatives that have been offered for international taxation, such as the Tobin tax[70] and the eco-taxes. The Tobin tax is a proposal to impose a modest tax on cross-border "hot money" flows or short-term capital movements. These short-term capital flows are highly volatile as they reflect speculative transfers, and as such they would present great difficulty in identification and collection, while also exposing revenue collection to high degrees of volatility. On the other hand, eco-taxes, such as carbon taxes on monoxide or carbon emissions in high-income countries, would amount to linking the size of the WDF on pollution in the North, and as these emissions decline in line with agreements such as the Kyoto Accords, the revenue yields would decline as well.

How should the WDF funds be utilized? They can be utilized either by international development agencies, such as the ILO as stated above, or directly by LDC governments or NGOs involved in human resource development. Requests for funding can be made by application to the WDF, which for reasons of transparency would clearly advertise its eligibility criteria and application procedures. It is important for efficiency reasons that the funds made available from the WDF should be subject to routine monitoring and evaluation, at least in part done by independent assessors.

The critical requirement for the disbursement of WDF funds is that they should be used for upward harmonization in the global labor market, i.e. to raise the productivity of workers, especially those from vulnerable groups, to protect workers under labor laws, and to enhance worker rights in society. Some of the notable projects that would qualify for funding under the WDF include:

1   skill development schemes, technical and vocational training on and off the job;
2   academic upgrading, including adult literacy;
3   labor market information programs;
4   credit and technical assistance, including entrepreneurship training for small and medium firms;
5   programs for strengthening labor laws and administration.

All factors considered, we believe our proposal for a development levy on MNEs is practical, defensible on economic and business criteria, and that it would provide a stable, autonomous fund to make upward harmonization in the global labor market a reality.

6 Toward global pluralism

There is a need to develop a new vision of global governance, economy, and law in order to ensure the flourishing of the human species within this precious biosphere we call Earth. We need to develop such a vision to make certain that the tragic flaw within the nature of humanity does not triumph. We also need such a vision to ensure that the wait for justice is not unbearably long for much of humankind. Some of the leading intellectuals in the world are focusing on the search for such a new vision.

In our view, one of the most convincing of these new visions being developed is that of Nobel Prize-winning economist Amartya Sen. Beginning his search for a new vision from the foundation of John Rawls' notion of justice as fairness,[1] Sen asks what would be the global "original position" from which one could formulate global principles of justice. He identifies two different conceptions of the global "original position":

- *Grand universalism.* The domain of the exercise of fairness is all people everywhere taken together, and the device of the original position is applied to a hypothetical exercise in the selection of rules and principles of justice for all, seen without distinction of nationality and other classifications.
- *National particularism.* The domain of the exercise of fairness involves each nation taken separately, to which the device of the original position is correspondingly applied, and the relations between nations are governed by a supplementary exercise involving international equity.[2]

Sen rejects both these conceptions of a vision of global justice and pursues the search for a third conception with "an adequate recognition of the plurality of relations involved across the globe."[3] We share Sen's dissatisfaction with grand universalism[4] because, like him, and as we have argued in Chapters 1, 2, 4 and 5, neither the United Nations, the WTO, the IMF, nor the World Bank are suitable institutions of global governance to implement any principles of justice hypothetically arrived at in the original position by the peoples of the world for the peoples of the world.

We also support Sen's reason for rejecting a nationalist particularist conception of global Rawlsian Justice, even though this is the conception that Rawls himself has indicated he would endorse in cross-societal and national linkages, thereby leading to "the law of the peoples."[5] While this is the present establishment conception of international law and justice, we have argued in every chapter of this book that the domain of international law and justice being limited to interactions between nations is breaking down. In Chapter 1 we saw the critical role that international solidarity on human rights between individuals and groups around the world has played in developing the body of international human rights law and justice, even within the United Nations agencies and bodies themselves. Likewise, we have seen how critical this same solidarity that transcends societies and nations has been in the establishment of the International Criminal Court and the banning of landmines. In Chapter 2, we have also discussed how individuals and groups have developed international solidarities against exploitation and for distributive justice, health and safety, and respect for the environment in the area of international trade and commerce. In Chapter 3, we have considered the impact of the emergence of supranational global players in international law, justice, and ethics. These global players are multinational enterprises (MNEs) that are now rivaling nation-states in power and influence. Finally, in Chapters 4 and 5 we have examined how it is the actions of individuals and corporations across borders and exploitation within those borders that give rise to the need for new rules of global governance.

Sen advocates a different conception of global justice, which he argues is neither as unreal as grand universalism or as separatist or unifocal as national particularism supplemented by international relations. He calls his different conception "plural affiliation."[6] The core of this conception is the recognition that all global players, including individuals, could have multiple identities which may "yield concerns and demands that can significantly supplement, or seriously compete with, other concerns and demands arising from other identities." Sen states that "With plural affiliation the exercise of fairness can be applied to different groups (including – but not uniquely – nations), and the respective demands related to our multiple identities can all be taken seriously."[7]

We adapt Sen's foundation of plural affiliation to offer our own vision of global governance for the twenty-first century, namely global pluralism. We suggest the core of this conception of global justice is a universal conception of human dignity that requires equal concern and respect from our multiple global identities as citizens of the planet and as citizens of national societies. Global pluralism requires that respective demands from our multiple global identities be taken seriously while attaching the concomitant responsibilities to this recognition, including the protection and promotion of universally accepted human rights. To adapt from the work of Ronald Dworkin,[8] it is not only fundamental human rights that must be taken seriously, it is also the demand of our multiple global identities, as members of national and supranational societies and as members of both national and supranational identity groups based on ethnicity, sex, religion, etc. If we accept that the demands of our multiple global identities are at the core of the concept of global pluralism, then we have rights and responsibilities in multiple contexts. Sen accepts this theory of justice and fairness that cuts across the grand collectivity of all peoples in the world and the more insular collectivity of the national society. He uses as an example the ethical duties of MNEs, the subject matter of our discussion in Chapter 3:

> How should a transnational conglomerate treat the local labour force, other businesses, regional customers or – for that matter – national governments or local administration? If there are issues of fairness involved, how should these issues be formulated – over what domain? If the spread of business ethics (generating rules of conduct, fostering mutual trust or keeping corruption in check) is a "global public good", then we have to ask how the cogency and merits of particular business ethics are to be evaluated ... All this calls for extensive use of the perspectives of plural affiliations and the application of the discipline of justice and fairness within these respective groups.[9]

It is clear from this example of Sen's that it is not only individuals but also organizations like corporations and institutions which have responsibilities to multiple stakeholders within the context of plural affiliation or global pluralism. While this is nothing new to the leadership MNEs, who have accepted that they have obligations beyond their shareholders to a variety of legitimate stakeholders, it is relatively new to some of the institutions of global governance. Within the context of global pluralism, institutions like the WTO, the IMF, and the World Bank must come to accept that, over and above their responsibilities to their member states or shareholders, they have responsibilities to the exploited in the Export Processing Zones or to the millions of people who see their livelihoods wiped out in financial crises. Likewise, the five permanent members of the Security Council must come to accept that they have fundamental duties to all actual and potential victims of human rights and humanitarian disasters, not just to the interests of their own governments and citizens. This exercise of global pluralism must be implemented in the daily actions of institutions of global governance rather than being left at the level of rhetoric or diplomatic niceties.

It is the refusal to accept these fundamental aspects of global pluralism that gives rise to the significant discontents with globalization.

Emerging from our discussion of evolution of the United Nations and international human rights law in Chapter 1, the vision of global pluralism would demand major reforms of the United Nations. In particular, there is an urgent need to democratize the Security Council of the United Nations to reflect a vision of global pluralism. After 11 September 2001, the need to reform the Council is even greater in order to avoid a "clash of civilizations" and, moreover, such reform is the key to sustaining the long-term battle against the new global evil of terrorism. In particular, as discussed in Chapter 1, global pluralism would demand an expansion of the permanent members of the Security Council to include all the major "civilizations" and regions of the world. Likewise, global pluralism could not support the veto power being available to a handful of nation-states that could stop timely action to prevent human rights and humanitarian disasters. As also discussed in Chapter 1, the emergence of the G8 as a powerful counterpart of the Security Council may be the first sign of a move to reform of the security institutions of global governance. However, even the G8 remains a relatively undemocratic global institution. Therefore, it is also encouraging that it is spawning other initiatives, such as the G20, which, as observed in Chapter 1, is beginning to show greater signs of implementing global pluralism.

A vision of global pluralism would also demand that we go back to the original vision of the global trade regime envisaged in the aftermath of the Second World War. The original vision of the Bretton Woods institutions was profoundly in accord with global pluralism. If it was clear in the aftermath of the war that trade, economic stability, peace, international security, and human rights are clearly linked, why have we lost that perspective today? As also discussed in Chapter 2, it is in the controversial areas of linkages between labor standards, the environment, and trade that the WTO and its member states must realize that global pluralism will demand that social and environmental justice be integrated into the trade regime for the sake of its own sustainability. In particular, we have argued that enforcement of existing trade rules in areas like export processing zones, to combat the exploitation of the most vulnerable, is essential to keep a "moral" level playing field in world trade. Likewise, we have argued that the governance of the WTO must become more pluralistic and democratic to ensure that it is accountable to the peoples of the world. The "Rule by the Quad" must become a thing of the past in terms of setting the agenda of the world trade regime. In the most recent Doha Round of multilateral trade talks, we have seen some of the emerging powers from the South refuse to accept the agenda of the North. We can expect to see more demands of global pluralism in the world trade regime from countries such as India, Brazil, and China, as well as from the Islamic world. Sadly, we can also expect increasing protectionist actions from the developed world, especially just before elections are held, which will undermine the ability of the developing world nations to grow themselves out of poverty. A perfect example is the US Farm Bill, passed in 2002, which increased agricultural subsidies to American farmers but will also drive many Third World farmers into greater uncompetitiveness and poverty.

On the optimistic side, it may well be in the context of building the multilateral trade and commerce regime that we will see a practical refutation of the central thesis of Samuel Huntington's "clash of civilizations."[10] Global pluralism demands that civilizations work together for the mutual benefit of all, rather than a zero sum game which involves conflict between civilizations. The American decision to promote China's accession to the WTO both externally and internally indicates that the so-called clashing civilizations are prepared to work together in the interests of citizens of both their countries.

One of the most potent forces of global pluralism will be the global private sector, as discussed in Chapter 3. We have argued that with the newly acquired economic, social, and even political power will come responsibility. Global pluralism encompasses not only rights but responsibilities. Responsibilities can be fulfilled through effective self-imposed ethical and moral codes. In Chapter 3, we have looked at the evolution of the huge array of corporate, sectoral, national, and ultimately global codes. We have seen how a failure to live up to their responsibilities or even their own voluntary codes has led to disastrous consequences for MNEs. It is in their own long-term sustainability and their corporate integrity environments that MNEs may regard themselves as major stakeholders in the global pluralism framework of global justice. We have suggested that, if MNEs ignore their fundamental responsibilities as stakeholders in global pluralism, their conduct will ultimately be regulated by the imposition of legal duties. We have already seen this in the areas of environmental damage, health and safety of employees and local communities, corruption, money laundering, and potential civil liability for complicity in gross human rights abuses.

Emerging from our discussion in Chapters 4 and 5, we assert that it is time that economics and economic experts came to terms with the reality of global pluralism. The world economic system must promote global economic justice as a fundamental tenet of global pluralism. Traditional Western economics has operated as an efficiency-driven system of resource allocation that has, in the past, ignored the vital aspects of global equity. In a world of cultural diversity, efficiency rules are insufficient; rules of equity that in deeds as well as the law distribute wealth equitably amongst all regions and peoples of the world must complement them.

Our discussion in Chapter 4 has demonstrated that a "race-to-the-bottom" economics is in no one's interest, least of all that of MNEs and their long-term sustainability. Modern capital and technology, combined with increased competition in the global marketplace, have greatly increased the mobility of Western resources. MNEs have successfully penetrated labor-abundant countries of the developing world. As a result, wages and working conditions in these host-countries have failed to keep up with the rapid expansion of labor forces.

Institutionally and from a legal standpoint, these host countries have avoided labor standards to protect workers. Inferior standards of occupational health and safety, as well as exploitation of the vulnerable groups, have been globalized. The position of women and children, in particular, has worsened. In general, however, urbanization, informalization, feminization, and causalization of employment have all contributed to declining real incomes and standards of living. Alienation and marginalization breed instability and, ultimately, spill over into violence and terrorism, making the entire world unsafe. The pursuit of orderly business becomes unsustainable in a world that ignores the imperatives of global pluralism.

Sustainability requires social justice in the global economy. Social justice is a normative objective which aims at paying labor of a given quality equitable wages due, regardless of location, ethnicity or gender. Given enabling institutional reform and adequate resources, social justice in the global marketplace would ensure that work of equal value in the production of traded goods and services is rewarded equitably in different national jurisdictions. Our concept of "labor's due" consists of two components. The first is upward harmonization regarding payment of equitable wages to workers of same productivity. The second component of labor's due refers to leveling the playing field in the global workplace. This requires that institutional and personal differences of global workers in terms of education, training, and legal rights pertaining, for example, to their rights of association and collective bargaining or overtime, are upwardly harmonized in the interests of global pluralism. Institutional reform, especially labor market reform, must be harmonized globally. We believe that such upward harmonization is the way to bring justice to global workers based on core labor standards as articulated, for example, in the ILO's Declaration of Fundamental Principles and Rights of Work, discussed in Chapter 2.

But declarations are not enough. Reform requires investment. Without resources to pay for needed reforms, the world sinks into conflict and instability. In Chapter 5 we have argued that the international financial institutions, as well as the private corporate actors, must adapt to the new responsibilities in an age of global pluralism. In particular, this chapter has proposed that the private sector must shoulder revenue-raising responsibilities for a new global Marshall Plan-type global development. Foreign aid flows, charitable donations through Western NGOs, or ad hoc contributions for Third World development are no longer adequate for the challenges of global pluralism. What are required are huge investments in equity-promoting HRD programs for human security in an integrated world. That is the logic of our proposal for a WDF.

Our vision is that a WDF must be the cornerstone of global governance. Without adequate revenue-raising capacity, lofty words are bound to remain as such. Funds are essential to promote all categories of human rights. So far the Western powers have given priority to civil and political rights, in part because they are cheaper to implement. But it is now time to "put the money where the mouth is" and invest in education, health, housing, and the other basic human needs. The goal of global governance in the twenty-first century should be to strive towards global social justice where all the peoples of the world have the opportunity to flourish within their own communities. It is the path towards a sustainable world based on diversity, tolerance, and interdependence.

In a recent controversial book titled *Globalization and Its Discontents*, written by one of the most inside of insiders in the institutions of global governance, there has been confirmation of much of the analysis of the authors of this text in the realm of the international financial institutions.[11] Joseph Stiglitz, a former White House adviser, World Bank chief economist and senior vice-president development economics, and winner of the 2001 Nobel Prize in Economics, has delivered a stinging attack, based on personal experience and information obtained as a discontented insider, on the failures of the international financial institutions, especially in the context of Russian and Asian financial crises. Echoing much of the views of Radelet, Sachs, and our own views discussed in Chapter 5, this former insider in the institutions of global governance also seems to confirm our perception of the problem of narrowly focused expertise and worldviews in the international financial institutions. He begins his closing chapter with the following statements:

Globalization today is not working for many of the world's poor. It is not working for much of the environment. It is not working for the stability of the global economy ... To some there is an easy answer: Abandon globalization. That is neither feasible or desirable. ... Globalization has brought better health, as well as an active global civil society fighting for more democracy and greater social justice. The problem is not with globalization, but with how it has been managed. Part of the problem lies with the international economic institutions, with the IMF, the World Bank, and WTO, which help set the rules of the game. They have done so in ways that all too often have served the interests of the more advanced industrialized countries – and particular interests within those countries – rather than those of the developing world. But it is not just that they have served those interests; too often, they have approached globalization from particular narrow mind-sets, shaped by a particular vision of the economy and society.[12]

The same narrowness of vision can also be found in the other institutions of global governance that we have discussed in this work. These institutions range from the United Nations to the de facto governance roles that the global private sector plays. We have also discussed throughout this work that, while both narrow perspectives and self-interest have undermined higher visions in the institutions of global governance, the human will toward justice has never failed to bear witness to the "tragic flaw" within the institutions of global governance. The next challenge is to develop global institutions of law and economics that are committed to the principles of global pluralism. This work, we hope, is another small step in that direction.

As with the controversy surrounding the work by Stiglitz, we anticipate the criticism of our ideas as utopian in an imperfect world. We do not deny that we seek a revolution in contemporary thinking about global governance, economy, and law. We do so in the belief that, as a species, humans are programmed for progress, and that progress is desperately needed at this time in our history. The mark of how far we have progressed as a species, and how civilized we really are, is how we treat our most vulnerable. The globalization of the local, propelled by international trade, finance, and emerging networks of civil society, must be accompanied by the globalization of solidarity and dignity for all members of the human family. This is imperative if globalization is to be sustainable. The ultimate frontier is the space that separates us from universal compassion for all members of the human family.

Notes

1 The "tragic flaw" of humanity reflected in the United Nations and the struggle for human rights

1 Paul Gordon Lauren, *The Evolution of Human Rights, Visions Seen* (Philadelphia: University of Pennsylvania Press, 1998), at pp. 141–2.
2 *Ibid.* at p.142. The Atlantic Charter is also discussed in T. Wilson, *The First Summit* (Boston: Houghton Mifflin, 1969).
3 *Ibid.* at p. 150. The Declaration is further discussed in Louise W. Holborn (ed.) *War and Peace Aims of the United Nations* (Boston: World Peace Foundation, 1943).
4 See Lauren, *ibid.* at p. 146. See also *Trials of Major War Criminals*, 42 volumes, Nuremberg Military Tribunal (Washington, DC: US Government Printing Office, 1947–9). For interesting extracts dealing with the Nuremberg Tribunal see H.J. Steiner and P. Alston, *International Human Rights in Context*, 2nd edn (Oxford: Oxford University Press, 2000), at pp. 112–26.
5 *Supra* note 1 at p. 160.
6 *Ibid.* at p. 166.
7 *Ibid.* at p. 170.
8 *Ibid.* at p. 165.
9 For a detailed history of this predecessor to the United Nations, see F.P. Walters, *A History of the League of Nations* (London: Oxford University Press, 1952).
10 *Supra* note 1 at p. 175.
11 *Charter of the United Nations*, 26 June 1945, 59 Stat. 1031, T.S. 993, 3 Bevans 1153, entered into force 24 October 1945. The full text of the Charter can be found at the official UN website at www.un.org/aboutun/charter (accessed: June 2001). For an analysis of the legal nature of these provisions, see R.B. Lillich, *International Human Rights: Problems of Law, Policy and Practice*, 2nd edn (Boston: Little, Brown, 1991).
12 *Supra* note 1 at p. 197.
13 *Ibid.* at p. 198.
14 For an analysis of how this provision and others relating to territorial integrity and political independence relate to the human rights provisions, see V. Leary, "When Does the Implementation of International Human Rights Constitute Interference into the Essentially Domestic Affairs of a State? The Interactions of Articles 2(7), 55 and 56 of the UN Charter" in J.C. Tuttle (ed.) *International Human Rights Law and Practice* (Chicago: American Bar Association, 1978) at pp. 15–21.
15 Quoted in A.H. Robertson, *Human Rights in the World* (Manchester: Manchester University Press, 1972), at p. 25.
16 *Supra* note 1 at p. 231.
17 *Supra* note 15 at p. 26.
18 *Supra* note 1 at pp. 231–2.

19 See *Trials of Major War Criminals, supra* note 4. See also Cherif M. Bassiouni, *Crimes against Humanity in International Criminal Law*, 2nd edn (The Hague, London, Boston: Kluwer Law International, 1999) at pp. 1–276; T. Meron, *War Crimes Come of Age: Essays* (Oxford and New York: Oxford University Press, 1998) at pp. 190, 198–203, 239–40; C.M. Bassiouni, "Nuremberg: Forty Years After" (1986) 80 *Proceedings of the Annual Meeting of the American Society of International Law* 59–65.

20 For the views of one of the principal architects of the Universal Declaration in this regard, see John Humphrey "The Universal Declaration of Human Rights: Its History, Impact and Juridical Character" in B.G. Ramcharan (ed.) *Human Rights Thirty Years after the Universal Declaration* (The Hague: Martinus Nijhoff, 1979) at p. 21.

21 Cited by Louis B. Sohn, "A Short History of the United Nations Documents on Human Rights" in A.H. Robertson, *supra* note 15 at p. 27.

22 See *Trials of Major War Criminals, supra* note 4.

23 For discussion of the impact of both the Nuremberg and Tokyo Tribunals see R. Falk, *Forty Years after the Nuremberg and Tokyo Tribunals: The Impact of War Crime Trials on International and National Law* (1986) 80 *Proceedings of the Annual Meeting of the American Society of International Law* 65.

24 For a historical account of the evolution of humanitarian law, see Henri Coursier, "L'Evolution du droit international humanitaire" (1960) 99 *Recueil des Cours de l'Académie de Droit International* 361.

25 For detailed discussion of these Covenants, see L. Henkin (ed.) *The International Bill of Rights: The Covenant on Civil and Political Rights* (New York: Columbia University Press, 1981); T. Meron, *Human Rights Law-Making in the United Nations. A Critique of Instruments and Process* (Oxford: Clarendon Press, 1986); M. Craven, *The International Covenant on Economic, Social and Cultural Rights: A Perspective on its Development* (New York: Oxford University Press, 1981); E. Asbjorn, C. Krause, and A. Rosas, *Economic, Social and Cultural Rights* (The Hague: Martinus Nijhoff, 1995).

26 See L. Henkin, *ibid.* at p. 259. See also D. Fischer, "Reporting under the Covenant on Civil and Political Rights" (1982) 76 *American Journal of International Law* 145; See also D. Kretzmer, "Commentary on the Complaint Process by the Human Rights Committee and Torture Committee Members" in Anne F. Bayefsky (ed.) *The U.N. Human Rights System in the 21st Century* (The Hague: Kluwer Law International, 2000) at p. 163.

27 See D. McGoldrick, *The Human Rights Committee: Its Role in the Development of the International Covenant on Civil and Political Rights* (Oxford: Clarendon Press, 1991); see also the annual reports of the Committee, located at www.unhcr.ch/tbs/doc.nsf (accessed: June 2001).

28 *Supra* note 1 at p. 259. See also the critical analysis of such treaty bodies in dealing with individual complaints by A. Byrnes, "An Effective Complaint Procedure in the Context of International Human Rights Law" in Anne F. Bayefsky (ed.) *supra* note 26 at p. 139. See also the collection of interesting and informative extracts on these civil and political rights treaties in H.J. Steiner and P. Alston, *supra* note 4 at pp. 136–7.

29 P. Alston, *Final Report on Enhancing the Long-Term Effectiveness of the United Nations Human Rights Treaty System*, UN Doc. E/CN4/1997/74 (27 March 1997) at para. 10.

30 Anne F. Bayefsky, *supra* note 26 at pp. xviii–xix. See also Anne F. Bayefsky, "The UN Human Rights Treaty system: universality at the crossroads," located at http://www.yorku.ca/hrights (accessed: April 2001).

31 *Vienna Declaration and Programme of Action*, UN GAOR, World Conf. On Hum. Rts., 48th Sess. 22nd Plen. Mtg., Part 1–Part 18.

32 *Ibid.*

33 Mary Robinson, "Addressing the Gap between Rhetoric and Reality" in Yael Danieli, Elsa Stamatopoulou, and Clarence J. Dias (eds) *The Universal Declaration of Human Rights: Fifty Years and Beyond* (New York: Baywood Publishing Company, on behalf of the United Nations, 1999), at p. 425.

34 *Ibid.* at p. 426.
35 Associated Press report, 20 March 2001, published in the *Daily Athenaeum Interactive*, located at www.da.wvu.edu.
36 "Chickens and Foxes," *The Economist*, 21 April 2001 at p. 41.
37 See B.W. Ndiaye, "Thematic Mechanisms and the Protection of Human Rights" in *The Universal Declaration of Human Rights: Fifty Years and Beyond, supra* note 33 at pp. 72–3. The author at the time of writing was a Special Rapporteur on Extrajudicial, Summary or Arbitrary Executions of the UN Commission on Human Rights.
38 See *The Report by the Special Rapporteur on Extrajudicial, Summary or Arbitrary Executions on His Mission to Rwanda*, 8–17 April 1993, UN Doc. E/CN.4/1994/7/Add.1.
39 Reuters, with files from Agence France-Presse, printed in the *National Post*, 5 May 2001 at p. A12.
40 Henry J. Steiner, "Individual Claims in a World of Massive Violations: What Role for the Human Rights Committee?" in P. Alston and J. Crawford, *The Future of UN Human Rights Monitoring* (Cambridge: Cambridge University Press, 2000) at p. 53.
41 See, to this effect, the decision of the International Court of Justice in *Reservations to the Convention on the Prevention and Punishment of the Crime of Genocide (Advisory Opinion)* [191] *ICJ Reports* 16, at p. 23.
42 (1951) 78 UNTS 277. For a critical analysis of the reservations by the United States and others to the Genocide Convention, see W. Schabas, *Genocide in International Law* (Cambridge: Cambridge University Press, 2000) pp. 521–8.
43 See Schabas, *ibid.* at p. 2.
44 *Ibid.*
45 *Ibid.* at p. 7.
46 Most vividly told in the great work of literature by A.I. Solzhenitsyn, *The Gulag Archipelago*, 3 volumes (New York: Harper and Row, 1973, 1974, 1979); see also Lauren, *supra* note 1 at p. 245.
47 For texts that are critical of both superpowers during the Cold War, see Noam Chomsky, *Superpowers in Collision: The Cold War Now* (New York: Penguin, 1982); See also Z. Karabell, *Architects of Intervention: The United States, the Third World, and the Cold War, 1946–1962* (Baton Rouge: Louisiana State University Press, 1999).
48 Quoted in P. Kennedy, *The Rise and Fall of the Great Powers* (New York: Fontana Press, 1989) at p. 479. The full speech of President Truman delivered 12 March 1947 can be found in *Public Papers of the Presidents of the United States – Harry S. Truman, 1947* (Washington, DC: US Government Printing Office, 1963) at pp. 176–80.
49 See Kennedy, *ibid.* at p. 479.
50 N. Chomsky, *The Chomsky Reader* (New York: Pantheon Books, 1987) at pp. 207–367.
51 S. Scarfe, *Complicity, Human Rights and Canadian Foreign Policy* (Montreal: Black Rose Books, 1996) at p. 35.
52 See Chomsky, *supra* note 50 at pp. 302–11.
53 *Ibid.* note 51 at p. 95.
54 *Ibid.* at p. 96.
55 See R. Clark, "'The Decolonization' of East Timor and the United Nations Norms on Self-Determination and Aggression" (1980) 7(1) *Yale Journal of World Public Order* at p.10.
56 *Supra* note 50 at pp. 307–8.
57 See M. Haas, *Genocide by Proxy: Cambodian Pawn on a Superpower Chessboard* (New York: Praeger, 1991).
58 See *supra* note 50 at pp. 302–11.
59 See Robertson, *supra* note 15 at p. 52.
60 *Ibid.* at pp. 53–4.
61 *Ibid.* at p. 55.

218 *Notes*

62 See C. Tomuschat, "Quo Vadis, Argentoratum? The Success Story of the European Convention on Human Rights and a Few Dark Stains" (1992) 13 *Human Rights Law Journal* 401–6.

63 M. Boyle, "Reflections on the Effectiveness of the European System for the Protection of Human Rights" in Anne F. Bayefsky, *supra* note 26 at pp. 169–70.

64 *Ibid.*

65 Substantially all of the European Convention was incorporated into British law by the Human Rights Act of 1998, which came into effect on 2 October 2000. For a rather uncritical but interesting perspective on the impact of the Act on Britain, see F. Klug, *Values for a Godless Age: The Story of the United Kingdom's New Bill of Rights* (Harmondsworth: Penguin, 2000).

66 *Supra* note 63 at p. 178.

67 *Ibid.*

68 See M. Nowak, "Human Rights 'Conditionality' in Relation to Entry to, and Full Participation in, the EU" in P. Alston., M. Bustelo, and J. Heenan, *The EU and Human Rights* (Oxford: Oxford University Press, 1999) at pp. 687–98.

69 *Ibid.* at p. 689.

70 *Ibid.* at p. 690.

71 For details about the Charter and the text of the Charter, see the official website of the EU Parliament at http://www.europarl.eu.int/charter/default_en.htm (accessed: June 2001).

72 For details of Human Rights Watch's pleas to the Council of Europe to censure Russia, see the official website of the organization at http://hrw.org/press/2001/01/chechnya0122.htm. (accessed: June 2001). The Council of Europe Parliamentary Assembly has also condemned Russia's actions in Chechnya, stating that it has breached its obligations under the European Convention of Human Rights; see the website of the Parliamentary Assembly at http://press.coe.int/cp/2000/260a(2000).htm (accessed: June 2001).

73 *Supra* note 68 at p. 692.

74 For a relatively recent assessment of the Inter-American Human Rights System, see S.C. Boero, "The Rebellion of the Vulnerable: Perspectives from the Americas" in *The Universal Declaration of Human Rights: Fifty Years and Beyond, supra* note 33 at p. 283.

75 *Ibid.* at pp. 288–93.

76 For the full text of the Quebec City Declaration of the Summit of the Americas, see the official Summit website, at http://www.summit-americas.org/eng-2002/previous-summits.htm (accessed: June 2001).

77 See V. Muntarbhorn, "Protection of Human Rights in Asia and the Pacific: Think Universal, Act Regional?" in *The Universal Declaration of Human Rights: Fifty Years and Beyond, supra* note 33 at p. 299.

78 *Ibid.* at pp. 299–307.

79 For a recent analysis of the African human rights system, see A. Dieng, "Interface between Global and Regional Protection and Promotion of Human Rights: An African Perspective" in *The Universal Declaration of Human Rights: Fifty Years and Beyond, supra* note 33 at p. 271.

80 *Ibid.* at pp. 275–82.

81 *Ibid.* at p. 281.

82 For further description and analysis of the new African Union organization, see the *Globe and Mail* (9 July 2002) at p. A9. For further reading on the African human rights system, see B.O. Okere, "The Protection of Human Rights in Africa and the African Charter on Human and Peoples' Rights: A Comparative Analysis with the European and American Systems" (1998) 6(2) *Human Rights Quarterly* pp. 141–59; C. Flinterman and E. Ankumah, "The African Charter on Human and Peoples' Rights" in H. Hannum (ed.) *Guide to International Human Rights Practice*, 3rd edn (Ardsley, NY: Transnational Publishers, 1999); H.J. Steiner and P. Alston, *supra* note 4 at pp.

920–37; see also J. Mayotte, "Civil War in Sudan: The Paradox of Human Rights and National Sovereignty" (1994) 47(2) *Journal of International Affairs* 497–524.

83 For a good, concise description of the US interests at stake in the Gulf, see J.M. Roberts, *The Penguin History of the 20th Century* (Harmondsworth: Penguin, 1999) at pp. 765–75.

84 UN Doc. S/Res/688. 1991; see also Payam Akhavan, "Lessons from Iraqi Kurdistan: Self-determination and Humanitarian Intervention against Genocide" (1993) 11(1) *Netherlands Quarterly of Human Rights* 41.

85 See *Final Report of the Commission of Experts established pursuant to Security Council Resolution 780* (1992) and its Annexes, 27 May 1994, UN Doc. s/1994/674. See also B. Ajbola, "Human Rights in the Federation of Bosnia-Herzegovina" (1997) 12(2) *Connecticut Journal of International Law* 189–96; D. Kresock, "Ethnic Cleansing in the Balkans: The Legal Foundations of Foreign Intervention" (1994) 27 *Cornell International Law Journal* 203–39; T. Meron, "Rape as a Crime under International Humanitarian Law" (1993) 87(3) *American Journal of International Law* 424–8.

86 *Final Report of the Commission of Experts established pursuant to Security Council Resolution 780*, *ibid.*

87 Human Rights Watch, "Bosnia-Hercegovina: The Fall of Srebrenica and the Failure of UN Peacekeeping" (October 1995) 7(13) *Human Rights Watch.*

88 For a discussion of the human rights situation in Bosnia after the Dayton Accords, see W. Benedek, *Human Rights in Bosnia and Herzegovina after Dayton: From Theory to Practice* (The Hague: Martinus Nijhoff, 1996).

89 *Report of the Secretary-General pursuant to General Assembly Resolution 53/35, The Fall of Srebrenica*, UN Doc. A/54/549 (15 December 1999).

90 See J.A.R. Nafziger, "The Security of Human Rights: A Third Phase in the Global System?" 1990 20(2) *California Western International Law Journal* 174–9; see also Lauren, *supra* note 1 at pp. 274–80.

91 Richard Curtiss, "In Somalia, the Goal Must Be 'Do No Harm' " *The Washington Report*, November/December 1993 at p. 38.

92 See the calculation of the scale of the genocide in A. Des Forges, *Leave None to Tell the Story: Genocide in Rwanda* (New York: Human Rights Watch, 1999).

93 Des Forges, *ibid.* at p. 20, describes in chilling detail how individuals representing Security Council members, and even President Clinton and French President François Mitterrand, seemed unable to dissociate Rwanda from Somalia, even though there were few comparisons.

94 See Des Forges, *ibid.* at pp. 16–26.

95 *Ibid.* at p. 18; see also pp. 150–4.

96 *Ibid.* at pp. 18–19, 595–634; see also Schabas, *supra* note 42 at p. 477, citing a study by S.R. Feil, *Preventing Genocide: How the Early Use of Force Might Have Succeeded in Rwanda* (Washington: Carnegie Commission on Preventing Deadly Conflict, 1998); see also L.R. Melvern, *A People Betrayed: The Role of the West in Rwanda's Genocide* (London: Zed Books, 2000). At p. 291 of the text, the author states:

> A political adviser in the State Department, Tony Marley described America's response to Goma as resulting from the "CNN factor", that a certain level of media coverage prompts action by governments. Marley also perceived a sense of guilt on the part of those who had obstructed any US action, or any US response to the genocide. "People had known earlier what was going on, but had done nothing," Marley claimed.

97 See Schabas, *supra* note 42 at pp. 495–6. For a devastating account by a leading US expert of how American self-interest has triumphed over concerns over massive human rights abuses and genocide in many of the genocides of the twentieth century, including Rwanda, see Samantha Power, *A Problem from Hell* (New York: Basic Books, 2002).

98 Des Forges, *supra* note 92 at p. 645.

99 Schabas, *supra* note 42 at pp. 459–62; see also Des Forges, *supra* note 92 at pp. 635–91.

100 Des Forges, *supra* note 92 at p. 25.

101 See *Report of the Independent Inquiry into the Actions of the United Nations during the 1994 Genocide in Rwanda*, http://www.un.org/News/ossg/rwanda_report.htm) (accessed: June 2001).

102 *Globe and Mail*, 15 April 2000, at p. A21 (a report from Associated Press, UN).

103 See Schabas, *supra* note 42 at p. 368 and pp. 378–86 for an analysis of the record of the International Tribunal for the Former Yugoslavia and the International Criminal Tribunal for Rwanda, as regards the indictments for genocide. See also R.J. Goldstone, *For Humanity: Reflections of a War Crimes Investigator* (Castle Lectures in Ethics, Politics and Economics; New Haven, CT: Yale University Press, 2000); Payam Akhavan, Theodor Meron, W. Hays Parks and Patricia Viseur-Sellers, "Conference on War Crimes Tribunals: The Contribution of the Ad Hoc Tribunals to International Humanitarian Law" (1998) 13 *American University International Law Review* at pp. 1509–39.

104 The best analysis of the Kosovo crisis, including the origins of the conflict, can be found in *The Kosovo Report* of the Independent International Commission on Kosovo, headed by Justice Richard J. Goldstone and Carl Tham (Oxford: Oxford University Press, 2000).

105 *Ibid.* at pp. 33–64.

106 *Ibid.* at pp. 67–92 and pp. 139–59.

107 *Ibid.* at pp. 92–4. For a fascinating account of the root causes and conduct of this "virtual war" see Michael Ignatieff, *Virtual War, Kosovo and Beyond* (Toronto: Viking, 2000).

108 *The Kosovo Report, supra* note 104 at pp. 166–76. For the view of an eminent international lawyer on these issues, see A. Cassese, "*Ex Inuria Ius Oritur*: Are We Moving towards International Legitimation of Forcible Humanitarian Countermeasures in the World Community? Comment on Bruno Simma" (1999) 10 *European Journal of International Law* 23.

109 This crucial distinction was made by Professor Mendes in discussions with the Independent International Commission on Kosovo and was endorsed by the Commission, see *supra* note 104 at p. 10.

110 *Ibid.* at p. 159.

111 *Ibid.* at pp. 140–2.

112 See Schabas, *supra* note 42 at p. 499.

113 *The Kosovo Report, supra* note 104 at p. 174.

114 *Ibid.* at pp. 95–7.

115 *Ibid.*

116 *Ibid.* at p. 99.

117 *Ibid.* at p. 97.

118 See International Council on Human Rights Policy, *Hard Cases: Bringing Human Rights Violators to Justice Abroad – A Guide to Universal Jurisdiction* (Versoix, Switzerland: International Council on Human Rights Policy, 1999) at p. 1. The report can be located at, http://www.international-council.org (accessed: June 2002).

119 *R. v. Metropolitan Stipendiary Magistrate, ex parte Pinochet* (No. 1) [2000] 1 AC 61 (House of Lords, 25 November 1998); see also Amnesty International, *United Kingdom: The Pinochet Case – Universal Jurisdiction and the Absence of Immunity for Crimes against Humanity*, AI Index: EUR 45/01/99, January 1999.

120 *Regina v. Bartle and the Commissioner of Police for the Metropolis and Others – Ex Parte Pinochet* (House of Lords, 24 March 1999) 38 *International Legal Materials* 581. See also International Council on Human Rights Policy, *supra* note 118 at pp. 29–34.

121 *Supra* note 118 at pp. 48–9. For an account of the trial of the four Rwandans in Belgium and discussion of the arguments in favor and against universal jurisdiction in this case, see the *Globe and Mail*, 9 June 2001 at p. A14.

122 See *The Princeton Principles on Universal Jurisdiction* (Program in Law and Public Affairs; Princeton, NJ: Princeton University, 2001). The full text of the decision of the International Court of Justice in the *Democratic Republic of the Congo v. Belgium* case can be located at http://www.icj-cij.org/icjwww/idocket/iCOBE/iCOBEframe.htm (accessed: February 2002).

123 *National Post*, 2 December 2000, at p. A14, reports by Reuters, Associated Press, and Agence France-Presse.

124 *United Kingdom: The Pinochet Case, supra* note 119 at p. 8.

125 *Ibid.* at pp. 14–22.

126 See further, R. Brody and M. Ratner (eds) *The Pinochet Papers: The Case of Augusto Pinochet in Spain and Britain* (The Hague: Kluwer Law International, 2000).

127 See D. Shelton (ed.) *International Crimes, Peace, and Human Rights: The Role of the International Criminal Court* (New York: Transnational Publishers, 2000), Introduction at pp. xiii–xiv.

128 *Ibid.*

129 Scharf, "The Politics behind the US Opposition to the ICC" (1999) 5 *New England International and Comparative Law Annual*, located at: http://www.nesl.edu/intljournal/vol5indx.cfm (accessed: May 2002).

130 For accounts of this historic ending of impunity of the individual who caused so much suffering and massive human rights violations in the entire Balkans, see *Globe and Mail*, 29 June 2001 at pp. A1, A8, A12.

131 Scharf, *supra* note 129.

132 *Military and Paramilitary Activities in and against Nicaragua (Nicaragua v. US)*, [1984] I.C.J. Rep. 392.

133 Scharf, *supra* note 129.

134 *Ibid.* at p. 3.

135 For detailed discussion of the Court see C.M. Bassiouni, *The Statute of the International Criminal Court* (Dobbs Ferry, NY: Transnational Publishers, 1998); C.M. Bassiouni (ed.) *The Statute of the International Criminal Court*, 2nd edn (Dobbs Ferry, NY: Transnational Publishers, 1999).

136 For a critical assessment of the doctrine of complementarity, see M. Morris, "Complementarity and Its Discontents: States, Victims, and the International Criminal Court" in D. Shelton, *supra* note 127 at pp. 177–201.

137 Scharf, *supra* note 129.

138 *Ibid.* at p. 4.

139 See D. Scheffer, "The United States and the ICC" in D. Shelton, *supra* note 127 at pp. 203–6.

140 *Ibid.*

141 See Human Rights Watch, "Getting Away with Murder, Mutilation, Rape. New Testimony from Sierra Leone" (July 1999) 11(3A) *Human Rights Watch*. This report can be located at http://www.hrw.org/hrw/reports/1999/sierra/ (accessed: July 2001).

142 See Amnesty International, *2001 Report on Sierra Leone*, located at http://www.web.amnesty.org/web/ar2001.nsf/webafrcountries/SIERRA+LEONE?Open Document (accessed: June 2001).

143 *The New York Times*, 13 May 2001 at pp. A1–A8.

144 See the US experts quoted in this regard in the *The New York Sunday Times*, 14 May 2000, Section 4 at p. 4.

145 *Supra* note 143 at p. A8.

146 *Supra* notes 141 and 142.

147 *Supra* note 143 at p. A8.

148 *Supra* note 141.
149 Charles Cobb, Jr, *Powell's Peacekeeping Promise* (24 May 2001) located at http://allafrica.com/stories/200105240382.html (accessed: June 2001).
150 For a detailed discussion of the Australian-led intervention, including the concern that Australia had to ensure that there were Asian contributions to the INTERFET force, see H.S. Albinski, "Issues in Australian Foreign Policy (East Timor)," (2000) 46(12) *Australian Journal of Politics and History* at p. 194.
151 United Nations, *INTERFET Security Force in East Timor Officially Replaced by UN* (Newswire, 23 February 2000) located at http://www.un.org/peace/etimor/news/N230200a.html (accessed: March 2000).
152 *National Post*, 31 December 1999 at pp. A1, A2.
153 See J. Kirton, "Creating Peace and Human Security: The G8 and the Okinawa Summit Contribution" (paper presented at Soka University, Japan, 26 May 2000). The paper can be located at the University of Toronto's G8 Information website at http://www.g7.utoronto.ca/g7/scholar/kirton200002 (accessed: June 2001). See also N. Bayne, *Hanging in There: The G7 and G8 Summit in Maturity and Renewal* (Aldershot: Ashgate, 2000); P. Hajnal, *The G7/G8 System: Evolution, Role and Documentation*, The G8 and Global Governance Series (Aldershot: Ashgate, 1999).
154 Kirton, *ibid.* at p. 3.
155 *Ibid.* at p. 4.
156 See Aileen McCabe, "G8 Unity Collapses over Chechnya Bombing: Russia Rejects International Calls for Ceasefire" *The Ottawa Citizen*, 18 December 1999 at p. E18.
157 See G8 Communiqué Okinawa 2000 (23 July 2000), located at http://acc.un system.org/-documents/repository/G8.communique.pdf. (accessed: July 2001). See also Kirton, *supra* note 153 at p. 3.
158 G8 Communiqué Okinawa, *ibid.* at paragraph 2 see also paragraph 72.
159 For the full text of the summit documents and the Chair's summary, see the Government of Canada's website at http://www.g8.gc.ca/kan_docs/chairsummary-e.asp (accessed: July 2001). See also *The New York Times*, 28 June 2002 at p. A1; *Globe and Mail*, 28 June 2002 at p. A1.
160 See *The Report of the Working Group on the Question of Equitable Representation on and Increase in the Membership of the Security Council and Other Matters Related to the Security Council*, UN GAOR, 52nd Sess. UN Doc. A/52/47 (24 August 1998).
161 Under Article 108 of the UN Charter.
162 See International Commission on Global Governance, *Our Global Neighbourhood* (Oxford: Oxford University Press, 1995) at pp. 239–41.
163 Kirton, *supra* note 153 at p. 4.
164 The World Bank has acknowledged the need to go in this direction; see the World Bank's *Development and Human Rights*, published on the fiftieth anniversary of the Universal Declaration of Human Rights. The full text can be found at http://www.worldbank.org/html/extdr/rights/ (accessed: July 2001).
165 Canada, as the architect of peacekeeping, has set up the Lester B. Pearson International Peacekeeping Training Centre in Nova Scotia, Canada, to train peacekeeping troops in these *new* military skills; see http://www.cdnpeace keeping.ns.ca (accessed: August 2001).
166 See D. Quayat, "The United Nations and Regional Organizations: A New Paradigm for Peace?" (Conference of Defence Associations Institute, 2–13 November 1999) at p. 12.
167 Speech by the secretary-general, Kofi Annan, to Georgetown University, February 1999, on the future of peacekeeping operations: UN DPKO, "Cooperation between the United Nations and Regional Peacekeeping Organizations/Arrangements in a Peacekeeping Environment: Suggested Principles and Mechanisms," March 1999.
168 UNDP, *Human Development Report 1994* (Oxford: Oxford University Press, 1994).

169 The full title of the Convention is: The Convention on the Prohibition of the Use, Stockpiling, Production and Transfer of the Anti-personnel Mines and their Destruction, established at Oslo, Norway, September 1997, even though it is commonly called the Ottawa Convention, given the lead of the Canadian government in creating it.

170 Lloyd Axworthy, "The New Diplomacy: The UN, the International Criminal Court and the Human Security Agenda" (speech given at Harvard University), located at http://www.dfait-maeci.gc.ca/foreign_policy/human-rights/statement-en.asp (accessed: June 2001).

171 These concepts are further elaborated by the Government of Canada in "Human Security: Safety for People in a Changing World" which can be found at http://www/dfait-maeci.gc.ca/foreignp/HumanSecurity/secur-e-htm (accessed: June 2001).

172 *Ibid.*

173 See *The Responsibility to Protect, Report of the International Commission on Intervention and State Sovereignty* (Ottawa: International Development Research Centre, 2001). The report can also be located at http://www.iciss-ciise.gc.ca (accessed: July 2001).

174 See *The New York Times*, 14 September 2001 at p. A1.

175 United Nations Security Council Resolution 1368 (2001), UN Doc. S/RES/1368 (2001).

176 United Nations Security Council Resolution 1373 (2001), UN Doc. S/RES/1373 (2001). Resolution 1373 also creates a committee to monitor implementation.

177 *The Economist* described the coalition in the following words:

> The coalition that America has assembled is extraordinary. An alliance that includes Russia, the NATO countries, Uzbekistan, Tajikistan, Pakistan, Saudi Arabia and other Gulf States as well as acquiescence from China and Iran would not have been imaginable on September 11, 2001.
>
> ("Closing In," *The Economist*, 29 September 2001, at p. 11)

178 *Ibid.*

179 See *The New York Times*, 15 December, 2001 at p. A1, describing how the United States hoped that release of this "smoking gun" would win over more of the Arab and Muslim world.

180 See *The New York Times*, 14 September 2001 at p. A17.

181 *Ibid.*

182 See the essay by Bill Keller in *The New York Times*, 6 October 2001, who states, inter alia,

> The original cold war taught us a good deal about the value of allies. It gave birth to the Marshall Plan and NATO, and those comforting arms control treaties that, at least until recently, the new administration belittled as constraints on our freedom. Now, the common fear of terrorism is beginning to drive us together, much as the fear of nuclear annihilation did. The new cold war has finally got us to pay our United Nations dues.

183 For an insightful view of Pakistan's role as both creator and victim of the Taliban and al-Qaeda terrorist network, see *The Economist*, 29 September 2001 at pp. 20–2.

184 *Ibid.*

185 See *The Economist*, 6 October 2001 at pp. 15–16; See also *The Economist*, 17 November 2001 at pp. 17–19.

186 Ultimately to secure the initial victory accomplished by a virtual war; see Ignatieff, *supra* note 107; putting large numbers of troops on the ground has proved a necessity in Afghanistan, see *The Economist*, 1 December, 2001 at pp. 20–1.

187 For a discussion of the possible expansion of America's war against global terrorism to Iraq, see *The Economist*, 8 December 2001 at pp. 19–21.

188 For discussion of the US anti-terrorism measures, see *The Economist*, 29 September 2001 at pp. 12, 35–6, and *The Economist*, 8 December 2001 at pp. 2930. For discussion of the Canadian measures, see the *Globe and Mail*, 20 November 2001 at p. A17.

189 For a discussion by leading human rights and constitutional experts in Canada on the relationship between anti-terrorism measures, human rights, and human security, see "Between Crime and War; Terrorism, Democracy and the Constitution," special issue of the *National Journal of Constitutional Law* (Toronto: Carswell, 2002).

190 See *The Economist*, 8 December 2001 at p. 18.

191 See *The New York Times*, 12 December 2001 at pp. A1 and A14.

192 See *The New York Times*, 8 December 2001 at p. A1.

193 See *The Economist*, 8 December 2001 at pp. 43–4. See also *The Economist*, 6 April 2002 at pp. 22–6; *The Economist*, 13 April 2002 at pp. 25–30.

194 *The Vienna Convention on the Law of Treaties*, 23 May 1969, 1155 U.N.T.S. 331 at 339 (entered into force 27 January 1980); see *The New York Times*, 7 May 2002 at p. A11.

195 See this and other critical statements of Senator Russell D. Feingold of the US Congress, *The New York Times*, 7 May 2002 at p. A11.

196 See Curtis A. Bradley, *U.S. Announces Intent Not to Ratify International Criminal Court Treaty*, American Society of International Law Insights (May 2002) available at: www.asil.org (accessed: June 2002).

197 See the statements by US Undersecretary of State John R. Bolton and Defense Secretary Donald H. Rumsfeld in this regard: *The New York Times*, 7 May 2002 at p. A11.

198 *Ibid.*

199 *Ibid.*

200 See *The New York Times*, 5 May 2002 at p. A18.

201 *Ibid.*

202 See *The New York Times*, 3 and 4 July 2002 at p. A1.

203 See *The New York Times*, 13 July 2002 at p. A3.

2 World trade: for whose benefit?

1 See Paul Gordon Lauren, *The Evolution of Human Rights, Visions Seen* (Philadelphia: University of Pennsylvania Press, 1998) at p. 142.

2 See John H. Jackson, William J. Davey, and Alan O. Sykes, Jr, *Legal Problems of International Economic Relations*, 3rd edn (St Paul, MN: West Publishing, 1995) at pp. 278–9.

3 *Ibid.* at p. 279 .

4 *Ibid.* at pp. 293–4.

5 *Ibid.*

6 *Ibid.* at p. 295.

7 Cited by Raj Bhala, "Clarifying the Trade–Labor Link" (1998) 37(1) *Columbia Journal of Transnational Law* at pp. 30–1.

8 See Tony McGrew, "The World Trade Organization, Technocracy or Banana Republic?" in Annie Taylor and Caroline Thomas (eds) *Global Trade and Global Social Issues* (London: Routledge, 1999) at pp. 197–216.

9 *Supra* note 2 at pp. 314–17.

10 *Ibid.* at pp. 301–10.

11 *Ibid.* at pp. 289–91; see also Asif H. Qureshi, *The World Trade Organization, Implementing International Trade Norms* (Manchester: Manchester University Press, 1996) at pp. 10–45.

12 *Ibid.*

13 *Report of the Standing Committee on Foreign Affairs and International Trade: Canada and the Future of the World Trade Organization, Advancing a Millennium Agenda in the Public Interest*

(Chair: Bill Graham, MP) (Ottawa: House of Commons, Canada, 1999) at p. 11-7 (SCFAIT Report). For an extensive discussion of the social dimensions, or the lack thereof, of the WTO, see the SCFAIT Report.

14 See Qureshi, *supra* note 11 at p. 11.
15 See SCFAIT Report, *supra* note 13 at p. 12-9.
16 For a discussion of the future of the WTO in the aftermath of the debacle at Seattle, see J. Schott (ed.) *The WTO after Seattle* (Washington, DC: Institute for International Economics, 2000).
17 The Canadian Constitution is probably one of the best examples to illustrate this point. The Supreme Court of Canada has, since the birth of the county in 1867, drawn on principles found in the preamble to the Constitution Act, 1867, to rule on some of the most important constitutional issues facing the country. The best example is the decision of the Supreme Court of Canada on the issue of whether the separatist government of the province of Quebec had the right to unilaterally secede from the rest of Canada. In ruling that there was no such right to unilaterally secede, but that the rest of Canada would have a fundamental duty to negotiate if the people of Quebec on a "clear question" and a "clear vote" opted in favor of secession, the Court referred to fundamental constitutional principles, most of which had their origins in the preamble to the Constitution Act, 1867. For an in-depth discussion by Canada's leading constitutional experts see the *Reference Re Secession of Quebec* (1998) 2 S.C.R. 217 at 1; see also "Special Issue on the Quebec Secession Decision" (1999) 11 *National Journal of Constitutional Law* at pp. 1–168.
18 For support of the view that the Marrakesh Agreement preamble qualifies the rest of the WTO Code, see Qureshi, *supra* note 11 at p. 4.
19 *Ibid.*
20 *Ibid.*
21 *Ibid.*
22 SCFAIT Report, *supra* note 13, at p. 11-5.
23 The summary of the online discussion with selected examples of participation, including the ones quoted here, can be found at http://www.panos.org.uk/environment/globalisation_and_poverty_online.htm (accessed: May 2000). The World Bank Development Forum on Globalization and Poverty involved the participation of over 5,000 persons across the world during May 2000. The online forum was co-moderated by the Panos Institute, London. The purpose of the forum was described by the Panos Institute as a debate which "was conceived after the anti-WTO demonstrations in Seattle. The [World] Bank recognised that Seattle marked a turning point; its 'clients' were no longer governments, but a much broader swathe of civil society."
24 SCFAIT Report, *supra* note 13 at p. 14-4.
25 Input by C. Osakwe, head of the WTO Working Group on LDCs, in the WTO–World Bank Online Forum on Trade and Sustainable Development which had over 1,000 participants from around the world. A summary of the discussion can be found at www.itd.org/forums/tsdsumm.htm (accessed: June 2001).
26 See Peter H. Lindert and Jeffery G. Williamson, *Does Globalization Make the World More Unequal?* National Bureau of Economic Research, Working Paper 8228, April 2001, located at http://www/nber.org/papers/w8228 (accessed: July 2001).
27 UNCTAD, *Trade and Development Report, Globalization: Distribution and Growth* (Geneva: United Nations, 1997).
28 For further elaboration of this perspective, see Ruth Mayne and Caroline Le Quesne, "Calls for Social Trade" in *Global Trade and Global Social Issues, supra* note 8 at pp. 91–113.
29 Quoted in SCFAIT Report, *supra* note 13 at p. 14-4.
30 See Charles Gore, *The Least Developed Countries 2000 Report, Aid, Private Capital Flows and External Debt: The Challenge of Financing Development in the LDCs* (Geneva: UNCTAD 2000). The full report can be located at http://www.unctad.org/en/pub/ps1ldc00.en.htm (accessed: June 2001).

31 See Ozay Mehmet, Errol Mendes, and Rob Sinding, *Towards a Fair Global Labour Market, Avoiding the New Slave Trade* (New York: Routledge, 1999) at pp. 40–58.
32 Charles Gore, *supra* note 30; see also SCFAIT Report, *supra* note 13 at pp. 14-1 to 14-7.
33 Charles Gore, *ibid.*
34 For a discussion of social dumping, see SCFAIT Report, *supra* note 13 at pp. 11-8 to 11-10.
35 See Peter Morci, "Implications of a Social Charter for the North American Free Trade Agreement" in *The Social Charter Implications of the NAFTA, Canada–U.S. Outlook* (Washington, DC: National Planning Association, 1997), at p. 8, quoted in SCFAIT Report, *supra* note 13 at p. 11-9.
36 Gilbert Winham and Elizabeth De Boer, "Trade Relations and Social Charters; The Case of the North American Free Trade Agreement" quoted in SCFAIT Report, *supra* note 13 at p. 11-9.
37 Quoted in SCFAIT Report, *ibid.* at p. 13-5.
38 Ozay Mehmet, Errol Mendes, and Rob Sinding, *supra* note 31 at p. 10.
39 *Ibid.* at pp. 70–4.
40 *Ibid.* at pp. 74–7.
41 *Ibid.*
42 *Ibid.* at p. 71.
43 *Ibid.* at p. 74.
44 For an excellent description of the structure of the WTO, see Qureshi, *supra* note 11 at pp. 5–9.
45 Mehmet *et al.*, *supra* note 31 at p. 78.
46 *Ibid.* at p. 81.
47 William J. Davey, "The WTO Dispute Settlement System" (2000) 3 *Journal of International Economic Law* 15–18.
48 International Labor Conference, ILO Declaration on Fundamental Principles and Rights at Work, 86th Session, Geneva, June 1998. The Declaration can be located at http://www.ilo.org/public/english/standards/relm/ilc/ilc86/com-dtxt.htm (accessed: March 2001).
49 See R.T. Stranks, *Look before You Leap: "Core" Labour Rights*, Policy Staff Commentary No. 14 (Ottawa: Department of Foreign Affairs and International Trade, 1996).
50 Mehmet *et al.*, *supra* note 31 at p. 89.
51 SCFAIT Report, *supra* note 13 at p. 13-8.
52 Mehmet *et al.*, *supra* note 31 at pp. 48–9.
53 For a discussion of the EPZs from the perspective of the World Bank, see *World Development Report: Workers in an Integrating World* (Washington, DC: World Bank, 1995); *Involving Workers in East Asia's Growth* (Washington, DC: World Bank, 1995). One author argues that Malaysia's EPZs do not fit the stereotype of abusive labor practices; see G. Sivalingam, *The Economics and Social Impact of EPZs: The Case of Malaysia*, ILO Working Paper No. 66 (Geneva: ILO, 1994).
54 For a more detailed discussion of the possible analogies of abusive labor practices to subsidies, see Mehmet *et al.*, *supra* note 31 at pp. 106–17.
55 *Ibid.*
56 *Ibid.*
57 For articles by a leading writer on the US ban on imports of prison labor and other areas that serve as a powerful analogy to dealing with other abusive labor practices, see S. Charnovitz, "The Influence of International Labour Standards on the World Trading Regime. A Historical Overview" (1987) 126 *International Labour Review* 565; S. Charnovitz "Environmental and Labour Standards and Trade" (1992) 15 *The World Economy* 335–56; S. Charnovitz, "The World Trade Organization and Social Issues" (1994) 28 *Journal of World Trade* 17–33; S. Charnovitz, "Promoting Higher Labor Standards" (1995) 18(3) *Washington Quarterly* 167–90.

58 For a discussion of these trends and the role of multinationals in EPZs see P. Bailey, A. Parisott, and G. Renshaw (eds) *Multinationals and Employment: The Global Economy of the 1990s* (Geneva: ILO, 1993).

59 OECD, *Trade Employment and Labour Standards: A Study of Core Workers' Rights and International Trade* (Paris: OECD, 1996).

60 For a discussion of how the ICFTU and other social clause advocates would structure such a clause and its enforcement, see R. Mayne and C. Le Quesne, *supra* note 28 at pp. 98–101.

61 *Ibid.* at pp. 101–2.

62 Mehmet *et al.*, *supra* note 31 at pp. 117–21.

63 *Ibid.* at p. 120.

64 For an in-depth analysis of how to deal effectively with hazardous and exploitative child labor, see UNICEF, *The State of the World's Children* (New York: Oxford University Press) at pp. 15–73.

65 See A.B. Zampetti and P. Sauve, "Onwards to Singapore: The International Contestability of Markets and the New Trade Agenda" (1996) 19(13) *The World Economy* 333; J.G. Ruggie, "At Home Abroad, Abroad at Home: International Liberalisation and Domestic Stability in the New World Economy" 24(3) *Millennium* 507; J. McKinney, "The World Trade Regime: Past Successes and Future Challenges" (1994) 49(3) *International Journal* 445.

66 Mehmet *et al.*, *supra* note 31 at pp. 202–4.

67 See Mayne and Le Quesne, *supra* note 28 at pp. 104–5.

68 For further discussion of the TPRM and the TPRB, see Qureshi, *supra* note 11 at pp. 108–25.

69 See Mehmet *et al.*, *supra* note 31 at pp. 201–2.

70 *Ibid.*

71 See Tony Evans, "Trading Human Rights" in *Global Trade and Global Social Issues*, *supra* note 28, at pp. 46–7; see also B.R Johnston and G. Button, "Human Environmental Rights Issues and the Multinational Corporation: Industrial Development in the Free Trade Zone" in B.R. Johnston (ed.) *Who Pays the Price?* (Washington, DC: Island Press, 1994).

72 Human Rights Watch, *Trading Away Rights: The Unfulfilled Promise of NAFTA's Labor Side Agreement* (April 2001) 13(2B) *Human Rights Watch*. The report can be located at www.hrw.org/reports/2001/nafta/ (accessed: June 2001).

73 *Ibid.* at pp. 14–23.

74 *Ibid.* at p. 32.

75 *Ibid.* at pp. 46–7.

76 *Ibid.* at p. 3.

77 For a detailed discussion of the USJFTA, with reference to key provisions, see Human Rights Watch, *supra* note 72, at pp. 10–13.

78 *Ibid.* at p. 11.

79 *Ibid.*

80 Quoted in Sheryl Dickey, "The Free Trade Area of the Americas and Human Rights Concerns" (2001) 8(3) *Human Rights Brief*. The article can also be located at www.wcl.american.edu/hrbrief/08/3ftaa.cfm (accessed: July 2001).

81 For the standard left critique of how industrial societies and development have produced this adapted litany of environmental ills, see Annie Taylor, "The Trade and Environmental Debate" in Annie Taylor and Caroline Thomas (eds) *Global Trade and Global Social Issues*, *supra* note 8 at pp. 72–90.

82 See the World Commission on Environment and Development (Brundtland Commission), *Our Common Future* (Oxford: Oxford University Press, 1987).

83 For the perspective that UNCED displayed a political consensus on the link between trade and the environment, see James Cameron, "What Now? Trade and the

Environment" in P. Geraint, A. Qureshi, and H. Steiner (eds) *The Legal and Moral Aspects of International Trade* (London and New York: Routledge, 1998) at pp. 166–82.

84 *Ibid.* at pp. 166–7.
85 Taylor, *supra* note 81 at p. 74.
86 Cameron, *supra* note 83 at p. 167.
87 For discussion of this perspective and others that focus on managing environmental protection in the development process, see P. Chatterjee and M. Finger, *The Earth Brokers: Power Politics and World Development* (New York: Routledge, 1994).
88 See Taylor, *supra* note 81 at pp. 78–9.
89 *Ibid.* at pp. 78–81.
90 See, for example, Cameron, *supra* note 83 at p. 168.
91 *Ibid.* at p.169.
92 The WTO website makes a special effort to detail the work of the CTE; see http://www.wto.org/english/tratop_e/envir_e/envir_e.htm (accessed: July 2001).
93 (1994) 33 *International Legal Materials* 842.
94 See Cameron, *supra* note 83 at pp. 170–1.
95 See the WTO website at http://www.wto.org/english/thewto_e/whatis_e/tif_e/bey4_e.htm (accessed: June 2001).
96 *Ibid.* For full text of the decision, see *United States – Import Prohibition of Certain Shrimp and Shrimp Products* (complaint by India, Malaysia, Pakistan, and Thailand) (1998) WTO Doc. WT/DS58/AB/R (Appellate Body Report), located at www.wto.org/english docs_e/docs_e.htm.
97 *Ibid.*
98 For a cogent argument that the WTO must take into account international law norms, including international human rights norms, in interpreting provisions of the WTO Code, see Robert Howse and Makau Mutua, "Protecting Human Rights in a Global Economy, Challenges for the World Trade Organization" in International Centre for Human Rights and Democratic Development *Rights and Democracy* (Montreal: International Centre for Human Rights and Democratic Development, 2000) at pp. 8–12.
99 This information is obtained from the website of the international environment NGO Friends of the Earth, at www.foei.org/trade/activistguide/turtle.htm (accessed: June 2001).
100 *Ibid.* In October of 2001, the Appellate Body handed down its decision in the latest of the *Shrimp–Turtle* disputes. Malaysia had brought a complaint to the WTO pursuant to Article 21.5 of the Dispute Settlement Understanding that the US was failing to comply with the previous Appellate Body ruling (which had found that the import ban discriminated between WTO members) by failing to substantially alter the requirements for shrimp importation into the US. However, the Appellate Body ruled that the changes made by the US to the ban, which now allowed shrimp to be imported from countries that had a comparable sea turtle conservation program to that of the United States, brought the import restrictions in line with the WTO rules. The Appellate Body considered that the changes made by the US meant that the ban no longer discriminated between WTO members. See *US – Import Prohibition of Certain Shrimp and Shrimp Products, Recourse to Article 21.5 of the DSU by Malaysia* (22 October 2001) WTO Doc. WT/DS58/AB/RW (Appellate Body Report), located at www.wto.org/english/docs_e/docs_e.htm.
101 Friends of the Earth, *ibid.*
102 Cameron, *supra* note 83 at pp. 177–80.
103 These and other MEAs are discussed as well as linked to other sites at the WTO website at http://www.wto.org/english/thewto_e/whatis_e/tif_e/bey4_e.htm (accessed: June 2001).
104 *Ibid.*
105 *Ibid.*

106 Cameron, *supra* note 83 at p. 178.

107 *Ibid.* at p. 177.

108 *Ibid.* at p. 179.

109 *Ibid.*

110 Report of the Appellate Body, World Trade Organization, in *European Communities – Measures Affecting Asbestos and Asbestos-Containing Products* (12 March, 2001) WTO Doc. WT/DS135/AB/R (Appellate Body Report), located at www.wto.org/english/docs_e/docs_e.htm

111 Howse and Mutua, *supra* note 98 at p. 12.

112 *Ibid.*

113 The following NGOs issued a joint statement which, in general praised the ruling of the Appellate Body that toxic asbestos is not the same as safer materials: Greenpeace International, World Wide Fund for Nature International, Ban Asbestos Network, International Ban Asbestos Secretariat, and the Foundation for International Environmental Law and Development. The statement can be located at www.field.org.uk/papers/tepap.htm (accessed: July 2001).

114 See the views of the European Trade Union Confederation in this regard at www.etuc.org/tutb/uk/asbestos.html.

115 Joint NGO statement, *supra* note 113.

116 The Executive Summary of the Global Health Council can be found at http://www.wto.org/english/tratop_e/trips_e/hosbjor_execsum_e.htm (accessed: July 2001).

117 International Institute for Sustainable Development (IISD), *Trade and Sustainable Development Principles* (Winnipeg: IISD, 1994). The Principles are also cited in full by Cameron, *supra* note 83 at p. 181; They can also be found on the IISD website at www.iisd.org/trade/princpub.htm (accessed: June 2002).

118 IISD, *The World Trade Organization and Sustainable Development: An Independent Assessment Summary* (Winnipeg: IISD, 1996). The report can also be located at www.issd.org/pdf/wto_assess_summ.pdf (accessed: June 2001); see also SCFAIT Report, *supra* note 13 at p. 12-11.

119 *Ibid.*

120 See SCFAIT Report, *supra* note 13, at p. 1-10.

121 For a discussion on this critical need for capacity building, see R. Blackhurst, "The WTO and the Global Economy" (1997) 20(5) *The World Economy* 527–44; C. Michalopoulos, "The Developing Countries in the WTO," (1999) 22(1) *World Economy* 117–43.

122 Blackhurst, *ibid.*

123 SCFAIT Report, *supra* note 13 at p. 1-10.

124 See the details of WTO engagement with NGOs/Civil Society from the WTO's own perspective at http://www.wto.org/english/forums_e/ngo_e/ngo_e.htm (accessed: June 2002).

125 See SCFAIT Report, *supra* note 13 at p. 1-11.

126 See C. Bellmann and R. Gerster, "Accountability in the World Trade Organization" (1996) 30(6) *Journal of World Trade* 54.

127 *Ibid.* at pp. 50–5.

128 For discussion of these parallels, see SCFAIT Report, *supra* note 13 at p. 1-13.

129 For discussion of the outcome of the Doha Multilateral Trade talks, see "Seeds Sown for Future Growth; The Doha Round" *The Economist*, 17 November 2001 at pp. 65–6.

130 *Ibid.*

131 *Ibid.*

132 *Ibid.*

133 For a discussion of the impact of the new US Farm Bill on the Doha Round of talks see *The Economist*, 11 May 2002 at pp. 14–16.

3 Power and responsibility: the ethical and international legal duties of the global private sector

1 Sarah Anderson and John Cavanagh, *The Top 200, The Rise of Global Corporate Power* (New York: Institute for Policy Studies, 1996). The report can also be found online at http://www.ips-dc.org/downloads/Top_200.pdf (accessed: July 2001).

2 *Ibid.* at p. 3. According to *Fortune* magazine, Wal-Mart became the largest corporation in the United States in 2001, surpassing manufacturing and industrial giants such as General Motors and ExxonMobil. The significance of this lies in the fact that it is the first time a service-orientated corporation has topped the list of the largest American companies since *Fortune* first published its list in 1955. See Cait Murphy, "The 2002 Fortune 500, Wal-Mart Rules" *Fortune*, 15 April 2002, online: www.fortune.com (accessed: June 2002).

3 Anderson and Cavanagh, *ibid.*

4 *Ibid.* at p. 4.

5 *Ibid.*

6 Commission on Transnational Corporations, *General Discussion on Transnational Corporations in the World Economy and Trends in Foreign Direct Investment in Developing Countries* (New York: UN Center on Transnational Corporations (UNCTC), 1993), UN Doc. E/C.10/1993/2 at p. 8.

7 See Allan Rugman, *The End of Globalization* (New York: American Management Association (AMACOM), 2001) at pp. 3–4.

8 *Ibid.* at p. 4.

9 United Nations Conference on Trade and Development, *World Investment Report* (New York: United Nations, 1998).

10 Anderson and Cavanagh, *supra* note 1 at p. 4.

11 *Ibid.* at p. 5.

12 Rugman, *supra* note 7 at pp. 5–6.

13 See S. Hawley, "Exporting Corruption: Privatisation, Multinationals and Bribery" located at www.thecornerhouse.org.uk (accessed: July 2001).

14 *Ibid.*

15 *Ibid.*

16 See C. Heymans and B. Lipietz, *Corruption and Development: Some Perspectives*, Monograph 40 (South Africa: Institute for Security Studies, September 1999). The monograph is located at http://www.iss.co.za (accessed: June 2001).

17 There are many sources on the Internet which give updates on the victims and ongoing controversies of the Bhopal disaster. Two of the most comprehensive can be found at http://www.bophal.net and http://www.bhopal.org. (accessed: June 2001). These sites contain information on developments in the ongoing litigation and NGO activity against Union Carbide and now Dow Chemicals. A more scholarly but now dated analysis of the disaster and the litigation in India and the United States can be found in Jamie Cassels, *The Uncertain Promise of Law: Lessons from Bhopal* (Toronto: University of Toronto Press, 1993).

18 Quotes taken from www.bophal.net, *ibid.*

19 *Ibid.*

20 *Ibid.* See also Dan Kurzman, *A Killing Wind: Inside Union Carbide and the Bhopal Catastrophe* (New York: McGraw Hill, 1987); D. Lapierre and J. Moro, *Five Past Midnight in Bhopal* (New York: Warner Books, 2002); "The Ghosts of Bhopal" *The Economist* 310: 7590, 18 February 1989 at p. 70.

21 Sources that offer other historical perspectives on the disaster include Michael Cross, "Minimata and the Search for Justice" *New Scientist*, 16 February 1991; Eugene Smith, *Minimata* (New York: Holt, Rinehart and Winston, 1975).

22 As with the Bhopal disaster, there are many sites on the Internet which give information on the *Exxon Valdez* disaster and its effect on the environment. Notable

among them is the site of the *Exxon Valdez* Oil Spill Trustee Council located at www.oilspill.state.ak.us (accessed: August 2001).

23 See the *Exxon Valdez* Oil Spill Trustee Council, which consists of three State and Federal trustees (or their designees) at www.oilspill.state.ak.us/facts/lingeringoil.html (accessed: June 2001).

24 These details are from Pamela A. Miller, "*Exxon Valdez* Oil Spill: Ten Years Later. A Technical Background Paper for the Alaska Wilderness League," (1999) 3 *Arctic Connections*. The paper can be found at http://arcticcircle.uconn.edu/SEEJ/ Alaska/miller2.htm.

25 For a discussion of the United States Supreme Court decision, see *USA Today* (2 October 2000). For a discussion of the 9th Circuit Court of Appeal decision, see the *Guardian*, 8 November 2001.

26 Miller, *supra* note 24.

27 *Ibid.*

28 *Ibid.*

29 For a detailed account of the role of Shell and other oil companies in Nigeria from the perspective of a leading human rights organization, see Human Rights Watch, *The Price of Oil, Corporate Responsibility and Human Rights Violations in Nigeria's Oil-Producing Communities* (New York: Human Rights Watch, 1999). The full document can be located at http://www.hrw.org/reports/1999/nigeria/Nigew991.htm (accessed: March 2001).

30 See Amnesty International, *Nigeria: Time to End Contempt for Human Rights* (London: Amnesty International, 1996), AI Index: AFR 44/14/96. The full text of the document can be located at http://www.amnesty.org/ailib/intcam/nigeria/con4.htm (accessed: March 2001).

31 *Ibid.* See also Amnesty International, *Nigeria, A Summary of Human Rights Concerns* (London: Amnesty International, 1996), AI Index: AFR 44/03/96. The report can be located at web.amnesty.org/ai.nsf/Index/AFR440031996?OpenDocument&of= COUNTRIES \NIGERIA (accessed: March 2001).

32 *Nigeria: Time to End Contempt for Human Rights*, *ibid.*

33 Charles Handy, *The Age of Paradox* (Cambridge, MA: Harvard Business School Press, 1994) at p. 153.

34 An international poll done by Toronto-based Environics International in collaboration with the Prince of Wales Business Forum, conducted in twenty-three countries using 23,000 adults in six continents, found that a majority, almost six in ten, identify broader corporate social responsibilities as key in shaping their views of particular companies. The poll, titled the Millennium Poll on Corporate Social Responsibility, revealed that one in five persons surveyed had "punished" irresponsible companies, either by avoiding their products or by speaking out against them. See the announcement of the results of the poll and means to obtain the full poll results from http://www.pwblf.org/csr/csrwebassist.nsf/content/f1e2d3g4.html (accessed: March 2002).

35 See Michael J. Mazaar, *Global Trends 2005: An Owner's Manual for the Next Decade* (New York: Palgrave, 1999) at pp. 230–1.

36 For the full text of the research see Errol P. Mendes and Jeffrey A. Clark, *The Five Generations of Ethical and Social Expectations by Corporate Stakeholders and Their Impact on Corporate Social Responsibility* (Ottawa: Human Rights Research and Education Centre, 1996) available at www.cdp-hrc.uottawa/publicat/five.html (accessed: June 2001).

37 For a discussion of the history and content of the FCPA, see George C. Greanias, *The Foreign Corrupt Practices Act: Anatomy of a Statute* (Lexington, MA: Lexington Books, 1992); See also Jeffrey P. Bialos and Gregory Husisian, *The Foreign Corrupt Practices Act: Coping with Corruption in Transitional Economies* (New York: Oceana Publications, 1997). For a discussion of how the Lockheed scandal involved the

corruption of the Japanese political elites, see Jacob M. Schlesinger, *Shadow Shoguns, The Rise and Fall of Japan's Postwar Political Machine* (New York: Simon and Schuster, 1997).

38 For a discussion of the history, operation and compliance focus of the Federal Sentencing Guidelines, see J.M. Kaplan, J.E. Murphy, and W.M. Swenson (eds) *Compliance Programs and Corporate Sentencing Guidelines: Preventing Civil and Criminal Liability* (New York: Boardman, Callaghan, 1997).

39 For a twenty-year analysis of the FCPA see "Symposium – A Review of the Foreign Corrupt Practices Act on its Twentieth Anniversary: Its Application, Defense and International Aftermath" (1998) 18 *Northwestern Journal of International Law and Business* 263.

40 On this point see Hawley, *supra* note 13, who provides ample evidence that the playing field is far from level. See also Kimberly Elliott (ed.) *Corruption and the Global Economy* (Washington, DC: Institute for International Economics, 1997); Peter Eigen, "Combating Corruption around the World" (1996) 7(1) *Journal of Democracy* 158–68.

41 The business case for ethical standards is strongest with the first and second generations. For this reason most MNEs will have policies dealing with the relevant stakeholders; see Simon Webley, *Codes of Ethics and International Business* (London: Institute of Business Ethics, 1997).

42 For details of the Nike controversy, see Christopher L. Avery, *Business and Human Rights in a Time of Change* (London: Amnesty International, 2000) at pp. 65–72. For an account kinder to Nike, see Peter Schwartz and Blair Gibb, *When Good Companies Do Bad Things* (New York: John Wiley and Sons, 1999) at pp. 51–5.

43 For an analysis of the Nestlé boycott, see Schwartz and Gibb, *ibid.*, at pp. 42–4. See Avery, *ibid.* at pp. 22–4 for recent polls and other evidence that consumers in Europe and North America are becoming more aware of their ethical buying power and are exercising it.

44 See, for example, the documentation of Human Rights Watch concerning how some United States corporations' suppliers treat garment workers in a maquiladora in Guatemala in "Corporations and Human Rights: Freedom of Association in a Maquila in Guatemala" (1997) 9(3B) *Human Rights Watch*. The report is located online at www.hrw.org/reports/1997/guat2/ (accessed: June 2001).

45 Wes Cragg, David Pearson, and James Cooney, "Ethics, Surface Mining and the Environment" (1997) 5(1) *Mining Environment Management* at pp. 10–13.

46 For discussion of this fifth generation of stakeholder expectations from a variety of perspectives, see Michael K. Addo (ed.) *Human Rights Standards and the Responsibility of Transnational Corporations* (The Hague: Kluwer Law International, 1999).

47 For a discussion of the content of codes of ten MNEs see Webley, *supra* note 41.

48 See the ILO Report *Overview of Global Developments and Office Activities concerning Codes of Conduct, Social Labelling and Other Public Sector Initiatives Addressing Labour Issues* ILO Doc. GB.273/WP/SDL/1 (Rev.1) (1998). One leading Canadian newspaper, the *Globe and Mail*, reported that in an international survey 75 percent of the corporations that had codes had not strictly adhered to them (*Globe and Mail*, 15 June 2000). Another survey of 1,000 Canadian corporations by the accounting firm KPMG in 1997 revealed that of the 251 companies responding, while 66 percent had codes, only 21 percent had any kind of training in connection with their ethics program. Over 60 percent had never undertaken a comprehensive review of their ethics-related policies and performance. In its 2000 Ethics Survey, KPMG found more positive numbers: 86.4 percent of companies that responded to a survey sent to 1,000 companies claimed they had some sort of document that outlined their principles and values. While 39 percent provided some form of training in ethics, of the companies that provided such training less than 10 percent provided more than eight hours of training per year to their managers. Moreover, almost one-third

provided for one hour or less of training per year, which rose to 42.1 percent of non-managerial staff who received one hour or less of ethics training a year, with about the same percentage receiving one to four hours a year. The survey can be located at http://www.kpmg.ca/english/services/fas/publications/ethicssurvey2000.html (accessed: July 2001).

49 See Mendes and Clark, *supra* note 36.
50 Schwartz and Gibb, *supra* note 42 at p. 28.
51 *Ibid.* at pp. 28–9.
52 *Ibid.* at p. 32.
53 See Shell, *People, Planet and Profits, The Shell Report, 2000* at p. 5. The report can be located at http://www.shell.com/shellreport (accessed: July 2001).
54 See both Avery, *supra* note 42, and Schwartz and Gibb, *supra* note 42, for details of the controversies surrounding these and many other companies who later attempted to develop ethical policies and practices.
55 See Avery, *supra* note 42 at p. 46. The Levi Strauss Co. "Global Sourcing and Operating Guidelines" can be located at http://www.levistrauss.com/responsibility/conduct/guidelines.htm (accessed: June 2001).
56 The Reebok production standards as well as the company's human rights initiatives can be located at http://www.reebok.com/Reebok/US/HumanRights/index.html (accessed: December 2001).
57 For information about The Body Shop's trading charter see http://www.the-body-shop.com/global/values/reporting/index.asp (accessed: June 2002).
58 For Nexen's extensive integrity program, which Professor Mendes has assisted in developing, see http://www.nexeninc.com/about/ethics.htm (accessed: June 2001).
59 See, for example, the ultimately positive reaction to the independent verification reports that contained both positive and negative findings on The Body Shop and Reebok in Avery, *supra* note 42 at pp. 52–7.
60 *Ibid.* at pp. 57–8.
61 See the documentation in note 48 above.
62 There is an ever-growing number of books, university and other courses, consulting firms, organizations and even professional associations (e.g. the Ethics Officers of America, the Ethics Practitioners Associations). The Prince of Wales Business Forum and the Business for Social Responsibility websites have an extensive list of some of the above resources, see http://www.bsr.org and http://www.pwblf.org (accessed: June 2001).
63 See Avery, *supra* note 42 at pp. 53–5.
64 For details on the Responsible Care sectoral initiative which was pioneered by the Canadian Chemical Producers Association (CCPA) see the CCPA's website at http://www.ccpa.ca/english/position/concerns/index.html (accessed: June 2001).
65 For details of the FSC see the FSC International website of this sectoral coalition at http://www.fscoax.org (accessed: July 2001).
66 The rival sectoral coalition in this area is the more radical group called the Certified Forest Products Council. For details of this organization see www.certifiedwood.org (accessed: July 2001).
67 A fuller discussion and details of the Sullivan Principles can be found in S. Prakash Sethi and Oliver F. Williams, *Economic Imperatives and Ethical Values in Global Business, The South African Experience and International Codes Today* (Boston: Kluwer Academic, 2001); Reid D. Weedon, "The Evolution of the Sullivan Principles of Compliance" (1986) 57 *Business and Society Review*.
68 For a discussion of the criticism, see Weedon, *supra* note 67.
69 For a discussion of the impact of the Sullivan Principles, see J. Perez Lopez, "Promoting International Respect for Workers' Rights through Business Codes of Conduct" (1993) 17 *Fordham International Law Journal* 1.
70 See Avery, *supra* note 42 at p. 31.

71 For more details on the ETI see the website of the organization located at http://www.ethicaltrade.org (accessed: June 2001). See also Paddy O'Reilly and Sophia Tickell, "TNCs and the Social Issues in the Developing World" in Addo, *supra* note 46 at p. 281.

72 *Ibid.*

73 For a detailed discussion of the EU initiative see Andrew McLean, "The European Union Code of Conduct on Arms Exports" in Addo, *supra* note 46 at p. 115.

74 The Voluntary Principles can be located at http://www.state.gov/www/global/human_rights/001220_stat_principles.htm (accessed: June 2001).

75 See the Confederation of Danish Industry publication "Industry and Human Rights" (April 1998) discussed in Avery, *supra* note 42 at p. 43; see also the Confederation of Norwegian Business and Industry's publication "Checklist for Corporations/Enterprises Interested in Investing Strategic Efforts in Human Rights Issues" also discussed in Avery, *supra* note 42 at pp. 43–4.

76 *Model Business Principles* (Washington, DC: US Department of Commerce, 1995). For critique of this initiative see Avery, *ibid.* at pp. 28–9.

77 See O'Reilly and Tickell, *supra* note 71 at pp. 274–5.

78 For details of the SA8000 see the website of the CEA at http://www.cepaa.org (accessed: July 2001).

79 See O'Reilly and Tickell, *supra* note 71 at p. 275. The Principles for Global Corporate Responsibility can be located at http://www.web.net/~tccr/benchmarks/ (accessed: June 2001).

80 The Caux Round Table Principles for Business and the activities around it can be located at http://www.cauxroundtable.org/ENGLISH.HTM (accessed: June 2001).

81 The Global Sullivan Principles can be found at http://globalsullivanprinciples.org (accessed: June 2001).

82 For a more extensive analysis by leading experts of the codes described in this chapter and other important ones such as the CERES Principles, see Oliver F. Williams (ed.) *Global Codes of Conduct: An Idea Whose Time Has Come* (Notre Dame, IN: University of Notre Dame Press, 2000).

83 For further discussion of this Declaration, see Avery *supra* note 42 at p. 27.

84 For further discussion see Joachim Karl, "The OECD Guidelines for Multinational Enterprises" in Addo, *supra* note 46 at p. 89. The OECD adopted a revised version of the Guidelines on 27 June 2000, which for the first time included a reference to human rights. For the full text of the revised Guidelines see the website of the OECD at http://www.oecd.org/EN/document/0,,EN-document-187-5-no-27-24467-187,FF.html (accessed: March 2001).

85 For the full text of the 1999 speech at the World Economic Forum in Davos, see UN Press Release SG/SM/6881. The speech can be found at www.un.org/partners/business/davos.htm (accessed: July 2001).

86 *Ibid.*

87 The text of the Global Compact and all associated activities can be located at http://www.unglobalcompact.org (accessed: July 2001).

88 *Ibid.*

89 *Ibid.*

90 *Ibid.*

91 *Ibid.*

92 *Supra* note 85.

93 We see this backlash even against the Global Compact by some activist NGOs who assert that the United Nations is being co-opted by the MNEs; see the harsh criticism at the website of one activist group, Corporate Watch, located at http://www.corpwatch.org/un/ (accessed: June 2001). This organization is also keeping a watch on corporations who have endorsed the Global Compact but who, in the view of the organization, are violating its principles. Insofar as these assertions

are accurate, this "watch" on the Global Compact will be of great benefit to prevent this initiative of the secretary-general from degenerating into a public relations exercise for some MNEs.

94 See e.g. Ian Brownlie, *Principles of Public International Law*, 4th edn (Oxford: Clarendon Press, 1990), at p. 58.

95 See International Council on Human Rights Policy, *Business Wrongs and Rights: Human Rights and the Developing International Legal Obligations of Companies, Draft Report* (Switzerland: International Council on Human Rights Policy, 2001) at pp. 45–7. The final report, *Beyond Voluntarism: Human Rights and the Developing International Legal Obligations of Companies* (Switzerland: International Council on Human Rights Policy, 2002) is located at http://www.international-council.org (accessed: June 2002).

96 *Ibid.* at pp. 46–7. According to one author, Radio-Télévision Libre des Milles Collines (RTML) was created in mid-1993 by "leading Hutu extremists" in the Rwandan government. However, despite being ostensibly controlled by Hutu extremists from various walks, including the government, RTML was established as a private jointly funded stock company. See J.F. Metzl, "Rwandan Genocide and the International Law of Radio Jamming" (1997) 91 *American Journal of International Law* 630.

97 Corporations operating in war zones such as the Sudan should be very careful about this type of scenario; see John Harker, *Human Security in Sudan: The Report of a Canadian Assessment Mission* (Ottawa: Department of Foreign Affairs and International Trade, 2000); see also the document by Amnesty International, *Oil in Sudan* AI-Index AFR54/001/2000, which can also be located at http://www.web.amnesty.org/ai.nsf/ index/AFR540012000 (accessed: June 2001).

98 Harker, *ibid.*; see also *The Price of Oil, Corporate Responsibility and Human Rights Violations in Nigeria's Oil Producing Communities, supra* note 29.

99 Harker, *ibid.* On the allegations of complicity by the oil corporation Unocal in forced labor and other human rights abuses by Myanmar, including the use of sanctions, see Schwartz and Gibb, *supra* note 42 at pp. 33–42.

100 There is a growing literature documenting this use of war and abuse of fundamental human rights to gain access to mineral wealth; see Global Witness, *A Crude Awakening: The Role of Oil and Banking Industries in the Angolan Civil War and the Plunder of State Assets* (London: Global Witness, 1999); David Keen, *The Economic Functions of Violence in Civil Wars*, Adelphi Paper No. 320 (London: Oxford University Press, 1998); Mark Duffield, "Greed and Grievance; Economic Agendas in Civil Wars" in Mats Berdal and David Malone (eds) *Globalization, Transborder Trade and War Economies* (Boulder, CO: Lynne Rienner, 2000); See also the Security Council-sponsored report of Canadian ambassador Robert Fowler on the subversion of the arms embargo against Angola by an international network of individuals and the Belgium diamond clearing house: *Report of the Panel of Experts on Violations of Security Council Sanctions Against UNITA*, UN Doc. S/2000/203, 10 March 2000. The report is located at http://www.un.int/canada/html/angolareport.htm (accessed: June 2001). See also the role of access to diamonds by rebels and corporate complicity in Sierra Leone in the document written by Ian Smillie, Lansana Gberie, and Ralph Hazleton, *The Heart of the Matter, Sierra Leone, Diamonds and Human Security* (Ontario: Partnership Africa Canada, 2000). The full text is located at http://www.sierra-leone.org/heartmatter.html (accessed: June 2001).

101 For a fuller analysis of corruption as a profound violation of the most fundamental of rights in the International Bill of Rights, see Errol P. Mendes, *Corruption: The Cancer of the International Bill of Rights* (Ottawa: Human Rights Research and Education Centre, forthcoming).

102 See Terry Carter, "Wide World of Payola: United States Pushes Action on Bribery Convention" (1999) 85 *American Bar Association Journal* 18.

103 There is an extensive literature on the history and evolution of the OECD Bribery Convention; see, for example, Barbara Crutchfield George, Kathleen A. Lacey, and Jutta Birmele, "On the Threshold of the Adoption of Global Anti-bribery Legislation: A Critical Analysis of Current Domestic and International Efforts toward the Reduction of Business Corruption" (1999) 32 *Vanderbilt Journal of Transnational Law* 1; See also, for the latest developments and implementation measures in OECD and other signatory countries, the website of the OECD, which has a special segment titled "Anti-Corruption Ring Online" located at http://www.oecd.org/daf/nocorruptionweb (accessed: June 2001).

104 See OECD Anti-Corruption Online, *ibid.*

105 See *ibid.* for an overview of developments in these multilateral institutions and regions and a host of other developments worldwide.

106 For more information and details about the FATF initiative, see the website of the OECD at http://www.oecd.org/fatf/AboutFATF_en.htm (accessed: July 2001).

107 See *Business Wrongs and Rights: Human Rights and the Developing International Legal Obligations of Companies*, *supra* note 95 at pp. 31–7.

108 *Ibid.* at pp. 37–8.

109 *Ibid.* at pp. 15–16.

110 *Ibid.* at p. 16, citing the UN Committee on Economic, Social and Cultural Rights, General Comment 12, "The Right to Adequate Food" 12 May 1999, UN Doc:E/C.12/1999/5, CESCR, at para. 27.

111 *Ibid.* at p. 16, citing the UN Human Rights Committee, General Comment 16, "The Right to Respect of Privacy, Family, Home and Correspondence and Protection of Honor and Reputation (Art. 17)" 8 April 1988, at para. 1.

112 *Ibid.* at p. 17, citing the European Court of Human Rights decision in *X and Y v. The Netherlands*, 91 ECHR Series A (1985), para. 23.

113 See the discussion of the problems of enforcement and compliance in *ibid.* at pp. 62–109.

114 See the discussion of the litigation under ACTA and litigation against MNEs in other countries in *ibid.* at pp. 102–5.

115 For discussion of the Enron, Andersen and WorldCom scandals, see *The Economist*, 9 February 2002 at pp. 9–10 and 57–60; *The Economist*, 5 July 2002 at pp. 9–10, 57–8 and 67–8.

4 From a "race-to-the-bottom" to social justice in the global labor market

1 A summary of the debate on the Asian Miracle can be found in O. Mehmet, *Westernizing the Third World*, 2nd edn (London and New York: Routledge 1999) at pp. 117–20.

2 For a comprehensive assessment of the social costs of the Asian Currency Crisis, see E. Lee, *The Social Impact of the Asian Financial Crisis* (Bangkok: ILO Regional Office, 1998). See also Ann Booth, "Impact of the Crisis on Poverty and Equity" (December 1998) 15(1) *ASEAN Economic Bulletin*.

3 See *The Social Impact*, *supra* note 2 at p. 57. See also E. Lee, "Trade Union Rights: An Economic Perspective" (1998) 137(3) *International Labour Review*, at p. 315 where it is argued:

> [O]ne cannot convincingly attribute role to labour market institutions when explaining differences in employment performance. Other factors such as macroeconomic policy, the degree of regulation of product markets, and the effectiveness of skill development and active labour market policies are probably of greater significance.

4　See United Nations, "Internationalization of Production, Reorganization of Work and 'Flexibilization' of Labour" in UN, *1999 World Survey on the Role of Women in Development: Globalization, Gender and Work* (New York: United Nations, 1999). See also M. Cornoy, "The Family, Flexible Work and Social Cohesion at Risk" (1999) 138(4) *International Labour Review* 411.

5　M. Buvinic, "Women in Poverty: A New Global Underclass" (Fall 1997) 108 *Foreign Policy*. See also M. Chen, J. Sebstad, and L. O'Connel, "Counting the Invisible Workforce: The Case of Homebased Workers" (1999) 27(3) *World Development*, 603.

6　See O. Mehmet, E. Mendes, and R. Sinding, *Towards a Fair Global Labour Market* (New York and London: Routledge, 1999) especially chapters 1 and 2.

7　In the literature on international migration, HICs are often referred to as "welfare" countries to indicate their attraction for potential migrants looking for higher incomes and better jobs as well as the benefits of social safety nets. For an extended discussion of economic migration, see Mehmet *et al.*, *supra* note 6 at pp. 53–8. For a discussion of social and welfare policies in HICs in the context of international social policy, see R. Mishra, "Globalisation and Social Policy: Defending Social Standards" in J. Drydyk and P. Penz (eds) *Global Justice, Global Democracy* (Winnipeg and Halifax: Fernwood, 1997).

8　For an extended discussion of the Informal Sector debate, see H.D. Evers and O. Mehmet, "Risk Management: The Informal Trade Sector in Indonesia" (Winter–Spring 2001) 22(1) *World Development*, 1; and the issue of *SAIS Review*, XXI(1), devoted to this topic (Winter–Spring 2001).

9　For a recent review of this subject see B.N. Ghosh and R. Ghosh, "The Problem of Brain Drain" in B.N. Ghosh (ed.) *Contemporary Issues in Development Economics* (London: Routledge, 2001).

10　See Evers and Mehmet, *supra* note 8.

11　See the OECD website: http://www1.oecd.org/daf/nocorruptionweb/moneylaundering/bib.htm (accessed: July 2001).

12　*The Ottawa Citizen*, 31 October 2001, p. B16.

13　Donna M. Hughes, "The 'Natasha' Trade: The Transnational Shadow Market of Trafficking in Women" (2000) 53(2) *Journal of International Affairs* 625.

14　Andrea M. Bertone, "Sexual Trafficking in Women: International Political Economy and the Politics of Sex" (2000) 18(1) *Gender Issues*, 4–22; and Janie Chuang, "Redirecting the Debate over Trafficking in Women: Definitions, Paradigms and Contexts" (1998) 11 *Harvard Human Rights Journal*, 65–107.

15　Chuang, *ibid.* at p. 68. For the provisions of the UN 1949 Convention for the Suppression on the Traffic in Persons and of the Exploitation of the Prostitution of Others, see the website: http://www.unhcr.ch (accessed: July 2001). On the work of the International Organization for Migration in this field, see Bertone, *supra* note 14.

16　*United Nations Convention for the Suppression of the Traffic in Persons and of the Exploitation of the Prostitution of Others*, GA Res. A/317(IV), 2 December 1949.

17　*Ibid.*, Article 2.

18　J. Salt, "A Comparative Overview of International Trends and Types" (1989) 23(3) *International Migration Review* 431; N.M. Shah, "Structural Changes in the Receiving Country and the Future of Labor Migration – the Case of Kuwait" (1995) 29(4) *International Migration Review* 1000–22; M. Abella, "Asian Labour Migration: Past, Present and Future" (1995) 12(2) *ASEAN Economic Bulletin* 125.

19　ILO, *World Employment Report 1998–99* (Geneva: ILO, 1999) at p. 139.

20　Buvinic, *supra* note 5.

21　On the topic of informality, see *SAIS Review*, XXI(1), specially devoted to this subject (Winter–Spring 2001).

22　For the latest data on the changing labor force status of the world's female workforce, see the UNIFEM website at http://www.unifem.undp.org/progessww/2000/charts.htm (accessed: July 2001). For statistics of increasing female economic activity participation in the world's economy, see UNDP, *Human Development Report 2000* (New York: United Nations, 2000), Table 29 at p. 262.

23 World Bank, *Workers in East Asia's Growth* (Washington, DC: World Bank, 1995) at p. 20.

24 See Chen in *SAIS Review*, *supra* note 21.

25 ILO, *Labour Practices in the Footwear, Leather, Textiles and Clothing Industries* (Geneva: ILO, 16–20 October 2000). The document is also available at the ILO website at http://www.ilo.org/public/english/dialogue/sector/techmeet/tmlfi00/tmlfir.htm (accessed: July 2001).

26 See http://www.globalmarch.org/worstformsreport/world/india.html (accessed: July 2001).

27 See Mehmet *et al.*, *supra* note 6 at pp. 50–1.

28 See for example, K. Maskus, *Should Core Labor Standards Be Imposed through International Trade Policy?* World Bank Policy Research Working Paper No. 1817 (Washington, DC: World Bank, 1997).

29 Birdsall and Lawrence in I. Kaul, I. Grunberg, and M. Stern (eds) *Global Public Goods, International Cooperation in the 21st Century* (New York and London: UNDP and Oxford University Press, 1999) at p. 128.

30 Thus we agree fully with him that it is necessary to safeguard the ability of the state "to generate the public funds needed to finance social insurance schemes." D. Rodrik, *Has Globalization Gone Too Far?* (Washington, DC: Institute for International Economics, 1997) at p. 73.

31 Anderson in F. Bergston and M. Noland (eds) *Pacific Dynamism and the International Economic System* (New York: Institute of International Economics, 1993).

32 E.B. Kapstein, "Distributive Justice as an International Public Good" in Kaul *et al.* (eds) *supra* note 29 at pp. 88–115.

33 *Ibid.* For an opposing view, see E.B. Kapstein, "Distributive Justice as an International Public Good" in Kaul *et al.*, *supra* note 29 at pp. 105–7.

34 J. Bhagwati, "Trade Liberalisation and 'Fair Trade' Demands: Addressing the Environmental and Labor Standards Issues" (1995) 18(6) *The World Economy* 745–59.

35 For a sample of these views, see P. Boettke (ed.) *Collapse of Development Planning* (New York: New York University Press, 1994).

36 See D. Lal, "The Third World and Globalization" (2001) 14(1) *Critical Review*, 43. See also D. Lal, "Social Standards and Social Dumping" in Herbert Giersch (ed.) *The Merits of Markets* (Berlin: Springer-Verlag, 1998).

37 See D. Lal, "The Third World and Globalization," *ibid.*

38 On the case of Asian countries, see A. Chan, "Labor Standards and Human Rights: The Case of Chinese Workers under Market Socialism" (1998) 20 *Human Rights Quarterly* 886–904. See also Mehmet *et al.*, *supra* note 6 at pp. 34–9.

39 See K.A. Swinnerton, "An Essay on Economic Efficiency and Core Labor Standards" (1997) 20(1) *The World Economy* 73.

40 See the discussion on "deep integration" by Birdsall and Lawrence, *supra* note 29 at p. 128.

41 M. Olson, *The Rise and Fall of Nations* (New Haven, CT: Yale University Press, 1982).

42 For a case study of Indonesia under Suharto, see O. Mehmet, "Rent-Seeking and Gate-Keeping in Indonesia: A Cultural and Economic Analysis" (1994) 27(1) *Labour, Capital and Society* 56.

43 See J. Bhagwati, *supra* note 34 at p. 745.

44 There is a huge volume of literature documenting the rising power of MNEs. For recent studies on the subject, see R. Barnet and J. Cavanagh, *Global Dreams* (New York: Simon and Schuster, 1994); D. Korten, *When Corporations Rule the World* (London: Earthscan, 1995).

45 Quoted in *The Economist*, 29 September 2001, "Survey on Globalisation" p. 9.

46 Stefan H. Robock and Kenneth Simmonds, *International Business and Multinational Enterprises*, 3rd edn (Homewood, IL: R.D. Irwin, 1983) pp. 511–12.
47 The full case study of Indonesian rent-seeking is in Mehmet, *supra* note 42.
48 For a recent review of this subject in the context of post-Seattle global governance and civil society, see R. Wilkinson and S. Hughes, "Labor Standards and Global Governance: Examining the Dimensions of Institutional Engagement" (2000) 6(2) *Global Governance* 259.
49 See discussion in the next chapter.

5 The failure of the international financial system and paying for upward harmonization

1 For a recent comprehensive discussion of this, see I. Kaul, I. Grunberg, and M.A. Stern (eds) *Global Public Goods, International Cooperation in the 21st Century* (New York and London: UNDP and Oxford University Press, 1999). On global governance, visit the website: http://www.cgg.ch/ (accessed: July 2001) for latest information on the work of the Commission on Global Governance.
2 See "Helping the Poor Manage Risk" in World Bank, *World Development Report 2000/1 Attacking Poverty* (Washington, DC: OUP for the World Bank, 2001). Chapter 7 of the same report, "Removing Social Barriers and Building Social Institutions," focuses in particular on the creation of social capital in development projects.
3 In the *World Development Report 2000/2001 Attacking Poverty, ibid.* at p. 23 (Table 1.1), it is stated that absolute poverty, defined as people living on less than US$1 a day, was virtually constant during 1987–98, rising marginally from 1.18 billion to 1.2 billion. However, poverty rose sharply in sub-Saharan Africa as a result of war and conflict.
4 C. Kindleberger, *Manias, Panics and Crashes: A History of Financial Crises* (New York: Basic Books, 1989).
5 L.Y.C. Lim, "Whose 'Model' Failed? Implications of the Asian Economic Crisis" (1998) 21(3) *Washington Quarterly* 25. For an extended discussion, see O. Mehmet, *Westernizing the Third World*, 2nd edn (London and New York: Routledge, 1999), pp. 117–19.
6 See in particular the articles by D. Lal, "The Third World and Globalization," and J. Sorens, "The Failure to Converge: Why Globalization Doesn't Cause Deregulation" (2001) 14(1) *Critical Review* 43 and 19–46 respectively.
7 See the exchange between G. Soros and B. Eichgreen in (2001) 14(1) *Critical Review* 69–88.
8 See Steven Radelet and Jeffrey Sachs, "Lessons from the Asian Crisis" in B.N. Ghosh (ed.) *Global Financial Crises and Reforms: Cases and Caveats* (New York and London: Routledge, 2001) at pp. 295–316.
9 Joseph P. Daniels, "Supervising the International Financial System" in Michael Hodges, John J. Kirton and Joseph P. Daniels (eds) *The G8's Role in the New Millennium* (Aldershot: Ashgate, 1999), pp. 112–113.
10 Radelet and Sachs, *supra* note 8 at p. 6
11 *Ibid.*
12 *Ibid.* at pp. 307–13.
13 *Ibid.* at p. 311.
14 *Ibid.* at pp. 303–4.
15 *Ibid.* at pp. 312–13.
16 *Ibid.* at p. 308.
17 Yilmaz Akyuz, *The Debate on the International Financial Architecture: Reforming the Reformers* UNCTAD Discussion Paper No. 148 (Geneva: UNCTAD, 2000).
18 *Ibid.* at pp. 3–4.
19 *Ibid.*
20 *Ibid.*

21 *Ibid.*

22 Stephen Fidler, "Who's Minding the Bank?" (2001) September–October *Foreign Policy* 40–1. Fidler also cites Sebastian Edwards, now a UCLA professor and a former World Bank senior economist, who has criticized Wolfensohn's own actions, including a bad temper and poor stewardship, as reasons for the internal weakness of the Bank. Despite these criticisms, however, Wolfensohn won a second five-year term as president, through to June 2005.

23 For example, the CATO Institute and the former US Secretary of State George Shultz take perhaps the most extreme abolitionist position, charging that the Fund has undermined the "information standard" of financial markets. They argue that it would be better to do away with the Fund altogether and let the apolitical financial market signals and actors deal with world currency markets. See G. Shultz, W.E. Simon, and W.B. Wriston, "Who Needs the IMF?" online at http://www.imfsite.org/abolish.html (accessed: July 2001). Also see Steve H. Hanke, "Abolish the IMF" online at http://www.cato.org/dailys/04-14-00.html (accessed: July 2001).

24 D. Osterfeld, "The World Bank and the IMF: Misbegotten Sisters" in P.J. Boettke (ed.) *Collapse of Development Planning* (New York: New York University Press, 1994) pp. 205–20; quote is taken from pp. 205–7.

25 Meltzer Commission on International Financial Institutions, *Final Report*, August 2001. Online at: http://csf.colorado.edu/roper/if/Meltzer-commission-mar00/ (accessed: July 2001) at p. 21.

26 Bretton Woods Project, *Structural Adjustment for the IMF: Options for Reforming the IMF's Governance Structure* available at http://www.brettonwoodsproject.org/topic/ reform/sapimf.html (accessed: August 2001) at p. 2. The Fund's voting system, based on quotas, reflects each member country's economic power. At the present time (2002), the USA holds 17 percent of the total votes, Japan has the next largest quota with 6.16 percent, and Germany is third with 6.02 percent. France and the UK each have 4.97 percent. The Third World, especially Africa, is heavily underrepresented in this system. Moreover, changing the system is virtually impossible because, under Article III, an 85 percent majority is required for any change in the quotas.

27 Group of Seven, *Final Report: Reducing Poverty*, available at http://www.g7.utoronto.ca/ g7/summit/1995halifax/communique/poverty.html (accessed: September 2001).

28 Akyuz, *supra* note 17 at p. 5.

29 *Ibid.*

30 *Ibid.*

31 *Ibid.* at p. 6.

32 *Ibid.* at p. 7.

33 *Ibid.* at p. 8.

34 *Ibid.* at p. 10.

35 *Ibid.* at p. 12.

36 *Ibid.* at p. 13.

37 UNCTAD uses a "transnationality index" in its classification, which is defined as "the average of three ratios: foreign assets/total assets, foreign sales/total sales, and foreign employment/total employment." See UNCTAD, *World Investment Report 2001* (Geneva: UNCTAD) at p. 19.

38 *Ibid.* at p. xiii.

39 World Bank, *World Development Report 2001*, *supra* note 2 at p. 279, Table 2.3.

40 See for example, L.D. Howell and B. Chaddick, "Models of Political Risk for Foreign Investment and Trade: An Assessment of Three Approaches" (1994) 29(3) *Columbia Journal of World Business* 70; A. Vives, "Private Infrastructure: Ten Commandments of Sustainability" (1997) 3(1) *Journal of Project Finance* 20–30.

41 There is a large literature on this new concept. For an earlier discussion see J.S. Coleman, "Social Capital in the Creation of Human Capital" (1988) 94 *American Journal of Sociology* S95–S120. For a recent discussion, see Francis Fukuyama, "Social Capital and Civil Society and Development" (2001) 22(1) *Third World Quarterly* 7–20; M. Woolcock and D. Narayan, "Social Capital: Implications for Development Theory, Research and Policy" (2000) 15(2) *The World Bank Research Observer* 225–49.

42 See J.D. MacArthur, "Stakeholder Roles and Stakeholder Analysis in Project Planning: A Review of Approaches in Three Agencies: WB, ODA and NRI", Development and Project Planning Center, University of Bradford Discussion Paper No. 73, March 1997. There are also several new websites on this topic. See, for example, www.worldbank.org/wbi/sourcebook/sb0302t.htm (accessed: November 2001); www.dams.org (accessed: November 2001).

43 See the World Bank, *World Development Report, Knowledge for Development* (Washington, DC: World Bank, 1998/9).

44 The GEF was set up after the UN Conference at Rio on Environment and Development with an annual estimated amount of $125 billion required for essential investment in global environmental security. See, for details, "Tokyo Declaration on Financing Global Environment and Development" (1992) 22/4 *Environmental Policy and Law* 265.

45 Under the Montreal Protocol, developing countries are subject to emission ceilings, but they are also entitled to "compensation" from industrial countries for the incremental costs of compliance. "These side payments ensured that developing countries are not worse off for signing," S. Barrett, "Montreal versus Kyoto, International Cooperation and the Global Environment" in I. Kaul, I. Grunberg, and M.A. Stern (eds) *Global Public Goods, International Cooperation in the 21st Century* (New York and London: UNDP and Oxford University Press, 1999) at pp. 210–11.

46 For an historical overview and economic analysis of international taxation, see the paper and references therein by M.J. Frankman, "International Taxation: The Trajectory of an Idea from Lorimer to Brandt" (1996) 24 *World Development*. Available online at www.globalpolicy.org/socecon/glotax/general/loribran.htm (accessed: July 2001).

47 For a discussion of this idea see the interesting essay by E.B. Kapstein, "Distributive Justice as an International Public Good" in Kaul *et al.*, *supra* note 1 at p. 109.

48 T.W. Schultz, "Investment in Human Capital" (1961) 51 *American Economic Review* 1–17. For an extended discussion, see O. Mehmet, *Human Resource Development in the Third World, Cases of Success and Failure* (Kingston, Ont.: R. Fryre, 1988) chap. 1.

49 There is now extensive empirical evidence demonstrating high social (as well as private) rates of return on investment in education. For a world survey of these rates see G. Psacharopoulos, "Return to Investment in Education: A Global Update" (1994) 22(9) *World Development* 1325.

50 Mehmet, *supra* note 48.

51 Myanmar's military regime is arguably the worst offender on slavery and forced labor conventions. On India, which has the world's most extensive system of bonded slavery system, see, for example, Human Rights Watch, *The Small Hands of Slavery: Bonded Child Labor in India* (1996) located at http://www.hrw.org/children /labor.htm (accessed: July 2001). In China there is a notorious case in the Labor Education Program under which workers sentenced for petty offences are obliged to work in conditions approaching near slavery in contravention of ILO Conventions.

52 World Bank, *The East Asian Miracle* (New York: Oxford University Press, 1993).

53 Mehmet, *supra* note 48, ch. 2.

54 World Bank, *supra* note 52; see also J. E. Campos and H. Root, *The Key to the Asian Miracle: Making Shared Growth Credible* (Washington, DC: The Brookings Institution, 1996) at p. 176.
55 Campos and Root, *ibid.*
56 A Gini coefficient of 1 implies maximum inequality in income distribution, whereas 0 implies perfect equality. Consequently, the aim of an egalitarian policy (e.g. HRD, income tax or subsidy program) is to lower this coefficient.
57 For supporting evidence, see Campos and Root, *supra* note 54 at p. 9.
58 World Bank, *World Development Report 1997* (Washington, DC: World Bank, 1997).
59 See R.E. Lucas, "On the Mechanics of Economic Development" (1988) 22 *Journal of Monetary Economics* 3; P. Romer, "Endogenous Technological Change" (1990) 98(5) *Journal of Political Economy* S71–102.
60 For an extended review of the evolution of human capital theory, see Mehmet, *supra* note 48, ch. 1.
61 S.P. Scott, "Education for Child Workers in Bangladesh: A Case Study of the Memorandum of Understanding Involving the ILO, UNICEF, and the Bangladesh Garment Manufacturers and Experts Association" (unpublished MA thesis, Department of Adult Education Community Development and Counseling Psychology, OISE, University of Toronto, 1997).
62 See generally Psacharopoulos, *supra* note 49.
63 The literature on social capital is expanding rapidly. See Woolcock and Narayan, *supra* note 41.
64 I. Sirageldin, *Sustainability and the Wealth of Nations: First Steps in an Ongoing Journey*, EDS Monograph Series No. 5 (Washington, DC: World Bank, 1996) p. 6.
65 According to the OECD's Development Assistance Committee that monitors ODA and has published an annual report concerning such assistance, total ODA declined from $56 billion in 1999 to $53 billion in 2000. Source: www.oecd.org/oecd/pages/home/displ.nt-15-nodirectorate-no-12-5120-15,FF.html (accessed: July 2001).
66 O. Mehmet, "An International Development Levy on Multinational Corporations" (1980) 7(2) *International Interactions* 101–22; Brandt Report, *North–South: A Programme for Survival* (London: Pan Books, 1980).
67 UNDP *Human Development Report 2000* (New York: Oxford University Press, 2000).
68 UNCTAD *World Investment Report 2001*, *supra* note 37, ch. 3.
69 For a proposal along these lines, see H.M. Wachtel, "Tobin and other Global Taxes" (2000) 7(2) *Review of International Political Economy* 335–52. Wachtel argues that a merit of taxing the profits would be its "tax fairness" relative to transfer pricing.
70 See James Tobin, *Essays in Economics: Theory and Policy* (Cambridge, MA: MIT Press, 1982) at pp. 488–94. For a recent review of this literature, see Wachtel, *supra* note 69. The Tobin tax was on the agenda of the Halifax G7 Summit where it met little support. See Rodney Schmidt, "A Feasible Foreign Exchange Transaction Tax" (Ottawa, Ont.: North–South Institute, September 1997).

6 Toward global pluralism

1 See John Rawls, *A Theory of Justice* (Cambridge, MA: Harvard University Press, 1971).
2 Amartya Sen, "Global Justice, beyond International Equity" in I. Kaul, I. Grunberg, and M.A. Stern (eds) *Global Public Goods, International Cooperation in the 21st Century* (New York and London: UNDP and Oxford University Press, 1999) at pp. 116, 118.
3 *Ibid.*
4 *Ibid.* at p. 119.

5 *Ibid.* See also John Rawls, *The Law of Peoples* (Cambridge, MA: Harvard University Press, 1999).

6 *Ibid.* at p. 120.

7 *Ibid.*

8 Ronald Dworkin, *Taking Rights Seriously* (Cambridge, MA: Harvard University Press, 1978).

9 Sen, *supra* note 2 at pp. 122–3.

10 See Samuel P. Huntington, *The Clash of Civilizations: Remaking of the World Order* (New York: Touchstone, Simon and Schuster, 1997).

11 Joseph Stiglitz, *Globalization and Its Discontents* (New York: W.W. Norton, 2002). For an equally stinging rebuttal of Stiglitz's views, see the open letter to Mr Stiglitz by the current chief economist, Kenneth Rogoff, on the website of the IMF at http://www.imf.org/external/np/vc/2002/070202.htm (accessed: June 2002). See also the equally critical review of Stiglitz's book by *The Economist*, 8 June 2002 at p. 78.

12 *Ibid.* at pp. 214–15.

Bibliography (selected)

Addo, M.K. (ed.) *Human Rights Standards and the Responsibility of Transnational Corporations* (The Hague: Kluwer Law International, 1999).

Alston, P., *Final Report on Enhancing the Long-Term Effectiveness of the United Nations Human Rights Treaty System*, UN Doc. E/CN4/1997/74 (27 March 1997).

Alston, P. and J. Crawford, *The Future of UN Human Rights Monitoring* (Cambridge: Cambridge University Press, 2000).

Alston, P., M. Bustelo, and J. Heenan, *The EU and Human Rights* (Oxford: Oxford University Press, 1999).

Anderson, S. and J. Cavanagh, *The Top 200, The Rise of Global Corporate Power* (New York: Institute for Policy Studies, 1996).

Asbjorn, E., C. Krause, and A. Rosas, *Economic, Social and Cultural Rights* (The Hague: Martinus Nijhoff, 1995).

Avery, C.L., *Business and Human Rights in a Time of Change* (London: Amnesty International, 2000).

Bailey, P., A. Parisott, and G. Renshaw (eds) *Multinationals and Employment, the Global Economy of the 1990s* (Geneva: ILO, 1993).

Barnet, R. and J. Cavanagh, *Global Dreams* (New York: Simon and Schuster, 1994).

Bassiouni, C.M., *Crimes against Humanity in International Criminal Law*, 2nd edn (The Hague: Kluwer Law International, 1999).

——"Nuremberg: Forty Years After" (1986) 80 *Proceedings of the Annual Meeting of the American Society of International Law* 59.

——*The Statute of the International Criminal Court* (Ardsley, NY: Transnational Publishers, 1998).

——(ed.) *The Statute of the International Criminal Court*, 2nd edn (Dobbs Ferry, NY: Transnational Publishers, 1999).

Bayefsky, Anne F. (ed.) *The U.N. Human Rights System in the 21st Century* (The Hague: Kluwer Law International, 2000).

Bayne, N., *Hanging in There: The G7 and G8 Summit in Maturity and Renewal* (Aldershot: Ashgate, 2000).

Benedek, W., *Human Rights in Bosnia and Herzegovina after Dayton: From Theory to Practice* (The Hague: Martinus Nijhoff, 1996).

Berdal, M. and D. Malone (eds) *Globalization, Transborder Trade and War Economies* (Boulder, CO: Lynn Rienner Publishers, 2000).

Bergston, F. and M. Noland (eds) *Pacific Dynamism and the International Economic System* (New York: Institute of International Economics, 1993).

Bialos, J.P. and G. Husisian, *The Foreign Corrupt Practices Act: Coping with Corruption in Transitional Economies* (New York: Oceana Publications, 1997).

Boettke, P.J. (ed.) *Collapse of Development Planning* (New York: New York University Press, 1994).

(The) Brandt Report, *North–South: A Programme for Survival* (London: Pan Books, 1980).

Brody, R. and M. Ratner (eds) *The Pinochet Papers: The Case of Augusto Pinochet in Spain and Britain* (The Hague: Kluwer Law International, 2000).

Brownlie, I., *Principles of Public International Law*, 4th edn (Oxford: Clarendon Press, 1990).

Campos, J.E. and H. Root, *The Key to the Asian Miracle: Making Shared Growth Credible* (Washington, DC: The Brookings Institution, 1996).

Chatterjee, P. and M. Finger, *The Earth Brokers: Power Politics and World Development* (New York: Routledge, 1994).

Chomsky, N., *The Chomsky Reader* (New York: Pantheon Books, 1987)

——*Superpowers in Collision: The Cold War Now* (New York: Penguin, 1982).

Craven, M., *The International Covenant on Economic, Social and Cultural Rights: A Perspective on Its Development* (New York: Oxford University Press, 1981).

Danieli, Y., Elsa Stamatopoulou, and Clarence J. Dias (eds) *The Universal Declaration of Human Rights: Fifty Years and Beyond* (New York: Baywood Publishing Company, on behalf of the United Nations, 1999).

Daniels, J.P. and A. Freytag (eds) *Guiding Global Order: G8 and Governance in the Twenty-First Century* (Aldershot: Ashgate, 2001).

Des Forges, A., *Leave None to Tell the Story: Genocide in Rwanda* (New York: Human Rights Watch, 1999).

Drydyk, J. and P. Penz (eds) *Global Justice, Global Democracy* (Winnipeg and Halifax: Fernwood, 1997).

Dworkin, R., *Taking Rights Seriously* (Cambridge, MA: Harvard University Press, 1978).

Elliott, K. (ed.) *Corruption and the Global Economy* (Washington, DC: Institute for International Economics, 1997).

Geraint, P., A. Qureshi, and H. Steiner, *The Legal and Moral Aspects of International Trade* (London and New York: Routledge, 1998).

Ghosh, B.N. (ed.) *Contemporary Issues in Development Economics* (London: Routledge, 2001).

——(ed.) *Global Financial Crises and Reforms: Cases and Caveats* (New York and London: Routledge, 2001).

Giersch, H. (ed.) *The Merits of Markets* (Berlin: Springer-Verlag, 1998).

Goldstone, R.J., *For Humanity: Reflections of a War Crimes Investigator*, Castle Lectures in Ethics, Politics and Economics (New Haven, CT: Yale University Press, 2000).

Gore, C., *The Least Developed Countries 2000 Report, Aid, Private Capital Flows and External Debt: The Challenge of Financing Development in the LDCs* (Geneva: UNCTAD, 2000).

Greanias, G.C., *The Foreign Corrupt Practices Act: Anatomy of a Statute* (Lexington, MA: Lexington Books, 1992).

Haas, M., *Genocide by Proxy: Cambodian Pawn on a Superpower Chessboard* (New York: Praeger, 1991).

Hajnal, P., *The G7/G8 System: Evolution, Role and Documentation*, The G8 and Global Governance Series (Aldershot: Ashgate, 1999).

Handy, C., *The Age of Paradox* (Cambridge, MA: Harvard Business School Press, 1994).

Hannum, H. (ed.) *Guide to International Human Rights Practice*, 3rd edn (Ardsley, NY: Transnational Publishers, 1999).

Henkin, L. (ed.) *The International Bill of Rights: The Covenant on Civil and Political Rights* (New York: Columbia University Press, 1981).

Holborn, L.W. (ed.) *War and Peace Aims of the United Nations* (Boston, MA: World Peace Foundation, 1943).

Huntington, S.P., *The Clash of Civilizations: Remaking of the World Order* (New York: Touch-stone, Simon and Schuster, 1997).

Ignatieff, M., *Virtual War, Kosovo and Beyond* (Toronto: Viking, 2000).

Independent International Commission on Kosovo, headed by Justice Richard J. Gold-stone and Carl Tham, *The Kosovo Report* (Oxford: Oxford University Press, 2000).

International Commission on Global Governance, *Our Global Neighbourhood* (Oxford: Oxford University Press, 1995).

International Council on Human Rights Policy, *Hard Cases: Bringing Human Rights Violators to Justice Abroad – A Guide to Universal Jurisdiction* (Versoix, Switzerland: International Council on Human Rights Policy, 1999).

International Institute for Sustainable Development (IISD), *Trade and Sustainable Development Principles* (Winnipeg: IISD, 1994).

Jackson, J.H., W.J. Davey, and A.O. Sykes, Jr, *Legal Problems of International Economic Relations*, 3rd edn (St Paul, MN: West Publishing, 1995).

Johnston, B.R. (ed.) *Who Pays the Price* (Washington, DC: Island Press, 1994).

Kaplan, J.M., J.E. Murphy and W.M. Swenson (eds) *Compliance Programs and Corporate Sentencing Guidelines: Preventing Civil and Criminal Liability* (New York: Boardman, Callaghan, 1997).

Karabell, Z., *Architects of Intervention: The United States, the Third World, and the Cold War, 1946–1962* (Baton Rouge: Louisiana State University Press, 1999).

Kaul, I., I. Grunberg, and M. Stern (eds) *Global Public Goods, International Cooperation in the 21st Century* (London and New York: UNDP and Oxford University Press, 1999).

Keen, D., *The Economic Functions of Violence in Civil Wars*, Adelphi Paper No. 320 (London: Oxford University Press, 1998).

Kennedy, P., *The Rise and Fall of the Great Powers* (London: Fontana Press, 1989).

Kindleberger, C., *Manias, Panics and Crashes: A History of Financial Crises* (New York: Basic Books, 1989).

Klug, F., *Values for a Godless Age: The Story of the United Kingdom's New Bill of Rights* (Harmondsworth: Penguin, 2000).

Korten, D., *When Corporations Rule the World* (London: Earthscan, 1995).

Kurzman, D., *A Killing Wind: Inside Union Carbide and the Bhopal Catastrophe* (New York: McGraw Hill, 1987).

Lapierre, D. and J. Moro, *Five Past Midnight in Bhopal* (New York: Warner Books, 2002).

Lauren, P.G., *The Evolution of Human Rights, Visions Seen* (Philadelphia: University of Penn-sylvania Press, 1998).

Lillich, R.B., *International Human Rights: Problems of Law, Policy and Practice*, 2nd edn (Boston, MA: Little, Brown, 1991).

McGoldrick, D., *The Human Rights Committee: Its Role in the Development of the International Covenant on Civil and Political Rights* (Oxford: Clarendon Press, 1991).

Mazaar, M.J., *Global Trends 2005: An Owner's Manual for the Next Decade* (New York: Palgrave, 1999).

Mehmet, O., *Human Resource Development in the Third World, Cases of Success and Failure* (Kingston, Ont.: R. Fryre, 1988).

——*Westernizing the Third World*, 2nd edn (London and New York: Routledge, 1999).

Mehmet, O., E. Mendes, and R. Sinding, *Towards a Fair Global Labour Market, Avoiding the New Slave Trade* (New York: Routledge, 1999).

Melvern, L.R., *A People Betrayed: The Role of the West in Rwanda's Genocide* (London: Zed Books, 2000).

Meron, T., *Human Rights Law-Making in the United Nations: A Critique of Instruments and Process* (Oxford: Clarendon Press, 1986).

——*War Crimes Come of Age: Essays* (Oxford and New York: Oxford University Press, 1998).

OECD, *Trade Employment and Labour Standards: A Study of Core Workers' Rights and International Trade* (Paris: OECD, 1996).

Olson, M., *The Rise and Fall of Nations* (New Haven, CT: Yale University Press, 1982).

Power, S., *A Problem from Hell* (New York: Basic Books, 2002).

(The) Princeton Principles on Universal Jurisdiction (Program in Law and Public Affairs; Princeton, NJ: Princeton University, 2001).

Qureshi, A.H., *The World Trade Organization, Implementing International Trade Norms* (Manchester: Manchester University Press, 1996).

Ramcharan, B.G. (ed.) *Human Rights Thirty Years after the Universal Declaration* (The Hague: Martinus Nijhoff, 1979).

Rawls, J., *The Law of Peoples* (Cambridge, MA: Harvard University Press, 1999).

——*A Theory of Justice* (Cambridge, MA: Harvard University Press, 1971).

Report of the Standing Committee on Foreign Affairs and International Trade: Canada and the Future of the World Trade Organization, Advancing a Millennium Agenda in the Public Interest, Chair Bill Graham, MP (Ottawa: House of Commons, Canada, 1999).

Roberts, J.M., *The Penguin History of the 20th Century* (Harmondsworth: Penguin, 1999).

Robertson, A.H., *Human Rights in the World* (Manchester: Manchester University Press, 1972).

Robock, S.H. and K. Simmonds, *International Business and Multinational Enterprises*, 3rd edn (Homewood, IL: R.D. Irwin, 1983).

Rodrik, D., *Has Globalization Gone Too Far?* (Washington, DC: Institute for International Economics, 1997).

Rugman, A., *The End of Globalization* (New York: American Management Association (AMACOM), 2001).

Scarfe, S., *Complicity, Human Rights and Canadian Foreign Policy* (Montreal: Black Rose Books, 1996).

Schabas, W., *Genocide in International Law* (Cambridge: Cambridge University Press, 2000).

Schlesinger, J.M., *Shadow Shoguns, The Rise and Fall of Japan's Postwar Political Machine* (New York: Simon and Schuster, 1997).

Schott, J. (ed.) *The WTO after Seattle* (Washington, DC: Institute for International Economics, 2000).

Schwartz, P. and B. Gibb, *When Good Companies Do Bad Things* (New York: John Wiley and Sons, 1999).

Sethi, S.P. and O.F. Williams, *Economic Imperatives and Ethical Values in Global Business, The South African Experience and International Codes Today* (Boston, MA: Kluwer Academic, 2001).

Shelton, D. (ed.) *International Crimes, Peace, and Human Rights: The Role of the International Criminal Court* (Ardsley, NY: Transnational Publishers, 2000).

Smith, E., *Minimata* (New York: Holt, Rinehart and Winston, 1975).

Solzhenitsyn, A.I., *The Gulag Archipelago*, 3 volumes (New York: Harper and Row, 1973, 1974, 1979).

Steiner, H.J. and P. Alston, *International Human Rights in Context*, 2nd edn (Oxford: Oxford University Press, 2000).

Stiglitz, J., *Globalization and Its Discontents* (New York: W.W. Norton, 2002).

Taylor, A. and C. Thomas (eds) *Global Trade and Global Social Issues* (London: Routledge, 1999).

Tobin, J., *Essays in Economics: Theory and Policy* (Cambridge, MA: MIT Press, 1982).

Trials of Major War Criminals, 42 volumes, Nuremberg Military Tribunal (Washington, DC: US Government Printing Office, 1947–9).

Walters, F.P., *A History of the League of Nations* (London: Oxford University Press, 1952).

Webley, S., *Codes of Ethics and International Business* (London: Institute of Business Ethics, 1997).

Williams, O.F. (ed.) *Global Codes of Conduct: An Idea Whose Time Has Come* (Notre Dame, IN: University of Notre Dame Press, 2000).

Wilson, T., *The First Summit* (Boston, MA: Houghton Mifflin, 1969).

World Bank, *The East Asian Miracle* (New York: Oxford University Press, 1993).

(The) World Commission on Environment and Development (Brundtland Commission), *Our Common Future* (Oxford: Oxford University Press, 1987).

Further reading

Adelman, H. and A. Suhrke (eds) *The Path of a Genocide: The Rwanda Crisis from Uganda to Zaire* (Somerset, NJ: Transaction Publishers, 1999).

Akyuz, Y., *The Debate on the International Financial Architecture: Reforming the Reformers*, UNCTAD Discussion Paper no. 148 (Geneva: UNCTAD, 2000).

Alfredsson, G. and A. Eide, *The Universal Declaration of Human Rights: A Common Standard of Achievement* (The Hague: Martinus Nijhoff, 1999).

Amer, R., *Foreign Military Interventions and the United Nations: Looking beyond the Charter*, Working Paper no. 149 (Canberra: Australian National University, Peace Research Centre, 1994).

Annan, K.A., *We the Peoples: The Role of the United Nations in the 21st Century* (New York: United Nations, 2000).

Arambulo, K., *Strengthening the Supervision of the International Covenant on Economic, Social and Cultural Rights: Theoretical and Procedural Aspects*, School of Human Rights Research Series vol. 3 (Oxford: Intersentia, 1999).

Arend, A. C. and R.J. Beck, *International Law and the Use of Force: Beyond the UN Charter Paradigm* (London and New York: Routledge 1993).

Bailey, S.D., *The UN Security Council and Human Rights* (New York: St Martin's Press, 1994).

Bellmann, C., *Accountability of the World Trade Organization (WTO)* (Lausanne: Swiss Coalition of Development Organization, 1996).

Booth, K. (ed.) *The Kosovo Tragedy: The Human Rights Dimensions* (London and Portland, OR: Frank Cass, 2001).

Buckley, M., *et al.* (eds) *Economic and Social Rights: Fifty Years after the Universal Declaration* (Vancouver: University of British Columbia Faculty of Law, 1999).

Century Foundation, Twentieth Century Fund Task Force on Apprehending Indicted War Criminals, *Making Justice Work: The Report of the Century Foundation. Twentieth Century Fund Task Force on Apprehending Indicted War Criminals* (New York: Century Foundation Press, 1998).

Ferencz, B.B., *From Nuremberg to Rome: Towards an International Criminal Court* (Bonn: Development and Peace Foundation, 1998).

Glazebrook, S., *The Role of the Rule of Law in the Asian Economic Crisis* (Tokyo: Inter-Pacific Bar Association, 1999).

Graham, D.T. and N.K. Poku (eds) *Migration, Mondialisation and Human Security* (New York and London: Routledge, 2000).

Harris, D. and S. Livingstone (eds) *The Inter-American System of Human Rights* (Oxford: Clarendon Press, 1998).

Heijden, B. van, and B. Tahzib-Lie (eds) *Reflections on the Universal Declaration of Human Rights: A Fiftieth Anniversary Anthology* (The Hague: Martinus Nijhoff, 1998).

Hodges, M.R., J.J. Kirton, and J.P. Daniels (eds) *The G8's Role in the New Millenium* (Aldershot: Ashgate, 1999).

Holm, H.-H. and G. Sorensen (eds) *Whose World Order? Uneven Globalization and the End of the Cold War* (Boulder, CO: Westview Press, 1995).

Howse, R. and M. Mutua, *Protecting Human Rights in a Global Economy: Challenges for the World Trade Organization* (Montreal: International Centre for Human Rights and Democratic Development, 2000).

Joseph, S., J. Schultz, and M. Castan, *The International Covenant on Civil and Political Rights: Cases, Materials, and Commentary* (Oxford: Oxford University Press, 2000).

Kaiser, K., J.J. Kirton, and J.P. Daniels (eds) *Shaping a New International Financial System: Challenges of Governance in a Globalizing World* (Aldershot: Ashgate, 2000).

Kirton, J.J. and G.M. von Furstenberg (eds) *New Directions in Global Economic Governance: Managing Globalisation in the Twenty-First Century* (Aldershot: Ashgate, 2001).

Kirton, J.J., J.P. Daniels, and A. Freytag (eds) *Guiding Global Order: G8 Governance in the Twenty-First Century* (Aldershot: Ashgate, 2001).

Morsink, J., *The UN Declaration of Human Rights: Origins, Drafting and Intent* (Philadelphia: University of Pennsylvania Press, 1999).

Parry, G., A. Qureshi, and H. Steiner (eds) *The Legal and Moral Aspects of International Trade: Freedom and Trade*, vol. III (London: Routledge, 1998).

Thomas, C. and P. Wilkin (eds) *Globalization, Human Security, and the African Experience* (Boulder, CO: Lynn Rienner, 1999).

Index